D0251367

THE BATTERED STARS

Errata

page iv: Credit for "A Prayer in Spring" excerpt should read:

> Excerpt from "A Prayer in Spring" from *The Poetry of Robert Frost* edited by Edward Connery Lathem, © 1969 by Henry Holt and Company. Reprinted by permission of Henry Holt and Company, LLC.

page 75: "Oh, give us pleasure in the grass today;" should read "Oh, give us pleasure in the flowers today;"

THE BATTERED STARS

One State's Civil War Ordeal
During Grant's Overland Campaign

❖

From the Home Front in Vermont
to the Battlefields of Virginia

HOWARD COFFIN

The Countryman Press
Woodstock, Vermont

Library of Congress Cataloging-in-Publication Data
Coffin, Howard, 1942–
The battered stars : one State's Civil War ordeal during Grant's overland campaign : from the home front in Vermont to the battlefields of Virginia / Howard Coffin.
p. cm.
Includes bibliographical references and index.
ISBN 0-88150-487-4
1. Vermont—History—Civil War, 1861–1865—Social aspects.
2. Vermont—History—Civil War, 1861–1865—Personal narratives. 3. Virginia—History—Civil War, 1861–1865—Personal narratives. 4. Virginia—History—Civil War, 1861–1865—Campaigns. 5. Grant, Ulysses S. (Ulysses Simpson), 1822–1885. 6. United States—History—Civil War, 1861–1865—Campaigns. 7. United States—Civil War, 1861–1865—Personal narratives. 8. United States—History—Civil War, 1861–1865—Social aspects. I. Title.

Published by The Countryman Press, P.O. Box 748, Woodstock, Vermont 05091

Distributed by W. W. Norton & Company, Inc., 500 Fifth Avenue, New York, NY 10110

Jacket and text design by Chris Welch
Maps by Jacques Chazaud, © 2002 The Countryman Press

Cover painting of *Civil War Battle Scene: A Moment of Decision* by Julian Scott reproduced courtesy of The Warner Collection of Gulf States Paper Corporation, Tuscaloosa, Alabama

Excerpts on pages 55, 72, 73, 74, and 103–4 from *Stillness at Appomattox* by Bruce Catton, courtesy of Doubleday, a division of Random House, Inc.

"A Prayer in Spring" on page 75 excerpted from *The Poetry of Robert Frost*, edited by Edward C. Lathem, courtesy of Henry Holt and Company.

Printed in the United States of America

10 9 8 7 6 5 4 3 2 1

Grant has come East to take up his last command
And the grand command of the armies.
It is five years
Since he sat, with a glass, by the stove in a country store,
A stumpy, mute man in a faded Army overcoat,
The eldest-born of the Grants but the family-failure,
Now, for a week, he shines in the full array
Of gold cord and black-feathered hat and superb blue coat,
As he talks with the trim, well-tailored Eastern men.
It is his only moment of such parade.
When the fighting starts, he is chewing a dead cigar
With only the battered stars to show the rank
On the shoulderstraps of the private's uniform.

Excerpt from Book Eight
John Brown's Body
by Stephen Vincent Benet

CONTENTS

FOREWORD

On three occasions since 1993 I have been privileged to read manuscripts and prepare forewords for publications center-staging Vermonters and their role in the Civil War. Howard Coffin authored two of those books. I have known Howard since 1991, when he joined me as a member of the congressionally man-dated Civil War Sites Advisory Commission.

The first of Coffin's two aforementioned books, published in 1993, is *Full Duty: Vermonters in the Civil War*, followed by *Nine Months to Gettysburg: Stannard's Vermonters and the Repulse of Pickett's Charge*. The last of the trio of books mentioned above is Jeffrey Marshall's *A War of the People: Vermont Civil War Letters,* off the press in 1999. Coffin's *Full Duty* and Marshall's *War of the People* are similar in that they do not ignore the people at home and their interaction with the soldiers as they campaigned.

Equally important, thanks to the state's enlightened public school system at the time of the Civil War, most adults in Vermont were liter-ate. Consequently, a surprising number of wartime collections of let-ters have survived, along with soldiers' journals. Newspapers were popular in the Green Mountain State, and provide grist for the enter-prising researcher. The paper trail left by the people of more than 135 years ago gives insights into a period that, like the American Revolution, tried men's and women's souls.

Because of past experience, I welcomed Howard Coffin's invitation to read and write the foreword for *The Battered Stars: One State's Civil War Ordeal During Grant's Overland Campaign.* Steeped by heritage and a lifelong interest in Vermonters in the Civil War, Coffin in his latest work meets the difficult challenge of integrating experiences of the combat soldier with those on the home front during what for a small populated state was a horrific six weeks. Never before or since have so many American servicemen fallen in so brief a period.

Coffin employs the words of the participants, be they soldier or civilian, family or friend, found in their letters, journals, newspapers, and reports from the field to tell it as they saw it. We share their experiences, triumphs, and heartbreaks as they wrote, not as interpreted by the words of historians, journalists, and novelists.

If this approach to what is happening to people, friends and families more than 400 miles apart, is to be successful, the author must have a firm grasp on the ebb and flow of the armies and the lay of the countryside that forms the backdrop and gives a sense of time and place. The same applies to the home front and the people there and the landscape. In that respect Coffin is a master with few peers. He has tramped the Virginia battlefields hallowed by the sacrifices and blood of the Vermonters, along with that of thousands of fellow soldiers in blue and gray. He knows the roads and byways, as well as the towns and farms, of the Green Mountain State.

A sixth-generation Vermonter, whose forebears fought the good fight that brought forth a new birth of freedom and a reunited nation, Coffin is endowed with a special talent for understanding what is special about Vermonters and their state. In 1775 this spirit gave the nation Ethan Allen, Seth Warner, and the Green Mountain Boys. In the Civil War it was Lewis Grant and his Old Brigade and the nine-month men who followed George Stannard to Gettysburg and those on the home front who in Coffin's latest get their just due. In 1898 it was Admiral George Dewey at Manila Bay. In 1936 the state's individualism was demonstrated in "as Maine goes so goes Vermont." In World War Two, Leonard "Red" Wing bravely led the 43rd Infantry

Division in the Pacific, then in 1947 Red Mike Edson of the First Raider Battalion came home to Vermont to head the Vermont Department of Public Safety. Senator Ralph Flanders stood tall in the early 1950s against McCarthyism, as did Warren Austin in the United Nations standing up against the Soviets during the Korean conflict. Then, in late May 2001, Jim Jeffords put principle before party loyalty, and turned over control of the U.S. Senate to the Democrats.

Vermonters have a long history of independence and freedom and in this latest book, Coffin enables readers to better understand this legacy.

Edwin Bearss
Historian Emeritus
National Park Service

PREFACE

What was the Civil War really like? I mean, what was it like to be alive and at war in the years 1861 through 1865? My first two Civil War books concentrated on the personal experience of people at war. But as I wrote those books, I began to wonder more and more about the total experience of people who lived in those momentous times, not only of the men fighting, but of those who remained at home. My earlier books had brief accounts of the home front, but over time I became interested in trying to write a book that would deal much more equally with the goings-on at home. The task of writing such a book on, say, New York State, with nearly two hundred regiments off to war, seemed impossible. But writing about my home state of Vermont, which raised just eighteen regiments—an admirable total from a wartime population of 315,000 people—*that* seemed manageable.

Several years ago, I came into possession of a somewhat battered and slightly water-damaged book that contained a monthly record of the clothing issued to members of a Vermont infantry company during seven months of the Civil War. The record had been carefully penned by an officer (probably Capt. William Pierce, of Wolcott) of Company G of the Third Regiment of the First Vermont Brigade. The regiment included men from an unusually wide range of towns throughout the state. One evening, inspecting the book, I looked at the clothing record for May 1864. The names of the fifty-five officers and men serving in the unit when the month began were neatly set down on two lined pages, and the issues to each of the soldiers were noted beside their names in columns headed "shirts," "trousers," "drawers," "shoes," "blouses," and so on. The May record nearly filled two facing pages of the sizeable book. I then turned the page expecting to see the June clothing record. There was none, probably because the recorder was too busy. Again turning the page, I encountered the listing for July 1864. The left column of the left page was about two-thirds filled with soldiers' names, while the right page was completely blank. Only 24 of the 55 names remained. What had happened to all those men? Could all of them have been lost in the May and June battles of the Army of the Potomac in 1864? What I suspected I was seeing was the most graphic example I had yet encountered of the terrible cost paid by the state of Vermont in Ulysses Grant's Overland Campaign. Sure enough, on further inquiry I discovered that 31 of those 55 men had been either killed or wounded during the 40 days of almost ceaseless fighting. During that time Grant led the Army of the Potomac from its winter encampment at Brandy Station, Virginia, to lay siege to the vital Confederate railroad center of Petersburg, south of Richmond.

The names of men who had been shot in the terrible conflicts at the Wilderness, Spotsylvania Court House, and Cold Harbor had disappeared from the book. Among them, Cpl. David Rattray and Privates David Connell, Hazen Hooker, and George Newton had been killed in the Wilderness. Privates Erastus Scott, James Simpson, and Hugh Crow had been shot dead at Spotsylvania's Bloody Angle. Privates Anson Writer and Wallace Paige had breathed their last at Cold Harbor. I had long known of the Vermont Brigade's heavy casualties in the Wilderness, and of the losses that it and other Green Mountain State units had suffered at Spotsylvania and Cold Harbor. But never had the reality hit me as when I turned the pages of that battered book. I was determined to have a look, in depth, at the Overland Campaign.

The roster of that shattered company contained one name familiar to me, that of Pvt. Erastus Scott. In my book *Full Duty: Vermonters in the Civil War* I quoted a letter written by Scott's young wife when she received news of his death. Her anguished "all my hopes in life are o'er" remains the single most agonizing statement of grief I have yet found from the Civil War period in Vermont. Her words furthered my resolve to delve into the subject of the home front. Then I revisited the remarkable diary kept by William Henry Herrick of St. Johnsbury that I had first seen five years earlier. In taking another look at Herrick's diary I discovered the richness of his account of the days of the Overland Campaign here in Vermont. The idea of a book combining the war front and home front became ever more intriguing.

So I began to look for more home front sources and soon came upon the letters of Olive Cheney, a farm wife in Stowe Hollow and the mother of four sons serving in Vermont regiments. I was touched by the words she wrote to her daughter: "It is strange what makes the boys want to go to war," and, speaking of her husband's struggle to keep the farm going, "It wears upon him with his work he looks quite poor to what he did last winter." Then I found a newspaper account of a large crowd that turned out in the rain in Rutland, while the fighting raged at Cold Harbor, to greet the famed showman Tom Thumb. Through it all it seemed that life, on the surface at least, had gone on so little changed. A book focusing on one state, both at home and at war, indeed seemed possible, certainly if it covered only a limited period such as that leading up to, and encompassing, the Overland Campaign. Vermont was small enough that the total wartime experience of a brief, terribly violent time in the Civil War could be given its due. Thus *The Battered Stars* was begun.

The research and writing of *The Battered Stars* became the most complex and difficult challenge of my three Civil War books, weaving together as it did the stories of the Vermont military units, the overall campaign, and the voices of more than 200 characters speaking from the front and at home. It was a task that took years, and I could not have completed it without considerable help. My thanks go to a Vermont foundation that wishes to remain anonymous for its generous support of the book. I am deeply indebted to the Brattleboro Historical Society, especially to Wayne Carhart and John Carnahan, for its sponsorship of this book, as it sponsored *Nine Months to Gettysburg*. I

Clothing issue roster for Company G of the Third Vermont Regiment for May 1, 1864, just before the start of the Overland Campaign. HOWARD COFFIN COLLECTION

5" Reg.t Vermont Vol.s for the month of May

	Light Coats	Blouses	Trousers	Shirts	Drawers	Shoes	Stockings	Forage Caps	Blankets Wool	Blankets Rubber	Haversacks
Alson Lothrop	1				1				1		
C J Inman											
A S Jenkins						2					
L B Miles											
Porter Morse				1	1					1	
Chas McCarthy											
John McDonald					1						
Joseph Nos					1						
Joseph Norton				1	2						
George Hinston				1	1						
John Nugent											
Rafiel Olmes					1						
Wm O'Brien					2						
W W Paige				1							
M G Paige											
G M Paint											
Alonzo Packard											
E H Scott											
F E Sargeant											
W B Shadrick					3/2						
A B Stone				1	2						
L H Simpson											
A S Writer										1	
David Wishart											
Clark Oliver	1										

Clothing roster for Company G, Third Vermont, at the close of the Overland Campaign. HOWARD COFFIN COLLECTION

owe thanks to the generosity of Vermonters Ken Squire of Waterbury; Nancy Spencer of Shrewsbury, in honor of her son Mitch; and Carl Taylor of Woodstock. In the course of research, I received enthusiastic assistance from many individuals, prominently including Paul Carnahan and Marjorie Strong of the Vermont Historical Society; Jeffrey Marshall and the Special Collections staff of the University of Vermont's Bailey/Howe Library; Kelly Nolin, archivist and savior of the

Vermont adjutant general's papers, who allowed me access to her immense work in progress at the state archives at Middlesex; Peggy Pearl and fellow staffers at the Fairbanks Museum in St. Johnsbury; the staff of the Sheldon Museum in Middlebury; the staff of the Brooks Memorial Library in Brattleboro; Paul Zeller of Newport News, Virginia; David Jamieson of Worcester; William Jenne of the Vermont Historic Sites Division; the late T. D. Seymour Bassett of South Burlington; Eunice Gates of Jeffersonville; remarkable Rokeby in Ferrisburg; and many others. Again, I owe great thanks to my friend

Robert Krick and his staff at the Fredericksburg and Spotsylvania National Military Park in Fredericksburg, Virginia, prominently including Donald Pfanz; to Richard Somers of the U.S. Army Military History Institute at Carlisle Barracks, Pennsylvania; to the staff of the Vermont State Library in Montpelier; to the Rutland Historical Society and the Rutland Library; to the Woodstock Historical Society; to the Windsor Library; to the staff of the St. Johnsbury Athenaeum; to David Blow at the archive of the Diocese of Burlington; to State Senator Hull Maynard and his wife, Taffy, of Shrewsbury for making available to me their wonderful Charles Mead diary; to Donald Miner and the St. Albans Historical Society; to Prof. Graham Newell of St. Johnsbury, a longtime friend and former teacher; and to the late Marjorie Pierce of North Shrewsbury, a dear friend who ever inspired and encouraged. I also owe thanks to many other people throughout the state of Vermont, most especially Wes and Miriam Herwig of Randolph Center for their constant encouragement and for making available to me the Randolph Historical Society's Civil War volumes; to countless Vermonters who came forward with letters, diaries, legends, books, and pieces of information that all combined to make possible the telling of a complex long-ago story; and most especially to Susan Limoge, for her patience, advice, endless support, and encouragement.

As always, I owe a tremendous debt to George Grenville Benedict, Vermont's official Civil War historian. After again making heavy use of his remarkable two-volume *Vermont in the Civil War*, and probing deeply into his personal papers, this time I accorded him the role of primary source. Though he was not a part of the Overland Campaign, as a result of his exhaustive and meticulous research, the fruits of which are preserved in several cartons at the University of Vermont, I decided to let him speak as one who was there.

Many books were of great value to me. Several chapters in *The Wilderness Campaign*, edited by Gary Gallagher, were of immense help, particularly Carol Reardon's pioneering examination of Lewis Grant's Vermont Brigade in the Wilderness. Gordon Rhea's concise *The Battle of the Wilderness, May 5–6, 1864*, was ever valuable, as was Robert Garth Scott's *Into the Wilderness with the Army of the Potomac*, and *Bloody Roads South*, by Noah Andre Trudeau. Also, Bruce Catton's *A Stillness at Appomattox* and *Grant Takes Command*, William Matter's *If It Takes All Summer*, Shelby Foote's *Red River to Appomattox*, Ernest B. Furgurson's *Not War But Murder*, William McFeely's *Grant: A Biography*, Jeffrey Marshall's *A War of the People*, and many others.

Also, I thank the readers of this manuscript: Jeffrey Marshall and Donald Wickman, two Vermonters who know the Civil War history of their state; and to Edwin Cole Bearss, who once again wrote an eloquent foreword for a Howard Coffin book. One of the joys, and great honors, of my life has been to call Mr. Bearss a friend. He is both a living encyclopedia of the Civil War and a fine human being who has, quite rightly, become a legend in his own time.

The subject of the Civil War home front is one that, it seems to me, needs further exploration. As I have said, Vermont's small size, by geography and population, and its limited number of military units, made it a manageable study. Still, the subject was highly complex, and material was often hard to come by. I found that several promising Vermont diary collections were lacking a diary for the year 1864, a fact due, I suspect, to the trying times the year produced at home.

I doubt that any northern state suffered proportionally more severe losses during a limited period of time than did Vermont during the Overland Campaign. The fact that the soldiers, and their friends and families at home, bore the trials almost without complaint seems a wonderful testimony to the Vermont people of the mid-1800s. As this book, I hope, makes clear, they seem generally to have constituted a supportive, self-reliant, stoic, religious, industrious, even gallant lot, who bore the great trial imposed by Ulysses Grant's drive from the Rapidan across the James with remarkable fortitude. To the Vermont people of that era, at home and at war, I dedicate this book, in admiration and amazement. Especially, I am thinking of Pvt. David Moody Jillson, of the 10th Vermont Regiment, my great-great-uncle, wounded at Spotsylvania, again at Third Winchester, and finally, mortally, at Petersburg on April 2, 1865, as the Vermont Brigade finally broke Lee's lines; and of William Henry Herrick, soldier and faithful, insightful, and remarkably honest diarist. Lastly, I express the hope that as the American nation moves into this new century, it will more fully realize the value of the historic places where the drama of the Overland Campaign, at home and at the front, was played out. What survives of the landscape where the war took place—not only the battlefields, but the routes of march, even the campgrounds—should be preserved. Likewise, the old places where the people at home persevered during a mighty time of war should be saved. Their loss would be our loss. Far too much is already gone forever, and more is being lost with each passing day. I recall the inscription above the altar of the handsome old church in West Calais where Vermonters worshiped during the Civil War, and where several soldier funerals took place:

REMOVE NOT THE THINGS THY FATHERS HAVE SET.

THE BATTERED STARS

MAP OF
VERMONT
HISTORICAL

Chapter One

REVEREND PARKER
JOURNEYS SOUTH

The lowering, late-afternoon sun of a spring day in 1864 had lengthened the woodland shadows, sending dim rays through the choked and tangled woodland, as the men, lined two ranks deep, received the order to advance. Smoke from the intermittent firing that had crackled during the previous four hours lay low amid the thick, leafy saplings and brambles, its acrid smell nearly obscuring the soft, sweet aroma of Virginia springtime. Ahead, as everyone knew, were Confederates, unseen through the maze of second-growth forest and thorny underbrush. As always, the men in blue knew, the first shots directed their way would come from a thin line of pickets, well out from the main enemy battle line.

They moved forward cautiously, on a broad front, and soon some of the men were surprised to come upon comrades on their own picket line, not advancing to find the enemy, but lying low and warning of Rebels just ahead. How far the long ranks walked, rifle-muskets at the ready, before everything exploded is not known for certain. Some men spoke of 50 yards, others 200. Suddenly, from the junglelike greenery, the crash of a heavy volley, not the scattered shots of pickets, exploded almost in their faces.

Men fell, as one commander said, by the hundreds. Thousands of shots ripped through the leaves and branches, striking faces, chests, stomachs, arms, and legs. Men were dead before they hit the ground, or dropped bleeding and in dreadful pain. Officers, for a few fatal minutes, doing what they were trained to do, walked the lines of their quickly prone men, giving orders and encouragement. They made the best targets, and colonels and majors, captains and lieutenants, were ripped by the Rebel fire. The men in the ranks who were still able were down and firing on instinct, like good veteran soldiers. They shot at an unseen foe, somewhere close ahead in the green confusion, a bank of smoke and muzzle flashes all that betrayed its position. The soldiers in blue would lie in the choking smoke and gloom, fighting as best they could amid an ever-increasing number of dead and wounded comrades, until darkness settled on the torn and bloodied landscape of this place, so aptly called the Wilderness.

In the night, men crawled forward into the no-man's-land between the hidden lines, risking life and limb to find friends, dead or alive. When it was all over, the toll of the dead, wounded, and missing on that fatal May 5, 1864, in that small section of the great battlefield, would be counted in the thousands. And one thousand of the casualties, out in front of a country crossroads that the generals knew must be held at any cost, would be from a single small and rather faraway place, the New England hill farm state of Vermont.

The Green Mountain State had been dealt a sudden blow perhaps unequaled, considering its small population, in all the northern states during the American Civil War. Vermont, quite simply, had been battered, and the fearful carnage on that Northern Virginia battlefield would even bring the state's governor hurrying south, with a hastily assembled team of civilian doctors, to care for the wounded.

But all that horror and carnage, bleeding and dying, were nearly three months into the uncertain future as, on a February day in Vermont, a man of the cloth, in the thriving railroad town of Waterbury, bid farewell to his beloved wife and family and headed down the main street to catch a train bound south. Ice and snow gleamed brilliant white on the nearby rocky, leonine summit of Camel's Hump, as the Rev. Charles Carroll Parker boarded a passenger car hitched behind a puffing, hissing steam locomotive at the little red Waterbury train station. The harshest of all the Yankee winter months was a week old as the forty-nine-year-old Congregationalist minister began what was likely the most momentous of his earthly journeys. Taking temporary leave of his devoted parishoners at the Waterbury Congregational Church, standing ornately steepled and Gothic along the town's busy Main Street, Reverend Parker answered the call of the United States Christian Commission in its efforts to uplift the moral and religious spirits of the Union's fighting men. Parker was bound for the Army of the Potomac, commanded by the victor of Gettysburg, Maj. Gen. George Gordon Meade, in its vast winter encampments on the hills and fields of Northern Virginia.

Though Parker's concern would be the souls of all the soldiers in the great army, the men in the 10th Vermont Infantry Regiment and the First Vermont Cavalry Regiment would be his special charge. A bit old to fight, Reverend Parker had for three years been doing what he could for the northern cause, gaining a reputation as a firebrand advocate of the Union and the defeat of slavery. A local historian would later write of Parker that his "ministrations during the Civil War kept at white heat the spirit of patriotism locally." Parker had also begun, soon after the rebellion broke out in the spring of 1861, urging the town fathers to erect a monument honoring Waterbury's Civil War soldiers. And he had gained a reputation as an adept amateur historian, sometimes lecturing on the subject of Waterbury's settlement and early history.

A native Vermonter, a poor boy who worked his way to earning a degree at the University of Vermont, Parker also graduated from the Union Theological Seminary in Albany, New York. After serving his first pastorship in the little hill town of Tinmouth, in southwestern Vermont, Reverend Parker had become a prominent religious figure in the state. In 1854 he accepted the position of minister to the Congregationalists in bustling and influential Waterbury, in the north-central part of the state, just a dozen miles from the state capital at Montpelier.

Reverend Parker's way that winter day in 1864 led south and east along the Winooski River, frozen nearly solid in the grip of a mid-Vermont winter. The train surely carried a sizeable number of Vermont soldiers, returning to the ranks from winter furloughs granted after the

Abraham Lincoln,
commander in chief.
LIBRARY OF CONGRESS

fighting in the east of 1863 had ended with a frigid standoff late in November and early December, along a stream called Mine Run. With luck, a solider could board a train at Brandy Station, Virginia, near the upper Rappahannock River, in the midst of the Army of the Potomac's winter encampment, and step onto a Vermont platform within two days.

Making its way through Montpelier Junction, Reverend Parker's train went up the valley of the Dog River and down into the valley of the White River. Chugging along the winding course past innumerable small farms and handsome clapboard villages, in perhaps three hours the train puffed into the busy railroad hub of White River Junction, on the banks of the Connecticut River. There the reverend changed trains for a detour down to Boston, where he intended to enjoy a stop in the so-called hub of New England, the region's largest city.

The highlight of his brief stay there was a visit to Faneuil Hall, that old shrine of freedom and rebellion, hard by the Boston waterfront.

Within the hall's hallowed walls that once rang with the voices of patriot firebrands urging revolution, Parker heard a stirring address by Edward Everett, the Boston orator whose long speech had preceded Abraham Lincoln's few appropriate remarks at the Gettysburg cemetery dedication the previous November. Surely inspired, Reverend Parker was soon back on a coach bound south, changing trains in New York City and taking cars down the eastern seaboard to Washington. There he crossed the Potomac River to Alexandria, Virginia, and headed west into the war zone. Along the way, the train passed through a portion of Northern Virginia already heavily fought over. Parker wrote that he caught glimpses of three major battlefields: Bull Run, where heavy fighting had occurred in the summers of 1861 and 1862; Bristoe Station, where a retreating Union army had inflicted a bloody ambush on a pursuing Rebel force; and Rappahannock Station, where an isolated Confederate force had been battered the previous November.

On arrival at the Army of the Potomac on February 12, the reverend wrote home,

> Here I came at the safe end of my journey. We left Washington at 10 & reached this place at 2½, distance some 60 miles. We went thro Alexandria, by Cloud's Mills, Union Mills, looked upon the Bull Run battlefield, as much as is in sight of the railroad, passed Warrenton Junction, Bristow & Rappahannock where battles have been fought & stopped at this desolation. Indeed from Washington here we did not pass a house that looked like a civilized home. I supposed the region was much broken, but instead it is one wide expanse, much like the gently rolling ridges of the west. All along were encampments of soldiers & contrabands. The latter were extremely engaged in drawing wood with a cart & four mule team, the darkey riding the near wheel mule. The wrecks of cars burned, rail road iron twisted strew the way along. Not a fence or rail was seen after we left Alexa[ndria].

The next morning, the reverend struck out from Brandy Station to locate the 10th Vermont Regiment, whose second in command was a fellow Waterbury resident, thirty-three-year-old Lt. Col. William

Henry. The regiment was camped a mile south and west of the railroad depot, in the fields of John Minor Botts, a prominent Virginia plantation owner and Union sympathizer. Parker wrote on February 13,

> The [Christian Commission] agent here said he had nothing in particular for me to do & I might go where I pleased. I was not long in determining to spend the day with the 10th . . . I slung my haversack, to make believe work, & I started across the fields to the camp. A young Maryland teamster overtook me & gave me a ride. On our way we met a guard coming in with four "Johnnies" as the boys call the Rebels here. They were sorry looking fellows, very lean & shabby, every one in butternut.

Parker joined Colonel Henry and fellow officers of the 10th Vermont at their noontime meal. Then,

> After dinner Col. h proposed a ride to the signal station on Pony Mt. some six miles distant, the highest point in all the region . . . We reached

Lt. Col. William Henry, commanding the 10th Vermont, seen through the mists of time, was a friend of Reverend Parker, a fellow resident of Waterbury. VERMONT HISTORICAL SOCIETY

the top of the Mtn which is about 1,000 feet high, entirely isolated & about half way between the Rappahannock & Rapidan . . . The view is one of the finest in the world, from the Bull Run Mts in the far N. E. round to far beyond Orange Court House, the beautiful range of the Blue Ridge with its gaps & gentle outline was in full view. The sun was shining clear and the Blue was intense. All round from the South West to the N. E. the horizon was in the farthest distance . . . It was a view unsurpassed by any thing I had seen except for Mansfield & Camel's Hump & very unlike them. The headquarters of Gen. Meade & all the encampments of his army with their white tents & blue smoke stretching scores of miles from Cedar and Slaughter Mountains far away to Warrenton was in full view. The big glass on the observatory was trained on the Headquarters. We could see in the West . . . the smoke of Lee's Army stretched along for scores of miles. At my request the Capt. in charge trained his glass on those camps. We could see them distinctly. I did not clearly see a person, but distinctly saw a team coming in.

The key Union signal and observation station on Pony Mountain, as Parker had described, commanded a sweeping view of Northern Virginia, and was capable of keeping a long-distance watch on the winter camps of Robert E. Lee's Army of Northern Virginia, which stretched for 20 miles along the south bank of the Rapidan as they awaited Grant's advance. A tributary of the Rappahannock, the Rapidan joined the larger stream after it passed the northern fringe of an area to the south and slightly east known as the Wilderness. Also within view would have been the key Confederate observation station, atop rocky Clark's Mountain, 15 miles south.

The following evening, Sunday, February 14, Reverend Parker composed a letter to his "dear ones at home." He wrote,

A strange but intensely interesting sabbath has passed. The whole world around has been a little less busy, little less confused than any other day. [No] Men galloping hither and thither, supply trains & ambulances coming & going, cars running and engines screaming, a general uproar on all hands . . . This evening we had a conference and prayer meeting, the tent was filled, mainly with soldiers. We spent nearly two hours with interest intense and unabated to the end. Many of the soldiers spoke telling in unadorned but touching language their experiences in the army, their trials and temptations & how precious they found Jesus to them in every place. The oldest man in the commission said they had seldom had such a meeting in the army.

The next day another Waterbury resident, Maj. William Wells, of the First (and only) Vermont Cavalry Regiment, contacted the visiting pastor. Parker wrote,

I went out by invitation of Maj. Wells to see a grand review of the two divisions of cavalry by Gen. [Alfred] Pleasonton, the commander of all the cavalry . . . As we rode thro Stevensburg, a village now in ruins, we saw the Cavalry gathering on a large plain at the West of the village. We rode directly for the field & soon found our Maj. Wells commanding. The Maj. received me with great cordiality and introduced me to nearly all the commanders of companies . . . After maneuvering for a long time the two divisions were arranged for review. It was grand beyond description. The Maj. said he had seen nothing like it before. One might be in the army years & never see the like. The cavalry proper was preceded by flying artillery, all the horses to the guns & cassons were mounted. It took more than an hour for the whole to pass the Gen. & when extended the column was fully two miles long.

A week later, the reverend visited an army hospital, then wrote,

At this visit we found the surgeons dressing the wounds & stopped while they dressed two whose legs have been amputated near the body. Never have I had my sympathies so moved for the brave and suffering fellows as while witnessing. These hospitals are in tents in a grove, with beautiful walks & cedar hedges & every arrangement to make them comfortable and cheerful.

He continued,

Saturday PM I went to Culpeper where several of the [Christian Com-

Sad-eyed George Gordon Meade, victor of Gettysburg, led the Army of the Potomac in 1864.
HOWARD COFFIN COLLECTION

mission] delegates are stationed & in the evening walked out a mile & preached in a gospel tent filled with soldiers belonging to Batteries— there is a good deal of religious interest there & it was pleasant talking to them . . . Sabbath morning I returned to Brandy Station . . . In the p. m. I rode five miles to Stevensburg & preached to the Vermont Cavalry. The chapel was full & I enjoyed it much. I went out at the request of Maj. Wells. At the close Col. Sawyer [Col. Edward B. Sawyer, commander of the Vermont Cavalry] invited me to come next Sabbath if it was pleasant and preach to the regiment in their camp . . . As I rode from the Cavalry to the 10th I passed the encampment of one division of the 2nd Corps. The men were all out on dress parade, with bands playing on all sides. It was not easy to realize it was the closing hour of the holy Sabbath . . .

On February 24 Parker wrote that a new chapel tent, measuring 30 by 18 feet, had been erected between the camps of the Second Vermont Regiment and the Sixth New York Cavalry Regiment. He noted that both units had seen hard fighting since early in the war, and that the cavalry flag fluttered before its headquarters "all in tatters."

On February 29:

> I ride horseback every day & enjoy it exceedingly. Ride which way we will it is like riding on parade. Men are marching, trains of teams are moving, music is sounding & horses are galloping on all sides. We never get out of sight or company. In passing from our station to Brandy we pass Gen. Meade's head quarters which is in a tent in a pine grove some half mile square which is filled with tents and camps. On each side of his tent are the tents of his staff in the form of a crescent. In front is a beautiful court surrounded by a hedge of pine bows & entered by beautifully arched pathways. The whole has a singularly Eastern and fairy look . . .

Parker wrote on March 9,

> Yesterday I attended the funeral of a young French boy by the name of Goodrich from Williston . . . About sunset we followed young Goodrich to the grave . . . The procession was long. At the grave after the coffin was lowered three volleys were fired over the grave by eight soldiers. This is the usual ceremony.

The next day, the reverend reported that he witnessed in the rain the latter part of a review of the five regiments of the Vermont Brigade. Had it been pleasant, he wrote, it would have been "a fine affair." Still, he said, "The review closed with a charge of the Whole Brigade in line across the field with bayonets gleaming before them with a horrid shout they rushed across the muddy field like demons. I do not wonder an enemy runs before such a sight & sound." On the way back to his tent, he saw a far less imposing sight. "As I was going out to the review I pass the Guard House. A poor fellow was pacing up & down before it in the rain with a great block of wood on his shoulder, a punishment for some misdemeanor. He looked very sorry, his slouched hat over his face & rain dropping from every garment."

Having become fond of military pageantry, the reverend accepted another invitation to attend a review, this one of artillery. Parker said that from a hillock he and many mounted officers watched five batteries with four cannon and four caissons, each drawn by six to eight horses, maneuver on the plain below.

Nearly all the commands were given with the bugle. As we were watching their movements—turning our eyes we saw a cavalcade of horsemen riding out from the pine grove in which are the Headquarters of Gen. Meade. As they drew near we saw it was the Gen. himself with the staff and orderlies coming down for the review. They trotted very quietly to the emminence where we were standing—Gen. Meade in full Military dress wearing his military cap and riding a white faced bay horse. As he rode up all the batteries came like magic into line. He asked the Capt. commanding the Brigade if they were ready & being told they were immediately put his horse into a gallop & rode entirely around them followed by his staff. It was a very fine sight as he went streaming around. Then taking his stand again [on] the emminence with Gen. Williams, Gen. Torbert, Gen. Hunt, joined subsequently by Gen. Sedgwick & a part of his staff making a fine show. Then all the batteries, with their tattered battle flags, filed along before him, the commanders saluting him with their swords & he returning it by raising his cap so that we had a distinct view of his face. After deploying before him the Batteries went through all the evolutions of a battle, upon the run. At times they seemed as confused as though they were all running helter skelter & would all be smashed, then in a moment they would all come into line as if by magic & to my great surprise & delight.

He continued,

After the review . . . I rode over to near Gen. Meade's Headquarters and had a meeting with a few blacks. They did the singing & I the talking. I never heard any thing so plaintive and touching as the singing of those men. One of them would read two lines and then the whole would lift up their heads and sing as though their whole souls were going out on the wings of their song. All had been slaves. Many of them had wives or children or friends still slaves. Perhaps they were thinking of this & of that land where there is no bondage, but all are free & where they shall meet those they love so well. Tears came from the eyes of one fine looking old man as he sang & they lacked little of coming from mine. For a time I almost forgot whether I was in the body or out . . .

Four days later, Parker got a chance to visit the Army of the Potomac picket line. Borrowing a horse from a friend in the the cavalry, Parker rode with an officer of the 10th Vermont into the woods beyond the broad fields that held the army encampments. On the way, they passed the headquarters of Maj. Gen. John Sedgwick, commander of the Sixth Corps.

We came to a camp of soldiers with a rude shelter & a camp fire burning before them. They were the Reserve pickets, those by whom those on duty are relieved & who rally to their support in case of an attack. Going a little further on we saw the picket on a little eminence walking his beat back & forth. Riding up to him we could see others to the right & left with the same measured step pacing their beats. We rode along the line perhaps two miles finding occasionally one from our regiment . . . As we rode along we saw many of the Reserve Camps with their shelters & fires which reminded us strongly of sugar making in Vermont.

A day later, Reverend Parker visited General Sedgwick's headquarters and met the man who commanded the army corps in which the 10th Vermont, and the five regiments of First Vermont Brigade, served. There he found a friend, Capt. James Platte of Hartford, who introduced Parker to Sedgwick and his staff. Parker said,

The Gen. is the finest and most military looking man I have yet seen in the army. He is just a little less than six feet, firmly & stoutly built, with a large round head and frank open face, clear, steady penetrating blue eyes & and a mouth and chin indicating decisiveness & energy. Perhaps he is not more intellectual in his looks than Gen. Meade, but there were apparent more decidedly the qualities that make the great commanders. He commands . . . our Vt. Brigade & this gave a ready introduction . . . Gen. Sedgwick's quarters are in a large tent in the yard of a great mansion the whole of which is used for Head Quarters purposes.

In late March came the time when Reverend Parker had determined to begin his return to Vermont. He presided at his last military religious service on March 25, and wrote that the experience was very powerful. In fact, Parker said that he went away feeling that he should stay with the soldiers. But in the morning he stepped from his tent into a biting wind, finding "a terrible scowl on the whole face of nature & a biting pinch in her grasp." He said, "Before I got back to my tent my purposes were formed."

Parker left Brandy Station by train that afternoon.

While the vast eastern army of the Union passed the winter on the gentle hills and fields along Virginia's Rappahannock and Rapidan Rivers, some 600 miles to the north and east the war was ever a presence on the home front in Vermont, with thousands of Green Mountain State boys away in uniform.

In the northeastern Vermont manufacturing town of St. Johnsbury lived William Henry Herrick, a twenty-three-year-old employee in the shops of the big Fairbanks scale manufacturing enterprise. Herrick (called Henry by his friends) knew something of war, having served for slightly more than a year near its outbreak in the Third Vermont Regiment, albeit in the band. A faded photo of several band members in military uniforms taken in 1862 shows Herrick to be of average height, with a short, thin beard, appearing somewhat sad-eyed. After he was discharged when the regimental band was discontinued, Herrick continued his musical activities as a member of the choir in St. Johnsbury's North Congregational Church, and as a teacher of music. Indeed, music was Herrick's great interest, and he pursued it throughout his life. While in uniform, Herrick had seen fighting, since his term of service included the Peninsula Campaign of 1862 and its brutal "Seven Days," a major Union defeat.

It was Herrick's habit for much of his early adult life to keep a diary. He did so during his army days, and back home in Vermont for several

years. Every night in 1864, Herrick retired to his room in the board-
inghouse of a Mrs. Curtis, not far from the St. Johnsbury railroad station, to record the happenings of his day. On the evening of March 4,
he wrote,

> Mr. Paddock came into the shop this forenoon to know if I would come
> up to the church this afternoon and sing at Abel Hawkins' funeral—he
> went into the 11th [Vermont] Regt. from here last fall and died with
> the measles. last Friday his mother went out to him and was with him
> when he died. he was an only son and his parents feel very badly—he
> was very well known here and the funeral was well attended. Mr. Cum-
> mings read some selections from the Bible and offered prayers. Mr.
> Brustin made the address and we sang two hymns . . . The services
> were solemn though quite brief—the coffin was covered with an amer-
> ican flag, and a beautiful bouquet lay on the opened lid—the body was
> dressed in full uniform with the cap by his side.

Herrick opened his journal for 1864 with an item written the night
of New Year's Day, the first evening of what was to be the bloodiest
year in America's history. As he made clear, a mighty cloud of war was
casting a great shadow over his, and the nation's, future. Herrick was
deeply concerned about his threatened country, and was well aware of
the possibility that he might be called back into uniform in its
defense. Yet he set an optimistic tone when he wrote:

> Standing on the threshold of another year one's thoughts naturally go
> backward and forward in conjecture of what the new has in store, but
> the past has gone forever and its records are sealed. But the future lies
> open before us, pure and unsullied as the pages on which I am writing,
> and I frequently offer the prayer "Lead us not into temptation" that no
> dark blots may deface the fair pages of the new year. My heart is full of
> gratitude to night for many blessings the old year has brought me, and I
> can only hope they may be continued to me; that my health may be
> preserved; that reasonable prosperity may attend me and a fair share of
> the world's goods reward my honest and earnest labor; that friends who
> are so dear to me may not grow estranged or cold; and that I may con-

sistently lead a "quiet peaceable life." But if this is not to be and duty calls me to the field to risk my life in the country's cause may I do it cheerfully and manfully. As the year opens, the nation is not yet delivered from its troubles. When it closes may it find us a free united people and again at peace.

Herrick's nightly commentaries constitute the best known personal record of the home front experience in Vermont during the Civil War. His journal well reflected the growing anticipation in Vermont as winter became spring and the resumption of fighting neared. In early April, Vermont's chief executive, Gov. John Gregory Smith, spoke to that anticipation when he issued a proclamation from his home in St. Albans, a railroad town in northwestern Vermont. It began:

As a fitting occasion for the people of this State unitedly to humble themselves before the Almighty God, and in observance of a custom, which finds its sanction and approval in the best promptings of the Christian's heart, I do hereby appoint THURSDAY, THE SEVENTH DAY OF APRIL NEXT, to be observed as a day of PUBLIC FASTING, HUMILIATION AND PRAYER. And I do earnestly invite the people of the State, on that day to lay aside all secular employment, and to assemble in their accustomed places of worship . . . Let us deplore before Him our sins as a nation, and beseech Him to grant us His favor, that he will give wisdom to all in authority, that he will grant success to our army and navy, and crown the year with an enduring peace. Let us seek His blessing upon the brave soldiers, that whether in the camp, or in the field of battle, in the hospital, or languishing in captivity, He will be near them to protect and bless, to comfort and sustain them, and, having accomplished their sacred mission, return them in safety to their families and their homes. Thus may our Fast be ever much as the Lord hath chosen, that our light may break forth as the morning . . .

Two weeks later, in Vermont's largest city, Burlington, on the shore of Lake Champlain, the daily *Burlington Free Press* printed the following brief editorial:

THE OPENING OF THE CAMPAIGN

We may prepare ourselves for events of the utmost interest and importance on the soil of Virginia. The season for active operations has arrived. Gen. Grant's splendid army is stripping for a fight. There are indications, it is said, of an advance on Gen. Lee's part. That the rebel general will take the initiative, we greatly doubt; that nothing would suit Grant better than such an advance is highly probable. Gen. Lee can move forward, doubtless, when he sees fit; but he will find that such a movement will result in no hurrying back of the army of the Potomac over the old "express route." Whichever moves first, it is not likely that a collision will be long avoided, and when it comes it will be no boy's play.

The great "collision" about to occur would, of course, commence in the war-ravaged area of Northern Virginia just south of where the two great armies faced each other along the Rapidan River in the winter of 1864. It was from the Union camps that Charles Parker had departed for his Vermont home. But it turns out that the reverend did not go directly to Waterbury and his church, home, and family. As on his southward trip, when he made a stop in Boston, on the way north he dallied a day or two in Washington. On arrival, Parker reported that he found the city a depressing place with "a furious gale blowing up the Avenue & the whole heavens vile with the dust of the city." He wrote,

> I have seldom seen nature more wrathful in her look & the wild whistle of her voice. Very soon snow began to fall & and with its fall the wind began to abate & pretty soon sidewalks & street, houses & trees were covered with virgin white and nature's face looked much better . . . Before leaving camp, I had seen in the papers that the President had a reception every other Tuesday evening from 7 to 11 & I also learned from a clerk in one of the departments who was down to the Army that I was in luck, this being the week for the reception.

Parker reached the White House at 8:30 PM, but he and other gentlemen (women were admitted on arrival) were forced to stomp about in the cold for a half hour "before we heard the welcome click & the door flew open." He related,

We first went into a large room where were waiters to take our coats & hats and give us checks. We then stepped into what I think is called the Green Room and lifting up our eyes to the Blue Room which opens out from this, we beheld the tall, gaunt, angular, unmistakable form and features of honest old Abe with his deep large eyes wide open towards the crowd . . . in a jiffy we were before him, had him by the hand & were saying "How do you do" and then we were out of his way for the next comer. Passing the president we paid our obeisance to Mrs. Lincoln, who was sitting to the right & rear of the President & near the middle of the room. No contrast can be more complete than between the looks of the President and his wife. He is sharp and angular to the last degree, as though he had been shaped by a rail splitter. She is round and soft as though she had been molded out of the nicest dough. On every feature of the man is written character—high—true—sterling—native character. On every feature of the woman—if perfect roundness has a feature—was plainly written CHARACTERLESS. With all his homely features, Mr. Lincoln looked like nature's nobleman & when a smile came over his ordinarily intensely solemn face & he was about to make a funny speech, his face was singularly pleasant—every rough feature radiant with the kindness & humor & geniality of his soul. Mrs. Lincoln was like a big doll, as emotionless as the lesser types of porcelain and china—so it seemed to me as I looked at one & then the other. The President was dressed in full black with white kid gloves covering the extremities of his huge, long, ape-like arms & his collar low & turned down as you always see it in the pictures. Mrs. Lincoln was dressed very neatly & as described in the notices of the reception I cut from the *Republican* of the next day & which I inclose. I think of nothing in addition but a gold comb in her hair.

The observant reverend continued,

After our introduction & obeisance we passed on into the East or Red Room—the large room for promenade, where we circulated or stood. Soon the room was filled but not crowded. In an adjoining room was a big band of twenty-four players who almost constantly made music for us . . . Occasionally I went round to the first or Green Room & quietly watched the President as he received the stream of old men & women, young men & maidens. To all he gave a smile & a word. Every now and then his eyes would twinkle & his face would light up with fun & gladness & before they were passed there was pretty sure to be a burst of laughter—the President bowing & swinging himself from side to side. Evidently an old friend had come & a funny story had been told. The moment they were passed and there was a break in the current, he would lift his eyes & look through the doorway to see what next was coming & his whole look would be as solemn as though it was never blest with a smile. In a moment a familiar face would send sunshine all over it again. Near the close he took his seat & received the guests sitting. Among the guests was Mr. Colfax, Speaker of the House [Schuyler Colfax of Indiana]. As he passed the president with a lady on each arm, he stopped & they had some very pleasant talk about Mr. Lincoln's likenesses. The President asked him if he had seen the one taken in Chicago with the long hook nose—taking hold of his nose as he said it & then joining a hearty laugh. He then spoke of another one and Mr. Colfax asked him if it was good. He replied—y—e—s—if you call an accurate likeness good—& then both joining in a laugh. The President then asked if he had ever had his bust taken & described in a laughable way the process of lathering the face with the soft plaster & the sensation produced. Two boys could not have talked with more child-like simplicity than they. A crowd gathered around then and I was fortunate enough to be so near as to hear . . .

The time for the end of the reception had come. "The President rose & walked around past Mrs. Lincoln," Parker wrote,

& with a smile and queer wrinkles at the spring of his nose such as we sometimes see when one feels funny and a little silly, he offered his arm—not to Mrs. Lincoln—but to a not handsome, but nonetheless elegant looking lady of middle age & marched to the East Room and began the promenade with which all such receptions close. Mrs. Lincoln followed them in four couples behind on the arm of Gen. Schenk, now member of the house [Congressman Robert C. Schenk, of Ohio]. Perhaps the lady on the President's arm was Mrs. S. As I looked at the President, tall, awkward, but dignified and solemn, as he walked around the room leading the whole throng & thought of him as a once poor boy—a rail splitter & flat boat man—now having in his hand power hardly surpassed by any man on earth & with cares & responsibilities such as perhaps no other man ever had, a feeling not much removed from awe came over me & I felt I would pray for him as I had never done before.

In the spring of 1864, as the time for war came once again to the battered country, as Reverend Parker correctly surmised, no man in all the land held power so awesome as Abraham Lincoln; his was the power to direct the course of the great civil war that had divided the American nation. With the tall, awkward westerner, come east to lead the nation's threatened federal government, lay the might to seek with the southern Confederacy some kind of peace, or to drive the North's military forces on toward a final, complete, military victory. Lincoln had, of course, chosen the course of all-out war and total victory. In no way had he made that intent more clear than by his appointment, on March 9, of Lt. Gen. Ulysses S. Grant, the great hero of the war in the west, the victor of Fort Donelson, Missionary Ridge, and Vicksburg, to command all the Union armed forces. Grant fought like no other Union high commander, Lincoln well knew, and he had told the general to come east and personally accompany the big eastern Army of the Potomac, that hard-fighting but poorly led and largest of all the federal legions, on its coming offensive. "He fights," Lincoln had said, and Grant would prove those words deadly true.

Ahead was a grim military campaign that would surpass in bloodshed and suffering anything the nation had known. Grant would drive the Army of the Potomac south across 100 miles of Virginia, a mostly rural landscape already considerably marked by war. But the people who made the farms and roadside villages in that portion of Virginia Tidewater their home had seen nothing like the fury that was to come. Ahead lay desperate struggles in the Wilderness, around Spotsylvania Court House, along the North Anna River, and at a rural crossroads called Cold Harbor. In the great eastern battles of the last spring and early summer of 1864, no northern state, certainly on a per capita basis, would pay a higher price than little Vermont. Before the coming forty days of fighting had ended, scarcely a Vermonter, whether in uniform or out, would escape the blows of what the world would come to know as Grant's Overland Campaign.

※

Because the largest cavalry battle of the Civil War was fought near Brandy Station, Virginia, a long fight has been waged in recent years to preserve the historic landscape. Thanks to the determined efforts of the Brandy Station Foundation and its many friends, much of the lovely landscape around the still-rural village has been saved from development. Included in that acreage is at least some of the site of the Vermont Brigade's camp. There the lads doomed to the fury of the Wilderness, Spotsylvania, and Cold Harbor spent a relatively happy winter, overshadowed by the mighty campaign all knew must commence with the coming of the traditional time of hope—the coming of spring.

The battlefield is located on some of the most handsome land in all of Virginia, whose high points command views of the rolling hills and fields along the Rappahannock River stretching off to the Blue Ridge. To the south are Pony Mountain, where Reverend Parker got his long-range view of the Confederate camps, and Clark's Mountain, now festooned with communications towers, where Lee and his generals gathered on the eve of the fighting. To the east, around Stevensburg, the wide expanse of fields where the Union cavalry regiments camped and paraded remains much as it was, though the land is unprotected and likely to someday be developed. Anyone interested in the places where the Civil War took place in Virginia should visit them as soon as possible, for the state is growing relentlessly and development is spreading at an alarming rate.

Some 600 miles to the north, in Waterbury, Vermont, the white Waterbury Congregational Church stands along the village's Main

Street. There Reverend Parker preached against slavery and in favor of a war to destroy it and to save the Union. The exterior of the church, which received a Gothic redesign shortly before the war began, looks much as it did in 1864. In July 2001, the church observed the two hundredth anniversary of its founding with a bicentennial service on a blue-sky Sunday morning. Late in the service, the doors of the sanctuary were opened and the minister told the congregation to listen. What they heard was the ringing of the church's long-silent bells, the same bells that had called the people of Waterbury to worship during the Civil War. Greetings were brought to the congregation on the historic occasion by the new leader of Vermont's United Church of Christ, the Rev. Arnold Thomas. A black man, Thomas is the great-great-grandson of people who had been slaves on plantations in Georgia and Alabama.

Chapter Two

BEFORE THE STORM

O n February 6, 1864, a new recruit arrived at the Brandy Station, Virginia, camp of the Army of the Potomac. Pvt. George S. Lyon, from the southern Vermont town of Winhall, had enlisted in Company E of the Fifth Vermont Regiment in early January. Lyon traveled by train to the war zone. He had just completed his first long journey anywhere and, for all he knew, his days might be numbered. A week after arriving, he wrote to a friend back home:

Dear friend,

I have seen some pretty hard times and some good times. I had a chance to see some of the country and some of it I did not see while coming out here. had a good long ride on the cars and some other things to numerous to mention . . . I stood on guard last sunday night and it was dark as a pocket and rained quite hard, made me think of home but I commenced to whistle and sing . . . and I was all right, have not been homesick nor sorry I enlisted atall whatever. The Rebs are coming onto our lines every day I should not think they could stand it a good while longer if a great many more desert. I have seen the rebs they look rather tough . . .

On the day he wrote that letter, Private Lyon had one day less than three months to live, for he would die of a Rebel bullet in the green hell of the Wilderness on May 5. At his funeral in Manchester, Vermont, a month later, the Rev. J. S. Goodall would face the dead soldier's friends, family, and neighbors from the little village and hill farms that had constituted George Lyon's small, beloved world and would ask the question, "To what purpose is this waste?"

Any Vermont soldier joining the Army of the Potomac in the winter of 1863–64 was sure to find in the ranks a good many friends and neighbors from back home. Vermont was well represented in Maj. Gen. George Meade's vast army by six infantry regiments, a cavalry regiment, and three sharpshooter companies. Many of the members of those fighting units had spent previous winters with the great eastern army, and all knew they were now experiencing the most pleasant winter encampment thus far. The first winter of fighting, the five regiments of the First Vermont Brigade, bivouacked a few miles south of the Potomac River near Alexandria, Virginia, had seen their ranks decimated by disease. Hundreds of men died, and the following winter, in camps near Fredericksburg along the Rappahannock River, the sick lists had again been far too long. In this third long cantonment, men were still taking sick and dying, but at a much reduced rate. The Brandy Station winter would be widely remembered by veterans of the Army of the Potomac as the best war zone respite of the war.

In the ranks at Brandy Station, and making up the First Vermont Brigade, fondly known as the "Old Brigade," were the Second, Third, Fourth, Fifth, and Sixth Vermont Regiments. On the fields of the Peninsula Campaign, at First Fredericksburg, and at Crampton's Gap, those veteran combat units had earned the Vermont Brigade a reputation as one of the best fighting outfits in the Army of the Potomac. During the storming of Marye's Heights, at the second battle of Fredericksburg in 1863, and then in protecting the Sixth Corps' retreat as Joseph Hooker went down to defeat at Chancellorsville, the brigade had again shone. Its reputation had grown in the summer of 1863 as it led the Sixth Corps' forced march to Gettysburg. Brig. Gen. Martin T. McMahon, corps adjutant, in a rousing tribute to the Old Brigade delivered after the war, said:

They were strangely proud, not of themselves individually, but of the brigade collectively; for they knew perfectly well they were the best fighters in the known world. They were individually self-reliant and skillful in the use of arms; and they honestly believed that the Vermont Brigade could not be beaten by all the combined armies of the rebellion.

The brigade had the rare distinction of having been formed entirely of regiments from a single state. Its commander (the brigade's third) was Brig. Gen. Lewis Addison Grant, born in Winhall, Vermont, a former schoolteacher in Massachusetts and New Jersey who had returned to his native state to practice law. Competent and unspectacular, with a quiet, easy manner, a receding hairline, and a rather prominent nose, the Vermont Brigade commander became known around the army for obvious reasons as "the other Grant." For reasons unclear, the men of his brigade had a rather uncomplimentary nickname for their thirty-six–year-old leader. "Aunt Lydia," they called him.

Also in the ranks at Brandy Station was the 10th Vermont Regiment. Mustered into service in the fall of 1862, the 10th had done patrol duty along the Potomac west of Washington until it moved with the Army of the Potomac in late November down to Mine Run. There the 10th had seen its only combat thus far, sustaining sixty-three casualties in a bold uphill attack on a wintry afternoon near Orange Grove, Virginia.

Just to the east of Brandy Station, around the war-battered hamlet of Stevensburg, were the camps of the Army of the Potomac's cavalry. Among them was the First Vermont Cavalry Regiment, Vermont's only mounted unit, already a veteran of many conflicts, including a running fight with the late "Stonewall" Jackson's horsemen during his Shenandoah Valley Campaign of 1862. The regiment had distinguished itself in several bloody clashes during the Gettysburg Campaign, and a portion of it had obediently followed the ill-considered orders of Judson Kilpatrick, joining a costly, brave, but unnecessary attack late on July 3, 1863, after Pickett's Charge had been repulsed. The Vermonters had also held their own in several clashes with the Confederate raider John Singleton Mosby.

As spring arrived, the Vermont cavalry had a new commander, a

Brig. Gen. Lewis Grant, "the other Grant," a native Vermonter, led the Vermont Brigade through the Overland Campaign.
HOWARD COFFIN COLLECTION

longtime veteran of the regiment, Lt. Col. Addison Preston. A dashing fellow, with thinning blond hair and intense eyes, Preston was a native of the beautiful northern Vermont hilltop town of Danville. For a time a student at Brown University, Preston had been forced to drop out of school because of ill health. On the advice of a doctor, he had embarked on a sea voyage to Australia. Then he sailed to California, where he stayed for several years. But with the outbreak of war, Preston was back in Danville, where he married before enlisting in the First Vermont Cavalry. A born leader, he was immediately elected a company commander and quickly gained a reputation as a fearless fighter. In 1863, he was wounded twice, once in a clash with J. E. B. Stuart's troopers near Gettysburg.

Also in the Army of the Potomac's ranks were three veteran companies of Vermont sharpshooters, Company F of the First U.S. Sharpshooter Regiment, and Companies E and H of the Second U.S. Sharpshooter Regiment. The Union armies counted among their sharpshooters proportionally more men from Vermont than from any other Union state. Vermont lads could shoot and they had proven their worth as marksmen in combat on many bloody fields, including Gettysburg.

Seth Eastman, a Sixth Vermont veteran and a private in the Old Brigade, summed up the experience of camp in the winter of 1863–64: "Our camp at Brandy Station [was] the most pleasant that I had while in the army."

The Rev. Edwin E. M. Haynes, chaplain of the 10th Vermont, wrote:

We went into winter quarters near the house of John Minor Botts, our regiment occupying a site which a few weeks before had been selected by the rebels for their winter quarters . . . The position on the left of our brigade, assigned the Tenth, was pleasantly chosen. It was a comparitively smooth piece of ground, sloping to the south, and backed by a grove of nearby oaks, which, however, the men were not allowed to cut down, both on account of the protection they afforded from the north wind, and the sturdy loyalty of the owner. [Botts, though a slave owner, was an avowed Union sympathizer] . . . It was commonly reported that the army encamped at Brandy Station, but it was scattered over the ground in this vicinity for six miles or more around . . . There were few things that the soldier needed that he could not purchase. There were sutlers for each regiment, and "purveyors" for corps, division and brigade head-quarters. Some of them opened clothing stores, and nearly all tried to keep on sale what there was a demand for, and through them anything that was kept in the markets of Washington and New York could be procured upon short notice at small (?) profits . . . The occupations of the men during these winter months were various—*they were Yankee.* Their quarters were comfortably arranged; some of them were ingeniously fitted up and fancifully adorned. Harper's and Leslie's Illustrated furnished many a soldier's hut with tasty decorations, after he had profitably read them. Some of their tents were turned into cobbler's shops and tailoring establishments, where the occupant, with true Yankee enterprise, would repair the clothes and shoes of his neighbor; some of them, besides all the other purposes they served, were converted into jeweler's shops, and watches were actually well cleaned and repaired in the camp. All kinds of craftsmen were found among the volunteers of our army, and details were easily made for the telegraph office, the forges, and all the workshops of the Quartermaster-General . . . these men were good for all work, from the tinkering of a tin cup and the digging of a ditch to the building of a railroad. All professions were also represented in the ranks . . . Our military duties at this time were light, details, only once in two or three weeks, being required for picket duty.

The men of the Army of the Potomac, camped around Brandy Station, lived under a cloud. The veteran soldiers knew, and certainly made the newcomers well aware, that some sustained and vicious fighting would commence with the coming of spring. A sense of foreboding, even of doom, was ever present. The routines of camp life, which included drills, duties, reviews, and picket duty, still left the men with time on their hands—perhaps too much time—for thinking.

"Day before yesterday we had a General's inspection and yesterday a Corps review," Pvt. Edwin Hall, of the 10th Vermont, wrote to his parents in Brookfield:

We were reviewed by Gens. Meade and French and some said that Uncle Abe was there—but there were so many there that I could not tell the man. It was a pleasant day—but cold . . . All the Infantry, Cavalry, Artillery, Train, Wagons, and Ambulances that belonged to the Corps were out in full uniforms and presented an imposing spectacle. Such a one as only those belonging to the army can appreciate.

Hall added to his letter the next day, "I have helped pay to send home the boys that have died and have bought some butter and a number of things and have had to pay double prices for everything."

Perhaps the most prolific writer within the ranks of the Vermont

Brigade was Pvt. Wilbur Fisk, product of a hill farm above the valley village of Tunbridge. Fisk not only carried a rifle-musket, but the former schoolteacher also served as a war correspondent for the *Green Mountain Freeman*, a newspaper in Montpelier. He signed his published letters with the pseudonym "Anti-rebel." From the camp of his Second Vermont Regiment, Fisk reported in March on one of the diversions organized to help pass the time and divert the mind. "Horse races were sometimes organized," he wrote:

> There was a big crowd of spectators in the hollow below us of men and officers the most of the latter being on horseback. When the time had come for the great drama to be enacted these last took a position in a straight line along the track and the men on foot got the most favorable positions for a sight that they could . . . The two competitors took their positions at the end of the allotted ground. A little negro boy was selected to ride the gray horse, a little boy that wasn't a negro was selected to ride the other. The signal was given and they started. At the very first the gray horse was behind but he soon picked up his feet and passed by the other and he kept about twice his length ahead all the way. The riders clung on to each like little monkeys in a circus riding around the ring. The bet was for $100 so I understand.

On February 3, Cpl. Edwin Horton, Fourth Vermont, wrote to his wife, Sally, in the mountain town of Chittenden, on the western slope of the Green Mountains. Mrs. Horton had tried her best, like so many loved ones at home, to improve their soldiers' lot. The corporal wrote,

> I received the box I got today the pies and the oysters was spoiled the play had gone out of the oysters . . . and the oyster juice had run in the pies and they are all jammed up and mouldy and the oysters all sowered on account of their loasing the juice. the rest of the box was all right I shall think of you sally when I am drinking that wine and eating those preserves. I wish I was up there so you could help eat them if I could see you sally I would divide willingly I wouldn't play hog at all I would just say Sally sit up and we will take a little grub.

Always, there were thoughts of home. Eugene Joslyn, a private in Company H, Second U.S. Sharpshooters, wrote to his mother in Waitsfield on February 22:

> Tell Charlie I mean to be home and help him get out the old pine next winter . . . It is very sad to hear of so much sickness and death among you at home. Those who remain at home are reminded that death is just as certain too them as to the soldier.

Two weeks later he wrote,

> We have been having some excitement about changing our blue clothing for green (to distinguish us from infantry). Our company did not wish to do so as they nearly all had blue suits which were good & they did not wish to lose them just to gratify a whim of the old Col. Well, the Capt. took sides in with the boys & tried to avoid it & the Col got mad & put him under arrest & took his sword from him. But he got it back again this morning & we were finally obliged to draw suits. I think the clothing is better than our other.

A keen observer of events in the Army of the Potomac that winter and spring was Dr. George T. Stevens, a surgeon in the 77th New York Regiment, from the Saratoga region, near the Vermont border, assigned to the same Sixth Corps division as the Vermont Brigade. He wrote,

> A course of literary lectures was . . . delivered in the chapel of our Third brigade, and Washington's birthday was celebrated in it with appropriate ceremonies and addresses. The chapel tent was also a reading room, where, owing to the energy of Chaplain Fox, all the principal papers, secular and religious, literary, military, pictorial, agricultural and scientific, were furnished; and these were a great source of pleasure and profit to the men.

And Stevens added, "The only military movement of the winter was Kilpatrick's great raid on Richmond, in which the lamented Dahlgren lost his life."

But for that "great raid," the winter encampment for the Vermonters would have been free of any fighting and hard marching. But Green Mountain State troops, both cavalry and infantry, were roused from their camps in late February to participate in a complex undertaking aimed at thrusting a Union force into the Confederate capital of Richmond. The idea was concocted by Brig. Gen. Judson Kilpatrick, a flamboyant, reckless New Jersey man who, in midwinter, won from Washington permission to launch a mounted raid on Richmond. The objective was threefold: to free Union prisoners, to torch Rebel storehouses, and to distribute, down toward the Rebel capital, thousands of amnesty proclamations that Abraham Lincoln very much wanted to get into Confederate hands. The pieces of paper stated that any citizen of the rebellious states pledging allegiance to the federal government would be given amnesty by that government.

Starting from the Union cavalry camps at Stevensburg on the evening of February 28, Kilpatrick led four thousand horsemen, including the First Vermont Cavalry under Addison Preston, south toward Richmond. To distract Confederate attention from the move, George Custer led more Union cavalry in another direction, on a foray toward Charlottesville, Virginia. As Kilpatrick's main body mounted up, a five hundred-man detachment under brave, one-legged Ulric Dahlgren, including a small detachment of Vermonters, crossed the Rapidan at Ely's Ford, captured a handful of Confederate pickets to clear the way for the larger force, then moved south to Spotsylvania Court House. There the daring Dahlgren swung to the southwest, intent on crossing the James River and advancing on Richmond from the south. Meanwhile, Kilpatrick continued due south and on March 1 was facing the formidable Richmond fortifications.

Rebuffed, he moved to the Mechanicsville Turnpike. At 10 PM he summoned Colonel Preston to his tent and asked if the Vermonter would lead a raid into the heart of the city to free Union prisoners from Libby Prison, near the Richmond waterfront on the James River, and from the prison on Belle Isle, midstream in the James. Preston readily agreed and prepared his Vermont regiment, with a small group of other handpicked men, for the strike. Preston spent the night readying for the move, but before dawn Kilpatrick received word of an attack on his rear guard that caused him to abandon the plan. Kilpatrick then determined to strike eastward and head for the safety of Union-held Yorktown on the Virginia Peninsula. He got most of his main body safely there on March 3, after considerable skirmishing.

Dahlgren's smaller force was far less lucky, encountering a flooded James River blocking its planned route. In the end, the hard-luck detachment had to fight its way up from Richmond. Dahlgren was killed along the way, and when Kilpatrick's battered command finally reassembled, well down the peninsula toward Williamsburg, any thought of an overland return to the Army of the Potomac was abandoned. Transports were sent to Fort Monroe, and the tired cavalrymen were given a boat ride back up to Alexandria. The cost of the failed adventure had been considerable, about 350 casualties. The First Vermont Cavalry had 12 men wounded, and reported 59 men missing, a good many ending up in Rebel prisons. Kilpatrick was soon transferred out of the Army of the Potomac, and certainly no Vermonters shed any tears.

The whole adventure also resulted in some hard marching on the part of the Sixth Corps, including the Vermont Brigade. Starting February 27, the corps was sent on a tramp toward Madison Court House, 23 miles southwest of Brandy Station, in support of Custer's diversionary strike. The expedition lasted five days and failed to produce any serious fighting. The march was described by Private Fisk:

We came in yesterday from a reconnaissance out to Madison Court House . . . We accomplished nothing wonderful, and did no deeds of mighty valor . . . We have marched out to Madison Court House and we have marched back again. We had rather a tedious time of it, but it is over with now and I am glad of it.

Fisk went on to note,

The weather when we started was as fine as could be desired . . . We marched through Culpeper, then bore to the right from the railroad towards Robertson Creek. Things did not look at all warlike in and around Culpeper. Ladies on horseback were riding gaily about with officers, and seemed to be having a merry time generally . . . We halted near Robertson Creek, stacked arms . . . in a few minutes more every rail in that near vicinity had been appropriated. Secesh pigs and chickens fared no better . . . A couple of sheep got frightened into the crowd and captured, for somebody a fine supper . . . We remained in that place till Wednesday morning when we came in. It commenced storming Monday night, and the rest of the time it was wet, nasty and disagreeable enough everywhere. Sometimes it rained, sometimes it snowed, and sometimes it did both at once . . . we had no tents . . . The cavalry had gone out and come in again, and from what the cavalry boys said it was evident that they considered their expedition anything but a successful one. Wednesday morning we had orders to return . . . The roads were the opposite extreme from dusty. We made the whole distance back to camp that day. The distance will not vary much from twenty-five miles. Many fell out completely exhausted and helpless as infants.

With the brief campaign ended, the routine of camp life resumed. But on March 14, a bit of military pageantry livened things up. Fisk wrote,

We had a brigade review last Monday, and one again Thursday, notwithstanding it rained the last time, there were some distinguished Vermont citizens, and a few ladies, present to witness it. We have a first rate ground in front of our camp for parades and reviews, and we have had some first rate parades and reviews on this ground. The Vermont Brigade took their places in line here,—and it makes a pretty long line now—and when the order was given "Prepare for review," and we had opened ranks so that the reviewing officer could see both the rear and the front rank at once, Col. Grant rode around the line to the rear and front, followed by his staff officers, citizens and visitors, who appeared to be well pleased with our appearance. Gen. Sedgwick couldn't resist the temptation to come and see us too. I noticed the old fellow was looking remarkably good-natured, as he passed by the front of where I stood, and he seemed to be talking with considerable animation to the officers that rode by the side of him; pointing occasionally to us, as if he was afraid they would overlook some of the excellencies which he saw. I couldn't tell what he said exactly, but I knew well enough, he was telling them how quick he could take Richmond if he only had Vermonters enough to do it.

Fisk also took note of a church presence in camp, including that of a certain minister from Waterbury. "We are having good religious meetings in our regiment," he wrote:

> The Christian Commission has two delegates here, the Rev. Messrs C. C. Parker and J. W. H. Baker, both from Vermont. They have put up a large chapel tent, capable of seating about two hundred men. They hold meetings here every evening, and almost every time the tent is filled to overflowing . . . Cheerful sacred singing and speaking is pleasant always; but I believe a soldier enjoys them the best of anybody. It is very natural from his circumstances that he should.

Certainly, not all the men in the ranks were churchgoers. Pvt. Tabor Parcher wrote his wife in April mentioning fellow Waterbury resident Reverend Parker, and that Vermont governmental staple, March town meeting:

> I doant think that Parker started many revivles in the armey as at least what you write is the first that I herd about it I did not go to hear him while he was here I doant go to meating much I have had a paper of the proceedings of town meeting so you will not nead to send eny.

The biggest stir of the winter encampment came with the earth-shaking change of command of all Union forces engineered by Abraham Lincoln. Pvt. Oscar Waite, in the 10th Vermont, wrote,

> Well, we have our wish. The Washington "Chron—i—kill." says:— The rank of Lieutenant General, revived by act of Congress passed February 14th, has been conferred upon General Grant by the President. The General will, by virtue of his office, take command of all the armies in the field. It is also understood that he will make his headquarters with the army of the Potomac and direct its operations in per-

son. This certainly means fighting; and fighting that will be kept up until the rebels are whipped, or we are.

Waite continued,

I don't think the Yankees, taken as they run, are very bloodthirsty, but since this job must be done, all hands seem anxious to pitch in and finish it. We are sick and tired of this everlasting, useless racing, and we rejoice in the fact that Grant doesn't belong to the retreating class. Yes, the "Bulldog of Donelson" is now boss of the whole job, and whatever his programme, it is perfectly safe to say that it doesn't include falling back to Washington every time a rebel happens to look in that direction.

Ulysses Grant arrived at Brandy Station on March 10, and thirteen days later a sweeping order was issued, directing a thorough reorganization of the Army of the Potomac. The aim was to get a tighter rein on the big army, and Grant directed that its five corps be consolidated into just three. The revamped corps were the Second, commanded by Winfield Scott Hancock, the Fifth, under Gouverneur K. Warren, and the Sixth, led by John Sedgwick. The Vermont Brigade remained in the Sixth Corps, to which was added a Third Corps division under James Ricketts, a crusty old West Pointer who had had two horses shot from beneath him at bloody Antietam. That division included the brigade of Brig. Gen. William H. Morris, and one of its regiments was the 10th Vermont. Thus six Vermont regiments were now serving in John Sedgwick's corps. In addition to Ricketts' division, the other two divisions of the Sixth Corps were commanded by Horatio G. Wright and George W. Getty. Getty replaced as commander of the Vermont Brigade's division Albion Howe, who was reassigned to oversee the artillery defending Washington. George Getty came to his new assignment with a sterling reputation, having distinguished himself in the Seven Days fighting of the Peninsula Campaign, and at Antietam, among other places. A native of Georgetown, in the District of Columbia, bearded and dark-haired with piercing eyes, Getty was married to a southern woman, though his devotion to the Union cause was unquestioned. He was a battler and under him, in "Getty's division," the Vermont Brigade would see its hardest fighting of the Civil War. Getty's brigades would be led as follows:

First Brigade, Brig. Gen. Frank Wheaton.
Second Brigade, Brig. Gen. Lewis A. Grant.
Third Brigade, Brig. Gen. Thomas H. Neill.
Fourth Brigade, Brig. Gen. H. L. Eustis.

Grant's reorganization also had its effect on the First Vermont Cavalry, just in from the failed ride against Richmond. First, a new top man was placed in command of all the Army of the Potomac's horsemen. Tough Philip Sheridan, short and wiry, was a favorite of Grant's brought from the west, where he had distinguished himself as a leader of infantry. G. G. Benedict, veteran of the Second Vermont Brigade and author of the official history of Vermont in the Civil War, wrote, "Aware that he had been an infantry division commander, the cavalry looked hard at him at first; but it was not long before they all owned that Grant knew his man, and that the man was equal to the place." Sheridan took the place of Alfred Pleasonton, sent to the west along with Kilpatrick. The Army of the Potomac's cavalry contained three divisions, and the leadership of the Third Division, formerly Kilpatrick's, which contained the First Vermont Cavalry, was handed to Brig. Gen. James H. Wilson, like Grant an Illinois man and a friend of the commanding general who had only limited combat experience.

Sharpshooter Thomas Brown wrote to his wife in Ryegate on April 6 about Grant's reorganization:

General Grant is tairn the army of the Potomac all to peses and giting redy to make a move on the Rebs. Grant has took the Third Corps and poot it into the 2 corps and 6 corps so you see this is now 3 corps I am in the 2 corps now I will tell you about the wether it is cold and rainy and it has raind and snod for about a week.

The winter wore on with some early signs of spring suddenly erased. Wilbur Fisk noted on March 17,

The equinoctial storm seems to be upon us in all of its violence. More snow has fallen here within the last six hours than we have had before this winter and still it comes. The prospect this evening is that it will snow all night—and, for all of any signs that are apparent now, it may keep on snowing forever . . . It is a regular northeaster, and beats right through the tent on to my sheet of paper here as if it was used to the business and liked it . . .

Fisk on March 23:

We had some glorious sport this forenoon, snowballing. The weather was fine and the snow just right. The 2nd and 6th Regiment had a regular pitched battle, which resulted in the discomfiture of the latter. A squad of our boys, principally from Co. C, went up to the Sixth, and stumped the crowd for a snowball fight. The Sixth came out and drove them back. It was now evident that the squad from the Second must have reinforcements or call themselves whipped. Some of our officers, eager for fun, collected quite a force, and headed by our Major, we rallied to the assistance of the defeated party. Snowballs flew thick and fast, some of the foremost on each side getting completely plastered over with them, head, ears, neck, and all. A reserve of reinforcements coming up in the nick of time, virtually decided the contest. They all charged on the Sixth, shouting and snowballing to their utmost. The Sixth was obliged to fall back, fighting variously as they retreated. We saw our advantage and followed it up till we drove them clear back to their camp . . . Both regiments left off snowballing and set to shaking hands with each other.

Other forms of entertainment could also get a bit rough. A friend wrote of the experience of Capt. Edward W. Carter, Fourth Vermont, a Brattleboro resident:

To pass the time away, the officers would get up games of foot ball, choose sides, and with fierce determination, each would fight with all of a soldier's courage for the game. During one of these games Captain Carter got the ball well over near the bounds and was working it along with his foot, when the Sergeant-Major, who was his opponent in the game, came bounding forward, the Major being a heavy weight, weighing about one hundred and ninety pounds . . . The Captain threw himself directly in the Major's path, when, with the force of a catapult, the Major struck him and fell heavily across his chest and stomach, knocking him senseless. He was put upon a stretcher and carried to the hut, where he lay for an hour unconscious.

Carter lapsed into a coma for several days, but was back in good health in time for the spring campaign. Again, Private Eastman:

Card games, poker and three-card monty with lively betting; was one of the forms of amusement during the idle hours in camp. Football, boxing, wrestling and baseball were popular at times . . . Another very amusing game was to catch some stranger in the camp and put him in a blanket and toss him up in the air. I have seen lots of fun in this way . . . Two or three men at each end of a strong rope would run up one company's street and down another, and sweep everything before them. There was no getting out of the way. I got caught in the game once, and in attempting to jump over the rope, got a fall that laid me up a day or two with a lame back.

Eastman and friends one day found some bags containing rain-dampened gunpowder, discarded by an artillery unit. "There was a very large stump, perhaps three feet in diameter," he wrote,

a rod or so back from my tent, and it had a small hollow in the center, about four or five inches across, and if one of these bags of caked powder dropped into this hole with a coal of fire, an explosion would follow, the report of which was the same as the report of a small cannon. This could be heard for miles, or all over the camp of the Army of the Potomac . . . We organized a fake company of artillery, had a fake captain, and drilled all day . . . Hundreds of officers and men collected around at a safe distance to see the sport. The stump got afire and we used water freely, but at last, the stump got so shattered that there was no report and we gave up the game, but it lasted till dark.

The 10th Vermont's Pvt. Samuel Parker, a soldier from Chelsea, jotted a brief entry in his diary each day. He recorded a week in his soldier life:

> March 27, Sunday today it fair and warm we had an inspection and at night we had dresperrade and we had a meating
>
> March 28 Monday today went on gard and we was gard mounted and they had a brigade review and at night they had a brigade dresperrade
>
> March 29, Tuesday i com of from gard this morning and the pickets went out and in the after noon it rained hard and rained all night
>
> March 30 Wednesday today I went down to warren junction [Warrenton Junction] and rid on flat botoms cars from brandy station and the wind blew and it was dam cold
>
> March 31 Thursday today i and some of the rest of the boys staid thare and loded the wood and the rest went into the woods and loaded wood and some was pickets [serving on picket, or outpost, duty]
>
> April 1 Friday today them that loaded staid here yesterday had to go into the woods i had to help load the wood and some of them had to be pickets
>
> April 2 Saturday today it rained and we don nothing but stay in our tents our tent leaked some tonight I stole 3 loaf of bread

Another documentation of camp life came from Pvt. Charles Mead, a Vermont sharpshooter. From his diary:

> April 5. My birth day—21 years old—henceforth I "paddle my own canoe" It rained nearly all day.
>
> April 21. Sanford and I went over to the target A. M. and fired about thirty rounds. My sights are improved and Sanford's gun shot very acurate. Shot at 3 and 500 yards.
>
> April 22. Marched at 7 AM beyond Stevensburg to a Corps review. It was a grand scene—some 50,000 infantry, cavalry, and artillery massed on the vast plain. Bright colors, fluttering standards, and magnificent music as the vast no's united to make it one of the most splendid reviews ever witnessed. We passed Grant, Meade & Hancock surrounded by a brilliant crowd of officers . . .

Mead and his brother, Pvt. Carlos Eugene Mead, grandsons of the first settler of the industrious southern Vermont community of Rutland, served in Company F of the First U.S. Sharpshooter Regiment. Charles, a handsome twenty-two-year-old with a carefully trimmed mustache and soft, distant eyes, had a literary bent. In his youth, he had drafted many compositions. In one called "Thought," he wrote,

> One of the most wonderful of man's faculties is that of thought . . . he can picture to himself scenes transpiring all over the world. He can in the shortest space of time travel to the most remote parts of the world and observe scenes as though he were there and they were actually present to his sences. He travels forward to the time when all things earthly shall be naught; he even tries to stretch his mental vision to the utmost tension in order to comprehend a boundless and a never ending Eternity.

Mead occupied much of his idle time in camp with letter writing.

Homesickness was an ever-present malady afflicting many of the young men far from home. Jerome Cutler, a private in the Third Vermont from the northern Vermont town of Waterville, betrayed a longing for home in a letter written on March 23 to his wife, Emily:

> I learned of the sudden death of Aunt Mairind in mothers letter . . . Grandmother and her makes two that have gone since I left home, and in this world I shall never see again but as you remarked we may all be prepared to follow them to the land of rest . . . Tell the children they must eat my share of the sugar this spring.

A week later:

> You spoke of its being a delightful spring morning when you finished your letter I can imagin something how it appeared and looked, there is something different up among the old hills of Vermont and here there is more of a contrast between the cold bleak days of winter and the returning warm and balmy days of summer. I wish that I could be there to enjoy them, (wouldn't I liked to have been up in the old sugar place

whare I have worked so much when you was there) there!

Orville Bixby, from Chelsea, a captain in the Second Vermont, wrote in late March to his wife, Frances,

I am very much oblige for the apples they are very nice and I will remember you in kindness when I eat them, it makes me think of home and friends to eat them. Kilpatrick returned with his raiders last night they looked rather careworn. We have an order last night to be ready to move at-once with three days rations but guess there is nothing up to move us just yet . . . There is quite hard cannonading at the present time it sounds as though it was at or near Mortons Ford. Am a little afraid it will disturb us but will not seal this up till night and let you know if anything unusual takes place before night. My health is very good.

As Bixby made clear, the soldiers lived with the knowledge that on some nearby day, orders for the army to march would come. But certainly, no major movement would occur as long as the winter persisted. On March 20, Captain Bixby wrote,

A soldier's life is a dreary one being entirely secluded from the society of his near and dear friends. Oh when he lays himself down at night for a little rest how little he knows what will awake him. Perhaps it will be the clean sound of a bugle which will remind him at once that he must be up and doing. he rises at once, cooks a little coffee takes it with his hard bread and makes out a hearty breakfast and then he is ready to obey any orders that he may receive. Or perhaps he may be awakened by the belching forth of shot and shell from the enemies guns . . . only two months and ten days more if nothing happens I will be a free man again how thankful I will be when that times comes then I can return to my family and friends but there is many a dark cloud to pass through before that time comes I hope I will come out all right . . .

Bixby continued, "Gen. Grant reviewed our Corps yesterday, so I had a pretty good look at him. He looks very much like his photography. I think he is a pretty smart man, but hardly think he can run the Army of the Potomac."

Not all the Vermonters who would soon be campaigning with Grant were bivouacked at Brandy Station. Off to the east, in the forts around Washington, D.C., doing service in the defenses of the capital, was the largest regiment the Green Mountain State sent to the Union armies. The 11th Vermont, trained as infantrymen, on reaching Washington in the fall of 1862 were turned into artillerymen. Thus, for nearly a year and a half, the 11th, with an authorized strength of eighteen hundred men, had been known as the First Artillery, 11th Vermont Volunteers, and had lived a comparatively easy life in the forts protecting the nation's capital. They were well removed from the fighting, though the rumble of distant cannon sometimes reached them, but the time of fortified confidence and considerable comfort was about to end. George Bridge, a private in the 11th from Morristown in the Lamoille Valley, described life as an artilleryman in a letter written in the winter months of 1864. "Our barracks were 100 feet long," he said,

with a wood heating stove at or near each end . . . [We had] drills and marching and faceings and instruction in the manual of arms. Also guard and picket duty and fatigue duty work on the Fort and rifle pits, and details to cut 4 foot wood 2 or 3 miles from Fort . . . This for heating our barracks and cooking. Also for officers quarters, several of which had their wives with them, with dress parade a short time before sundown and inspection every Sunday and batalion drills every little while. These little duties kept us some busy. Yep, I guess so. We also had white gloves and brass ornaments for shoulders. These called scales, were removable, and had to be kept bright and shining, as also our buttons, belt plates, also muskets had to be in the pink of conditions. The inside so that the head of ramrod would leave no mark on a white glove when inspected by an Officer. Also our shoes neatly blacked and roll call early in the morning, again at 9 o'clock PM About 9:30 Taps, when all lights of private soldiers had to be extinguished. All these drills and other duties were sounded on a bugle. I believe I have not mentioned drills on the big guns in the Fort, also mortars, and light artillery pieces. These latter were taken out of the fort for drill with. A pass to go to the City of Washington could be obtained occasionaly, good from 9 o'clock a. m. until 9 o'clock PM Our Regt. had a pretty good brass band, and as Col. James Warner, Commander of the Regt., had his headquarters at Fort Slocum, the band was there.

The 11th Vermont helped man several forts north of Washington, sited on prominent hilltops that commanded long views of open farm country and key roads approaching the city. Vermonters served in Forts Slocum, Totten, Thayer, Saratoga, Lincoln, and Bunker Hill. For a time, Colonel Warner commanded seven miles of the Washington defenses, with his headquarters at Fort Bunker Hill.

Pvt. Charles Porter, of Ferrisburg, was stationed at Fort Slocum. "While in Fort Slocum," he recalled in a memoir written four decades after the war,

> our time was taken up first with learning the facings, manual of arms, and platoons, drill, drills of the company, etc. . . . . All the companies [in the 11th Vermont] had nicknames, most of which I have forgotten—a few were "gambling B" "fighting E" "drunken L" "Lousy M" . . . Dress parade every afternoon, picket practice and drill on the big guns . . . There were 25 guns in the fort and the timber had been felled for more than a mile north to give range to the cannon and to prevent the enemy from approaching too close . . .

Another member of the 11th, Pvt. Jonathan Blaisdell, wrote to his father in Cambridge, in the shadow of Mount Mansfield, on March 31, with a considerable wish list:

> Dear Father,
> . . . I want you to send me a box send some dried apples some butter and cheese I will send some money as soon as I get some and I want you should send a little sugar I should like to have after you get to making sugar to have a box of about 75 pounds of small cakes it will cost 5 or 6 cts a pound to espress it and I can sell the sugar for 50 cts a pound.
> I want you should send a little can of molasses a little bottle of cam-

phor a pair of boots some horse radish scraped up and put in a bottle
and some vinegar put in with it and cooked up tight and as much other
stuff as you have in mind. The weather is vere fine the frogs are out we
see wild geese going north most every day. I must close for it is getting
bed time.

Though few letters from 11th Vermont soldiers made mention of it,
within its ranks was a growing speculation that the regiment might
soon end up campaigning with Ulysses Grant.

Back at Brandy Station, of course, no one doubted that hard
marching with the three-star general was in their future. But one of
the Leach boys from the little northern Vermont town of Fletcher,
who served in Company H of the Fourth Vermont, would not be going
along. Charles Leach was a lieutenant, while brother William was a
private. Charles wrote to his wife:

All's well except William, & he is very sick. The Dr. says he has the
Typhoid Fever, & I am afraid he is not going to wear it out. He has very
bad spells where he can hardly breathe or talk, & wants water to drink
all the time . . . Before you get this he will probably be better, or else he
may never be better. He wanted to know the other day if I had written
anything to his folks about his being sick. I told him I had written to
you & the rest of the folks would hear it by you.

The lieutenant added,

An order has been issued that in consequence of the nearness of the
time when this army may resume active operations, all females are
ordered to be removed beyond the limits of this Army, except such as
are connected with charitable institutions and the like. I presume there
are six or eight hundred women, wives of Officers, now in the Army, &
I presume a great many that are not wives. Any time there is anything
going on, more or less, females are mixed with the Spectators. We have
but three in our Regt. & those are Dr. Sawin's wife, Capt. Cady's wife,
& Lieut. Robbins' wife.

On March 26, Charles sent sad news of brother William:

Thursday morning the flush had gone from his cheeks, & more death like color was on him, otherwise, he appeared about the same only weaker & the nervousness of the day before had left him. I saw him last about 11 O.C., & about 2, they sent down word that he was dead. I started as soon as possible to make arrangements to send his body home. I learned that there was an office of embalming at Brandy Station, so I got an ambulance and went there Thursday afternoon, got a coffin to take the body in, & sent it to the station that night . . . I would very much like to have taken the body home, myself, but I knew there was no use to try, therefore, have done all that I can do, & hope it may reach home without any accident. There will be some of his clothes in the box, & if I had thought about it before I went to the Station, should have sent everything he had that was worth sending, as it would cost nothing, & help hold the coffin steady in the box . . . Thursday, the day Wm. died, was a very pleasant day, & reminded me of a first-rate sap day in Vt., after a big snow storm.

Still, despite such sad events, the winter encampment remained generally pleasant. Martin McMahon, the Sixth Corps adjutant general, recalled it in an address delivered to Vermont veterans at Montpelier in 1880. Speaking of corps headquarters and commander John Sedgwick, he said,

Through all this winter of delights no man looked forward to the future except to plan amusements for the ensuing winter for, strangely enough, we had got the idea that this war was to be continued indefinitely and during the rest of our lives. We were not prophets nor the sons of prophets. What knew we then of the lurid fires that would lighten the Wilderness within a few short months. The angel of death hovered over many but no prophetic shadow fell from its wings.

The waiting for action was, for some, becoming more and more difficult. Lt. Col. Samuel Pingree, of the Connecticut River Valley town of Hartford, second in command of the Third Vermont, wrote to his cousin, Augustus Huntoon, in Bethel:

> The army are now waiting with constrained patience for the order to go forward . . . I think the army was never so big with expectation of complete triumph as at present . . . We expect to encounter the same old army always brave and now desperately so, commanded by the highest order of military talent,—all posted behind the most formidable entrenchments,—so it has always been, but we feel an advantage not sensible to us before . . . There is enough visible to satisfy me and all, that the pulling is all one way now and such activity and earnestness indicates that the sensible conclusion has been arrived at, that cost what it may Richmond must fall at once.

The time for campaigning, when spring would be in full bloom, and the old dirt roads of Virginia sufficiently dry for the movement of armies, had obviously nearly come on April 10. That day Dr. Joseph Rutherford, a surgeon with the 10th Vermont, wrote to his wife, Hannah, back home in Newport, near the Canadian border. "The weather," he told her,

> has been horrid all this month till this morning the sun rose to an unclouded sky and every tree was alive with the songsters of the forest and made the air melodious with their sweet songs. There is a sweetness in their music that I never experienced in the feathered songsters of our more northern climes. All nature seemed to clap her hands with joy as the God of day presented himself in all his splendor to this admiring gaze.

The Vermont Brigade camps were on high ground, above and to the west of Brandy Station, land fought over in the great cavalry clash of June 9, 1863, that had preceded the march to Gettysburg. The camps commanded a striking view of surrounding Virginia, down to and beyond the Rebel signal station on Clark's Mountain. On the horizon to the west was the long crest of the Blue Ridge Mountains, with its well-known gaps made famous by the passing of armies blue and gray.

Surgeon Joseph Rutherford wrote to his wife of camp life at Brandy Station.
VERMONT HISTORICAL SOCIETY

The ridge had a certain resemblance to the long spine of the Green Mountains back home, and the Vermont boys closely watched its coating of snow, knowing that as it disappeared the time for war was near.

As April ended, another Vermont infantry unit arrived in Virginia, just in time for the fighting. The 17th Vermont Regiment had been raised at the order of Governor Smith, who was convinced that many veterans of the Second Vermont Brigade would join. The Second Brigade, which served only nine months, had won glory at Gettysburg in the final days of its enlistment by breaking the flank of Pickett's Charge. But its men, who had been smack in the midst of the war's largest and deadliest battle, did not hurry to re-up. When the 17th came south in late April, it had in the ranks only about 450 men, half the intended number. Consequently, it was, as planned, not commanded by a full colonel, Francis Voltaire Randall, a leader of the attack on Pickett. Instead, a lieutenant colonel, Charles Cummings of

Brattleboro, a veteran of the Second Brigade and a newspaperman back in his hometown, led it. The 17th arrived in the Washington area on April 22 and was immediately assigned to the Ninth Corps of Maj. Gen. Ambrose Burnside. It was Burnside who had led the Army of the Potomac to its crushing defeat at Fredericksburg in December 1862, following his dismal performance at Antietam. Nevertheless, the old Rhode Islander with the famous sidewhiskers still held a major command. Though Burnside would fight with the Army of the Potomac, his Ninth Corps would not technically be a part of that army until late May.

On April 29, cavalryman John Q. French wrote to his family in Proctorsville,

> We have been having very pleasant weather here for two or three weeks, 'till last night when we had quite a hurricane, which lasted about ten moments. It first started way over beyond the rebel camps, where it done things up Brown in the way of carrying off their tents as the air was almost full of them . . . It passed over us without doing much harm except almost choking us with dust . . . General Grant is getting a great many troops together in this particular place and almost every spot fit for a regiment to camp in, is filled for three or four miles around. We had Review of this Divison yesterday and they looked splendidly. I wish you could have seen them.

On April 29, a soldier in the Fourth Vermont wrote a letter to the *Watchman and State Journal* in Montpelier (popularly known as *Walton's Journal*) that was published unsigned:

> The preliminary reviews and inspections have taken place, all extra goods and baggage have been sent to the rear, including the canvas of our rude chapels . . . we expect next week will witness our advance and encounter on some new field of blood.

The soldier went on to judge it fair to "reasonably hope" for a decisive victory. Then he undertook a comparison of present campaign prospects with the military situation of a year past. In the spring of

1863, the Army of the Potomac was poised to move across the Rappahannock and begin the doomed Chancellorsville Campaign. The letter continued,

> How bright is our present prospect compared with a year ago this morning, when we gazed across the Rappahannock on the battle plain of sad memories, with gloomy forbodings, soon to catch a glimpse of sunshine on Marie's Heights and then plunge into a darker than the natural night which shrouded us at Banks' Ford, a night whose dawn arose only on the gory heights of Gettysburg! Here on the threshold of conflict, beyond the mist and gloom of the valley of tribulations below, rises the acme of our hopes resplendant in as unclouded sunlight as this morning gilds the leafing trees, expands the blossoms of the peach, the pear, the cherry, and opens the buds of the lilies. Spring is upon us in smiling beauty, brightening the few oases amid the desolations of war . . .

With the onset of spring, Ulysses Grant had formed his plan for the coming great offensive. Starting simultaneously with the Army of the Potomac's advance against Lee, in the west Grant's close friend William Tecumseh Sherman would lead his legions south with the aim of defeating Joseph Johnston's army. Down toward Richmond, the hapless but politically powerful Maj. Gen. Benjamin Butler would lead his Army of the James in a strike against the Confederate capital city. And a Union force would be active in the Shenandoah Valley, keeping the Confederates at bay there. Grant's instructions to the men who would lead this grand, coordinated offensive were, as always, concise. If Grant was a fighter, as Lincoln well knew, he was also a master of the craft of writing. His orders to Meade were whittled down to the absolute essentials, typically Grant: "Lee's army will be your objective point. Wherever Lee goes, there you will go also . . ."

Were the Vermonters ready? Dr. Rutherford, in the 10th Regiment, thought so. He wrote to his wife, Hannah, on April 21,

> The time is rapidly drawing near for our departure from this. every thing is veiled in mystery and uncertainty—except it is very certain

that we are to move to the front. We all feel that many who are with us to day will in all probability be numbered with the dead before another sabbath draws upon us and the thought makes us feel sad. Officers and men all feel it . . . There has been a Sabbath stillness in our camp for days past. Men collect in little knots and with a sub-dued manner and hushed voices talk of coming events. Officers meet one another with looks that speak louder than words and expressions that are none the less deep for their being noiseless. Oh! this stillness is awful and anxious. But with all this there is a look of terrible determination in every man's countenance, a look that plainly says—we conquor or die. It is the calmness that preceeds the coming tornado. And this is not confined to a part of the army, but is one and universal.

The doctor went on to inquire of his wife whether Vermonters back home were "sending up prayers to the God of battle for us today in their quiet congregations." He wrote, "We would feign believe they are, for we do feel pervading our atmosphere that is not common, a feeling of strength that is not our own."

The Army of the Potomac, by 1864, had known several comman-ders. Irvin McDowell had led it to defeat at Bull Run. George McClellan had failed it, rallied it, then failed it again. Burnside had directed it to slaughter at Fredericksburg. Joe Hooker had been flanked at Chancellorsville, then had led his army, still full of fight, in retreat across the Rappahannock. George Meade had directed the army in turning back Lee at Gettysburg, but had failed to deliver a resulting death blow to the Army of Northern Virginia. Now Grant was here, not commanding the army in title, but to be ever at Meade's side—in effect, leading this old and battered, but still grand army of the American republic. Grant was the boss. No private soldier believed otherwise. As he ended his letter home, Rutherford turned to the subject of Grant, and perhaps echoed the feelings of many men in the ranks:

I have seen it stated that the appearance of Genl. Grant among us, is the cause of so much enthusiastic determination and that we are ready to worship him—don't believe it—we are no hero worshipers and if we were he has yet to do something to earn our reverence. The time is past when the Army of the Potomac is ready to tear the trim of his hat for any general officer . . . When Genl. Grant proves himself worthy of such honors as none but the soldiers can give then he will receive such honors as are due him . . . He is a noble man and officer and deserved all his honors he has received—now let him earn new laurels, then be crowned with them.

At the beginning of May, Capt. David White, Second Vermont, wrote to his new wife, Marie, in Ludlow:

I too think early spring a little bit dull but when the leaves begin to spring out and the birds sing and the flowers present thin variegated hues to the eye, I think it the most pleasant season of the year for it reminds one of youth when the mind is light and buoyant and the spirits vivacious and no trouble hangs like a dark pall over the mind. I remember well what reflections and impressions I had when I saw these beauties of nature of what I would do when I was a man. I never dreamed of a war among ourselves or that I would ever witness a battle or much less participate in one, but we see by this how short sighted we are and how little we know of the future or the manner in which we may be affected by it and it is well we do not. Those remembrances are among the happiest of my life, yet I little knew I was happy, but was constantly looking forward to the time when I should be a man and act for myself, but I think even in this could I only be with my wife I could be perfectly happy, but for a while at least I must forego the pleasures of her society.

In less than a week Captain White would be severely wounded, but he recovered and eventually returned home to Marie.

Chapter Three

THE HOME FRONT WAITS FOR WAR

O n February 22, 1864, as snow covered the state of Vermont and the Virginia mountains, and as the Army of the Potomac's winter camp wore on, the people of central Vermont received a harsh reminder of the grim reality of war in *Walton's Journal*:

Died in camp near Brandy Station, Feb. 22, corporal George Temple, Co. G., 10th Regt. Vt. Volunteers, aged 30, of measles. He was the only son of Caleb Temple Esq. of Randolph, to which place the remains were brought, and there they were honored by appropriate and affecting funeral services in the Congregational Church . . . Young Temple was a conscientious, honorable and estimable man, who left wife, child, friends . . . George Temple had a neighbor and friend George Perry, also enlisted due to Temple's example. He, too, was stricken at the same time and died by the same disease. The affection was so strong that a comrade said, "If Temple shall die, I believe Perry will follow him." And so it was . . . Such are the sacrifices of Vermont on the altar of patriotism. While the fathers and mothers give their sons ungrudgingly, yet well may they cry—Oh Lord, how long?

In 1864, in the Stowe Hollow section of the mountain town of Stowe, lived Olive Cheney, a farm wife and the mother of four sons serving in the Union armies, including Pvt. William Cheney, 11th Vermont, and Pvt. Edwin Cheney, Fourth Vermont. She also had a son-in-law on her mind, Cpl. Chandler Watts, a Stowe man, married to her daughter, Jane, who was living in Orford, New Hampshire. Mrs. Cheney wrote to Jane on March 5, the day after Kilpatrick's battered troopers reached the safety of Union lines:

> The family are well with the exception of your Father. he has been sick with a hard cold for a few days past . . . last Monday morning your father took Edwin and went to the Centre. Ed enlisted for the war . . . 3 other soldiers, Eugene Stockwell, only 15, a young Houstin and a brother of Deliza Cadys girls husband those three were going into the 5th Reg. Edwin has enlisted for the 7th [Vermont] . . . he has got to enlist in Stow in order to draw the town bounty . . . to war he must go and said he SHOULD go, if his Father did not give his consent for him to go now he should go the first chance he got, we made up our minds he might as well go now as ever he said he could not work nor did not much . . . it comes pretty hard for your Father to give him up he has made so much calculation for him to stay at home . . . I could not reason the case with him at all he said it was no worse for us than others that had given up their boys dont suppose it is any worse than it is for a good many others. it is strange what makes the boys want to go to war I suppose it is all right—if the boys hated to go as bad as the folks hated to have them there would not be much fighting done could they . . . O that their lives may be spared and the boys return to us again but it is not very probably they all will if any of them.

In the winter of 1864, the 300,000 people remaining in the state of Vermont knew full well that spring and summer would bring a bloody resumption of all-out war in Virginia. More than 25,000 of the state's young men had already put on uniforms, depriving Vermont of some of its most able bodies. As mother Cheney indicated, it was hitting the farms hard, and in Vermont in the 1860s there were more than 30,000 farms, mostly small hill farms like the Cheneys'. Blessedly, the winter of 1863–64 seems to have been a somewhat mild one for Vermont, and spring produced a bumper crop of maple syrup. Vermonters watched still another regiment, the 17th Vermont, forming to go off to war. The people did not know, though certainly they had hoped, that it would be the last. Some four hundred members of the Eighth Vermont Regiment were headed home for a month's furlough as a reward for reenlisting. The winter and spring brought much illness to Vermont, with outbreaks of smallpox and scarlet fever (called canker rash), particularly in the Champlain Valley. Women labored in the evenings to sew clothing for the troops away at war. Efforts were made to lift spirits—concerts were presented and plays put on, including a production of *Julius Caesar* in Bennington. Life went on while the newspapers foretold, with the easing of winter, the resumption of military campaigning along the eastern front.

In Vermont, many of the hardships of the wartime home front fell on the women. Not only did they struggle with tasks previously done by men now in uniform, they also labored to make and gather articles to be shipped to Vermont soldiers in their winter encampments. In mid-March, the *Vermont Phoenix* of Brattleboro reported the ladies of that town had sent south to the Sanitary Commission:

> 21 pair flannel drawers, 27 pair stockings, 39 flannel shirts, 6 cotton shirts, 7 pillow cases, 34 handkerchiefs, 5 pair slippers, 8 packages maizena, 2 bags dry apples, 1 bag hops, 1 package of larkspur seed, 1 bag chestnuts, 1 bag dried currants and blackberries, 1 doz. cakes soap.

Those efforts were overshadowed by the output in much bigger Burlington, where in a single month the ladies turned out 80 haversacks, 164 woolen shirts, 168 drawers, 185 towels, 80 sewing kits complete with New Testaments, 30 sheets, 21 bed gowns, 12 pillowcases, 12 bed ticks, 12 ring pads, 10 surgeon's pincushions, and two sacks of bandages. A Vermont historian writing a century later would rightly observe that during the war, Vermont women "served for the duration."

Up in St. Albans, in his elegant hilltop mansion with a splendid view across Lake Champlain, the governor of Vermont, John Gregory

Smith, returned in early March from a visit to the Vermont regiments at Brandy Station. Now he was spending a considerable amount of time trying to form another Vermont infantry unit. Smith, in civilian life a railroad executive, was an efficient businessman, used to seeing his wishes become commands. But his attempts at creating the 17th Vermont Regiment had foundered. As a result, the governor had issued a decree that was posted throughout the state:

> The Seventeenth Regiment *must be filled.* The men already enlisted are idle, waiting for the completion of the organization, large expense to the State has already occurred, which must be lost unless the regiment is filled; and the honor of our State is involved, that the thing be speedily completed . . .

On March 8, Ulysses Grant, just arrived from the west, was a guest of Abraham Lincoln at a White House reception. In Burlington, diarist William Henry Hoyt, a printer, took note of the early springlike weather. "Mild morning," he wrote. "Slight S. wind, a deep snow upon the yd, a foot or more and covering trees, house etc. The blue lake . . . widely open in spots & strips. Mild, thawing and sloppy, the snow poaching into mud in the roads making poor sleighing."

On March 10, the day Lieutenant General Grant appeared for the first time at Brandy Station, Hoyt wrote of an event that brought to Burlington one of the nation's best-known abolitionists: "Evening at church til nearly 9 then went to town hall to hear Wendell Phillips' lecture before the Young Men's Association. Went down to the lake after mass to see the men getting out ice . . ." Vermont had long been a hotbed of abolition, and advocates of the cause kept stoking the fires of freedom in Vermont throughout the war.

A week later, Hoyt took note of St. Patrick's Day observances in Burlington by the city's sizeable Irish Catholic population. His journal entry on March 17 read:

> *St. Patrick's Day. Clear, bright and fine morning. A great crowd of people in town today and all seeming to enjoy themselves finely. A flag presentation to the Hibernian Soc. at 9 o'clock at the Town Hall and a*

procession with brass band & a military band to the church where, at 10,
the Bishop's High Mass, pontifically, church densely crowded . . . Evening
a grand supper at American Hotel at which time 200 . . . sat down and
had a merry time of it till nearly or quite 2 o'clock at night. Capt. Loner-
gan presided.

John Lonergan, a prominent local Irishman, had recruited a company
for the 13th Vermont Regiment, then bravely led it at Gettysburg.
During St. Patrick's feast, glasses were raised to "the successors of St.
Patrick—the priesthood of Ireland," to "Vermont, a state of happiness
where friends will find a welcome, foes a grave," to "our adopted country, the United States of America," and to "the Army and Navy—we
will Grant to no country a better general than he who now leads our
army." That night at Brandy Station, the Army of the Potomac was
being battered by what Private Fisk described as an "equinoctial
storm."

By late March, Vermonters were learning more and more details of
the cavalry raid toward Richmond. On March 23, the *Burlington Free
Press* contained the following item:

In Kilpatrick's last "On to Richmond" was a soldier boy by the name of
Edwin A. Porter, whose mother lives in Wells, Vermont. In one of the
skirmishes, he rode up fearlessly to a squad of rebels. The officer
demanded of him to surrender. He replied coolly, "don't see it." And
suiting his actions to his words, he instantly drew his sabre with which
he cleft the head of the officer, at the same time instantly wheeling his
horse to join his company, the rebels firing a volley at him, of which
shower the lad carried off in his person four bullets, and joined his
company G. He kept his saddle for more than one hour, and is now
doing well.

On March 28, with thirty-seven days remaining before the commencement of campaigning in Virginia, the *Free Press* ran an advisory
on shipping home the bodies of soldiers from Washington, D.C., area
hospitals. It stated in part,

The bodies are embalmed at the Campbell and Armory Hospitals free of expense, but if done elsewhere it costs from $18 upwards, according to the ability of the parties to pay, while it is not so well done as at the hospitals. The undertaker charges for an outside case and for delivering to express company $6, and $8 for disinterring one body.

Certainly, the military did not have a corner on all Vermont tragedy. As Vermonters were getting word of the big and playful snowball battle in the Vermont Brigade on March 23, they were also reading in the newspapers of a horrible happening in Guilford, on the Massachusetts border. There, the four-year-old daughter of Russell Roberts died when she fell into a kettle of hot maple syrup. Along the New York border, in Fair Haven, Joseph Sheldon, a railway worker, fell from a freight train and died after crawling to a nearby house. Another railroad worker was near death in Bennington after having been, as the papers said, "caught between the cars." The March 28 *Burlington Free Press* stated, "Two more doctors declare that Burlington HAS got small pox."

April arrived in Vermont bringing in mild weather. On April 1, a farmer in the north-central Vermont town of Berlin came on a sign of an early spring. The papers reported that Joseph LaClare found a grasshopper "alive and brisk in his mowing field." According to the *Manchester Journal*, "The first day of April was an eventful one for Mr. L. Phillips of Winhall. On that day his wife gave birth to twins, one sheep of his flock to twin lambs, and his cat to four kittens." On April 1, the start of the great eastern campaign was but 34 days away.

April Fools' Day was observed in the Fairbanks shops in St. Johnsbury. Henry Herrick wrote that night in his diary,

About the shops . . . various tricks, some of them pretty smart and others not so much so. Randall was the first victim by having his dinner taken out of the pail, and when he came to open it found nothing but an iron weight and the label "april fools" . . . Randall prepared an apple by skillfully taking out the core, and soaking the inside with brine which tastes horribly—when it was done he gave it to Sanborn but he was too shrewd for him, but put it on the bench, and soon after Albert Daniels stole it, and began eating it as soon as he was out of the door and a scene followed.

The enjoyment of the day soon faded for Herrick, with an incident that involved his coworker, and very close friend, Zenas. Herrick wrote,

> Another thing happened which was not so pleasant to-day. Mr. Eastman called Zenas into his office and told him that we being so much together in the shop made some remarks among the hands, and that they perhaps thought he was not doing his duty in allowing it—that he did not think we lost any more time than others. But from our being always together it was more noticed—he cared nothing about it himself, but spoke for our interest. Perhaps there is some reason for rebuke, but he shall never have occasion to speak of it again.

That night, Herrick attended a St. Johnsbury lecture by abolitionist Phillips, and noted in his diary:

> 10 o'clock P. M. I have passed one of the pleasantest evenings of my life listening to Phillips. I had heard of silver tongued eloquence before, but hardly appreciated what it meant, but now I understand— the subject was the "Reconstruction of the Union" which was made very interesting—his language was perfectly plain and simple, but who shall describe the charm of the style—strong, earnest—never excited—but always flowing on quietly like the calm current of a mighty river, carrying me along . . . I remember it was like beautiful music. The church was filled and perfectly quiet, except a baby cried and was carried out. Why will people be so foolish as to bring the little innocents.

Serious illness was spreading in Vermont that winter and spring of 1864. On April 6, in Woodstock, in south-central Vermont, Mrs. Cordelia Luce Gilbert wrote a letter to her daughter, Abbie, in Amesbury, Massachusetts, where the young lady had gone to work in the woolen mills. As usual, mother reported to daughter on local matters:

A group of soldiers from the Third Vermont Regiment poses for a photograph during a respite in the Peninsula Campaign of 1862. The bearded private standing to the right is Henry Herrick, band member and diarist. FAIRBANKS MUSEUM

Your ever welcome letter came to hand today & has been read & reread with pleasure . . . Last Sunday the mud was so plenty that I did not venture out to church . . . yesterday afternoon they sent for Dr. Frost to go up & lance a sore on Mrs. Bridges face he lanced it & she was comfortable in a short time droped to sleep & rested nicely for two hours a thing she has not done for two weeks before. canker rash prevails to a great extent about here. Your Father and I are well as usual his shoulder does not trouble him much now he works all of the time. & I keep the needle going steady most of the time.

Though Mrs. Gilbert made no mention of it, Woodstock was, in 1864, the most important place in Vermont from a military standpoint. The handsome, tree-shaded village, believed by many to be the most beautiful in Vermont, was the home of the man who administered the state's war effort. Local lawyer Peter Washburn, perhaps the finest of all attorneys in Windsor County, served from the autumn of 1861 until the war's end as Vermont's adjutant general. From an office in the Phoenix Block on the south side of the village square, Washburn administered the state's war involvement. Reports, discharges, requisitions, death notices, draft calls, and correspondence of every kind flowed into and out of Woodstock on a daily basis. Woodstock was, in effect, the Pentagon of Vermont.

But war was not the only interest of Woodstock residents in early 1864. They eagerly awaited construction of a railroad into their village. The previous fall, the decision had been made to bring a spur line from the busy railroad center of White River Junction, 14 miles east along the Connecticut River. Indeed, it was thought the route would eventually be continued westward across the main ridge of the Green Mountains to another rail center, Rutland. A town meeting was approaching in Woodstock that would see voters approve an investment in stock for the Woodstock Railroad. One of the line's founders, in addition to local rail magnate Frederick Billings, was Governor Smith, of St. Albans.

Of far more overall importance than the railroad planning in Woodstock was, of course, the quiet, diligent work going on in the office of the adjutant general. Washburn was well familiar with war, having led Vermonters into combat for the first time, in the opening battle of the war—at Big Bethel on the Virginia Peninsula in June 1861. With the disbanding of the First Vermont Regiment after its ninety days of service, Lieutenant Colonel Washburn left the service and ran successfully in the general assembly for the post he now held. As was customary at the time, the adjutant general set up shop in his hometown. Washburn and a handful of clerks labored daily on their seeming mountains of paperwork. Washburn was strongly expecting to hear from Washington, in the very near future, concerning the need for more men for the Union armies. As the start of what would likely be the most important, and costliest, campaign of the war neared, Washburn fully expected to soon order more Green Mountain State boys into the ranks.

The first week in April, the *Burlington Free Press* contained the following brief, but interesting, item: "Col. Chas. B. Stoughton of the 4th Vt. Regiment has resigned his office and is going to study law with his brother the General, at Bellows Falls." The brother, Edwin Stoughton, once the youngest brigadier general in all the Union armies, had commanded the Second Vermont Brigade. But Stoughton's military career had come to a disastrous end on the wintry night of March 8, 1863, when he was captured from his bed by the Confederate cavalryman John Singleton Mosby. Now he was practicing law in Bellows Falls, with his brother Charles, who had been forced out of the war by a wound.

In Virginia, at Brandy Station on April 7, orders were given throughout the Army of the Potomac that all camp sutlers and excess baggage should be sent to the rear. The next day, in Vermont, was a day of fasting proclaimed by Governor Smith in hopes that Vermonters would attend chuch and offer up prayers for the success of the upcoming campaign. The *Free Press* reported: "The houses of worship were open, and the various sermons were listened to by the average Fast-day audiences. There was rather less than the average amount of ball-playing and riding-out, we thought . . ." That same day, in Brattleboro, the local paper said that a Mrs. Emma Thayer "has been acquitted of the charge of murdering two infant children at Burlington." The *St. Albans Messenger* said: "Edgar Anderson, of East Franklin, hung himself in his wood-shed . . . No reason was assigned for the rash act. He was discharged from the army, not long since, on account of ill health."

On April 9, in Windsor, the *Vermont Journal* delivered some remarkable news from the town of Perkinsville. A young man named Darley, the paper said, an employee of the soapstone factory owned by a Mr. Tailor,

> Went into the wheel-pit . . . to tighten some nuts, and while there was caught by his coat sleeve upon a two inch horizontal shaft, and after being carried around the shaft 15 or 20 times with fearful velocity was thrown into the inside of a large breast wheel and brought to a small door where it left him in a perfect state of nudity. Strange as it may appear, hardly a scratch could be found upon him, though he fainted.

On April 8, the *Brattleboro Phoenix* had predicted that campaigning in Virginia would be delayed due to "severe storms of late [that] have

Peter Washburn served as Vermont's adjutant general through most of the Civil War after having become the first Vermonter to lead troops into combat, at Big Bethel, Virginia, in June 1861. Note the resemblance to Lincoln.
VERMONT HISTORICAL SOCIETY

made the roads so deep that some time will be required to dry up the ground before the army can move." Two days later, on April 10, that spell of bad weather ended with a brilliant sunrise illuminating the Virginia Piedmont. And that week in Bristol, Vermont, overlooking the Champlain Valley, Royal Peake wrote in his diary, "Willis went to the pond got some pickerel." Vermont ponds are not often thawed in the first part of April, so winter was apparently breaking early.

On a mid-April evening in Burlington, William Hoyt wrote in his diary that he welcomed Louis de Goesbriand, the Catholic bishop of Burlington, to his home for dinner. A likely topic of discussion was the new Cathedral of the Immaculate Conception, standing unfinished on Burlington's St. Paul Street. The bishop of all Vermont Catholics had suspended work because of a manpower shortage. But with spring coming rapidly in 1864, de Goesbriand was about to order resumption of the stonework. It would be welcome news in the Queen City, with its many Irish and French Catholics. Religion played a considerable role in the lives of most Vermonters at the time of the Civil War. In Hyde Park, along the Lamoille

River, papers reported that five Protestants had been baptized by total immersion, though the ice of the river had to be broken for the dunkings.

With the start of military operations in Virginia little more than a month and a half away, Governor Smith received word of violence in the 17th Vermont Regiment's camp at Burlington. A violent death had occurred there, with a resulting court-martial. Nowhere was that incident of more interest than in the thriving Lamoille Valley community of Morrisville. The victim in the Burlington incident was a local lad, Pvt. James Sweeney. A page one story in the *Morrisville Newsdealer*, with the headline HOMICIDE IN THE SEVENTEENTH, was based on testimony before a military court-martial convened at Burlington. Several witnesses stated that Private Sweeney had repeatedly tried to escape from the camp guardhouse the night of April 17. He was stopped by two guards, Privates Henry Luce of Wolcott and Francis Gokey of Morrisville. Pvt. Lucien Bingham, corporal of the guard and also from Morrisville, said under oath,

> The second time the deceased tried to escape, I saw him getting nearly by Luce. I had just relieved private Gokey of Company C who was on the same relief. Gokey said he would like to assist Luce, and I told him he might. I could see both Gokey and Luce doing something with their guns, but it was too dark to see distinctly.

What the two guards were doing with their guns, further testimony revealed, was bayoneting Private Sweeney nine times. The court-martial found the two guards not guilty, determining the killing to be "justifiable homicide." Gokey would be wounded in the Wilderness and thus discharged from the army. Luce would be killed in fighting near Petersburg in late July.

The night of the bayoneting in St. Johnsbury, in his rented room, Henry Herrick was feeling introspective. He mused on his departure from his childhood home in the village of Cabot, 20 miles east, to find employment:

> I have been thinking this evening that this is an anniversary, that of my

first leaving home, and coming to St. Johnsbury—that and the few days preceeding it were not pleasant days of my life—as what days can be that mark the breaking up of pleasant associations and the parting from cherished friends, even from home and parents. And to-day as I think of them something of the old ache comes to me; but still I am glad the separation was necessary and that I am sure it was for my good, it is through trial that strength comes and little of manliness and self-reliance as I have to boast of . . . These years, so sadly begun, have been by no means sad years to me.

As April passed the midpoint, almost everyone in Vermont was busy as the growing season was fast approaching. On his farm in West Windsor, Jabez Hammond, a veteran of the Second Vermont Brigade, made the following diary entries:

> *Mon 16—Gathered sap tubs and washed them out Done some choring . . .*
> *Tue 17—Ploughed some drawed off some stone harrowed and sowed the wheat & oats up in the orchard . . . ploughed the garden*
> *Wed 18—Ploughed the little orchard below the barn sowed it to wheat sowed the grass seed in the orchard*
> *Thu 19—picked up 1¼ acres of stone sowed my onions and planted my peas*
> *Fri 20—Sowed some ashes and some grass seed on to the dry spot down in the mowing in the fornoon tagged the sheep in the afternoon . . .*

The *Bennington Banner* said in mid-April that a local farmer, S. F. Harris, was planning to grow a southern crop, tobacco, on five of his acres.

Somewhat like returning migratory birds, April brought to Vermont a sizeable portion of the veteran Eighth Vermont Regiment, home from service along the Mississippi River. Commanded by Col. Stephen Thomas of West Fairlee, a former Democratic member of the state legislature, the Eighth had seen combat at Port Hudson and in the bayou country. The *Vermont Watchman* noted that four hundred members of the regiment, who had agreed to reenlist, reached Montpelier on April 16 by train, with a sizeable crowd out to greet them. En route, the

Woodstock's village square at the time of the Civil War. Adjutant General Wash-burn's offices were located in the Phoenix Block, the prominent three-story commercial building. Woodstock was the Pentagon of Vermont's war effort.
Woodstock Historical Society

troop train stopped a dozen miles south, at Northfield, before proceeding to the capital city. "The arrival of the train at Northfield," the *Watchman* reported, "bearing these brave defenders, was duly signaled by the ringing of bells and ere the train arrived a multitude of people swarmed in the depot and railroad grounds, who loudly cheered as the train rested." The men of the Eighth went on to Montpelier, where a celebration was held in front of the Pavilion Hotel, near the State House. The soldiers then headed home for monthlong furloughs.

On April 21, perhaps the best known of all American Irishmen paid Burlington a visit. Most Vermont papers reported on the arrival of Brig. Gen. Thomas Francis Meagher, the fiery Irish nationalist and leader of the famed Irish Brigade of the Army of the Potomac. "The General was received at the wharf by the Hibernian Society," said the *Free Press*, "headed by an extempore drum corps, and escorted to the American Hotel. Immediately on his arrival, a salute of 11 guns was fired from the battery." General Meagher gave a lecture that night to an enthusiastic crowd of Burlington-area Irishmen. The start of campaigning in Virginia was but 14 days distant.

On April 22, the *Brattleboro Phoenix* reported:

> Seven companies of the 17th Regiment under command of Lt. Col. Cummings passed through this place on their way to Annapolis, where they were ordered to report; it is understood they will go into active service under the command of Gen. Burnside. They are a hardy set of men, and look as if they would do good service on the field of battle.

The paper failed to note that the regiment had gone off to war at only half strength. Still, up in St. Albans, Governor Smith no doubt breathed a sigh of relief.

Also on April 22, a ceremony was held in the U.S. Marine Hospital in Burlington. In the third winter of the war, two military hospitals were operating in Vermont at Burlington and Brattleboro, while a third was being rushed to completion at Montpelier on the old town fairgrounds. The new facility there would be called Sloan Hospital, in honor of William J. Sloan, medical director of the U.S. Military Department of the East. The Brattleboro hospital had been built at the insistence of Vermont's second war governor, Frederick Holbrook of Brattleboro, after a considerable debate with the War Department, which considered the care of soldiers a federal responsibility. Its wooden buildings now stood on the drill field just outside town. At Burlington, so few soldiers were being treated at the U.S. Marine Hospital south of the city on Shelburne Road that plenty of time was available for diversion. The *Burlington Free Press* reported on a grand event there:

> One of the largest gatherings of the season . . . took place on Tuesday evening last, in connection with the meeting of the Hospital Literary and Debating Club. J. S. Adams, Esq., was present and gave a lecture on "Lyceums"—inimitable and soul-stirring. During the evening, Surgeon Samuel W. Thayer, in charge of the hospital, came in . . . Doctor Thayer [Vermont's surgeon general and formerly a teacher of medicine at the University of Vermont] was then presented with a sword and sash as a token of affection from staff and patients.

Though the patient load was light, workers were busy building an addition to increase the number of beds. The *Free Press* also remarked on slow times at the Brattleboro hospital, but added a somber note to its brief report. "Less than a hundred patients now occupy the general hospital there, all available men having gone to the front. A large number of patients however may soon be expected."

Also on April 22, the *Brattleboro Phoenix* carried this item of "Local Intelligence," concerning an incident at one of Brattleboro's springhouses, where people came from far and wide for the curing mineral waters:

> A colored boy about 15 years of age, of the milk and molasses stripe, came to this village a few days since, and from his stories was taken as a contraband. He was kindly taken in by Mrs. Francis at the Wesselhoeff Water Cure . . . He stole $54 from one of the inmates and made tracks. He was found in Whitaker's saw mill in Marlboro, and now has quarters at Newfane [site of the Windham County jail].

Always, Vermonters kept a sense of humor. Under the headline WATER BET was the following item in the *Bennington Banner*: "Two Stamford chaps made a bet the other day, as to how much water they could drink respectively, and managed to worry down, the one 11, and the other 12 full glasses in less than an hour." That paper also noted that a woman in nearby Pownal had said she would never allow the erection of a telegraph pole in her dooryard, "And every time I spank my children have it go all over the country."

In late April, the *Rutland Herald* noted, "The performance of Shakespeare's tragedy 'Julius Caesar' by the Bennington 'Thespian Club' is said to have been a great success." The people of Burlington were treated, the last week in April, to a performance by the noted American pianist and composer Louis Moreau Gottschalk. The *Free Press* opined that the maestro's playing of his own "Fantasia on National Airs" "shows so well his marvelous power over the piano, from which he brings forth tones and effects attained by no other mortal hand."

In Morrisville, plans were announced for a dance at the Waterville

House on May 5. Music would be provided by the band of the Eighth Vermont Regiment. The local paper noted that members of the regiment were having trouble adjusting to the climate back home in Vermont, "So Montpelier ladies, who give their time, money and labor to the Sanitary and Christian Commissions, went straightaway to work on the blessed Sabbath day, making woolen shirts for the soldiers."

As musicians and actors displayed their talents, two Vermonters published books that attracted considerable attention. One was destined to fundamentally affect humankind's view of planet Earth. The other, while much more discussed at the time, would be rather soon forgotten. The *Burlington Free Press* ran a severe editorial criticism of the latter book, by the Rev. John Henry Hopkins, Episcopal bishop of the state, titled *A Scriptural, Ecclesiastical and Historic View of Slavery*. Hopkins was a considerable figure in Vermont, and his opinions were of interest. A man of formidable abilities, the prelate was an artist, a lawyer, an amateur architect, and the father of eleven children, as well as having become the first Episcopal bishop of the Green Mountain State. Now he had written a book the Republican *Free Press* found considerably too tolerant of slavery. The paper noted, at the end of a lengthy and scathing review:

> A good many will say of the Bishop . . . the fallacies and irrelevances and inaccuracies as to facts, in the book, are not surpassed by any thing which we ever saw in a book this size. But we have already given more space to it than we intended. We presume it will serve as a sort of pro-slavery gospel for copperhead politicians, though not few, even of them, will say they cannot quite stand all that. We do not think the book will do much harm except to its author.

The more lasting book of note was written by a native of Woodstock, a remarkable man serving in Rome as United States minister to Italy—George Perkins Marsh. In the spring of 1864 he published his best-known work, *Man and Nature*. *Walton's Journal*, in Montpelier, wrote,

> The title is not so attractive as we think the book will be; at least, we suspect the title does not give a very clear idea of the work. We con-

dense a statement of purpose by Mr. Marsh when we say: his purpose is to show the changes in the physical conditions of the globe produced by human action—to point out danger from interfering on a large scale with natural arrangements of the organic and inorganic world—to suggest modes of improving waste and exhausted regions—and to show that man is, in both kind and degree, of a higher order than any of the forms of animated life nourished by the table of bounteous nature.

A man ahead of his time, Vermonter Marsh had written in *Man and Nature* the first great tract describing the effect of humanity on the environment.

With spring blossoming in Vermont, smallpox was taking an increasingly heavy toll. In Vergennes, Mary Tucker noted in her diary on April 30:

Last night I witnessed a midnight funeral and burial of a case of small pox, from our chamber window. It was one of the saddest scenes I ever witnessed, the lonely slow jiggling funeral cart, with its solitary attendant with a lantern wending its way to the new cemetery through the silent sleeping village to the city of the dead, oh how sad.

While Mrs. Tucker wrote, 600 miles to the south Generals Ulysses Grant and George Meade were meeting to make final plans for the spring campaign, now less than a week from commencing.

At about the same time, Dr. E. H. Sprague wrote to the *Middlebury Register* in the Champlain Valley college town of Middlebury to give advice concerning the illness plaguing a nearby town:

Through your columns it may be thought advisable to lay before your readers a short exposition on the real character of the disease which has prevailed to considerable extent in Weybridge within the last two weeks. If I am correctly informed, there have been as many as six or seven deaths with this new disease—The patients were taken with chills, shivering, and a livid or purple hue; the blood, as it were, settled under finger nails, the cheeks and lips of the same lurid hue, the pulse very small . . . soon loss of consciousness . . . While the patient is in the cold or congestive stage, I should immediately immerse him in a warm bath somewhat above the blood heat, and as soon as the blood will flow open a vein in the arm and allow it to run until the pulse may be felt in the wrist, and by this time get your family physician.

Death was a dark and ever-present companion in the Vermont of the 1860s, not only because of war, but because death came too often, and often too soon, in a time without modern medicines and with the ever-present dangers of farm and factory life. Every newspaper had its reports on nonmilitary tragedies. A sampling from the spring of 1864:

Eddie Smith, the only son of Frederick Smith of St. Johnsbury, while playing about the dam at Miller's carriage shop, Monday afternoon slipped into the current above the flume, and was immediately drawn under the ice and drowned. His playmates gave the alarm but before a hole could be cut in the ice and his body recovered it had been in the water twenty minutes or more, and life was extinct.

Mr. James Briggs of Lincoln, while at work in the Plow Factory at Bristol, had his left hand sawed off close to the thumb, by a circular saw.

While a little daughter of Mrs. James Sprague, a widow lady of Wells, was playing with her young brother last week, the latter dropped a lighted match upon her dress. The dress was immediately in flames, and the clothes were nearly burned from the child's body. The little one lingered about twenty hours when she died.

Charles Woodruff, of Cambridge, was badly hurt a few weeks ago, while in the woods hauling wood. He was at work for Chauncey Warner, and driving a pair of oxen somewhat inclined to have their own way. He started down a hill in the woods, with a long log on a sled, and in his efforts to control the team, was caught between the end of the log and a tree, while oxen were going at a rapid rate. The oxen broke the yoke and cleared themselves from the sled, leaving him fastened between the log and the tree, unable to extricate himself. Another man being in the woods, came to his relief, and he was taken to the house, with his leg badly smashed

As April ended and May commenced, Mercy Eddy, on a farm in Wallingford, south of Rutland, each night made a brief diary entry at the end of her day that mixed farm labors, housework, and news of the war:

> *Fri 29 Mother is not here and I am not well this spring*
> *Sat 30 I am baking and mopping. Gen Grant takes the department of the Army of the Potomac as commander in chief I had my stomach cramps this afternoon*
> *Sun May 1st Mother come last night Picked some cow slips*
> *Mon 2 Mother is washing I am doing house work*
> *Tues 3 rains all day I am not well to day received news that D. Chapin is dead died with small pox. Mother Stafford is 62 years old today*

The fateful May of 1864 had arrived. In St. Johnsbury, Henry Herrick penned in his rented room the night of May Day: "If April went out 'in a blaze of glory' as I wrote yesterday, May has come in gloomy and weeping enough—it was raining when I woke up this morning and has rained by terms all day." On May Day, in a schoolhouse somewhere along the Lamoille River Valley, a teacher named Dana made an entry in his diary indicating that spring fever had infected his classroom:

Have had a hard week indeed. Monday was a cold cheerless day without, not less within. Do not know when I have been so severely tried. Almost lost my patience. The Old Nick seemed to possess the pupils. Some were cold and some wanted more fire, others were warm and wanted the windows open. So it went all day, pretty much, was greatly annoyed . . .

In the Union army camps in Virginia, as May arrived, activity was increasing with the start of marching a matter of hours away. In Norwich, Vermont, on the Connecticut River, doubtless many young men enrolled at the local military college were wondering if the war would last long enough for them to make a mark. Many cadets had not waited for graduation and left Norwich University for the military without waiting to complete their education. The Class of 1864, nearing graduation, had entered the school in 1861 about one hundred strong. The time for awarding degrees was fast approaching, but only seven would be present to accept them. The university's armory had just received one hundred new Springfield rifles, and an assortment of other up-to-date military equipment, which certainly served to heighten campus war fever. The military school would be well represented in the Army of the Potomac when it moved south. A total of sixty-four men of Norwich would march in its ranks, with fourteen serving in the Vermont Brigade.

If spring was in the air in Vermont, so was politics, for 1864 was an election year. Indeed, the political events of the coming summer and fall would determine whether Abraham Lincoln would continue to serve as the nation's chief executive. Lincoln's general election opponent would be Democrat George Brinton McClellan, once the leader of the Army of the Potomac. In early May, Vermont newspapers ran notices of conventions to be held for the selection of candidates for state offices, and to choose delegates to the Republican National Convention. (Few Vermont papers mentioned the Democratic National Convention.) The *Free Press* announcement stated:

> A Mass Convention of the Freemen of Vermont, without distinction of party, will be held at Burlington . . . to nominate candidates for Governor, Lieutenant Governor and Treasurer, to be supported at the ensuing election. Also to appoint delegates at large to the National Convention to be held at Baltimore, on the 7th day of June next, to nominate candidates for President and Vice President of the United States to be supported at the coming election. All those in favor of sustaining the Government in its efforts to suppress the rebellion and to re-establish the Union in its integrity, are cordially invited to attend.

That announcement was placed by Vermont members of the Republican Party, Lincoln's party. Vermont was overwhelmingly Republican. In the presidential election of 1860, Vermonters had voted five-to-one for Lincoln, though he was opposed by a Green Mountain State native, Stephen Douglas. As a sure indication of the state's current political bent, only nineteen Democrats held seats in Vermont's 240-seat House of Representatives in 1864.

In the marble quarries west of Rutland, Irish quarrymen were involved in a tough political struggle of their own that spring, fighting for better wages while the company was threatening them with eviction from their company-owned housing. The *Rutland Herald* said,

> The proprietors . . . have given notice, that they will pay quarry-men $1.50 per day—eleven hours work—from and after to-day; and that all men in their employ must vacate houses belonging to them (such proprietors) on or before the 15th inst.

In early May, production was also nearing an interruption at the Robbins & Lawrence factory at Windsor, on the Connecticut River, but not because of labor troubles. In the spring of 1864, a contract for the manufacture of rifles was running out at the tall brick armory and machine shop. The factory, which supplied rifles for the British army in the Crimean War, had produced 50,000 weapons for the Union with its revolutionary machine tools. Robbins & Lawrence was now converting from the manufacture of Springfield rifles to a new weapon, the Palmer rifle. But none of the latter would be used in the Civil War.

In early May, a wounded cavalryman whose days of fighting were over and who was now assigned to duty at the military hospital in Brattleboro as a member of the Veteran Reserve Corps, and sent a letter to his parents in the northern Vermont town of Craftsbury. Pvt. Augustus Paddock wrote,

> I have just come from our usual game of quoits, after dinner, and will try to answer your kind letter that was received last evening. I suppose that this quoit pitching will do but very little toward putting down this wicked rebellion, but it is all the style here now. The steward has been over to take a game this afternoon, & even the Surgeon is out often pitching. There are but 78 men here now, consequently very little to be done at either offices . . . I do so hope Grant will be successful and this

cruel war be closed soon. The sad news is that a Mr. Holt of Co. B., 4th
Vt. Regt. [Pvt. Samuel B. Holt, of Morristown] died this afternoon of
small pox. He is all rotten with it, or his boddy is, I should say . . .

In Stowe Hollow, Olive Cheney wrote to her daughter Jane on May 1:

Your father went to the village last night and waited for the mail and
fetched home two letters one from you and one from Wm. so that paid
pretty well for the waiting . . . the papers say there is not going to be
any more communication with the Army of the Potomac for the present
I suppose they are going to fighting now soon Ed writes he is in a hurry
to be on the move is tired of stying there it is such lazy work but guess
he will wish he was at home in the mill to work before another month
rolls round.

The first week in May, from Warren in the Mad River Valley, a worried Vermont farm wife, Esther M. Thayer, struggled to write to her soldier husband, Willard, a private in the 10th Vermont at Brandy Station:

Dear husbin,
mine it seems so plesent too day I thought i must sete mi self to write
to you for semes tho i cold write A leter . . . Your leter of the 19 come
too hand in good time & how glad i was too hear from you & too hear
you was so well in mind & body oh I am thankful for helth. The wee are
all well & so is the rest of our Folks . . . i worry more this spring then i
have this winter for tha say tha are goin in too action but I hope yo will
come out safe oh if I cold trust in the Lord as some doo i should bee
happy i spose instide of fearing for the worse but all cant fly frome deth
it will over take us . . . George [identity unknown] says they talk out
there as though they were going to release the drafted men in June and
he was coming home but I am afraid he will be disappointed aint you.
there will be a great slaughter before that time.

At the same time, in a far more learned hand, Judge Royall Tyler
wrote from his home in Brattleboro to his nephew at Brandy Station,
Lt. Col. John S. Tyler, of the Second Vermont Regiment. The previous

day, Colonel Tyler had celebrated his 21st birthday. Already a three-year veteran of the war, the tall blond officer had just been promoted to the number two position in the Second Regiment, commanded by Col. Newton Stone of Bennington. Before the war, John Tyler had begun to study law with his uncle, but left Brattleboro in June 1861 for war service. Judge Tyler's letter began with congratulations on the recent promotion:

> Dear Col.
> When you left us, now nearly three years ago, I didn't expect to be addressing you at this time. I believed you would do well, but did not look for your attaining this position so soon. I am glad now that you owe nothing to favor. You owe nothing to anyone. You have fought your way up . . . There will be terrible fighting sometime, & I suppose in the course of May, or June. In all the battles you have been in you have escaped wounds wonderfully. I hardly know why it is, but I feel more oppressed with apprehension for your Safety in the approaching Campaign than ever before . . . However, we will not dwell on this view of the Subject. We shall try to be as hopeful for you, & for us all as possible. Present my regards & congratulations to Col. Stone . . .

On May 2, in Virginia, Ulysses Grant announced that the spring movement of his forces would begin two days hence. That same day, Gen. Robert E. Lee took his generals to the top of Clark's Mountain, just below the Rapidan River, to discuss the coming fighting. The Confederate brass had a sweeping view of the theater of war, including the Union camps. Lee called their attention to the Rapidan crossings and predicted correctly that Grant would move south by way of Germanna Ford to the north and Ely's Ford to the east. In Vermont that day, the *Burlington Free Press*, under "War News," stated: "Advices from Culpepper Court House [Grant's headquarters] of Saturday evening report everything quiet in that vicinity." The paper also editorialized:

> A considerable portion of our church-going community were shocked yesterday by an uncommon sight in Burlington—nearly a dozen grown

men, with a smaller number of boys, *playing ball* throughout the afternoon. On the open space between Main and College streets, by the old railroad track, in the heart of our village. If we have those among us who have neither respect for the Sabbath themselves, nor decent regard to the feelings of those who do respect the day, we trust our officers will enforce the laws of the state against Sabbath-breaking.

So a bit of spring fever was in the air. After all, high spring had come to Vermont, with rushing, flashing little brooks carrying the last mountain snow away. In the fields and woods spring pools were drying, but still producing nightly their deafening choruses of peepers. Apples trees had blossomed, mayflowers carpeted the hillsides, the lilacs were about to bloom. Hay fields were again green and growing. Yet spring in Vermont, always a time of hope, this year also brought a terrible sense of dread. In the spring of 1864, on the upland farms, in the valley factory towns, in the busy little cities, every Vermonter knew that a bloody campaign was about to commence in Northern Virginia. Nightly, in countless darkened homes, help was quietly asked from on high for the boys far away and in peril. The people of the Green Mountain State that spring would well have understood words written four score years later by a poet who would, one day, grace their Yankee land with his words:

Oh, give us pleasure in the grass today;
And give us not to think so far away
As the uncertain harvest; keep us here
All simply in the springing of the year.

The words are Robert Frost's, the first lines of his poem "A Prayer in Spring."

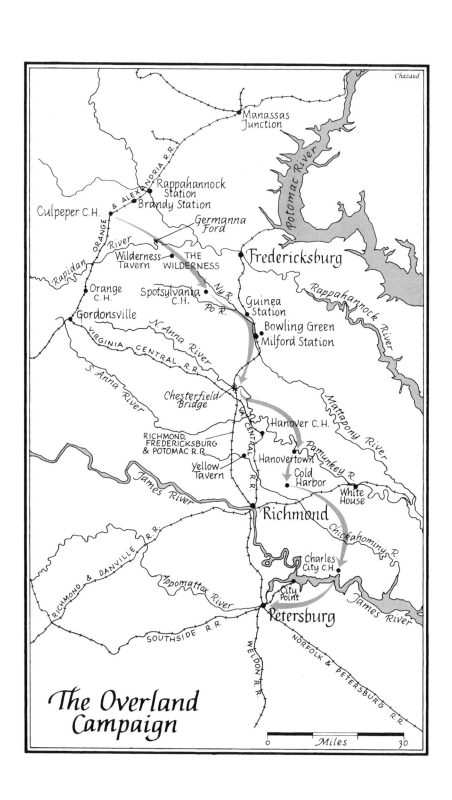

Chazaud

The Overland
Campaign

Miles
0   30

Chapter Four

OVER THE RIVER

On May 3, at Brandy Station, Dr. Rutherford wrote to his wife, Hannah: "We are packing for a march . . . the order came at 1 to day to move at 4 tomorrow morning, so you see we have got to get up and dust . . . We shall probably leave . . . before day light. I said three weeks ago that when we left it would be in the night. God bless you all and believe as ever."

Private Edwin Hall, 10th Vermont, wrote his parents in Brookfield the evening of May 3,

> We are ordered to be ready to march tomorrow morning at 4 AM. We are all ready and in good spirits with 3 days rations and 50 rounds of ammunition and tomorrow night may find us South of the Rapidan. Troops have been coming in all day and we start with a large force . . .
> It is getting dark and I must stop. Don't worry about me for there is an eye that is ever watching over us and shields us from the dangers of the Battlefield. If I do not have another chance I will say farewell—May we meet again.

Certainly many in the ranks dreaded the campaign. In the Sixth Vermont, Sgt. Edward Holton of Williston was engaging in some wishful thinking. He wrote on May 3, "Now Katie, do not fret and worry about me as I do not hardly think that Lee will give us battle short of his fortifications around Richmond." Erastus Scott, a private in the Third Vermont, had written to his sister Harriet in South Reading, Massachusetts, a month earlier: "The tops of the Blue Ridge are capped with snow & as long as that lasts we may look for cool weather. It wont hurt my feelings a bit if the army does not move for a Munth and a half yet." But now the snow was long gone and orders had been received to prepare for the march. Just where the army was going was a secret known only to Ulysses Grant and his top commanders. But the soldiers were speculating, and one private in the Vermont Brigade thought he knew where the fighting would take place. He was betting on an area of Northern Virginia, just south of the Rapidan River, known to much of the army from its campaigning the previous year. Pvt. Oscar Waite, of Sheldon, wrote:

Old Mr. Bowen, the miller, knows all about the Wilderness . . . I find that dreaded, gully-scarred triangle is about thirty miles on a side,—a gruesome kind of half-desert, where for a hundred years, off and on, people have been getting out surface streaks of iron ore and cutting the timber for charcoal to smelt the ore with. It is too poor in spots to raise even bushes, and most of the balance is thickly covered with almost every conceivable tree, bush, or vine that would interfere with military manoevre and any other known operation. A few sandy spots are covered with scrub pines so thick that a man cannot see a rod in advance and then he will come to a mess of vines and savage cats-paw briars that a dog can't get through. Old men who have hunted there all their lives say that much of it can still be marked "unexplored territory." We have already seen the edges of the place. We have tried to penetrate some of the jungles and given up. There are several good roads which would let a big army through in a couple of days, provided it was let alone; but just think of an army of a hundred thousand men, with three or four thousand wagons, getting caught in such a hole! It would fare about as well as a woodchuck in a brush heap, surrounded by a lot of schoolboys.

On May 1, a private in the Third Vermont, Curtis Cobb, from Morgan, wrote to his wife indicating that he, and the army, were well prepared for the coming campaign:

> I am in the Sixth Army Corps Second Brigade Second Division. General Gettie is the General of this Division and General L. A. Grant is General of this Brigade General U. S. Grant is the Commander in Chief. We are in the Army of the Potomac and it is a big thing and I hope that thare will not be a Rebel on Earth in one month from to day. I think Gen. Grant is going to do the thing up this Spring but I cannot tell but you will hear of some big fiting ere long and may God be with each and every soldier.

On May 3, Pvt. Erastus Worthen wrote a letter to Rutland that was interrupted by the long-awaited orders:

> Friends Wilson and Mary it is with great pleasure that I take this opportunity to write a few lines . . . very glad to hear from you and to hear that you wer well for I am well & enjoy life pretty well at the present time hope these few lines will find you in the enjoyment of the richest of heavens blessings, health peace & prosperity. Well Wilson we have just received orders to march to morrow morning at 4 o'clock with six days rations dont know where nor which way we shall go but shall probably find out where I am in the corse of a month I tell you this there is going to be some pretty hard fighting done this summer we have got about 130,000 men in the army of the Potomac and it is reported the rebs has got 20,000 Cavelry and 80,000 infantry in front of us ready for a battle. tell you when those two armys come in contact with each other, there is going to be some blood spilt before either side will back scatter. I wish that I could contrive some plan to get out of this first battle but I don't see any chance for me to get out of it . . .

One of the last letters sent from Brandy Station by Lt. John A. Smith, Fifth Vermont, to his sister Lucia Gilman in Sutton, Quebec, contained the following snippet of verse:

Who will cair for Mother now
Soon with angels I'll be Marching
With bright angels on my brow
I have for my country fallen
Who will cair for mother now.

Smith would survive the coming campaign, but fall mortally wounded at Petersburg the following spring, with but a week remaining before the surrender at Appomattox.

To Tunbridge came a letter dated May 3 from Captain Bixby, written to his wife, Frances:

Thought I would just write . . . to tell let you know that we move tomorrow morning at 4 o'clock. So you musent think it strange if you do not hear from me again for some time. I wrote you Sunday no news here excepting the move. My health is good. Can't write any more good by with the true love of your Orville to my own Dear Wife, Heaven bless you.

In the envelope, Bixby enclosed a lock of his brown hair.

In the Third Vermont, Pvt. Seth Eastman wrote,

The first that we knew that a movement of the Army was about to occur, we had orders to draw six days' rations to be packed in our haversacks, and three days rations to be packed in our knapsacks, and each man had to take twenty cartridges in his pockets. We all knew that these kinds of orders meant business, but there was no backing out or saying that we felt discouraged. We were now under the command of U. S. Grant and everybody had the utmost confidence in him, as he had a reputation second to none as a fighting man, and all believed that our labor would amount to something.

Grant had chosen to move southeast, to strike past Lee's right flank and cross the Rapidan at Germanna and Ely's Fords. He had taken a long look at a swing to the west, out toward Gordonsville, far from the Wilderness. And he had considered a waterborne thrust south, as

Robert E. Lee, commander of the Army of Northern Virginia, waited south of the Rapidan to counter the Army of the Potomac's spring offensive. This photo, taken shortly after the war, shows the strain of four years' fighting. HOWARD COFFIN COLLECTION

McClellan had done in 1862. But in the end he chose to move by the most direct overland route, and risk a passage through the difficult woodland just south of the Rapidan.

Beginning the great campaign, the cavalry led the way. Riding out of its winter camp at Stevensburg, the First Vermont Cavalry was near the head of the column as James Wilson's division of Phil Sheridan's command set out southeast, mounting up at about 2 AM on May 4, bound for Germanna Ford. The miles-long column jingled down the long dirt roads, riding unhindered until it reached the Rapidan at Germanna. Confederate pickets were on the far bank, and they fired a few shots when the vanguard of the Union advance suddenly appeared out of the dim early morning.

Eri Woodbury, a private in the Vermont Cavalry from St. Johnsbury who had left his beloved Dartmouth College to enlist, said, "Sunrise saw us emerging from the Ford of the Rapidan and tumbling up the steep bank into Rebel territory in a hurry; but little opposition met us . . ." Before dawn, the Rapidan was forded and Wilson's men settled down to await the arrival of the engineers who would construct pontoon bridges for the walking army and the long wagon train to follow. The first units to cross would be those of Gouverneur Warren's Fifth Corps, leading the infantry. Behind it came John Sedgwick's

Tough Ulysses Grant was photographed about the time the Overland Campaign began, with his new lieutenant general's stars. HOWARD COFFIN COLLECTION

Sixth Corps. To the east, the Second Corps under Hancock was moving on Ely's Ford.

Wilson's cavalry waited at Germanna Ford until the engineers came up, then moved down the Germanna Plank Road to Wilderness Tavern, in open country on the northern edge of the Wilderness. There, the Orange Turnpike, one of the two major east–west roads that crossed the densely wooded area, came through. The other main road through the tangled woods, the Orange Plank Road, lay some two miles to the south. Wilson waited at the tavern until the head of the Fifth Corps appeared, then headed his men south and west. After a couple of hours they reached their objective, Parker's Store, on the Orange Plank Road. At this little farm country hamlet west of the Wilderness, Wilson set up headquarters and sent scouts to the west. They saw little to indicate that an enemy army was moving their way. Cavalryman Horace Ide, however, noted some ominous signs. He wrote that night,

We moved up the Turnpike towards Robinson's Tavern and then took across the fields to the Plank Road, which we struck about two miles east of Parker's Store . . . We advanced to Parker's Store where nearly the whole division went in to bivouac but a detachment was sent further up the road under Maj. Bennett and had a little skirmish with a small squad of the enemy cavalry. About dark I was sent out with ten men on a wood road to the east which I followed about 2 miles to the Catharpin road, where we found pickets from the 3d Ind. Cav. The pickets reported seeing a cloud of dust to the south and citizens said that a train of artillery had moved in that direction.

Col. George Chapman, commanding the brigade that included the Vermont Cavalry, reported, "We bivouacked and threw out strong pickets on all approaches. During the march nothing was seen of the enemy save a small mounted force, which retreated rapidly before our advance."

Wilson commanded the smallest of the Army of the Potomac's three mounted divisions. It was bedded down to the west of the Wilderness, sleeping along a road on which a full corps of General Lee's army was approaching. The other two cavalry divisions had gone off southeast with Sheridan toward Chancellorsville, protecting the army's trains and keeping a lookout for J. E. B. Stuart, said to be over toward Fredericksburg. James Wilson had made the first foray into and through a portion of the Wilderness safely, and had arrayed his force well in case Rebels should move his way in the morning. What he had failed to do was to act in the key role of cavalry, as the army's eyes and ears. On May 4, Wilson failed to discover that two-thirds of Lee's infantry was close by the Wilderness, just off to the west along the Orange Plank Road and the Orange Turnpike. When those Rebels came marching in the next day, Ulysses Grant's army would be strung out north and south, ill prepared to meet a heavy infantry assault on its flank. One key road intersection would be totally undefended. A heavy price would be paid for that lack of warning, and nobody would bear the cost more dearly than the Vermont Brigade.

Horace Ide said of Wilson, after the war,

Gen. Wilson never was a good Cavalry officer and never knew how to use them mounted. He almost invariably dismounted them and sent the horses to the rear and it was a standing joke for us to say that "our horses have started towards the rear and would keep agoing till we overtook them and consequently the one that started first would fare best."

The infantry had moved out of Brandy Station in the darkness. As the sun appeared and the day warmed, the marching columns saw one of those perfect spring days developing that often favor Northern Virginia in high spring. Bruce Catton, nearly a century after the Civil War, may have caught it best:

> Beside the roads the violets were in bloom and the bush honeysuckle was out, and the day and the year had a fragile light that the endless columns would soon trample to fragments . . . The men . . . who marched away from winter quarters that morning took a last look back and saw a golden haze which, even at the moment of looking, they knew they would never see again. They tell how birds were singing, and how the warm scented air came rolling up the river valley, and how they noticed things like wildflowers and the young green leaves, and they speak of the moving pageant which they saw and of which they themselves were part.

The Sixth Corps, including the Vermont Brigade and the 10th Vermont, began the tramp from Brandy Station at 4 AM. Private/correspondent Wilbur Fisk, in the Second Vermont, said,

> We left our camp at early dawn, and took the war path once more. The morning was bright and clear, the air cool and refreshing, as we bid adieu to our winter's home, and started on what we knew to be the most perilous campaign of the war. We took the same line of march that we did last fall, marching direct to Germanna Ford, and halting for the night two or three miles beyond.

Private Seth Eastman:

We started in the twilight of that early morning with gloomy forebodings as to what the next few days would mean to us. We marched all day, crossed a small river on a pontoon bridge, and camped for the night without seeing or hearing any danger.

Looking back on that day years later, Luther Harris of the Fourth Vermont, from the little remote northeastern Vermont town of Sutton, recalled the Rapidan and "the blue line crossing, every soldier in that immense line seemed a hero, the great throng seemed made up of individual athletes, and the spectacle was grand." Harris said he took a piece of paper out of his cartridge box and wrote his sweetheart that "the sight was magnificent, that the line looked like a huge projectile worming its way toward the enemy." He then wrote, "After crossing

Philip Sheridan, surrounded by fellow cavalry officers. From left are generals Wesley Merritt, David McM. Gregg, Sheridan, Henry Davies, James Harrison Wilson, and Alfred Torbert. Wilson led the division that included the First Vermont Cavalry. HOWARD COFFIN COLLECTION

the Rapidan the undulating plains were covered by a dense growth of second growth scrub oak . . ."

Harris said he sat on a high bluff to watch the passing of the army. He did not explain how he managed to get away from the marching columns to make such an observation. Perhaps the march was interrupted for a rest with the crossing of the Rapidan. However he got there, Harris had chosen the best observation point along the roadway from Brandy Station to the river to view the march. There was, indeed, a high bluff on the south side of the Rapidan, overlooking the pontoon bridges. Ulysses Grant had noticed that and had, for a time, seated himself on the porch of a farmhouse to watch his soldiers tramp by.

One wonders: When viewing the passing of the Vermont Brigade, was it possible to distinguish its soldiers from others in the miles-long column? Early in the war, when the Vermont troops went south and passed through the big eastern cities, people remarked on how tall the men were, on how well they marched. In his famous tribute to the Vermont Brigade, Sixth Corps Adjutant McMahon said after the war that the Vermonters "swaggered, in a cool, impudent way," and "had a long, slow, swinging stride on the march, which distanced everything that followed them." So perhaps some watcher on the bluff that day might have picked up something different about the Vermont Brigade, noted the long, loping farm boy stride, caught something of a swagger. Certainly, the tattered old flags, veterans of many a hot fight, would have identified the Green Mountain Boys, some displaying the state seal with a cow in a pasture by a tree, and a green mountain rising beyond.

Watching the march of the Old Brigade on May 5, one would have seen Lewis Grant, "Aunt Lydia" to his men, all round-faced and serious, riding near the head of the column. To the front of the brigade would have been the Second Vermont Regiment, the oldest of the brigade's units, first bloodied on Chinn Ridge, way back at First Bull Run. Riding alongside his men was Col. Newton Stone, regimental commander, raised in the southern Vermont mountain town of Readsboro, where his father was pastor. Stone was a lawyer in nearby Bennington when the war began. Now he led the biggest regiment in the brigade, numbering somewhat fewer than eight hundred. He'd been the Second's colonel for less than a month, having replaced Col. James Walbridge, who had resigned because of illness. Likely riding by Stone that day was his second in command, another minister's son and student of the law, newly promoted Lieutenant Colonel Tyler.

The six hundred men of the Third Vermont Regiment marched that bright May day led by their veteran commander Col. Thomas O. Seaver, a resident of the central Vermont farming town of Pomfret. Seaver was a lawyer with a practice in the thriving neighboring town of Woodstock. The Third Vermont had distinguished itself on many fields and was particularly proud of its bold part in the storming of the heights at Fredericksburg under Seaver's leadership the previous spring.

A new commander led the Fourth Vermont on its march that morning. Big Col. George Foster, from Walden in north-central Vermont, had gained a bit of command experience before the war as a teacher in a rural district school. The tall Foster was known as one of the most handsome men in the brigade, and was a great favorite among the troops. Now he had been elevated to lead the Fourth after the resignation of the wounded Col. Charles Stoughton, who lost an eye at Funkstown, just after Gettysburg. Stoughton had gone home to recuperate, but was never able to shake the effects of the severe wound, and had sent in his resignation.

The Fourth had done the hardest fighting of all the Vermont regiments at First Fredericksburg. Now it crossed the Rapidan with about six hundred men. Near the front of the Third and Fourth Regiments were two men who, not surprisingly, bore a strong resemblance, the Pingree brothers from Hartford. Lt. Col. Samuel Pingree was second in command of the Third, and Lt. Col. Stephen Pingree was second in command of the Fourth. Both were Dartmouth College men.

The Fifth Vermont had seen hard combat during the Peninsula Campaign at Savage's Station. Advancing too eagerly into a wooded area thick with Rebels who were supported by artillery, the regiment sustained the most severe loss of any Vermont regiment in the entire war. Formerly commanded by Lewis Grant, the Fifth, as it tramped across the Rapidan, mustered a bit fewer than five hundred men. Now leading the regiment was Lt. Col. John R. Lewis, a Burlington dentist who had

Pontoon bridges at Germanna Ford, on the Rapidan River, where the Sixth Corps crossed. HOWARD COFFIN COLLECTION

entered the service as a captain. The previous winter he had taken his men home on furlough and they had been reviewed at Burlington by Governor Smith, just before their return. At the occasion, Lewis spoke, "Pledging anew the loyalty of the regiment to the cause of the Union and faithful regard for the honor of Vermont."

The Sixth Vermont Regiment that May morning, rounding out the Vermont Brigade as it stepped across the Rapidan, had some 550 men present for duty. They were led by Col. Elisha Barney, a merchant before the war in the northwestern Vermont community of Swanton, up near Lake Champlain. Popular with his men, though known as a tough disciplinarian, Barney had survived a severe wound in fighting at Crampton's Gap, just before Antietam. He came from a Vermont family that furnished six sons to the Union armies. One brother was second in command of the Ninth Vermont Regiment, down in North Carolina. Near Fredericksburg a year previous, a colonel of the Seventh Louisiana had surrendered his sword to Elisha Barney.

As the Vermont Brigade tramped toward the Wilderness, Sgt. Ransom Towle of Rochester, in the Fourth Vermont, had time to make a brief diary note: "Passed by General Grant in plain dress on a wiry little pony. Grant looks plain, important, icy & thoughtful."

An observer watching the armies pass would need to have been well downstream that bright May morning to see Vermont's three companies of sharpshooters cross the Rapidan. They served in Hancock's Second Corps, which was moving down toward Chancellorsville, on the eastern edge of the Wilderness. Even from a distance, the marksmen would have stood out from the long lines of blue-clad soldiers, for they wore distinctive green uniforms, made for camouflage. Through the course of the war, the Green Mountain State sent 620 sharpshooters to serve, the highest number per capita of all the northern states. Vermont Company F, of the First Sharpshooter Regiment, was led by newly promoted Capt. Charles Merriman, a Brattleboro man, and was assigned to Brig. Gen. Alexander Hays' Second Brigade of Brig. Gen. David Birney's division of the Second Corps. Vermont Companies E and H served in the Second Sharpshooter Regiment, commanded by Lt. Col. Homer Stoughton, a Vermonter from Randolph. Capt. Seymour Norton of Burlington led Company E, while Capt. Albert Buxton, from Londonderry in southern Vermont, led Company H. The companies were attached to Brig. Gen. J. H. Hobart Ward's brigade, also of Birney's division. The three Vermont companies, with authorized strengths of one hundred men each, were all well undersized. Company F had just forty-three men in the ranks as it crossed the Rapidan.

Back at Germanna Ford, Dr. Joseph Rutherford, 10th Vermont, looked back on the long day and wrote years later,

Early on the morning of May fourth, the movement silently and ernestly commenced; and when the sun rose it shone, never brighter, upon the deserted camps of the Union Army, and revealed to the rebel commander, no doubt, from his signal station on Clark's Mountain, a scene that plainly said, "We are coming—coming to finish up the tragedy" . . . Somehow it seemed to every man, all of whom had crossed that same stream several times before to fight the enemy and then retreat, that we had now come to stay.

In his diary the night of May 4, Rutherford wrote,

Over the River! We are all here, and Mr. Lee, though he did not for-
mally invite us, has not yet decided to object to our staying. Cheerily
have the men pushed on to-day—fifteen miles and not a sore foot, not
a struggle—the column came in solid. What next we do not know; but
we shall sleep soundly to-night, right under the shadow of Grant's bat-
tle-flag, charmed by the music of the Rapidan. Sleep soldier! May God
bless thy numbered slumbers.

Also on the march was the understrength 17th Vermont, just down
from Vermont and now a part of Burnside's corps, under the command
of Brattleboro's Lt. Col. Charles Cummings. The regiment had been
assigned to the Second Brigade of the corps' second division, which also
included three New Hampshire regiments and a Maine regiment, all
led by Col. Simon Griffin of New Hampshire. The brigade was part of
the division of Brig. Gen. Robert Potter, a New Yorker. The 17th had
marched from Alexandria with Burnside on April 27 and arrived at Beal-
ton Station, a railroad stop in broad, open farming country a few miles
north of the Rappahannock, on May 4. That night the Ninth Corps was
poised to move down to Germanna Ford and become the last Union
corps to cross the Rapidan. The route of march out from Alexandria had
been along the Orange & Alexandria Railroad via Fairfax and Bristoe
Station. Cummings, leading the regiment, had marched through territory once familiar to the Second Vermont Brigade, in which he was an
officer. He wrote to his wife,

We started Wednesday morning and marched to Fairfax Court House
that night when we encamped on precisely the same ground on which
the 16th [Vermont] pitched the night of the 11th December 1862. I
immediately left the regiment and went to the home of Spencer Jackson, where I boarded when I was provost marshall and when I was sick
in Feb. 1863. The people were quite glad to see me and gave me a nice
supper.

Cummings then noted that when the fighting began, it was likely his men would be placed in some kind of support role. "I am glad of some such arrangement just now," he wrote, "for I could not take such undrilled troops into the field without some misgivings."

Back in the Sixth Corps, the night of May 4, Brig. Gen. George Getty, commanding the Second Division, including the Vermont Brigade, summed up his day by noting,

> Marched to and crossed the Rapidan at Germanna Ford, and encamped on Flat Bush Run, 2 miles from the ford; in position covering the Germanna plank road; pickets connecting on the right of the First Division of this corps, and on the left with the Fifth Corps.

In his diary, Wilbur Fisk wrote,

> We halted that night about three miles from the river on the rebel side. It was late in the afternoon and we were all tired and some were foot sore and nearly exhausted. We spread down our blankets . . . very few thinking it worth while to put up any tents as the weather was clear and fair. Hart Smith and I spread down our blankets to sleep together. It was quite cool in the morning there was considerable frost.

On his Vermont farm, far north in West Windsor, farmer Jabez Hammond recorded that same night that the weather was "warm and pleasant." He added, "Watson worked a ploughing with his oxen." The *Free Press* of May 4 was busy with Vermont news, including the following account of a recent tragedy in Cabot, some 60 miles east:

> Henry Durgin, a young man of 20, and a small boy who was in a boat with him, were drowned in Molly's Pond in Cabot, last week Wednesday. They had a load of young trees and it is supposed a sudden gust capsized the boat, but no one saw the accident.

In the far north of Vermont, in Brownington, Edson Tinkham's diary reported on the burial of a local soldier, a war casualty:

May 4 Chamberlain buried. He was starved at Belle Isle [a Confederate prison at Richmond].

Alvira worked for father. Sophia helped tie up hops. Planted potatoes in sheep pasture. Built big barn. Sold gray mare got gray kicker off Uncle Eli.

In Barre, students at the local academy heard a lecture on the battle of Gettysburg given by G. G. Benedict, who had been an aide to the commander of the Second Vermont Brigade, George Stannard. Benedict would one day be awarded a Medal of Honor for his battlefield service. The newspaperman/historian was traveling about the state delivering popular talks on the great battle.

In St. Johnsbury, Henry Herrick wrote at bedtime, May 4,

Still another drizzly gloomy day and to-night it is very cold—Zenas came down street to-night, the first time in a good while. Went into the Hotel to look at the dailies as I was coming home, but there is hardly any news. It seems to be a time of busy preparation with the army of the Potomac, but I am almost losing patience that it does not move—it is there, if anywhere, that we are to look for a turn of the tide of our military misfortunes and it is hard waiting. It seems as though this campaign must be a decisive one, at any rate it must be a most important one, and if victory is with us, we may hope for a speedy end of the war; but if it is against us—it is hard to calculate the results. Such a responsibility as rests on Gen. Grant hardly any man ever had before . . .

Back in the war zone, Maj. Richard B. Crandall of Berlin, near Montpelier, another Dartmouth man and a beginning lawyer, was on picket with his Sixth Vermont that night south of the Rapidan. Surely the men were looking anxiously to the west, peering through the dark in the direction from which they knew Lee's army must soon approach. It has been written that some soldiers in the Army of the Potomac the night of May 4 could hear the distant rumble of an army on the move. In point of fact, the lead elements of Lee's advance were but a few miles distant. If Crandall heard anything of their approach, he didn't note it. He wrote in his diary, "The day excessively warm . . . We are 400 strong. I wonder how it will be in another week."

Chapter Five

MAY 5, 1864

T he deadliest day in the history of the state of Vermont began both at home and in the fields and tangled woods of Northern Virginia with a brilliant sunrise announcing the arrival of a warm and beautiful spring morning. In West Windsor, Vermont, on May 5, 1864, Jabez Hammond pronounced the day "warm and pleasant" and passed it plowing with a pair of oxen borrowed from neighbor J. W. Perkins. In St. Johnsbury, Henry Herrick wrote of a "pleasant and very warm" day. He worried about a letter from his mother, back at the family place in Cabot, imploring him to come home for a visit. "She hopes I should come alone, for she has a feeling that it is to be our last," Herrick wrote. Though mother Herrick was apparently feeling her mortality, her son chalked it up to her only being "childish and low spirited." Herrick also made it clear he was not pleased that his mother had implied that his friend Zenas would not be welcome at the Herrick house.

In the war zone early that morning, the Army of the Potomac continued to move across the Rapidan and into the Wilderness. Gouverneur Warren's Fifth Corps and John Sedgwick's Sixth Corps were massing on the northern edge of the Wilderness, near Wilderness Tavern on the Orange Turnpike. And Generals Grant and Meade were

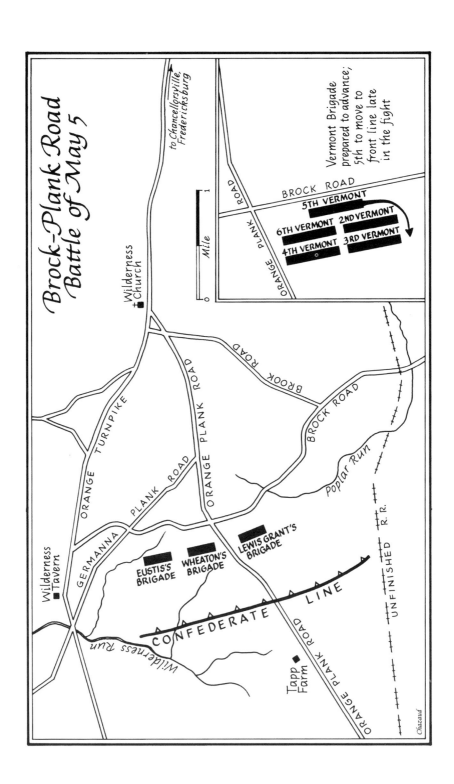

Brock-Plank Road
Battle of May 5

to Chancellorsville,
Fredericksburg

Wilderness
Church

Vermont Brigade
prepared to advance;
5th to move to
front line late
in the fight

BROCK ROAD

5TH VERMONT

6TH VERMONT   2ND VERMONT

4TH VERMONT   3RD VERMONT

ORANGE PLANK ROAD

Mile

ORANGE TURNPIKE

GERMANNA PLANK ROAD

ORANGE PLANK ROAD

BROOK ROAD

BROCK ROAD

Poplar Run

UNFINISHED R.R.

Wilderness
Tavern

EUSTIS'S
BRIGADE

WHEATON'S
BRIGADE

LEWIS GRANT'S
BRIGADE

CONFEDERATE LINE

Wilderness Run

Tapp
Farm

ORANGE PLANK ROAD

Chazaud

coming down to set up headquarters on a nearby knoll beside the turnpike. Grant hoped to move his army south of the Wilderness without a fight, and he already had Hancock's Second Corps well to the south. A key problem was the need to protect the army's supply train, the thousands of wagons bearing vital supplies of food and ammunition. The trains could not be left behind at the mercy of Confederate raiders, and they were slowing the march.

As General Warren reached Wilderness Tavern, he ordered a division to march west, along the Orange Turnpike, just in case any enemy were in the vicinity. It had gone less than a mile before Rebels were spotted in the distance. Soon both sides had deployed and a brisk, groping fight was under way. There would be no getting through the Wilderness without a battle. General Lee's Army of Northern Virginia was on the march from the west, its commander intent on striking Grant before he could move his army through the woodlands into the open country to the southeast. The soldiers Warren had encountered were part of Richard "Baldy" Ewell's corps, moving on the northern east–west road cutting through the Wilderness, the Orange Turnpike. To the south, on the Orange Plank Road, Ambrose Powell Hill's corps was also coming east, closing on Parker's Store where Wilson's cavalry division, including the First Vermont Cavalry, had spent the night. The third big Confederate fighting unit, James Longstreet's corps, was on the move from the west along first the Pamunkey and then the Catharpin Road, but still many hours from the field of battle. Its absence was keeping Lee from ordering a no-holds-barred advance by Hill and Early. By the time Warren got in a fight on the turnpike, a clash had already erupted to the south.

At early morning James Wilson and his Third Division of cavalry, some 3,500 strong, were alone, to the west of the Wilderness. At 5 AM Wilson, having left a single regiment on the Orange Plank Road at Parker's Store, moved the rest of his force south, toward the Catharpin Road that ran along the southern edge of the Wilderness. In the advance was Col. Addison Preston, ever eager for action, his Vermonters trotting along on their tough little Morgan horses. Reaching the Catharpin Road, Wilson had his men rein in. Then he sent George Chapman's brigade off to the west, bound in the direction of Craig's

Meeting House, a little Baptist church in open fields. G. G. Benedict wrote, "A squadron of the First Vermont, under Captain [William] Cummings, had the advance . . . At about eight AM the brigade reported a body of the enemy in sight." The Vermonters had run into Rebel cavalry under Thomas Rosser.

Lieutenant Horace K. Ide, from Barnet in northeastern Vermont, was in the advance. "We had passed through [a] clearing on one side of the road when the advance reported the enemy in sight," Ide wrote:

> Capt. Cummings [who like Ide came from Barnet] rode up to investigate and coming back in a hurry ordered me to take 6 men down to the left of the road while the rest were ordered into line. I took the squad into the woods and while we were tearing down the fence to our rear the rebels came charging down. We had struck Rosser's brigade who were marching without any advance guard and the instant they met us the whole command charged. The men in the road fired a volley and fell back while we to the left could not get back to the road. Geo. Austin of Co. B was struck by a rebel sabre at the first onset and "scalped" but made his escape. The column in the road kept rallying and checked the enemy.

The Battle of the Wilderness, with the commencement of the cavalry fight known as Craig's Meeting House, had begun for the state of Vermont.

Also in the fight was Pvt. Eri Woodbury, who said his company dismounted and took cover behind a fence:

> One of our co. came up on my right, and I moved about foot & half to left, he taking my place. In half minute ball hit him in temple & without a groan he was "mustered out." His warm blood formed a little pool in which his knees were steeped. Several balls cut through the rails in that very spot driving dirt into my face, but I was unharmed.

Ide said that he and six men jumped two fences to reach the main column on the Catharpin Road. On the way one man, Pvt. Dennison

Thomas Rosser led the Rebel horsemen that hit the First Vermont Cavalry near Craig's Meeting House. HOWARD COFFIN COLLECTION

Badger, was captured when his horse fell. "The balance of the distance to the brigade we made in pretty good time," said Ide, "occasionally turning round and giving a volley, but we did not stop long for as far as we could see the road was full of Rebel cavalry." As Ide reached his comrades, "The rebels were coming in so that they were unable to halt soon enough and some of them ran right into our ranks . . . After a few minutes of seemingly inextricable confusion the enemy began to give ground . . . They were forced back over the ground we had been driven to near where the fight began."

As noted, the Confederates were led by Thomas Rosser, a Texan and West Point graduate, one of the best of Lee's cavalrymen, who was about to put a stop to the retreat. Approaching Craig's Meeting House, the Rebels dismounted and an infantry-style fight developed with horses taken to the rear. It lasted only briefly as more southerners came up and the outmanned Union line soon gave way, as the enemy was discovered overlapping and moving past its left flank. Ide said there were calls from the Confederates to "surrender you damned Yanks." The Yankees, instead, sprang to their horses and galloped off east, according to Ide, "as the woods was on fire and the smoke quite thick we were soon out of sight." As the cavalry had discovered, the woods in and around the Wilderness were tinder-dry and ready to ignite, covered with dead leaves from the previous fall. That fact would bring indescribable agony to many wounded soldiers as the Battle of the Wilderness intensified.

Again a running battle developed, this time with the Confederates in hot pursuit. Ide wrote: "The enemy were following us vigorously firing into our rear and the whole division was retreating in confusion."

Along the way, Private Woodbury had his horse shot from under him. "After losing horse did some tall travelling for about three miles before getting another I never so tired in my life," he noted in his diary. He added, "By the way the horse I lost was a good one."

Not so lucky was Charles Chapin, a corporal from Williston in the Champlain Valley. He wrote, "Skirmished very hard . . . then was relieved got back to our horses & in 15 minutes was ordered out again & I was captured by a Reb in our uniform." Chapin would soon be on his way to the worst of all Confederate prison camps.

"There seemed to be no attempt to rally," said Ide, "till we crossed a deep valley through which ran Hunting Run." There, according to Ide, both Union and Confederate artillery unlimbered and exchanged fire, though he said, "they did not cross the run and after a while we withdrew several miles to the rear and eastward." By day's end, the Vermonters were positioned near Todd's Tavern, on the Brock Road south of the Wilderness, having linked up with the rest of Sheridan's command. For the time being, their fighting was done and the cost had been considerable. Benedict put the regiment's losses on May 5 at 4 killed, 31 wounded, and 14 missing.

Meanwhile, as the fight had developed along the Catharpin Road, the detachment left by Wilson on the Orange Plank Road was in desperate straits. Up there, dismounted Yankee cavalrymen faced A. P. Hill's infantry, and the pressure from growing numbers of Rebels was becoming unbearable. Fighting as they gave ground, the hopelessly outnumbered Union horsemen steadily retired along the Plank Road, back toward the Brock Road, the main north–south avenue through the Wilderness.

Early that morning, as the cavalry moved into action, the men of the 10th Vermont Regiment had been roused from sleep along the

Hard-hitting Ambrose Powell Hill led the Confederate advance toward the Brock and Plank Road intersection. HOWARD COFFIN COLLECTION

south bank of the Rapidan at Germanna Ford. The regiment was under a new commander, Lt. Col. William Henry, described as "tall and commanding," the friend and neighbor of Reverend Parker. Only days before, Henry had succeeded Col. Albert Jewett, who had led the 10th since it went south to serve in 1862. Jewett was said to be suffering from a kidney disease and had gone back to his home in Swanton. Regimental surgeon Dr. Rutherford wrote of the morning of May 5, "Our division remained at and near the ford, where we had crossed, until General Burnside, with the Ninth Corps, arriving from Warrenton, appeared on the other side of the river. The division was then ordered to move by the Germanna Plank Road, to the old Wilderness Tavern . . ." The arrival of the Ninth Corps and its subsequent crossing of the Rapidan brought another Vermont regiment, the little 17th, toward the Wilderness.

May 5 had begun in the Vermont Brigade, according to Pvt. Wilbur Fisk, when "We were called up before light and an hour given us to prepare our breakfast. We had fresh beef to cook and coffee to make and when this was done and our breakfast eaten it was time to pack up our things and fall in." George Getty, in his official report, stated that his Second Division of the Sixth Corps began the day as follows: "The division moved at 7 AM on the 5th to Old Wilderness Tavern, massed, and remained waiting orders until noon." Getty then noted that at 10:30 a brigade of his division, Neill's, was detached and ordered to report to Brig. Gen. Horatio Wright, commanding the Sixth Corps' First Division. So Getty's depleted division was at Wilderness Tavern, where to the west the sound of battle was growing as Baldy Ewell was pressing along the Orange Turnpike, piling in more and more men. The Fifth Corps soldiers facing him were under increasing pressure, and soon much of the Sixth Corps was ordered into that fight. But Getty's division remained in the fields near the tavern, awaiting orders. Indeed, according to Pvt. Luther Harris, the spirits of the men were high, partly because it appeared they had been desig-nated a reserve force that might not fight that day.

About noon, Getty received marching orders. He was to take his division south, down to where the Brock Road crossed the Orange Plank Road, "to support the cavalry," Getty said, "who were being driv-en in from Parker's Store." Vermont Brigade commander Lewis Grant said General Meade had sent instructions "to hold the cross roads at all hazards until the arrival of the Second Corps." It had finally dawned on the Union high command that the vital intersection of the Brock and Plank Roads was largely undefended. The advance of A. P. Hill's corps was making steadily for it, easily pushing back the small cavalry force Wilson had left at Parker's Store that morning. A major crisis had already developed in the growing battle, for Hancock's Sec-ond Corps, moving by way of Chancellorsville and the Catharpin Road, was now well to the south of the Plank Road. Were Hill to seize the intersection, the Army of the Potomac would be sundered. How much importance the Vermont Brigade's presence in Getty's com-mand bore on the decision to send the division for such important work remains a matter of considerable conjecture. Only one bit of eyewitness testimony seems to exist to indicate it was a key factor. Surgeon Samuel Allen, in the Fourth Vermont, serving as medical director on Getty's staff, told historian Benedict after the war that when the order to move was received, it was accompanied by a special direction that Getty should take with him the Vermont Brigade. Pvt. Seth Eastman, in the Sixth Vermont, had no doubts about such matters. "The men from Vermont were considered the very steadiest troops in the whole army," he stated, "and, therefore, were sent to the place where there was the worst danger."

So Getty took his division, with just three of its four brigades, off south, down the road from Wilderness Tavern. In the advance was the First Brigade, under Brig. Gen. Frank Wheaton, made up of four Pennsylvania regiments, the 93rd, 98th, 102nd, and 139th, and the 62nd New York. Grant's five Vermont regiments constituted the Second Brigade. The Fourth Brigade, commanded by Eustis, included the Seventh, 10th, and 37th Massachusetts, and the Second Rhode Island Regiment. In all, the man named after the father of his now divided country, George Washington Getty, had about 6,000 men. Getty's Third Brigade, led by Brig. Gen. Thomas H. Neill and made up of the Seventh Maine and the 43rd, 49th, and 77th New York Reg-

The Orange Plank Road, along which A. P. Hill's corps advanced and the Vermont Brigade made its stand. This photo, taken after the battle, shows the blasted tangle of the Wilderness. HOWARD COFFIN COLLECTION

iments, was left to the north, supporting the hard-pressed Fifth Corps along the Orange Turnpike.

Lewis Grant wrote: "The distance was nearly two miles, and part of the road was narrow and muddy, but the command pressed rapidly forward and reached the crossing not a minute too soon." Sgt. Marshall Twitchell, of Townshend, years later recalled the march with pride:

> Our division . . . was the strongest division in the army. Five of its regiments were from the Green Mountains of Vermont, and other regiments were perhaps equally good; and as a whole it partook of many of the qualities of the Swiss of Europe or the Highlanders of Scotland. It had been upon every large field of battle since the commencement of the war [and] had never been repulsed or driven from position. Two years service had weeded out all men lacking in courage or physically weak, while the division as a whole believed itself invincible. From all of these causes we reasoned that our movement must be important. With the regularity of clockwork, every few minutes the order would come from General Getty, "Keep your men closed up." Officers would repeat the imperative "Close up men" from the head of the column until the sound was lost to me as it was repeated backwards to the rear . . . We were moving rapidly southward, a narrow road in front, a thick wood on right and left.

Getty stated, "On approaching the cross-roads our cavalry was found hastily retiring. Hastening forward, with my staff, I reached the cross-roads just as the enemy's skirmishers appeared rapidly advancing to gain possession of this point." According to an officer who was there, Getty said, "We must hold this point at any risk, our men will soon be up." Getty himself wrote,

> The presence of my small retinue, consisting of my staff and orderlies, standing firmly at the point in dispute, although under fire, served to delay their advance for a few minutes, during which Wheaton's Brigade was brought up at the double-quick, faced to the front, and a volley poured in, which drove back the enemy's advance. Skirmishers were then immediately deployed, and advanced a few hundred yards, until they encountered the enemy's skirmishers.

Brig. Gen. George Getty led the division in which the Vermont Brigade served and, with his staff, was first to reach and defend the Brock/Plank crossroads. HOWARD COFFIN COLLECTION

It all had happened just in time. When the Union skirmishers moved into the woods, Getty said, "The rebel dead and wounded were found within 30 yards of the cross-roads, so nearly had they obtained possession of it."

In a dispatch sent at 12:30 PM, Getty told General Sedgwick, "Hill's Corps is reported on this road, Heth's division in advance. Have taken several more prisoners, wounded men." If the message betrayed a sense of urgency, it was understandable. Getty, leading an under-strength division, was acquiring information indicating that a full Confederate corps was bearing down on him along the Orange Plank Road. From wounded Confederates, Getty learned not only that he was already facing Maj. Gen. Harry Heth's division, but that it was supported by the division of fellow major general Cadmus Wilcox.

Lewis Grant put the strength of his Vermont Brigade at 3,000 men and, as Getty directed, he deployed them to the left of Wheaton's line, a bit to the south of the Orange Plank Road. North of the road, extending from the right of Wheaton's brigade, Eustis put his men in position. The Vermonters faced a wall of scrub woods and brambles lining the Brock Road. Indeed, the two roads and the tiny clearing where they crossed must have been the only open space visible to any of Getty's men. The cut-over Wilderness, now grown back a dozen years or so, with a thick undergrowth of brush and brambles, must have appeared all but impenetrable. The previous year, when Stonewall Jackson's men had charged through the nearby woods in their great flank attack at Chancellorsville, some had emerged naked after their plunge through the tangles.

Wilbur Fisk was at the crossroads, and he later wrote, "Here was a high point of land where the roads cross at right angles, and it is in the midst of an endless wilderness—'a wilderness of woe,' as the boys call it." Luther Harris said that when the Vermont Brigade neared the crossroads, it met "a few cavalry-men with their arms in slings and their faces tied up in handkerchiefs to nurse their sabre cuts leading three or four horses . . ."

To the front were Heth's battle-tested men, soldiers who had led the infantry advance on Gettysburg the previous summer. Two companies of the Fifth Vermont, under Capt. Charles Ormsbee, a Brandon man, were sent a bit forward as skirmishers. Behind, and in line side by side, were the Third and Fourth Regiments. The Second and Sixth Vermont were posted in a third line, with the Fifth Regiment held to the rear, for the present, as a reserve. North of the Plank Road, also in thick woods, Wheaton's brigade was similarly posted. Seth Eastman wrote: "As we took our position in line of battle at the crossroads, we, without any orders to do so, collected all the logs and rotten wood and fences that were lying around loose, and piled them in our front. We might need them in case we were attacked . . ." The men, he said, then set about "eating a few hardtack and drinking from the ever-present canteen." Now came a lull of perhaps two hours, punctuated by firing on the picket lines. The Confederates, having seen infantry in considerable numbers, and under orders from Lee not to bring on a general engagement, had withdrawn a short distance from the crossroads. By that stage of the war nobody had to tell veteran troops on either side to put up a breastwork when facing the enemy. The Rebels also piled up logs, and waited.

Once in describing the Vermont Brigade soldiers, Sixth Corps Adjutant McMahon stated,

When moving into action, and while hotly engaged, they made queer, quaint jokes, and enjoyed them greatly. They crowed like cocks, they ba-a-ed like sheep, they neighed like horses, they bellowed like bulls, they barked like dogs, and they counterfeited, with excellent effect, the indescribable music of the mule. When, perchance, they held a picket line in a forest, it seemed as if Noah's ark had gone to pieces there . . .

So it seems likely that as the Vermonters waited behind their rude breastworks and the afternoon warmed, in addition to the firing to the front, the sounds of a Vermont barnyard may have been heard amid the Wilderness greenery.

Meanwhile, Meade had rushed orders to General Hancock hastening troops north to bolster Getty's small force. Hancock quickly grasped the urgency of the situation and started men up the Brock Road, with David Birney's division in the vanguard. But artillery choked the narrow track, making progress slow. Hancock rode on ahead of his men, reaching the vital intersection well ahead of his regiments. Hancock the Superb found General Getty and assured him that help was coming as fast as possible. According to Benedict, it was about 3:30 PM when Getty's men began to see Second Corps troops coming up the road. But well before, an impatient Ulysses Grant, on his knoll up near Wilderness Tavern, had grown fearful of a heavy assault against the Brock/Plank Road crossroads, and its consequences. He sent orders for an immediate attack, instructing Getty to go forward without waiting for any help.

"So Getty's bugles sounded, high and thin over the noise of the firing, and the federal battle line went crashing forward through the timber," wrote Bruce Catton. "It got to close quarters at once, and in the pathless tangle on both sides of the Plank Road there was an enormous shock and crash of battle . . ."

The Vermonters were the first of Getty's men to move. "Officers and men leaped over the rude works they had been constructing," said Lewis Grant, "and plunged into the almost impenetrable forest. The thickly-standing trees, dense underbrush and tangling vines made the advance extremely difficult. As good a line as was possible was preserved, and it moved steadily on. No skirmishers were met—they had been driven back on their main line. Our first greeting was a terrific volley of musketry all along the line and from a few yards in our front."

Seth Eastman, Sixth Vermont:

We soon came to the skirmish line, all laying close to the ground, and as we stepped over them, they said to us, "You will catch hell, boys, the graybacks are in force not 10 rods in front." We had heard no firing anywhere on the line up until this time . . . After taking about ten steps from the skirmish line, the battle opened in earnest. Volleys of musketry broke out of the thickets and underbrush in our faces. We replied to the best of our ability and that was not slow. The rifle balls came in showers and cut the underbrush down to about as high as a soldier's belt, this showing how the enemy was trained to fire in battle. In a short time the air became thick and sulfurous and reduced the light down to twilight, but we fought on. Those who could of my comrades began to look like colored men from biting their cartridges and powder smoke, but we fought on hour after hour.

Said Lt. Col. John Lewis, Fifth Vermont, "Now came the holocaust." Without the warning of the scattered shots of enemy skirmishers, the Vermonters had been met by a withering fire coming from the very substantial main battle line of a virtually unseen enemy. In the bloodiest moments in the history of the state, Lewis Grant said, "Hundreds of our men fell at that first volley, but it was immediately returned, and the rattle of musketry continued until dark."

Colonel Thomas Seaver, commanding the Third Vermont:

After passing the skirmish line for about 200 yards, we met the enemy, who gave the first indications of his presence by delivering a full volley in our front, in consequence of which I lost many valuable lives. I had no means of guarding against this disaster, as the skirmishers were not moved forward, and were not under my control.

According to Eastman, Confederate prisoners taken the next day said they had orders not to fire at the Vermonters until they could see the whites of their eyes. "I laid down after this terrible volley had been received, on my belly," Eastman wrote, behind the stub of a tree . . . Many balls passed through this stub; it was rotten and afforded me no protection, but the balls went over my head. I was unhurt. Two of my comrades fell dead at my side . . . Moody Martin and Asa Whitcomb. They never spoke or uttered a groan, they were killed instantly. Our colonel was wounded by a musket ball and it made him crazy. He rode his horse down the line, shouting and giving orders that could not be executed. He had to be taken to the rear. His name was Elisha Barney of Swanton, Vermont, a very nice man and good looking . . . we all felt very bad to have him killed.

Henry Houghton, in the Third Vermont and from Woodstock, said, "We marched in on the left of the Orange Plank Road with scrub oak so thick that we could not keep any formation and the first we knew of the enemy we received a volley from a line of battle within a stone's throw." Houghton said that a man to his left was shot dead,

and a bullet went so near the face of the man in my rear that it took an eye out, two bullets went through my haversack and one through my canteen and another passed so near my neck that it burned the skin then entered my blanket and when I unrolled it I found 19 holes in it.

Lewis Grant recalled,

The density of the forest was so great that we could see but a short distance. The men aimed at the wall of fire and smoke in our front. The distance between the two lines was so short that under ordinary conditions we could have charged upon the enemy with the bayonet before giving time to reload. But here a bayonet charge was impossible. A line could advance only slowly and with great difficulty even when unopposed. Anything like a dash upon the enemy was simply out of the question. The best that could be done was to hug the ground and keep up an incessant firing.

Samuel Pingree reported that his Third Vermont was "met by a terrible fire from a concealed foe at a distance of less than 75 yards. The regiment stood bravely in their places, and the fire was returned from ranks being thinned every moment by the murderous fire of the enemy."

Still, brave efforts were made to close on the Rebels. Colonel Seaver, leading the Third, reported,

> After receiving the enemy's fire I ordered a charge, but the nature of the ground and the heavy fire made it impossible to move my men. The Fourth, on my right, seemed to be in the same condition, and the line at my far left had either wholly given way, or had not advanced so far, so that I received a partial cross fire from that direction.

In the Fourth, all officers of Company I were out of action, including the company commander Capt. Daniel Lillie. Nicknamed "Tiger" by his men, and one of the most popular officers in the Old Brigade, Lillie had just given the order "Forward," according to Sgt. Marshall Twitchell, when he was shot. Lillie would linger a day before dying,

The doomed Capt. Daniel Lillie, affectionately called "Tiger" by his men, led a company into the Wilderness. University of Vermont

then his body would be taken back to his hometown of Barnard in the green hills of central Vermont. His funeral, held in the little white church near Silver Lake, was the largest in the town's history. Sergeant Twitchell, suddenly in command of the company, did as he believed Lillie would have wished and ordered his men to move "Forward till you cover the wounded, and then lie down." He remembered,

> Instantaneously, that kneeling line, as if one monster animal by electric current moved, swept over . . . four rods and threw itself in line, rifle in hand, in front of the farthest wounded man. For a moment I stood proudly exulting over the heroic action of my comrades . . . when I, like my seniors, fell.

Twitchell had been shot in the head. He recalled,

> My company of fifty-three men was left in the command of the only sergeant standing, and he had but twenty-one men uninjured. I have heard that a sergeant of Company A carried me to the rear. It seems to me that I passed General Hancock and staff, but I more think it was a kind of dream . . .

At some point, Getty had artillery rolled down the Plank Road in support of his infantry, and it opened fire, rather blindly, in the supposed direction of the enemy. Luther Harris, in the Fourth, said, "two pieces of artillery were brought up and from the cross roads fired a few shots." Harris believed that Lewis Grant was personally directing their fire. "From the nature of the case," Harris said, "it was impossible for it to do anything but harm. The first shot killed eight men on the left of my company, a few more shots were fired when some soldiers got back to the guns and told the gunners what was being done." Seth Eastman was more optimistic:

> There were two 5 inch cannons, all that there was any room to use, placed at the crossroads. These were used constantly all afternoon throwing grape and cannister, and were double and treble shotted with this deadly material. This no doubt killed hundreds of our enemies and

added a base to the treble of musketry in the terrible music of that afternoon.

At some point early in the fight, Lewis Grant ordered the Second and Sixth Regiments forward to join the front line. According to Wilbur Fisk,

> They poured their bullets into us so fast that we had to lie down to load and fire. The front line gave way, and we were obliged to take their places . . . We were close on to them and their fire was terribly effective . . . Just a little to the rear of where our line was formed, where the balls swept close to the ground, every bush and tree was cut and splintered by the leaden balls. The woods was a dense thicket of small trees about the size of hop poles . . . I doubt if a single tree could have been found that had not been pierced several times by bullets, and all were hit about breast high. Had the rebels fired a little lower, they would have annihilated the whole line. They nearly did it as it was. Our Colonel was killed, our Lieut. Colonel and acting Major wounded, and only the three captains were left after the fight. We all had hairbreadth escapes to tell of . . . I had a bullet pass through my clothes on each side, one of them giving me a pretty smart rap, and one ball split the crown of my cap in two, knocking it off my head as neatly as it could have been done by a scientific boxer.

Corporal Erie Ditty, Sixth Vermont, had a close call as the fighting raged. The Roxbury lad, one of five sons, said that a comrade on his right carrying the United States flag was wounded, as was the corporal on his left. And another corporal standing just behind him was killed. "The firing came from the brush only a few rods away," Ditty said. He added that as his regiment fell back a short way, then advanced again, "A ball passed my head and entered my tent and rubber blanket."

Seth Eastman: "We had a new recruit in our company by the name of Daniel Craig [from Topsham]. He had never been under fire before, and one time when we fell back to form a new line, I was a little behind the main body and I met him going directly towards the enemy." Eastman warned the private to go no farther, but the young man replied that he'd accidentally fired his ramrod and had to find it. "He would not listen to me," Eastman said, "and I saw him walk into the Rebel ranks." Craig would die at Andersonville.

Another Second Vermont soldier, Pvt. Peter Chase, before the war a farmer in Weston, said that at one point in the fighting, Lieutenant Colonel Tyler had moved along the lines of his regiment and asked a Captain White to send Cpl. Albert May and sixteen men to cross and secure a little woods road that ran off through the Wilderness. "The corporal was the only man to cross the road," Chase said,

and he fell across wounded; all the rest were either killed or wounded before they could get over the road. About this time Col. Stone had come back to the regiment, after having his wound dressed. He was soon after killed while passing to the right of the line, cheering his men by his example of bravery. Many brave boys had fallen all along the line, and the groans of wounded and dying were heard on every

Capt. Orville Bixby, Second Vermont, was shot on May 5 and died in a Wilderness field hospital. VERMONT HISTORICAL SOCIETY

side; but the muskets still flashed forth their missiles of death, and the fight went on.

The Confederates, according to Lewis Grant, had a considerable advantage of position over his men:

Their line was partially protected by a slight swell of ground, while ours was on nearly level ground. The attempt was made to dislodge them from that position, but the moment our men rose to advance the rapid and constant fire of musketry cut them down with such slaughter that it was found impracticable to do more than maintain our present position.

G. G. Benedict spoke of

Unseen movements of troops, terrific volleys of musketry bursting at close range from the thickets; charges through woods so dense that a field officer could scarcely see more than a line of a company; sudden appearances and disappearances of bodies of troops through the smoke and jungle, regiments on each side hugging the ground for shelter, not daring to rise or either advance or retreat, yet keeping up incessant fusilades; an almost Indian warfare in the forest. Hill had almost two men to Getty's one, yet he secured no material advantage.

Indeed, Getty's division was greatly outnumbered. Lewis Grant met Cadmus Wilcox nearly a year after the Wilderness, at Appomattox Court House at the war's end, and inquired of the Confederate what numbers he had been up against. The reply, which must have shocked Getty, was that he and Heth had moved into battle with 14,000 to 15,000 men.

On went the struggle amid the constricting trees and saplings, brush and brambles, vines and thorns, a dim and green hell filled with smoke and thunderous noise. Death and maiming came from unseen sources. A Vermonter might catch a glimpse of some vague shape moving off to the front in the dense fog of battle. More likely, all that was seen of the enemy was the flash of muzzles and roll of smoke. Bullets clipped limbs and branches and mowed down saplings with a whipping sound. A telling thud too often meant that a comrade had been hit, and he would scream or moan, or more often roll over silently and endure, or die. No doubt in their agony some men called out for mother, father, a sweetheart, for someone 600 long and impossible miles away. The bullets struck everywhere, smashing faces, disemboweling, shattering arms and legs, ripping through chests, blowing away brains and hearts, bursting through lungs, destroying hands, feet, private parts. Men who had only recently discovered the joys of learning lost their powers of reason to a bullet in the head. Lads who worked dawn to dusk on the farm suddenly became cripples for life. Boys who loved to watch a pink sunrise or a golden sunset over the hills of home suddenly were without sight. Husbands and fathers, young lovers, in an instant were made eunuchs. Curses mixed with prayers amid the endless racket. Men saw best friends maimed, closest comrades die. As more and more officers were hit, those in the ranks experienced a frightening feeling of being leaderless. Bullets whined in, some nipping clothing, shoes, hats.

There seemed to be no clear battle lines, no clear targets. Sometimes artillery boomed, sending through the deadly twilight heavy discharges, meant for Rebels, that too often screamed perilously close to the men in blue. Hands and faces grew black and grimed with powder. In the din, even attempts to speak with one's nearest comrade often proved futile. Men had to wonder, were commands to advance, or retreat, being heard? Will we be isolated, flanked, because of some order not heard, some signal unseen? Blood reddened and browned the crisp leaves, the brittle carpet that could burst into flame at any instant. Death came unseen, sometimes from impossible directions.

In the final analysis, what seems to have survived was the remarkable, steely determination that certainly displayed itself along both of the sprawled, uneven battle lines. In the Vermont Brigade a sense of duty, put to the ultimate test, ruled in most of those young men. Perhaps it was something they learned on a below-zero farm morning when the chores had to be done; or around the supper table by lantern light, when their father or mother read from the Good Book. There was some quality that made them stay where they were, in front of that vital road junction that, on this hot and now airless Virginia day, had become the most important place on all the Earth.

Benedict:

General Getty well knew that he had two men in front of him for every one of his own; but he knew the importance of the duty assigned him. The situation required desperate effort; for if Hill had succeeded in reaching the Brock Road, it is hard to see how he could have been dislodged. It would then have been an easy matter for him to hold back Hancock—who as it was did not get into position till after four o'clock P. M.—with one of his divisions, while Wilcox pushed in on Warren's left flank with the other. The consequences can be imagined.

Though everywhere men of every rank were getting hit, it was the officers who sustained the highest percentage of the casualties. Benedict wrote,

In the Vermont regiments the carnage was fearful. The loss of field and line officers who were on their feet and moving along the lines, while the men hugged the ground, was especially severe. Colonel Stone, the gallant young colonel of the Second, fell with a ball through his thigh; retired to have his wound dressed, and returned to his post, soon to drop dead, shot through the head. Lieut. Col. Tyler took his place, till, an hour later, he too fell, with a mortal wound leaving the regiment without a field officer. Colonel Foster of the Fourth received a ball in the thigh and had to yield the command to Major Pratt. Lieut. Colonel Lewis, commanding the Fifth, fell with a shattered arm, and Major Dudley stepped into his place. Colonel Barney, of the Sixth, received a mortal wound in the temple, and was succeeded in command of his regiment by Lieut. Colonel Hale. Of the company officers, one after another fell not to rise again, or were born bleeding to the rear.

Capt. Edward Carter was severely wounded while leading his Fourth Vermont company on an attempted advance. The Brattleboro man was first hit in the thumb of his right hand. Moments later he

Col. Newton Stone, Second Vermont, mortally wounded in the Wilderness.

VERMONT HISTORICAL SOCIETY

was hit in the left thigh, knocking him to the ground. Carter rose briefly, but quickly fell forward onto his face. As he lay struggling to rise again, six bullets cut through his clothing. One struck him in the abdomen, exposing a portion of his intestines. He lay in agony, unable to move. Finally, some of his men dragged him over the rough ground to safety, but it was feared his wounds were fatal.

In the Sixth Vermont, eighteen-year-old Pvt. Henry Wright was fighting beside his father, David Wright, two farmers from the Connecticut Valley town of Ryegate. The son was shot in the bowels and taken from the field. Moments later, his father was hit by a bullet that blinded him. The younger Wright died hours later in a field hospital. The father would wander in the Wilderness for days, sightless, until he was found by a New York soldier. He survived the war.

Two of the comrades of Pvt. Charles W. Whitcomb, a St. Johnsbury soldier in the Sixth Vermont, saw a Rebel soldier rise up from behind a log and shoot their friend. The bullet passed through Whitcomb's thigh and groin, lodging in his wallet. His friends promptly rose and shot the Rebel. Whitcomb lay on the field two days before being taken to a hospital to begin his recovery.

Two brothers from Williston, Sgt. Edward Holton and Pvt. David Holton, were struck almost simultaneously. Edward, who had told his wife he doubted that Lee would fight outside his Richmond defenses, was hit just below the knee. Though he would survive, he was out of the war for good. David, beside him, was shot in the head and died instantly.

The day was a bad one for the northern Vermont hill town of Greensboro. In the Fourth Vermont, Sgt. Thomas Griffin was shot in the groin. In agony, he dragged himself to the rear, only to die in a field hospital that night. Pvt. Ephraim Hartshorn was hit as a Minié ball entered his side. He would suffer for eighteen days before succumbing. Pvt. Robert Rogers was hit in the arm and bled to death on the way to a hospital.

Four lads from the small northern Vermont town of Sutton were killed that day—Cpl. David Rattray and Privates Mark Gray, Aruniah Burt, and Joel Streeter. Warren, in the Mad River Valley, lost Privates James Maynard, Lewis Spaulding, and Horace Stoddard, all shot through the head. Sgt. Herbert Taylor, from the southern Vermont town of Guilford, was hit simultaneously by bullets in the heel and to the right of his spine. He survived.

Seth Eastman came upon a severely wounded man,

> Shot through the head, the ball entering his head at the temple, just back of the eye, and passing through. It came out in the same place on the other side of his head. Both his eyes were out of the sockets and located on his cheeks. He was moaning and said that he was blind and that all was dark . . . A drafted man came up, and he stood looking at the wounded man . . . He said it was too bad to use men in that way and that they had dragged him out here to fight against his will. He said he "would never fire another gun in this damn nigger war."

Eastman said the blind man survived to live a long life. The angry private soon had two fingers shot away.

"The fight was so sharp and persistent," said Luther Harris,

that the bullets wore away the scrub oaks, and the ground in the front
seemed mown as with a scythe . . . the fighting assumed an aspect of
tenacity—there was nothing of brilliancy or manouver in it . . . so far as
distance was concerned, stones could have been used as missiles.

Harris added,

Although from the nature of the circumstances the shots were unusually high, the slaughter was great, but the gaps were filled quickly and
when there was lack of men to take the places of the dead, the soldiers
would maintain their front by increased bravery.

"Each man seemed to vie with his comrade in doing his duty
bravely and fearlessly," said Lt. Col. Stephen Pingree, Fourth Vermont. Dr. George Stevens, nearby with the 77th New York Regiment,
said, "Our friends, the Vermonters, fought with gallantry which always
characterized the sons of the Green Mountain State. Their noblest
men were falling thickly, yet they held the road."

Bruce Catton wrote: "Getty had all his men in action and there
were not enough of them, not by half, and the Vermont Brigade hung
on with a thousand of its men killed or wounded, and the terrible little
flames came snaking through the dead leaves and dry pine thickets."

So the battle persisted and, to the Vermonters' discouragement,
despite all the casualties they must surely be inflicting, pressure from
the front increased. The firing even intensified. The fear grew that a
Confederate attack was likely coming. All the while, Hancock was
pushing reinforcements up the Brock Road, but two hours seem to
have passed before Birney's division, of his Second Corps, was formed
along the road and ready to go in.

Well into the fight, the nearly unscathed Fifth Vermont was ordered
forward from the Brock Road and placed on the left of the Old Brigade,
where the danger was greatest. There the brigade's left flank was unsupported and the chance of the line being rolled up was ever present. Capt.
Eugene Hamilton put the time of his regiment's advance at 5 PM. "As we

were preparing to obey this order," he said, "Lieut. Col. John R. Lewis was severely wounded, and carried from the field, and the command devolved on Maj. Charles P. Dudley." The Fifth moved into the dim, smoldering woods and immediately came under severe fire. The regiment was staggered and stopped, but not until it had moved slightly ahead of the battered Second and Third Regiments. Hamilton estimated the Fifth fought in its exposed position for a half hour.

With Birney's division of the Second Corps now up, Getty directed the Vermonters to withdraw. But how to do it? Lewis Grant decided to order an attack by the Fifth Vermont from his left, where reports indicated the Confederates might be weakest. The shock of a sudden attack might provide a brief opportunity for the other regiments to get away. Grant wrote in his official report,

> I went to Major Dudley, commanding the fifth . . . and asked him if he could, with the support of the two regiments in his rear [the Second and Third Vermont], break the enemy's line. "I think I can," was the reply of the gallant major. I went to the commanders of those two regiments, and asked them to support the Fifth in its advance. The men rose and answered with a cheer, "We will."

Captain Hamilton, in the Fifth, said,

> When the charge was being made, we suddenly found ourselves 40 or 50 yards in advance of the line, wholly unsupported and exposed, not only to front fire of unprecedented severity, but also to a raking fire on both flanks of the most galling description. The brigadier-general commanding, perceiving our situation, ordered an immediate withdrawal . . .

At about the time the Fifth made its charge, Private Chase, in the Second Vermont, was shot, bullets hitting his neck and each leg. Sgt. Fred Fish from Jamaica, Chase said, quickly bound up the wounds and stopped the loss of blood. But to his horror, Chase now saw that Confederates were beginning their own advance.

The Fifth Vermont's bold and costly push had achieved its purpose and now, seeing Confederates edging forward, the Fourth and Sixth

Vermont rose and beat a hasty retreat toward the Brock Road and the relative safety of the breastworks they had wisely erected earlier. Then came the Second and Third, with the Fifth not far behind, and as they rose to run, the Confederates came swarming forward.

Seth Eastman, of the Sixth, wrote:

Our ranks began to thin and the enemy came nearer. Things began to look desperate, and at last we fell back to our first position and behind the breastworks . . . This was a great help to us and we made a stand, but the Rebs came up and continued the battle.

The Vermonters took cover behind the low line of logs and rails they'd put up earlier and resumed firing. "We were," Eastman said,

better off than before and stood them off, and they could not drive us another inch. We got word that help or reinforcements were near at hand. We were, at this time, almost out of ammunition, and in a few minutes would be entirely out, but Hancock's men came and formed a line in our rear, and as it was most dark from powder smoke, they supposed they were on the front line and their men began to fall, so they opened fire to our rear, by which some of our men fell. We were between two very hot fires for a short time, but we quickly fell back behind their line and our work was slackened up for a time.

It was along the Brock Road, just before dark, that young Colonel Tyler of Brattleboro was shot in a leg. The ball struck the femoral artery and the colonel's boot rapidly filled with blood. Tyler ordered the men in his Second Vermont, who ran to assist him, back to the line of battle. But soon he had to surrender command of the regiment and allow himself to be carried to the rear. "I was within two rod of him when he was shot," said Capt. Rollin Ward, a Castleton man serving in the Second. "Why, John Tyler did not know what fear was, and there was not an officer or man in the regiment but worshipped him almost."

Out in front, amid the hundreds of dead and wounded, was Private Chase, thrice shot. As Sergeant Fish, who came to his aid, had risen to go, he told Chase that he should "keep a stiff upper lip." Chase:

> I now lay between both lines of battle. The firing on both sides being
> fearful . . . The rebels, with a small line of battle, had passed over me.
> What! A prisoner? Yes and on the field of battle among the dead and
> wounded who, but an hour before, stood with me in the line of battle
> in full vigor of manhood, now lay bleeding. The groans, the cries for
> help, and the prayers, may they never again pierce my ears or any of the
> young men of this fair land again.

Soon, Confederates in retreat from their attack on the Brock Road
came back past Chase, and he began to see a chance of rescue.
Bruce Catton:

> Getty's exhausted line was about ready to fall clear out of the war; and
> at last Hancock got a couple of brigades lined up and he sent them in
> to the attack. When they hit they hit hard—they were veterans . . .
> They overran Getty's tired men and bent the Confederates back . . .

Charles Mead, from West Rutland, a sharpshooter with the relief
force that was Birney's division, wrote the night of May 5,

> Marched till about 4 PM. We were deployed and advanced on the W.
> side of the [Brock] road. Firing commenced on our right and the battle
> was soon fairly opened. We "went in" on our skirmish and fought one or
> more lines of battle . . .

So the Vermonters were withdrawn across the Brock Road, for a
rest in the woods, while Hancock's men took over. The Brock/Plank
Road juncture had been held, at fearful cost. All Getty's depleted
brigade had battled for it, though the pressure had been by far the
greatest on the Vermonters. Yet the fight for the crossroads had been
but one violent part of a far larger battle.
On an uneven line running from south of the Orange Plank Road
to, and well north of, the Orange Turnpike, the Battle of the Wilderness raged into the night. It was strange and unorganized. While the

Vermonters were able to advance only yards, to the north some Union troops moved more than a mile forward and burst into a field to encounter some high-ranking Confederates. Had the men pressed ahead, they might have captured General Lee himself, with A. P. Hill and J. E. B. Stuart.

Still farther north, the battle seesawed along the Orange Turnpike. The 10th Vermont, in Ricketts' Sixth Corps Division, had marched down from the Rapidan in the morning and was positioned near Wilderness Tavern, away from the action. In the afternoon, the regiment was marched west along the turnpike and quickly came under artillery fire. Maj. Lemuel Abbott said,

> The enemy fired a solid shot straight along the pike which tore screeching through the air just a little above the heads of the men in column of our regiment till it struck the pike about midway the regiment, providentially where the men had split and were marching on either side of the road . . .

Miraculously, nobody was hurt, and the next shot that Abbott so dreaded, the one that would tear the length of the regiment, never came. Soon the 10th was moved into woods on the south side of the turnpike, to support a part of Sedgwick's line. Abbott said,

> Before Capt H. R. Steele had hardly finished dressing his company after forming line, a shell . . . exploded in the ranks of Co K, killing a private and wounding others. The shell had burst actually inside the man completely disemboweling and throwing him high in the air in a rapidly whirling motion above our heads with arms and legs extended until his body fell heavily to the ground with a sickening thud . . . We were covered with blood, fine pieces of flesh, entrails, etc., which makes me cringe and shudder whenever I think of it. The concussion badly stunned me. I was whirled about in the air like a feather, thrown to the ground on my hands and knees—or at least was in that position with my head from the enemy when I became fully conscious—face cut with flying gravel or something else, eyes, mouth and ears filled with dirt, and was feeling nauseated from the shakeup.

The 10th's Chaplain Haynes remembered, "Our brigade at dark occupied a position on the south of the pike, two hundred yards beyond, where we stayed in line of battle all night."

Also on the Wilderness battlefield, but not yet in action, were the less than four hundred men of the 17th Vermont, in Burnside's corps. Regimental commander Cummings said his men reached the battlefield about 2 AM on May 6 after a lengthy march. Historian Benedict wrote:

> The carnage of the first day's battle had just ceased; night had fallen on the field, and scarce realizing that they were in the lines of the Army of the Potomac, on one of the bloodiest battlefields of the war, and knowing little of the events of the day, the exhausted men dropped for a few hours rest.

Back in the 10th Vermont, word of the Vermont Brigade's heroics at the crossroads had spread fast. Chaplain Haynes wrote, "We had suffered but little in this first day's battle of the Wilderness. The 'Old Brigade' had suffered terribly, having born the brunt of the battle from noon till dark. The number of men slaughtered was shockingly great . . ."

At the vital crossroads, Pvt. George B. Godfrey, Fourth Vermont, summed up the day in his diary: "The Vermont Brigade alone lost more men killed and wounded on the 5th of May than the whole of the Second Corps all together on that day, and the Vermont dead were not behind . . . breastworks."

That night, Pvt. John Kelly, Second Vermont, exhausted, managed to record his usual brief diary entry. "May 5—Marched about 4 miles. fought in line of battle for about two hours Colonel Stone is Killed we lost about 250 officers and men they are burying the Colonel now, about 9 p. m."

Diary entries that day, if they were written at all, were understandably brief, and few if any letters home appear to have been written that May 5. Elijah Stone, in the Sixth Vermont, noted, "Heard skirmishing, muster, skirmish, hard fight. Had four killed." "The balls and shells flew round some," wrote Pvt. Samuel Parker, also in the Sixth.

Robert E. Lee, in his report written the night of May 5, seems to have paid an unintentional tribute to the men who held the Brock/Plank Road juncture against his advance:

The enemy subsequently concentrated upon General Hill, who, with Heth's and Wilcox's divisions, successfully resisted repeated and desperate assaults . . . By the blessings of God we maintained our position against every effort until night, when the contest closed. We have to mourn the loss of many brave officers and men.

A Vermont officer wrote to the *Bennington Banner* of having been at Lewis Grant's headquarters late in the day of May 5:

I found the general at his post with only *one* staff officer left . . . all the rest either killed or severely wounded. The general appeared almost worn out, and when he informed me that his losses in his brigade were near half of his command, and his staff all killed or disabled, his emotions were very great.

In Grant's official report on the day, he stated that

darkness came on and the firing ceased. One engaged in that terrible conflict may well pause to reflect upon the horrors of that night. Officers and men lay down to rest amid the groans of the wounded and dying and the dead bodies of their comrades as they were brought to the rear. One thousand brave officers and men of the Vermont Brigade fell on that bloody field.

Benedict wrote of the day's "terrible cost":

Of five colonels of the brigade but one was left unhurt. Fifty of its best line officers had been killed or wounded. A *thousand* Vermont soldiers fell that afternoon. The fighting along and near the Plank road ended about eight o'clock; but elsewhere, and especially in front of the Sixth Corps, there was skirmishing on into the night; and till two o'clock in the morning occasional volleys lit up the dark woods with flame. Along the fronts of the opposing lines strong picket guards faced each other with exhausting watchfulness. Behind them the burial parties and stretcher-bearers sought through the thickets for the killed or wounded, at the risk of their own lives, for the enemy's pickets fired at every sight or sound. In the debatable ground between them lay hundreds of dead and dying, whom neither army could remove. The men in the lines of battle lay on their arms behind their low breastworks, and got but brief and fitful sleep.

In portions of the Wilderness, the woods had caught fire and wounded men burned to death, but apparently the Vermont wounded were spared such a fate. As night came down, some friends of Private Chase's, led by Cpl. E. W. Prior, made their way into the no-man's land between the lines and found their wounded comrade. Four men carried Chase on a tent canvas for nearly three-quarters of a mile through the brush. Chase said,

The Corporal had a short piece of candle which he lit to help on the way, but as soon as the rebels saw the light they began to fire on it. The balls whistled so near us that it made us feel rather uncomfortable, and he was obliged to conceal the light under his coat. They soon had me on the plank road, where the ambulances were taking the wounded back. They laid me down and bade me goodby.

It was the last time Chase ever saw the men who carried him, Privates Elmer Holmes, George French, and Ira Clark. All three were killed in fighting one week later, on May 12.

"Most all of my friends lay dead or wounded, scattered in the field somewhere," said Seth Eastman, Third Vermont:

It was dark and I tried to find some of them, but could not locate any . . . We looked through the regiment to see who was left, and we found thirteen men of my company still unhurt. Co. F. of our regiment had only four men left, and the regiment had 94 muskets that night. All had not been killed; some had skedaddled and came back later when the danger was less. I had been in the army now more than two years and supposed I knew what a battle was, but I must say I had never seen a real fight until I was in the first day's Battle of the Wilderness.

In Eastman's shattered company, wounded Sgt. Nathaniel Sutherland was found and carried behind the lines. "He was supposed to be mortally wounded," Eastman said,

> a large hole was made in the left side of his abdomen . . . He said the ball was in his body and that it gave him great pain and that he had only a short time to live. His looks indicated as much . . . To make his last moments comfortable he suggested that we take off his shoes. We did so, and on removing his stocking, we found the ball in it. It was very much flattened out as a result of striking the bayonet shank.

Sutherland immediately began to feel better and, after a brief hospital stay, was back in the ranks. Eastman said that night he experienced "a nightmare of sleep." Years later, he summed up May 5:

> I cannot remember any of my comrades or myself felt in any way discouraged or like running away. We felt the same as usual and had the same courage that we always had, and we knew the battle was not ended and that it would be renewed in the morning. We knew that General Ulysses S. Grant would not fall back, and we saw no signs of the enemy falling back. He was laying on his arms in our front and we knew there was plenty of fight in him yet, as he fired at everything that he saw moving anywhere in the line all that night. How we ever kept our spirit up, I never knew; now, as I remember, we were cheerful as ever when we had our coffee and had time to eat and get a little sleep.

So a deep darkness fell on the Wilderness, and the exhausted, battle-weary Vermonters who remained fell into a stupor. Before sleep, Pvt. Lorenzo Watts, Third Vermont, wrote in his diary, upside down, "We were ordered to charge about 4 o'clock but were repulsed and the loss of our Regt was 226." In the Sixth, Maj. Richard Crandall wrote, "The fight was teriffic . . . At least one third fallen today." In the Fourth Vermont, Cpl. George Greene from the granite hills of

Williamstown noted in the space reserved for a May 5 entry: "Vermont Brigade all cut up." "It was," said Luther Harris, "the saddest night the Vermonters had ever known."

That night, back in Vermont, Burlington people settling down to read the local *Free Press* encountered the following, disturbing headlines on page two:

FROM VIRGINIA

ADVANCE OF THE ARMY

THE RAPIDAN CROSSED

A FOOTRACE FOR RICHMOND

BATTLE PROBABLE AT ANY HOUR

There followed a brief story, datelined Washington, D.C., that began:

We feel authorized to state since it cannot now afford information to the enemy, that the Army of the Potomac has advanced towards Richmond, and the struggle for the possession of the rebel capital is begun. Our army moved on Tuesday night and has crossed the Rapidan . . . Lee has been compelled to fall back from the strong position where he has held us at bay all winter, whether he makes a stand this side of the defenses of Richmond we are not advised. It is the opinion of some that he will fight at Chancellorsville. Any hour may now bring us news of a battle . . .

In Burlington that evening, Ellen Lyman attended the performance of "a tableaux," the portrayal, by costumed actors, of famous scenes from art and history. She noted in her diary that she appeared on stage in one scene, "Religion Consoling Justice," for which she was "all chalked up." And that night in Morrisville, all seemed bright and gay as the band of the Eighth Vermont Regiment provided lively music for a dance at the Waterville House.

Well to the south, in Rutland, readers of the May 5 *Rutland Herald* found, on page one, a poem by the well-known local poet Julia Dorr. Mrs. Dorr had seen three half brothers go off to war. One, Edward Ripley, commanded the Ninth Vermont Regiment, in North Carolina.

Another brother, William Ripley, had led a sharpshooter company until badly wounded at Malvern Hill:

A MEMORY

Under the pine trees, dark and still,
Standing like sentinels on the hill,
Where we walked in the long ago,
Falls, as of old, the sunset glow.
Tingeing the mossbank, till it seems
Fitting couch for fairy dreams;
Cloth of gold its drapery rare,
With velvet meant for a queen to wear.
Still does the river roll between
Flowery banks and meadow green;
Still do the mountains and the plain
All of their pomp and glow retain,
But thou and I! Ah! Years have flown,
Oft have the summer roses blown,
Oft have the roses died since we—
Mere boy and girl beneath this tree—
Watched while the daylight softly crept
Up from the vale where the waters slept,
Till the high mountain peaks grew dim,
And yon star sang as a vesper hymn.
I am older, and thou art—dead!
In a soldier's grave low lies thy head;
They who laid it gently down,
Saw it crowned with a martyr's crown;
Saw the palm in hands at rest,
Folded o'er a blood-stained breast.
Twice have the wild birds come and gone,
Since that crown and palm were won!
Woe that earth should be just as gay,
When a smile like thine hath passed away!
Woe that word nor sign may tell
If she mourns for one that loved her well!

A dozen miles south of Rutland, as she retired for the night on her farm, tired as ever, Mercy Eddy took a moment to make a daily diary note. The astounding faraway events were, of course, to her unknown. Though no existing records seem to hold mention of any significant celestial event having transpired that day, what Eddy penciled that spring night causes one to wonder if, somehow, all that blood and thunder in the woods far south had, mystically, had an effect high over Vermont. She wrote:

Thursday, [May] 5 Eclypse of the Sun.

Chapter Six

LIKE A DEATH WARRANT

O ur hours of sleep were few and brief," Wilbur Fisk said:

> At half past four o'clock we were ordered to advance into the same place again. There were pale and anxious faces in our regiment when that order was given. We had had insufficient rest for the two nights previous, and the terrible nervous exhaustion of fighting had left us in hardly a fit condition to endure another such ordeal so soon. There was so many men missing from our number that it hardly seemed like the same regiment.

So orders came early, to the Second Vermont and the entire Vermont Brigade, to go back into that terrible woods where they had fought so desperately just hours before. Lewis Grant said, "To me, personally, the order came like a death-warrant. If the struggle of the day before was to be repeated, it evidently meant death to many of us. I felt as I never felt at any other time. The premonition of death was upon me, and I could not throw it off." Grant gave his watch and wallet to his aides, told them how to dispose of them, and of his horses. Then, the brigade commander said, "The entire army attacked the enemy at daylight." Indeed, it had been the plan of both Ulysses Grant and Robert E. Lee to launch attacks early, to get the jump on their adversary. Lee got his men rolling first, just barely. But within 15 minutes Hancock struck, and his heavy battle lines hit the surprised and ill-prepared Confederates hard. Lee's divisions were soon giving ground, as the odds this day were quite different from May 5. Along the Plank Road, some twenty-five thousand federals were moving against fourteen thousand Confederates.

The Vermont Brigade caught a break early that morning. "There were two lines from the Second Corps in our front," said Lewis Grant, "and during the advance two lines from the Fifth Corps came from the right and filed in front of the others." The Vermont Brigade, to the rear of the assault, moved forward in two lines of its own, straddling the Plank Road. "At this time there was a general movement to the left," said the brigade commander, "and the brigade all came together on the left of the road." The brigade had been ordered to the left and was back on the road's south side, where it had fought so desperately the previous day.

Private Luther Harris noted, "On the second day instead of the one brigade of Vermont men, there was a great army and that . . . commanded by able generals. The rebel lines were beaten back . . ." Private Fisk said:

> We advanced directly down to the same place we had fought the day before. Our dead comrades lay on the ground, just as they had fallen, many of whom we recognized. We would gladly have fallen out to give them a decent burial, but we had no time to think of that. We drove the enemy this time and captured some prisoners. The prisoners were mostly North Carolinians, and some of them came into our lines swinging their hats and saying "the tar heels wouldn't stand [this] morning."

According to Luther Harris, "It was noticed that the enemy were not as persistent as the day before. They had less courage. Some of the prisoners . . . said that it was expected that we should retreat the first night, they were disappointed at finding us there in the morning."

Not far to the front the roar of battle grew, then receded, as this day the advance continued. "The enemy had fallen back a short distance during the night, and when met was driven back nearly a mile farther," Lewis Grant said. "During this advance, there being two and some-times four lines in front, this brigade suffered only from stray bullets and shells which came to the rear. Soon, however, the advance was checked and the enemy fought with great desperation."

To the front, high drama had unfolded. Hancock's heavy battle lines had caught the Rebels unprepared and the southerners gave way a mile or more, to the only large clearing in that part of the Wilder-ness, the site of a small farm owned by a widow named Catherine Tapp. "The lines moved forward till Lee's headquarters and the Con-federate trains and artillery were in sight, not far to the front," said Benedict. "Hill's corps was tremendously shattered. It looked much like a Union victory in that part of the field. At that time Longstreet arrived with two fresh divisions—those of Joseph Kershaw and Charles Field.

One of the war's famous moments occurred in the Tapp Farm clear-ing. There Lee himself, seeing the Union lines advancing into the open ground, rode forward to direct the assault of Longstreet's lead elements, just on the field after a long march. But with cries of "Lee to the rear," the soldiers implored their commander to retire from danger. Only when the general turned back from the front did his men advance, and the inspired Confederates soon brought Hancock's juggernaut to a halt.

Before Lee's counterattack came on them, the men of the Vermont Brigade spoke of a considerable lull in the fighting. When the Rebels advanced, they first hit the men of Birney's division up ahead. Sharp-shooter Charles Mead was there:

About 11 there was a lull of an hour. Some cannon have been heard away on the right. Soon the battle commenced again, and the firing on our left becomes very heavy. Our lines fell back and we were flanked. A retreat commenced. We rallied, drove the Rebs, and then retreated by the right flank. It was almost a stampede. Fell back till we reached our position of the morning.

The retreat of Hancock's troops suddenly left the Vermonters, as they had been the day before, out front and bearing the brunt of the fight. Lewis Grant:

> Longstreet had arrived with new lines of fresh troops, and there was severe fighting in front. Gen. Getty was wounded [in an arm and was out of the fight] and Gen. Wheaton succeeded to his command. It so happened that when the advance was checked and the serious trouble in front commenced, my brigade had just taken possession of two irregular lines of fieldworks, made of logs and decaying timber, which the Confederates had thrown together for their use. We necessarily took possession of the wrong side, but improved what time we had in adjusting them to our own use . . . These works were situated on a knoll or swell of ground commanding some distance in front and either side. The trees were larger and the forest more open than where we had been coming through. Altogether it was a position of advantage, and served our purpose exceedingly well.

So the Vermonters, known as crack shots, had a good defensive position in more open woods through which they could sight on men, not muzzle flashes and banks of smoke. Grant:

> The enemy's advancing lines came upon us in great force. They were met by a terrible fire of musketry, broken and sent back in confusion. They reformed, and with fresh troops returned to the attack to be again slaughtered and sent back. This was repeated, and each time the attack in our front was met and repulsed. But at each advance the Confederates gained substantial advantage on our right and left. Our line on either flank was pressed back, so that the Vermont Brigade stood well out in front, like a bulge or a great knot in the line.

"We were in the point of the letter V," said Wilbur Fisk, "and the rebels were fast closing up the sides. On they came, double quick, elated with the prospect of capturing a fine lot of Yankees."

Many troops in the Vermont Brigade recalled the fighting of May 6 as worse than the previous day. Seth Eastman said May 5 had been "a

summer calm compared to what was in store for us the very next day."
Veteran Cpl. Erie Ditty, in the Sixth, said, "I never remember hearing
such heavy firing of muskets." Pvt. Orvin Leach, of Woodstock, said,
"The roar of muskets was continuous, resembling a long train of cars
crossing [a] railroad bridge." Though the brigade's losses this day
would be less than one-fourth those suffered on May 5, many men
thought the firing was heavier. Apparently, what limited the Vermonters' casualties was the protection of those Rebel breastworks they had
strengthened, and their ability to see targets and keep the Confederates somewhat at bay.

*Maj. Gen. Winfield Scott Hancock directed the Union advance along the
Orange Plank Road the morning of May 6. Standing behind the Second Corps
commander are (left to right) Generals Francis Barlow, John Gibbon, and David
Birney.* HOWARD COFFIN COLLECTION

The Vermonters, in their V-shaped position, were again amid an unimaginable firestorm. The boys from the Green Mountain State stayed low and fired this day more slowly, more carefully, at targets they could sometimes see. To the front, when a lull came, they sometimes heard the commands of Confederate officers positioning their men to better deal death into the Old Brigade's ranks. Again Vermonters were being hit, scores and scores of men who had survived May 5 only to end up in this cauldron of battle. Again the bullets whipped in from front and flank. Again it seemed that the Vermonters were alone. Again, it was the Vermonters who must hold, for less than a mile behind them was that all-important place where those two woodland roads came together in a now shattered woodland, and where Ulysses Grant's army could be cut in two if it were lost. So they hugged the ground, rose up quickly to fire, then did the whole thing again and again, and watched the toll of dead and wounded among their ranks increase. But this day they saw better the carnage they were inflicting in the butternut ranks so close by. Once again, the Old Brigade held on and the interminable seconds became minutes, then hours.

"Bullets came from the right and left," said brigade commander Grant, "and my flanking regiments changed and directed their fire to meet that coming from the flanks." Grant said he then received support from a portion of Wheaton's brigade that moved in on the Vermonters' right and "directed its fire across the Plank Road." The effect, Grant said, was the enfilading of the enemy's line, preventing further advance by the Rebels on his right flank. Still, strong pressure came from the left. Grant: "How long we held that position I cannot say, but it was hours, and much of the time we were dealing death and slaughter in front and flank." Col. Thomas Seaver said the Vermonters held until 2 PM.

Luther Harris recalled that as the Vermonters fought, they became short of water: "The only supply . . . they had was what by accident was in their canteens in the morning, so that the suffering was considerable. Those who had had a small supply in the morning had for the most part let it go to the wounded in the early part of the day, for water is the first thing a wounded man calls for."

Maj. Richard Crandall, Sixth Vermont: "The battle raged hotly . . .

The 6th stood its ground and . . . drove back the rebel hordes, but our dead lie in winrows."

Lewis Grant:

Perhaps the valor of Vermont troops and the steadiness and unbroken front of those noble regiments was never more signally displayed. They stood out in the very midst of the enemy, unyielding, dealing death and slaughter in front and flank. Only the day before one-third of their number and many of their beloved leaders had fallen, but not disheartened the brave men living seemed determined to avenge the fallen, and most effectually they did it. For more than three hours did the brigade hold this advanced position, repelling every attack.

In the Second Vermont, Private Fisk saw a comrade beside him shot:

He, less timid than myself, had raised himself up, and was loading and firing as fast as possible. The ball struck near his heart. He exclaimed, "I am killed" and attempted to step to the rear, but fell on me and immediately died. Just then we were obliged to retreat.

When the Vermonters' position collapsed, it happened fast. Seth Eastman said,

Rob Taisey and I got behind a large tree, he firing from one side and I from the other . . . We could hear the Rebel officers commanding their men to take good aim and fire low. Many of our men lay dead or wounded and our powder was getting scarce. Also, our muskets were getting so foul and hot that our fight began to slack, and so did that of the enemy . . . We expected men to come and relieve us, but no men came. About this time Rob Taisey shouted to me and I looked towards the rear. There was a column of rebels double-quicking to our rear. I did not wait for any orders, but started to run to get around the end of the line of Rebs, so as not to be made a prisoner, and our whole line did the same. I threw away my musket as I thought I should not need it anymore and could run faster without it. Most of the men did the same.

Suddenly the Vermonters saw Confederates behind them, moving up from the south in considerable numbers. They would later learn the cause—a heavy surprise flank attack by General Longstreet and seven thousand Confederates launched from the bed of an unfinished railroad that led through the Wilderness below the Orange Plank Road. Threatened with being cut off by Longstreet's men, the Vermonters ran for their lives, making for the Brock Road and the protection of the breastworks they had built the day before. Eastman said that as he ran he heard Rebels shout "Surrender and halt." But he said, "I knew their guns were hot, and if they stopped to load them, I would be so far away as to be out of danger." Eastman recalled,

> One oldish man by the name of Stratton got a ball in the thigh as he ran. He was just ahead of me and it broke his thigh and he fell. I never heard of or saw him afterwards. [Probably Pvt. Moses C. Stratton, of Bradford, and the Sixth Vermont, who died in a Rebel prison.] Another of my friends by the name of C. P. Divoll [Pvt. Charles Divoll, of Topsham] was shot in the head. I never saw him again, but he was not killed outright and did get to Fredericksburg, Virginia and died there ten days later. Sergeant Austin Goddard [probably Charles A. Goddard, of Norwich] of my company was wounded in the leg near the ankle joint, but he could run. His leg was not broken and he managed to get away.

The scenes that confronted Eastman as he sped across the battleground stayed with him all his life. "As we ran," he said,

> we were obliged to run to the right of the line as the Rebels came in on our left flank. This took us over a part of the ground that had already been fought over that morning by another part of the army. The ground was covered with the dead and wounded in indescribable confusion. Hundreds of men in blue and gray clothing lay in every possible situation that could be imagined: on their backs with wide open eyes, on their faces, some with their legs bent under them, and others cut in two, as artillery had been used in this part of the field. A part of the ground was swampy and many had fallen in the mud. Others were in

the mud to their knees. One in particular was in the mud to his knees and had fallen over backwards. He was stone dead, but had, in some way, gotten out his bible and had it spread over his breast, as if that was going to do him some good. It was a run for life, and I made it all right, and got away all safe, but many of our men were captured. I never ran so fast in my life and I know I could run as fast as any rebel could run . . . The retreat ended at the crossroads, just where the fight began the day before, and from the place we had started that very morning.

Wilbur Fisk: "My legs saved me. We had to leave our dead and wounded, and without much ceremony, or ordered retreat out of that place, leaving all that we had gained in the hands of the enemy."

Lewis Grant:

Perceiving that it was worse than useless to attempt further resistance there, I ordered the regiments to rally behind the breast-works on the Brock road, at which point we had been ordered to rally in case of disaster. Our entire lines at this part of the army went back in disorder. All organization and control seemed to have been lost. But out of that disorder the Vermont brigade quietly and deliberately took its position in the front works on the Brock road, and awaited the enemy's advance. Other troops were rallied and placed on the right and left and rear, though thousands went beyond reach or immediate control.

Grant said the Vermont Brigade lost between thirty and forty men in the sprint to the Brock Road, with a few "not fleet of foot" probably captured. Along the Brock Road, before the attack hit, he said,

Gen. Hancock displayed almost superhuman efforts and ability in rallying the disordered troops and in reforming the line to resist attack. The attack came late in the afternoon. It was a sudden, vigorous, determined and desperate attack, and it was handsomely and effectively repulsed. The point of attack was about a hundred yards or more to my left, but it was so near that the brigade joined in the rapid musketry that repulsed and slaughtered the enemy.

Vermont sharpshooter George Jones, of the Second Sharpshooter Regiment, was killed near the Plank Road in the morning advance on May 6. DAVID JAMIESON COLLECTION

Wilbur Fisk found himself swept along in a tide of fleeing soldiers, all headed for the breastworks. He became separated from his regiment and found himself "with a squad belonging to the division that broke and caused the defeat." He wrote of officers with drawn swords trying to rally their men, and of "generals and their aides . . . giving and carrying orders in all directions." Fisk said he was "tired almost to death, and as hungry as a wolf." He wrote, "They tried to halt us at the first line of breastworks, but I saw fresh troops coming that hadn't been in the fight at all, and I thought they might as well hold the line as me. My object was to find a safe place in the rear and, in spite of revolvers, or swords, entreaties, or persuasions, I found it." The private from Tunbridge caught his breath, then went looking for his Second Vermont. "I found the regiment had moved to the right a little on the line," he said, "and were stationed behind a rude breastwork preparing to defend it against the enemy, which was momentarily expected." He added, "Our breastwork was not very high nor very thick. We had a poor place to stand. We couldn't dig any on account of the stumps and roots. The ground was higher just back of the breastwork and this made the rear rank almost as much exposed . . ."

To the front, the surging Confederates were also in some confusion. The architect of the great flank attack, General Longstreet, had fallen along the Plank Road, accidentally shot by his own men. Still the Rebels came on. Fortunately for the Vermonters, the weight of the flank attack had forced the Old Brigade to the Plank Road's north side. There along the Brock Road, they crouched behind low breastworks, thrown up the previous day by comrades in another Sixth Corps unit, and awaited the onslaught. It never hit them full force, though Hancock's men, just to the south, sustained the hammer blows of a heavy frontal assault.

Fisk wrote,

> to the left . . . they tried to break our lines and they tried it hard. They charged clear up to the breastworks, and fairly planted the colors on the top of it, but they did not live to hold them there long. The ground in front of the works was literally covered with rebel dead after they left. One Colonel lay dead clear up to the breastwork. Two were shot on top of the breastwork, and fell on our side. I believe I have never heard such a murderous roar of musketry as was made to repel that charge. The rebels fell back and did not renew the attack.

To the Vermonters' front, Fisk said the Rebels "made a faint attack on our part of the line but we drove them back after a few rounds had been fired. The roar of musketry was not so awful as on our left. We killed three or four rebels and I saw them there the next morning and they killed a man near me, but that was all."

Where the Confederates hit hardest, sections of the earthworks caught fire. Luther Harris wrote, "The woods took fire and many wounded ones were killed that could have lived but for the fire."

While the Brock Road fighting raged, to the north along the Orange Turnpike the Vermont's Brigade's fighting of May 5 was all the talk among the men of Col. William Henry's 10th Vermont. Maj. Lemuel Abbott wrote in his diary on May 6: "Rumored that the Vermont Brigade of our Corps was badly cut up yesterday afternoon, but I hope it's not true; it was hotly engaged, though, on our left." Abbott went on to report on the 10th's activities on May 6. "We were led further into the woods this forenoon to form another line of battle evidently, but general Seymour who was in charge seemed to be dazed and while poking around alone in front of and too far away from his command without a skirmish line in his front, was taken prisoner." Abbott was referring to Brig. Gen. Truman Seymour, commander of the Second Brigade of James Ricketts' Sixth Corps division, who was a native of Burlington. The thirty-nine-year-old West Point graduate soon was on his way to a brief stay in a Rebel prison.

Abbott continued,

> A portion of Morris's Brigade of the Sixth Corps, including the Tenth Vermont, was then moved to the north of the Orange Turnpike . . . we formed line behind some natural breastworks with the enemy's earthworks about fifty yards more or less across a pretty, level, green field, in the edge of the woods; this work of theirs was in front, I am told, of the enemy's main line. We were shelled more or less at times through the day until about mid-afternoon when we were let alone.

In late afternoon, the lull abruptly ended. "At once hearing firing on the right flank of our army not far away," said Major Abbott,

> Colonel W. W. Henry excitedly called us to attention, faced us to the right and then turning the head of the column directly to the rear we ran with all possible speed—there was no double quick about it—for a mile or more into the woods in rear of where the heavy firing on our right was, stumbling over logs, ditches, brush, etc., till our faces, hands and shins smarted from bruises and scratches, when we were halted all out of breath, and ordered to give the charging war cry . . .

Abbott said, "Panic-stricken men were hastening to the rear from our defeated right through our lines . . ." The cause of the great commotion was a late-afternoon attack launched against the north end of the long Union line. A Confederate force led by Brig. Gen. John B. Gordon had struck about a mile north of the 10th Vermont's earlier position, and the army's right flank was being driven in. Thus Lee had done to Ulysses Grant's northern flank what Longstreet had done to the southern flank, below the Plank Road, about noon. Gordon's attack lost its steam before the 10th Vermont was engaged, but just barely. Abbott said,

> We, together with the One Hundred and Sixth New York Volunteer Infantry and the Fourteenth New Jersey repeatedly gave the war cry as we had never given it before or did give it ever again afterwards. It reverberated again and again through the forest . . . This war cry had the effect not only to stop the enemy's firing but its advance, thinking probably it was a counter-assault to meet theirs, and it saved many a poor fellow from being captured . . .

The war whoops may have had some effect, but it took considerable fighting to the Vermonters' front before the surprise attack was stopped. With the coming of darkness, the battle in the northern sector of the Wilderness died away. That night, Major Abbott was surprised to meet, in the gloom, Army of the Potomac commander George Meade and John Sedgwick, leader of the Sixth Corps, as Abbott said, "returning from an investigation of that part of the battlefield." The major said they inquired what troops were positioned there, "And on being told it was the Tenth Vermont at that particular point, Sedgwick said to Meade, 'We are safe enough with that regiment.'"

In combat that day for the first time were the men of the 17th Vermont. In Burnside's corps, which had been late arriving to support Hancock's early-morning attack, the regiment was first pushed forward on a picket line. Later in the day, the 17th got into a stiff fight. Before arriving in the Wilderness, the regiment had suffered an epidemic of measles, and on the morning of May 6 it counted just 313 men present for duty. Lt. Col. Charles Cummings led his "undrilled troops" that day. He wrote home,

> Soon after sunrise we were in line of battle. The 17th drove in a skirmish line in a short time and held the position until noon when we were withdrawn . . . we lost one killed and fifteen or twenty wounded. In the afternoon we were removed further to the left and about 2 p. m. we were hotly engaged with Longstreet's troops. It was in the woods where artillery could not be used, so the engagement was close and the musket firing fearful. We made one charge on our own hook and captured one rifle pit but not being supported could not hold it, so were forced to withdraw two rods.

Maj. William Reynolds began May 6 as second in command of the 17th. The lawyer from Milton, in northwestern Vermont, wrote in his official report on the fighting, "At noon the regiment was ordered to move about one mile to the left, where it was immediately assigned the right of an extended line, then forming for a charge upon the enemy, posted behind log breastworks in a thick wood." The 17th was about a half mile from the Tapp Farm clearing, where Hancock's advance had been stopped. Major Reynolds: "In this position the regiment sustained a very galling musketry fire for some moments, during which Lt. Col. Cummings was wounded in the head and assisted to the rear." So Reynolds was temporarily elevated to command of the regiment. Cummings wrote to his wife:

> While on one knee, the better to discover the enemy, and to direct the fire of my men (smoking my pipe meanwhile) a minnie ball struck me on the right side of my head against my hat band. It cut a hole four inches long backwards and upwards—as my head was pitched forward at the time—and about two and a half inches long in the scalp. The blow did not make me reel but it bled with such profusion . . . that I concluded to go to the rear. I think I might have fainted if I remained.

Major Reynolds: "About two o'clock PM the charge was ordered, which resulted in driving the enemy from his log covering, and I take pleasure in saying, no colors were advanced beyond those of the Regiment." He added that during the remainder of the day the 17th was placed in the second firing line, and was not engaged. But the cost to the newest Vermont fighting unit had been considerable. In its first day at the front, 10 men were killed and 64 wounded. Ten of those wounded would die in the next few days.

Back to the south, the men of the Vermont Brigade, safe behind their Brock Road breastworks and with everything relatively quiet in front, fell into an exhausted sleep. Before turning in, Pvt. Samuel Parker, Sixth Vermont, summed up May 6 in his diary: "Today we laid in line of battle all day in the woods and the balls flew and the shells flew and killed some." John Kelly, Second Vermont, noted that night: "Went into the line at 4 a. m. and stayed until 12 O clock the rebels turned our left and we fell back we lost near 400 men both days."

Lewis Grant said, "Later in the evening the First (Wheaton's) and the Fourth (Eustis's) Brigades went back to join the Sixth Corps. It was said that this brigade could not be relieved from the important position it held until morning, when it could join our corps." Appropriately, the Vermont Brigade would be the last of General Getty's units to leave the junction of the Brock and Plank Roads.

Capt. Erastus Buck, ever popular with his men, fell in the Wilderness. Vermont Historical Society

Next morning, Saturday, May 7, the Old Brigade remained in place, facing the smoldering woods. Though the heavy fighting in the Wilderness had generally ended, still there was some serious soldiering to be done there. Maj. Richard Crandall was in command of the brigade's skirmishers that morning and was ordered to advance. "Two companies of sharpshooters are sent to assist," he said:

we drove the rebel sharpshooters & skirmishers back more than a mile, out of two lines of works & into strong entrenchments. Captured as many as 3000 rifles which the enemy had gathered and were carrying off. Secured the body of Capt. Bird [Riley A. Bird, of Bristol and the Sixth Vermont] and had him buried by the side of Col. Stone.

Seth Eastman also talked of the great harvest of rifles:

We gathered up muskets on our front on the ground, where the Rebels had charged over the day before. A man could go out toward the front and bring back a whole armful of muskets. These muskets we piled behind our line . . . We had cords of them. Their wounded men had all been removed in the night, but the dead still lay where they fell. The muskets were piled up, all pointing one way, and hay was tucked between then and fire was applied to them. The muskets were all loaded and when they burned, they went off, and the noise was like another battle . . .

Wilbur Fisk was on Major Crandall's picket line. "We took our stations several rods in advance of the breastwork," he said,

to keep watch if the enemy should approach. We kept our post there awhile and then had orders to advance. I can hardly say that I liked to hear that order. We were advancing on the enemy a feeble line of pickets without support. The enemy were there, we could hear them talk . . . We kept advancing occasionally giving and receiving a shot from the enemy. We halted just under the crest of a hill for some sharpshooters to take up their position. As they advanced one of them was shot dead. The rest turned like cowards and run . . . Pretty soon the order came to us "Forward." Some of the men hesitated. They hated to advance up that hill and meet those skulking sharpshooters and very likely share the fate of the man just killed . . . George Lyndon shouted "Come on boys" and I wasn't going to be behind Lyndon. I clenched my musket and pushed ahead . . . They fired but didn't hit us and we fired back and they retreated. We kept on advancing until we came to their works when they opened on us with grape and of course we had to fall back. The commander of the picket retreated faster than we could. He got safely back long before we did.

Though Fisk chided the sharpshooters, the green-clad boys in the three Vermont sharpshooter regiments did some hot work the morning of May 7, and took considerable losses. Company F of the First Sharpshooter Regiment, with Alexander Hays' brigade (this day the late Alexander Hays, for the general had been killed the previous day), and Companies E and H of the Second Regiment, with Hobart Ward's brigade, all advanced from the Brock Road. The official history of Company F states,

> The third day of the battle opened with the greater portion of the army quietly resting on their arms; but for the sharpshooters there seemed no relief or respite. At day break they were deployed, again on the right of the plank road, and advancing over the scene of the fighting of the two previous days, now thickly covered with the dead of both armies, encountered the rebel skirmishers at a distance of about four hundred yards from the Union line."

Union commanders were making certain that, by posting skirmishers with sharpshooters to the front, no such surprises as Gordon and Longstreet had sprung the previous day would occur. Charles Mead, in Company F, wrote,

> advancing drove the rebel skirmishers half a mile into their works. We were answered by a hot fire, and a volley drove us back. Lay behind a slight breastwork all the P. M. on the left of the plank road. In the evening we were withdrawn and told that the army had left.

Companies E and H, of the Second Regiment, also advanced into that no-man's-land and, according to Benedict, "were under heavy fire." A telling loss was that of Capt. Albert Buxton, of Company H. Hit by a Minié ball that shattered a leg, he died an hour later from the shock of amputation. The Vermont marksmen's losses in the Wilderness totaled 40 men, nearly a third of their number.

Compared to the previous two days of bitter battle, May 7 was a rather quiet one for the men of the Vermont Brigade as they held the Brock Road near the hard-defended intersection, with pickets advanced. Seth Eastman said,

> We remained in the same place all day, but no attack came . . . The Rebel picket line came up again to within speaking distance of our front. We asked them what was going on. They knew more than we did and told us that General Grant was moving by the left flank. I never knew how they found out.

According to Lewis Grant, the Vermont Brigade received orders to rejoin the Sixth Corps sometime during the afternoon of May 7. "The Sixth Corps was at this time on the extreme right of the army," he said, "with its right thrown back facing the Rapidan. We joined the corps about sundown . . ."

So the Battle of the Wilderness had ended for the Vermonters as they moved to the north to join their comrades in John Sedgwick's corps. In the Sixth Vermont, Erie Ditty summed up the battle: "It was a terrible slaughter. But we had a man at the head who intended to win if it took every man in the army."

As the Wilderness fighting finally died away, far to the north, back home in Vermont, life went on seemingly at a normal pace. Vergennes' Mary Tucker said May 6 had been "a warm and pleasant day, but cloudy." She added, "I have felt unwell," and went on to note that "Sue and Bell have worked most of the day in the garden . . . This afternoon I have been removing old postage stamps from letters . . . I have cut out 240 stamps to add to John's cousin's collection. He is trying to collect a million."

To the south, in Windsor, readers of the local *Journal* saw a disturbing item in the May 7 edition: "Arthur K. aged four years, a son of William W. Williams of South Reading, was instantly killed by being drawn over a shaft in a saw mill on Monday last. He was a very promising and intelligent lad, much missed and deeply mourned."

William Henry Herrick said that Saturday, May 6, in St. Johnsbury had been "warm and sultry." Herrick was planning a vacation, noting, "I have worked very steadily for the past six months, and think I deserve some rest." He added, "I was glad it was Saturday night." Herrick went to a barbershop for a shave, then took a bath "and felt better." Then he went out. "It was raining when I went over to the street. Zenas promised to meet me early, but I could not find him till nearly 8. Then we came over to my room played euchre a bit and going to bed early."

The May 7 *Burlington Free Press* ran a brief item on events in Northern Virginia: "The spring campaign has begun in Virginia. The Army of the Potomac started on Tuesday night crossed the Rapidan in four places without serious loss, and a great battle on the other side commenced on Wednesday; what will be the result it is yet too soon to predict." The paper also used a bit of space to boast that its report the previous day of the Army of the Potomac having begun its spring offensive had been an exclusive story in Vermont, and that Vermonters had read the news before readers in many other northeastern states.

The *Free Press* also reprinted an item from the *Boston Post*:

The practical result of the low wages of seamstresses and workmen was illustrated by an incident which came to our knowledge last night. A young girl, neatly though plainly dressed, was arrested by a police officer for improperly soliciting men upon the street. When taken to the station house she admitted the charge but said she was compelled to adopt that course of life or starve. She came from Vermont with her mother and sister, because they could find no employment there.

In Burlington, William Hoyt wrote the night of May 7, "Cloudy and cooler, the wind having changed to the North . . . the Army of the Potomac moved in the early part of the week, and the whole country is intent with absorbing interest upon the news." In Virginia, Grant's army was once again on the move, out of the Wilderness, marching south on the orders of Ulysses Grant. The battered Vermont Brigade, however, moved north to link up with the Sixth Corps before swinging off deeper into Virginia. So the five regiments marched away from the Brock and Plank Road junction, in the smoking jungle with its heavy odor of death. The crossroads had been held, at a frightful cost, and the Army of the Potomac had not been cut in two. Lewis Grant would later write,

> The list of killed and wounded contains the names of some of the most valuable officers of the service. Col. E. L. Barney, Sixth Vermont, who fell seriously wounded in the head and survived only a few days, was one of Vermont's purest and best. He was always prompt and faithful in the execution of his duties . . . Col. Newton Stone, Second Vermont, whose dead body was brought from the field the night of the first day's battle, had but recently been promoted to his command. He was a good officer, gallant by nature, prompt in his duties, and urbane in his manner. He was beloved by his command and all who knew him. Lieut. Col. John S. Tyler, Second Vermont, who received a severe wound, was a young offi-cer of great promise. Always cool, especially in battle, he could be relied upon. His loss is deeply felt . . . It was a terrible struggle, a time which "tried men's souls." The memory of those who fell will be sacredly cher-ished among the true and tried patriots of Vermont; and those who sur-vive, well may proudly say, "I, too, was in the battles of the Wilderness."

Lewis Grant did not find the time to write those words, part of his official and detailed report on the Wilderness, until late August. His-torian Benedict took long years to compile information on the Wilder-ness. When he finally put pen to paper, he stated,

> The killed and wounded of the Vermont Brigade numbered 1,200. The killed and wounded of the Army of the Potomac numbered 12,485. That is to say, the Vermont brigade, being one of thirty-two infantry brigades engaged, suffered one-tenth the entire loss of Grant's army in killed and wounded in the Wilderness.

The remains of a soldier killed in the Wilderness lie among the dry leaves and saplings cut low by the fire of rifle-muskets. HOWARD COFFIN COLLECTION

Benedict went on to calculate that 191 members of the Old Brigade had been killed in the battle, while 947 were wounded, 96 were missing, and that 151 later died of their wounds:

Of the missing, five were never accounted for; two deserted. Most of the rest were wounded men, who fell into the hands of the enemy, only a few unwounded Vermonters being captured. The loss of officers was especially severe, accounting in killed and wounded to three-fourths of all present for duty—a fearful percentage. The brigade had no less than twenty-one officers killed and mortally wounded, being more than the number of officers killed in all the rest of the Sixth Corps put together. Among them were some of the best soldiers in the brigade . . .

Benedict put the total number of Vermont Brigade casualties at 1,234. But the entire toll taken by the Wilderness on the state of Vermont's fighting units was considerably higher. Adding in the losses of the First Vermont Cavalry, the 10th and 17th Regiments, and the three companies of Vermont sharpshooters, the total for Vermont in the Wilderness seems to be 1,420 killed, wounded, captured, or missing.

Of course, the five regiments of the Old Brigade were hit by far the hardest. According to Benedict, the Second Regiment lost most heavily, with 297 men out of the ranks. The Third lost 239 men, the Fourth 250, the Fifth 230, and the Sixth 216. Two casualties were listed among Vermonters on General Getty's staff.

So the armies moved south, toward another little country crossroads soon to be famous around the world. And as the fighting would rage around Spotsylvania Court House, Lewis Grant on May 11 found time to send a brief report to Adj. Gen. Peter Washburn, back in Woodstock, Vermont. What he wrote at the headquarters of his battered little brigade remains the finest tribute ever composed to the Vermonters in the Wilderness. After listing his losses to that day, the quiet Vermonter stated:

> It is with a sad heart that I inform you of so great a loss of Vermont's noble sons, but it is with a certain pride that I assure you there are no dishonorable graves. The brigade has met the enemy in his strongholds, attacked him under murderous fire, and in the very face of death has repulsed with great slaughter repeated and vigorous attacks upon our lines, and on no occasion has it disgracefully turned its back to the foe. The flag of each regiment, though pierced and tattered, still flaunts in the face of the foe, and noble bands of veterans with thinned ranks, and but few officers to command, still stand by them; and they seem determined to stand so long as there is a man to bear their flag aloft or an enemy in the field.

✳

The Brock and Plank Roads intersection today is an increasingly busy meeting place of highway traffic, with but a tiny parking lot available for visitors. The remnants of trenches, built and occupied for a time by Vermonters, are visible. Several National Park

Service signs explain the fighting that took place there, though none mentions any Vermont units. The park service owns narrow strips of property around the intersection, the largest being 300 yards deep and running several hundred yards along the south side of the Plank Road. Thus a significant portion of the land on which the Vermont Brigade fought has been saved. Except for the traffic noise, which becomes muted as one walks away from the intersection, the scene of the heaviest fighting, in the intersection's southwest quadrant, is quiet and the aroma of the Virginia woods is ever present.

Some 250 yards west of the historic intersection, on the north side of the Plank Road, is a pull-off where a marker is set close to the site of James Longstreet's wounding. Look across the road, and one sees a cable blocking entrance to an old road leading into the woods. Step over the cable and begin to see traces of depressions that once were graves. Many of the Wilderness dead, certainly including many Vermonters, were buried there soon after the fighting in a hastily prepared cemetery. Eventually, they were disinterred and reburied in the vast national cemetery at Fredericksburg. Look west of the graves and the remnants of a trench are visible, likely built by Confederates to fight off the advance of the Vermonters. Walk more deeply into the woods and, moving west, one encounters a swampy area, likely the one Seth Eastman saw on his hasty retreat from Longstreet's flank attack. Beyond it is high ground, probably that occupied by the Vermonters on May 6, as they held their V-shaped lines "on a knoll," as Lewis Grant said.

Chapter Seven

SPOTSYLVANIA COURT HOUSE

Beloved" was the word Vermonter Seth Eastman chose to describe Maj. Gen. John Sedgwick, commander of the Sixth Corps. If the term was a bit strong for most soldiers from a state known for quiet people not given to overstatement, it nonetheless made clear that the corps commander was well liked by his troops. Eastman added, "We loved him as children love their father." Sedgwick was the most popular general in the Army of the Potomac. Stocky, bearded, and barrel-chested, with a look of kindness in his eyes, the general apparently drew men in the ranks to him. Sedgwick was a New Englander through and through, from hilly country in northwestern Connecticut. Cornwall Hollow was his home, a hamlet in a deep and green valley that Sedgwick was fond of describing as the most beautiful place on Earth. He had been born there in 1813, grandson of a veteran of the Revolution. It was to his own big white house, just above the hollow, that Sedgwick longed to return after the cruel war was over. He had seen much fighting in his nearly 51 years of life. After West Point, he had served under Winfield Scott in Mexico. Then he had soldiered out west, fighting Indians for six years. On the Civil War's commencement, Major Sedgwick was promptly promoted to the rank of brigadier general, and he led a division into combat during the Peninsula Campaign. Now he led the Sixth Corps on the march from the deadly Wilderness toward another battlefield that would perhaps equal its horror.

Martin McMahon, Sedgwick's faithful adjutant, after the war said of his friend,

> Sedgwick's compliments many times cost the soldiers from Vermont very dear; for they were the high compliments of placing them on many battlefields in the foremost position of danger—of placing on them the whole reliance of the corps.

McMahon then described an incident at the close of fighting in the Wilderness. According to McMahon, the Vermonters saw the general ride along their lines "as they were coming into bivouac," and

> they burst forth in a hearty spontaneous cheer that touched him to the very heart. And when the cheers subsided one of them stepped to the front and called out with a comic and yet touching emphasis, "Three more for old Uncle John!" The general's face flushed like a girl's; and as his staff laughed at his embarrassment, the laugh spread along the lines and the whole brigade laughed and cheered as if just returning from a summer picnic, and not from a bloody field, weary, worn and with decimated ranks.

Ulysses Grant was an admirer of Sedgwick's, believing his value to the army equal to that of a full division. Grant, on the night of May 7, had put his army on the march, bound southeast for the key crossroads village of Spotsylvania Court House. If other Union generals had been battered by Robert E. Lee in Northern Virginia and turned back north, Grant was made of different stuff. Though the best he could call the bloody slugging match in the Wilderness was a draw (he'd suffered far more casualties than Lee and had both his flanks smashed in), still with his bigger army he came on. And he knew that whoever reached Spotsylvania first would control the most direct route toward Richmond. Lee saw it too, and in the night he had his armies moving southeast, parallel to Grant. It was a grim race in the smoky darkness, moving down out of the Wilderness to more open country where Grant hoped to bring Lee out in the open for a show-down fight.

The four brigades of Getty's division, as they moved through the darkness, were being led by a temporary division commander. Brig. Gen. Frank Wheaton, former commander of Getty's First Brigade, had led the division since Getty's wounding. But on the reuniting of the brigade, according to Wheaton, on "connecting with the Third Brigade . . . Brigadier General Neill, he being my senior, I resumed command of the First Brigade." So Getty's division was now led by Thomas Hewson Neill and would be through the remainder of the campaign, as Getty's wound would keep him out of action for about six weeks. Getty kept in close touch with the division and still filed some of its official reports, and the men preferred to continue referring to their outfit as "Getty's division." Neill was a native Pennsylvanian and an 1847 graduate of West Point. A staff officer early in the war, he had led troops in combat on the peninsula and, during the Chancellorsville campaign, at Marye's Heights and Salem Church, where he received a brevet promotion to brigadier general.

Departing the Wilderness, most of the army moved directly southeast by the Brock Road, the shortest route. But the Sixth Corps swung off east, to Chancellorsville, before turning south. The Vermonters, dead tired from the fury of the previous two days, stumbled along the dusty dirt road in the darkness, bringing up the rear of their corps. Historian Benedict said, "The trains and artillery filled the roads, and the men were on their feet all night."

Wilbur Fisk: "We were tired almost to death and very much needed rest and sleep that night but instead of that we had orders to march and were on our feet all night." Seth Eastman:

> The night was very dark and a misty rain set in. So dark was it, that we could not see the man at our elbow to see who he was, and so, in the night, the men got into confusion. Companies and regiments became all mixed up and the organization was lost. Still we pressed on in this confusion.

Deep in the night, Eastman said that a friend whispered, "The damn Rebels are right among us." Eastman:

It was so dark that I had not noticed it, but in looking at the shadow forms about me, I perceived that this was the case. They were follow- ing us up and it was so dark that they did not know that they had mixed up with us. No one dared to speak at this time . . . I knew that they were Rebels, as I could see that they had their blankets in a roll over one shoulder.

Eventually, Eastman concluded that the Confederates were unarmed, and prisoners.

Well ahead of the Old Brigade, somewhere in the long column, was the 10th Vermont, which marched through Chancellorsville in the daylight. Chaplain Haynes:

In crossing the battlefield of Chancellorsville we saw many signs of the desperate conflict that raged there just a year before . . . The field was a sepulcher, silent, and full of dead men's bones. It seemed worse even than the one we had just left . . . Here was all the debris of battle, white and moldy; splintered gun carriages, torn saddles, broken mus- kets, battered canteens, shriveled cartridge boxes and knapsacks, blan- kets stripped into shreds and hanging upon the bushes, skeletons of horses and men scattered about the field and mingling in the common dust . . . Scores of human skulls were kicked over and went rolling away from the path we were treading to other scenes of carnage.

Lewis Grant said it was well into the morning of May 8 when the Vermont Brigade reached Chancellorsville. "From this point," he said, "the brigade was detailed to guard the train of the Sixth Corps, and soon became separated from the corps. The train went into park at 4 p.m., and the brigade halted, took dinner, and lay down to rest. Shortly afterward we were ordered forward to join the command . . . "

The road from the Wilderness to Chancellorsville led east, toward Fredericksburg, and when the Vermont Brigade turned south at the historic road crossing, the significance was not lost on the Vermon-

Maj. Gen. John Sedgwick and his staff before the Overland Campaign. The general stands with hand in coat. Note the white Sixth Corps crosses. HOWARD COFFIN COLLECTION

ters. "We marched through Chancellorsville and then turned right towards Spotsylvania Court House," said Private Fisk. "Fredericksburg Heights [where the Vermont Brigade had fought the previous spring] we were leaving in our rear. Of course then we could not be retreating."

The fight for Spotsylvania Court House would last nearly two weeks and cost many thousands of casualties. But early on the morning of May 8, Union cavalry, including the First Vermont, briefly occupied the place. Wilson's division was on the move early that morning and out ahead of the Union and Confederate infantry. They rode into the crossroads village unopposed. Sgt. Horace Ide accurately described Spotsylvania Court House, saying it "consisted of a court house, a jail and perhaps half a dozen other buildings situated at the junction of several roads . . . " He added that "towards this point Grant's and Lee's armies were moving at that moment and if we had had sufficient force to have held it the rest of the war would have been quite different . . . We soon found we were in danger of being run over by the Confederate army [and we] retreated across the Ny river." That night Company D of the Vermont cavalry was sent out on picket north of the village and brought in a dozen Confederate prisoners.

Lee's infantry won the race for Spotsylvania, just barely, driving out the Union cavalry and entrenching along a low ridge a mile northwest of the village. Fighting immediately developed as Union infantry tested, without success but with considerable loss, the strengthening Rebel lines. Both sides dug in. The 10th Vermont came on the field in midafternoon of May 8. Major Abbott said, "We advanced across the Ny river, a mere creek, but meeting with a sharp artillery fire from a rebel battery on the opposite ridge to us skirting the valley, we were ordered to halt." Abbott said the regiment was about three miles north of the village. Late in the afternoon, he said, the 10th participated in an unsuccessful attack across an open field against entrenchments "without effect except to be repulsed with the field covered with our killed and badly wounded." Abbott said his regiment suffered sixteen casualties. He added, "General Meade was in rear of our regiment which formed a rear line in our assaulting column, superintending the assault, and when jocularly reminded by a wag that he (Meade) was in a dangerous place, he graciously replied, 'It's safe enough behind a Vermont regiment anywhere!" The men of the 10th had been the first Vermonters to go into action at Spotsylvania and had gotten a good look at the lay of the land. Much of it was farm fields, with the enemy's works plainly in sight. To be out of the dense confusion of the Wilderness was a relief, but clearly any attack across this new and open ground would be costly.

As the army took position north of Spotsylvania Court House, a battery attached to the Sixth Corps was blasting away at a Rebel signal station in the top of a tree 1,500 yards distant. Along came Vermonters of sharpshooter Company F, and for a time the men watched the firing. Then they went into action, attaching sticks to their rifle sights to increase elevation for long-range shooting. The company's strength had been greatly reduced in the Wilderness, but soon twenty-three men opened fire. Signal flags stopped waving from the tall tree. General Hancock was watching with satisfaction and personally complimented the Vermont marksmen.

The Vermont Brigade, according to its commander, reached the battlefield and rejoined the Sixth Corps just before dark on May 8. As the five battered regiments came up, they were accorded perhaps their greatest tribute of the entire war. Lewis Grant said, "Striking the lines of battle near the right of the corps, we were ordered to the extreme left. As the brigade passed along the lines to its designated position on the left, it was greeted with hearty and repeated cheers from the other brigades of the corps." Seldom during the long grim war did soldiers raise a cheer for fellow soldiers. "The troops of the Sixth corps were standing to their arms and expecting momentarily to move into action," said historian Benedict:

> They could hardly be expected under the circumstances to expend much breath in compliments. But the fighting of the Vermonters on the Orange Plank road had been for two days the talk of the corps; and now as the brigade, reduced to half its former size, began to move along the line, the men nearest to it broke out into spontaneous and hearty hurrahs for the Green Mountain boys. The greeting was taken up by regiment after regiment and brigade after brigade in the line, as the Vermont brigade moved past them, and its march to the left was made under a continuous round of cheers. Its officers and men were sober from their losses, exhausted by four days of fighting, marching and want of sleep, and blown by double-quicking; but the welcome of their comrades put fresh heart into them . . .

Seth Eastman said that among the cheers he heard were: "Hurrah for the Green Mountain Boys, they can whip their weight in mountain cats," "There are no bullet holes in their backs," "They are good on their feet, but they can't run," and "Has old Ethan Allen or Seth Warner got the command of them?" He added that other comments were made that, in good taste, he could not repeat.

Though the Sixth Corps expected to go into action the night of May

8, the attack was suspended by General Meade. The Vermont Brigade was led, in the gathering darkness, through a ravine and up a wooded hill to a position facing the right of General Lee's lines. "Here, as darkness fell," said Benedict, "Brig. Gen. Grant discovered that his command was in front of the general line of the army, and in advance even of any skirmish line." The Vermonters must have experienced sudden flashbacks to their time spent isolated to the front in the Wilderness. According to Benedict,

> [Lewis Grant] knew not where the enemy was, whether near or far. Scattering shots, as of skirmishers, were heard on his flank and in his rear. The position was not a pleasant one, and he determined to seek some other, where he could at least be sure where the enemy was before and not behind him. After several hours of reconnoitering and wandering to and fro in the darkness, the brigade at last took a position behind a skirmish line. The men were thankful to have a chance to sleep.

The next day, May 9, the firing intensified as the Union and Confederate lines continued to be extended. Lee's army now was covering the crossroads at Spotsylvania with a great arc of entrenchments. Chaplain Haynes of the 10th Vermont said,

> Batteries were placed in position and the division got a terrific shelling in reply to their own batteries, besides being constantly annoyed by the enemy's sharpshooters. Those who had the opportunity sought the best cover they could from this close and deadly fire; both officers and men hugged the ground with an affection that was truly touching . . . At such times does each man feel that he weighs a ton, so far down does he imbed himself in the earth. It was with the utmost risk that the cooks prepared coffee, for the moment that a column of smoke rose above the woods, the rebel artillerists would train their guns and blaze away at the spot they supposed to be somewhere near its base. By this practice they spoiled several batches of coffee, designed for the men, destroying the kettles and scattering the firebrands around. Some were half buried beneath the furrows plowed by bursting shells—among them our brigade commander, General W. H. Morris.

That May 9 morning, General Sedgwick was out along the lines, in the area where the fight for Spotsylvania Court House had begun, near the Brock Road. His adjutant was with him as he visited an artillery unit, near the front lines. At one point, the general asked when the Vermont Brigade would be up. McMahon said,

> He seemed in excellent spirits although a little discouraged by the slow progress of the campaign, which seemed to be desperate fighting day after day with indecisive results. A few minutes before he had spoken of some of the young officers of his staff in tender and kindly terms of affection. He said a few jesting words to some of the men who passed before him as they moved into the rifle pits. His manner, attitude and gesture as he stood indicated to the enemy that he was an officer of rank and authority. He wore no uniform, not even a sword.

Confederate sharpshooter rounds were zinging in, and the general was told by soldiers nearby to beware. But Sedgwick tried to deflect their concern, saying, "Boys, they couldn't hit an elephant at that range." McMahon:

> From across the little valley which separated us from the enemy's line, from one of their sharp shooters concealed in the woods in front of us came the swift messenger of death. Slowly, without a word, with a sad smile upon his lips, John Sedgwick fell and his great heart ceased to beat, his life blood pouring a strong, steady stream from the wound spirited over me. I made an effort to sustain him as he fell and in so doing fell with him. He uttered no word and made no sign. It seemed to me if I could but make him hear and call his attention to the terrible effect his fall was having on our men he would by force of his great will rise up in spite of death. I called vainly in his ear—he made no answer. His favorite aid, General Charles A. Whittier, bent over him with streaming eyes. General Tompkins, the chief of artillery, and his surgeon Dr. Ohlenschlager raised him partly from the ground and the pale and anxious faces of the men in the long line of rifle pits were bent eagerly toward the group, but such was the force of discipline that although these men's hearts were filled with great sorrow, although

they knew that a terrible blow had fallen upon them, none left the ranks, and the silence which follows a great tragedy fell upon the summer woods of Spotsylvania on that morning of saddest memories.

So John Sedgwick was dead, almost instantly, shot in the face. The news raced through the Army of the Potomac. "'Johnny Sedgwick,' as the boys call him, was a favorite general with the boys of his corps," Wilbur Fisk wrote, "and they had unbounded confidence in his prudence and judgment. But he has died with his armor on, and we cherish his memory, emulate his bravery so that, though dead, he still lives with us." Chaplain Haynes noted, "His name and the glory of the old Sixth Corps are forever identical." Seth Eastman: "This incident made us all very sad . . ." He added,

> Because the sharp shooters were annoying us very much, a call was made for volunteers to set against them and put a stop to their deviltry. It was suggested that I should volunteer to go against them, but said no, that I would go when the company went, but would not go that day as a volunteer sharp shooter. I had a friend that said he would go [Pvt. Albert Craig, of Topsham] and he did. I bade him good-bye, as I never expected to see him again. He went and fought the Rebel sharp shooters all day and came in that night, all safe and sound.

Major Richard Crandall, Sixth Vermont, wrote the night of May 9, "Our dear corps commander John Sedgwick was to day killed by a rebel sharpshooter while reconnoitering. We loved him as our father. How priceless is the cost of liberty!"

Sedgwick's body was carried to Ulysses Grant's headquarters, where it lay in state for a day. Then the remains were sent north, back to Cornwall Hollow in Connecticut. Several days later, two thousand people came to the Sedgwick home for funeral services on the back lawn. Then he was buried, among his ancestors, in the hollow cemetery. Back at the front, Brig. Gen. Horatio G. Wright was named commander of the Sixth Corps. Like Sedgwick a native of Connecticut, the handsome, red-haired West Pointer had a familiarity with Vermont, having for a time attended Norwich University.

In Vermont on May 9, the *Rutland Herald* published an editorial titled "The Grand Conflict Begun." It said,

> Not only the two huge armies in Virginia, but the people of the whole Union, are trembling with the shock of the battle . . . There is "thunder all around" again, and this time with more hopeful prospects of success than ever before. God grant a final victory to the Republic will be on the anxious prayer of every patriot at home; while the brave defenders in the field are battling the hordes of rebellion in the great contest for freedom and the Union.

Vermonters were beginning to learn that something dreadful had happened the previous week in the Wilderness. The night of May 9, Henry Herrick, in his rented room, wrote,

> There has been news from the army by telegraph to-day telling of a terrible fight Thursday and Friday in which I think the advantage was with us, the losses were severe . . . there is much excitement, but not much confidence among the people now . . . these years have made us wiser and they have made us sadder, for in them we have learned such bitter lessons—but we eat and sleep and go about our lives as usual, so I have worked all day, though it has been very warm.

Back at the front, the morning of May 10 began with fighting along a portion of the Spotsylvania lines. Heavy engagements erupted along the Union right flank, along the Po River and at Laurel Hill. For the Vermont Brigade, the fiery day began with an advance by the Fourth Vermont. The purpose was to test the enemy's lines, with an eye toward finding an opportune target for a major attack. The Vermonters, as usual, undertook their assignment with vigor and drove the skirmishers in their front all the way into the Confederate entrenchments. At a cost of two killed and eighteen wounded, the Fourth obtained information that helped set the target for an assault late in the day. It would come because Ulysses Grant was most anxious to batter his way through the now tough Confederate entrenchments around Spotsylvania and, when a young

Emory Upton conceived and led the late afternoon assault of May 10. HOWARD COFFIN COLLECTION

colonel with a proven battle record came to him with a bold plan, he readily agreed.

North of Spotsylvania Court House the Confederate lines, following high ground, made a pronounced outward bend, in the shape, as the troops said, of "a horseshoe" or "mule shoe." The run of the lines thus created a salient, or bulge, which was notoriously hard to defend because guns within had difficulty concentrating fire. Col. Emory Upton, a New Yorker commanding a brigade in the Sixth Corps, proposed taking 12 regiments and launching a sudden attack on the west face of the salient, at a point where only about 200 yards of open field had to be crossed to reach the Rebel works. Upton would mass four thousand men in the woods in four battle lines. The Confederate defenses were formidable, two lines of deep entrenchments (Upton said the second line was 100 yards in back of the first) fronted by a line of abatis, or brush, and sharpened stakes. The plan was for the front rank to make a sudden rush across those 200 yards, have the men spring over the works, and fan out left and right shooting and stabbing the defenders. Then the next three ranks would pour in to secure the entrenchments, creating a major break in the Rebel lines. Only the front rank would advance with capped muskets. Thus the supporting three ranks would be prevented from stopping to fire while crossing the field, having no choice but to rush on. Three of the Old Brigade's five regiments were chosen for the attack—the Third Ver-

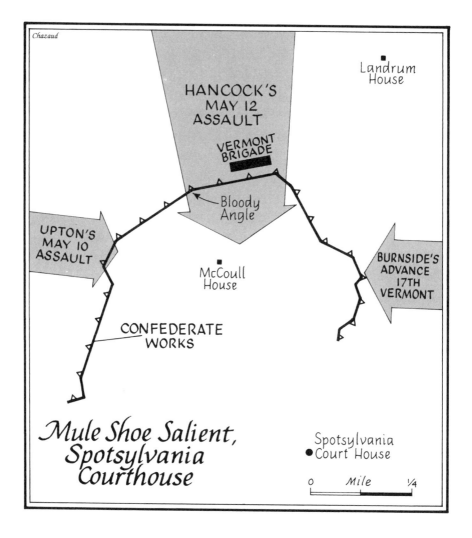

Chazaud

Landrum
House

HANCOCK'S
MAY 12
ASSAULT

VERMONT
BRIGADE

UPTON'S
MAY 10
ASSAULT

Bloody
Angle

BURNSIDE'S
ADVANCE
17TH
VERMONT

McCoull
House

CONFEDERATE
WORKS

Mule Shoe Salient,
Spotsylvania
Courthouse

Spotsylvania
Court House

0   Mile   ¼

mont, this day commanded by Samuel Pingree; Maj. Charles Dudley's
Fifth Vermont; and the Sixth Vermont, under Lt. Col. Oscar Hale.
Some men in the Third and Fourth Regiments also joined the assault.
All would be under the overall command of Col. Thomas Seaver and
they would make up the fourth line of the assault. Upton said, "All the
officers were instructed to repeat the command 'Forward' constantly,
from the commencement of the charge until the works were carried."

It was late afternoon when Upton got his regiments into line and
gave the order to advance. Wilbur Fisk said it was about 5 PM when

we piled our knapsacks and prepared for the bloody work. A brigade of the first division was to lead the charge, and we support them. A hundred rods or so in front of us, we came to an open space in the woods, of perhaps a hundred rods or more, and on the opposite side of this space was the rebel rifle-pits. We formed in a ravine, screened from the rebels' view, where we prepared to charge across this open space, and drive the rebels out of their rifle-pits if possible. Our batteries kept up a continual shelling as we were getting into shape, firing over the woods with a degree of accuracy truly remarkable. We formed in four lines of battle, three ahead of us. At the signal the first three lines sprang to their feet, and rushed across the field, determined to drive the enemy or die. We followed immediately after. The rebels mowed the men down with awful effect, but the advancing line was not checked.

G. G. Benedict said the men advanced "with hearty cheers" and were met "by a sweeping front and flank fire of musketry and canister." The men pushed on and, Benedict said, "reached and mounted the opposing breastworks; engaged the Confederates behind them in a hand-to-hand fight; took 900 prisoners, drove out the rest; and pressing forward to a second line of works, took them also, with a battery posted in them."

So for the moment, Upton had succeeded in smashing a hole in Lee's Spotsylvania lines. Now he needed support to exploit his breakthrough, reinforcements to pile in and make the breach a permanent one. It didn't happen, as troops from the Second Corps, under Brig. Gen. Gershom Mott, got hit by artillery as they moved up to help. Mott's men quickly halted their advance, and Upton's attackers were left alone in and along the Rebel entrenchments to fight as best they could. Lewis Grant: "The Vermont regiments, under Colonel Seaver, advanced and, under a most galling fire, occupied the rebel works, while the other regiments of the attacking column fell back." The Vermonters, with the way cleared for them by the front ranks, had surged on into the first line of Rebel trenches, then had rolled on and captured a portion of the second line. Once again, they were far to the front. Pvt. Charles Morey, Second Vermont: "We advanced to the enemy's works after they were carried and held them until after dark

Bringing up more troops, in the rain, to fight at Spotsylvania Court House.
HOWARD COFFIN COLLECTION

but nothing came up on our left and we were obliged to retire." Lewis Grant said, "Orders were given for all to fall back, but it failed to reach a portion of the Second Regiment, and some from each of the others, who remained obstinately holding them against all attacks of the enemy until late in the evening, refusing to fall back until they received positive orders to do so."

While the Vermonters hung on, Vermont sharpshooter Companies E and H were engaged in a supporting action, exchanging fire at long range with Confederate marksmen. Lt. Col. Homer Stoughton, an organizer of the Vermont sharpshooters back when the war began, was hit in the side, smashing two ribs. The tough colonel went back to his home in Royalton to recover, but was back at the front within a month.

In the captured Rebel works, the Vermonters stayed low and kept up a brisk fire as the Confederates moved in more and more men and the fire increased. As they held on, the Vermonters' dilemma became increasingly acute as Wilbur Fisk said they were "exposed to a raking cross-fire." Not only were they reluctant to give up the bloodied ground won at a dear cost, they also knew that to withdraw unsupported across 200 or 300 yards of open ground would expose them to heavy fire. A message was sent back from the captured works that the Vermonters, thank you, would stay where they were. Colonel Upton knew the game was up and bravely crossed the field to the Vermonters, to order them back. But according to Benedict, the response was, "We don't want to go. Send us ammunition and rations, and we can stay here for six months." Samuel Pingree, commanding the Third Vermont, said that his regiment "with many others intermingled held this line under a fire from the flanking work on the left & a direct fire in front." The *New York Herald* stated, "The blood of the Green Mountain Boys was up and they absolutely refused to budge a single hair from the field they had wrested from the enemy."

Years later, corps adjutant McMahon would say, in a speech to Vermont veterans in Montpelier, "Well, they held a sort of town meeting in the works, and they decided that those works belonged to them, and they would not leave . . . they had captured this point by a magnificent assault, and they felt that abandoning it was an injury to the cause." The obstinate Green Mountain lads had presented young Upton with a dilemma, and Sixth Corps commander Horatio Wright took it all the way to army headquarters. War correspondent Carleton Coffin was there and heard Wright tell Ulysses Grant that Vermonters were still in the salient and would not come away. "What shall I do?" the flustered Wright asked. "Pile in men and hold it," was Grant's reply. But by the time the Sixth Corps commander got back to the front, the Vermonters had received stern orders and, seeing their situation as hopeless, had come back, running, under the expected heavy fire. Lt. Chester Leach, in the Second, summed things up well: "Made a charge on the Rebel's works, & took a lot of prisoners, but had to get out of there." Lt. Col. Samuel Pingree said in a letter to his cousin,

> When I got by myself where I would not be ashamed of it I cried like a whipped spaniel—I saw many soldiers cry like girls, and many who took things less to heart, gave vent to their mortification at having lost

all they had gained so nobly—by the fault of others, by letting off unnumbered salvos of profanity—I believed while there, & I believe still that the only true way to save us was to send a column to take the enfilading work on our left. It might have cost 500 men that night. I do not think it would have cost a man more. The next day it cost us over ten times that number.

When it was all over, in the deep dusk of that May night in the Virginia woods and fields, eighty-eight more Vermonters had become casualties of the overland drive on Richmond. Among them was Major Dudley, who led the Fifth, so badly wounded that he would expire a few days later. Yet the Vermonters had helped to prove that Lee's lines could, indeed, be breached. Ulysses Grant liked what he saw and gave Emory Upton an instant battlefield promotion, to brigadier general. The general commanding also began to hatch a plan for a much heavier attack on the Confederate salient, Upton style. It would come two days later. But Seth Eastman thought the May 10 attack pretty much a waste. "Many of our men were disabled in this affair," he wrote. "It was a fool-hardy attempt to do an impossible thing, like the Charge of the Light Brigade at Balaklava . . ."

Charles Carleton Coffin, with the army, writing in the *Boston Journal,* said, "It is a proud thing for you, Vermont, that the patriotic fire which burned in your sires' bosoms in 1776 should burn in your sons in 1864 so bright a flame."

In Vermont, as the fighting intensified around Spotsylvania, public awareness of the magnitude of events in Virginia was growing. The night of May 10, as the battered Vermonters made their way back from the Rebel works, Henry Herrick made his usual diary entry. The former soldier was gaining an understanding of Grant's overall strategy, as was clear when he wrote,

The telegraph and the papers bring us news of continued fighting. Lee appears to be stubbornly retreating and contesting the ground foot by foot, while we are closely following and thus far the advantage is with us, meanwhile Butler is going up the James river in an attempt to take Richmond in the rear, and Sherman is advancing in Geo. "Thundering all around"—the fate of the nation seems to be in the balance and these are eventful days and yet they go by as other days, and only by our prayers, it may be, and by our sympathy, and worry, can we be of any use or assistance to the noble hearts who are fighting their battles as well as our own, to whole thousands of them will it be "their last battle." The 6th Corps were engaged in Thursday and Fridays battles and suffered surely. How many of our Vermonters are among the slain?

That night, as Upton's weary attackers rested in the woods, in North Springfield, Vermont, a very worried Helen Wheeler, staying with her mother in Weathersfield, wrote a letter to her husband, Pvt. Artemas Wheeler, in the 10th Vermont. "I am feeling anxious about you at this time," she wrote,

> but God will protect you if it is his will . . . Oh my darling think of us talking and thinking of you and praying, be of good cheer God will have it all right in the end . . . I have again to tell you that our little circle is well, my health is pretty good. Aunt's health is good, she has been engaged in planting. Mother grows weaker every day think we must give her up unless something turns in her favor . . . Keep your mind on God pray often.

At Spotsylvania, May 11 began for Ulysses Grant with the writing of a letter to Chief of Staff Henry Halleck, in Washington:

> We have now ended the 6th day of very hard fighting. The result up to this time is much in our favor. We have lost to this time eleven general officers killed, wounded and missing, and probably twenty thousand men. I think the loss of the enemy must be greater—we have taken over four thousand prisoners in battle whilst he has taken from us but few except a few stragglers. I am now sending back to Belle Plain all my wagons for a fresh supply of provisions and ammunition, and propose to fight it out on this line if it takes all summer.

Those words were released to the newspapers and the phrase "if it takes all summer" struck a chord across the Union. That statement of resolve proved to be much what the public wanted to hear as the bloody war moved relentlessly on.

The day of Grant's writing, May 11, was a relatively quiet day on the battlefield, though men continued to die. Many fell from sharp-shooter bullets. Charles Mead wrote that day,

> Rebel sharpshooters got a flanking fire on the breastwork and wounded a few men among them the color corporal co. A. Helped cook a turkey that Capt. Captured and had a magnificent breakfast. About 10 AM we were ordered back to check the rebel sharpshooters scattered around the buildings and hills and soon silenced them. The boys made some splen-did shots—shot 12 and 1400 yds hitting them. Rainy some P.M. In a lit-tle rifle pit. Got some close calls. At dark relieved, drew rations. Marched all night to the left reaching it just before day-light on the 11th.

The Vermont Brigade spent the day on the front line, sometimes under fire. That night it was withdrawn several hundred yards behind the lines and the men were allowed to rest. Maj. Richard Crandall wrote,

> Skirmishing all day on our front . . . the evening is rainy, the first since we crossed the river. A band is playing "Departed Days." Oh! The mem-ories it awakens.

The respite lasted but a few hours. As sharpshooter Mead had noted, much of the Army of the Potomac was moving that night, positioning itself for a massive attack planned for just before dawn the following morning.

While Grant's legions struggled through the mud and darkness of Northern Virginia, up in the state of Vermont, more news of the recent fighting was reaching the citizenry. Henry Herrick wrote May 11:

> There was a dispatch at the office announcing the death of Gen. Sedg-wick, who was shot by a sharp shooter—a great loss for he was a brave man and a good officer—another dispatch states a severe loss in the Vt.

Brigade, the killing and wounding of nearly all the Cols. and that only 90 men & 5 officers are left in the 4th Vt. It made me faint, and sick at heart, for I knew many in the Regt . . . Went down to work at 3—a dispatch came to Mr. Carpenter this afternoon announcing Capt. Carpenter's death has cast a gloom all over the whole community. It is coming very near to us.

(Capt. Joseph Carpenter, of St. Johnsbury, was leading a company in the Fourth Vermont on May 5 when he was killed by a bullet to the chest.) That evening Herrick read a Boston newspaper and wrote,

There are tolerably full accounts of the battles to-night, and they were terrible. I never read or heard of such desperate fighting—of fierce, dashing attack by the rebels and stubborn steady defence on our side. They are fighting with the energy and desperation of despair and upon the result is staked their cause . . . We are all gaining confidence in Gen. Grant, and if he is fully successful he is the idol of the nation— but our losses have been terrible, and the end is not yet.

On the battlefield, more than fifteen thousand men of Hancock's corps were massed in the darkness for a heavy, sudden onslaught against the north and northeast fronts of the Rebel salient. Burnside's Ninth Corps would be on the left of Hancock, with Wright's Sixth Corps on the right, both ready when Hancock needed support. And Warren's Fifth Corps was also placed on the alert. Ulysses Grant was going all out in this effort, committing much of his army. Lewis Grant said, "Early in the morning of the 12th the brigade moved with the corps to the left to co-operate with the Second Corps." Just before the assault the attackers got a break, as in the night Lee withdrew twenty-two artillery pieces from the apex of the Mule Shoe, guns that could have done fierce damage to massed troops advancing across open country.

As the eastern sky was beginning to show a first hint of light, Hancock's ranks, led by the division of Francis Barlow, surged forward, through the mud and rain. They plunged ahead, stumbling through woods to overwhelm a stunned Rebel skirmish line. Then they bulled ahead in the dim light into an open field, first stumbling downhill, then moving upward, as the flash of muskets along the awakening Confederate lines began to outline the object of their assault. The men in blue, in a huge, hollering mass, tore their way through the Rebel abatis and surged onto and over the entrenchments. Amid the shooting and stabbing, the Yankees came on an unexpected bonus of their surprise onslaught. Lee, just before the attack, had second thoughts about moving his artillery from the Mule Shoe's tip, and the heavy guns were on their way back when the Yankee mass swarmed in. Quickly, twenty of those cannon and more than three thousand prisoners were on the way to the Union rear.

Hancock's men rolled on, the disorganized juggernaut thundering down the salient. On they rushed, shouting and shooting, a mighty mob of men flushed with a sudden victory and seeming bent on running all the way to Richmond. But in the gloom and rain, with all military order gone and units mixed and confused, the grand assault lost its cohesion, and its force. Now there were Rebels in considerable numbers to the front, in line and firing fast in the dim early light. It was not long before the blue horde was bludgeoned to a halt. And soon Hancock's men were giving up the ground they had won. Robert E. Lee was present to personally direct an inspired Rebel counterattack, moving to seal the huge hole suddenly smashed in the center of his Spotsylvania lines.

Ulysses Grant said,

The victory was important, and one that Lee could not afford to leave us in full possession of. He made the most strenuous efforts to regain the position he had lost. Troops were brought up from his left and attacked Hancock furiously. Hancock was forced to fall back; but he did so slowly, with his face to the enemy, inflicting on him heavy losses, until behind the breastworks he had captured . . . Wright was ordered to reinforce Hancock, and arrived by six o'clock.

Lee's counterattack had driven Hancock's troops back to, and over, the high Confederate breastworks they had overrun at first light. There the federals made a stand as the angered Confederates came on in a heavy counterattack. As the fighting intensified and both sides poured in more men, only scant yards separated the two armies along a portion of the salient's west face. At a spot where the trenches made a slight turn, rank on rank of federals faced rank on rank of Rebels separated only by the long Confederate earthwork and the log parapet on its top. The place would forever be known as the Bloody Angle and there, in the muck and mist, the Civil War produced its most bitter close-in fighting. The battle for the salient would go on through the entire rainy day and into the early hours of the next morning as Lee fought for time to build a strong secondary line across the Mule Shoe's base. The combat would be relentless and utterly deadly.

Apparently it was sometime near 8 AM when the partially rested Vermont Brigade was called into action. Benedict stated, "The Sixth Corps had been ordered to support Hancock, and taking Russell's and Getty's divisions, General Wright advanced promptly up to the west angle of the salient." So, once again, the Old Brigade had been sent into the hottest portion of a big battle, this time into the area of the soon-to-be-infamous Bloody Angle. "As the Vermont brigade moved up the slope it came under a severe artillery fire from the enemy's guns on its right, and lost a number of men," said Benedict.

Lewis Grant first received orders to move north along the west face of the salient toward the apex of the Mule Shoe salient and relieve the hard-pressed troops of Barlow's division, who had led the predawn onslaught. Grant promptly formed his brigade, under fire, in a double line. Then the brigade advanced and opened fire upon the Confederates on the far side of the trenches. Hancock was nearby and, seeing fresh troops, the Second Corps commander changed Grant's orders, asking him to both hold his present position and send men to the assistance of Brig. Gen. David Russell's Sixth Corps division to the south, newly thrown into the fray but already in difficulty. Leaving the trusted Colonel Seaver in charge of three regiments, Grant took the Fourth and Fifth Vermont south. The two regiments then moved forward, with the Fourth in the forefront moving up close to the Confederate breastworks. Soon Seaver came up with the rest of the brigade, and another repositioning was made. Leaving the Fourth Vermont where it was and moving the Sixth back to a sheltered spot in the field, Grant maneuvered the Second, Third, and Fifth Regiments to a point where a crisis had developed just north of the Bloody Angle. There South Carolinians under Samuel McGowan had battled their way to the east side of the entrenchments. The Vermonters went in, pushing up near the west side of the earthworks, yards from the Rebels. The fighting quickly became brutal. "There began one of the most desperate struggles of the war, for the possession of the angle," said George Benedict.

Private Erie Ditty, Sixth Vermont, said, "It was like a slaughter pen." According to Lewis Grant, "It was literally a hand to hand fight. Nothing but the piled up logs of the breastworks separated the combatants. Our men would reach over the logs and fire into the faces of the enemy, and stab over with their bayonets. Many were shot and stabbed through crevices in the logs. Scores were shot down within a few feet of the death-dealing muskets." Seth Eastman: "The enemy was on one side of the breastworks and we were on the other side, and remained in this situation for several hours."

Private Henry Houghton, Third Vermont:

Sometimes a white flag would show above the rebels works and when our fire slackened some would jump over and surrender, and others would be crowded down to fill their places. I saw one man jump over and turn and take deliberate aim at his late comrades and fire, he said he was conscripted into their army but had never fired at the Yanks . . . It was a terrible battle, probably the fiercest and most deadly of the war.

Wilbur Fisk:

We could touch their guns with ours. They would load, jump up and fire into us, and we did the same to them. Almost every shot that was made took effect.

Along the dirt-and-log west face of the Mule Shoe, not far south of its tip, the most intense and sustained face-to-face fighting of the entire Civil War raged. And amid the smoke and blood, rain and mud, all the horror and dying, the bravery of Vermonters was again dramatically demonstrated. "Men mounted the works," Lewis Grant said, "and with muskets rapidly handed up, kept up a continuous fire until they were shot down, when others would take their places and continue the deadly work." Wilbur Fisk:

> Some of our boys would jump clear up on to the breastworks and fire, then down, reload and fire again, until they were themselves picked off. If ancient or modern history contains instances of more determined bravery than was shown there, I can hardly conceive in what way it could have been exhibited.

Command of the Second Vermont that May 12, because of the heavy losses in previous fighting, was in the hands of a captain, Dayton Clark, a Montpelier man. Years later he wrote,

> My duties caused me to move up and down the entire length of my line, and you may be sure I had all I could attend to. The men were reaching over the breast-works and firing into the confederates on the other side, as well as trying to punch them with bayonets, and the confederates were doing the same thing . . . During this time I noticed private Noyes standing on top of the breast-works within ten or fifteen feet of where a large number of confederates were lying low, and he was deliberately drawing a bead on each one of these as fast as his comrades could pass up freshly loaded muskets to him: the number of shots fired in this way I could not pretend to tell, but certainly there were not less than fifteen, and it may have been twice that number.

Bullets whistled around the man, and one knocked off his cap, but he was unhurt. The captain was referring to Pvt. William Wallace Noyes, a farm lad from East Montpelier, serving as a substitute for a Montpelier man, Joseph Sterling, who had bought his way out of the war. Many years later, Noyes received the Medal of Honor for his heroics.

Again Lewis Grant:

> Some men clubbed their muskets, others used clubs and rails. General

Upton personally attended to the serving of two pieces of artillery . . . [nearby] the celebrated tree (22 inches in diameter) was cut off by bullets; there that the brush and logs were cut to pieces and whipped into basket-stuff; there that fallen men's flesh was torn from their bones and the bones shattered; there that the rebel ditches and cross-sections were filled with dead men several deep. Some of the wounded were almost entirely buried by the dead bodies of their companions that had fallen upon them. In this way the Vermont brigade was engaged for about eight hours.

After the war, Benedict contacted Brig. Gen. Samuel McGowan, who fought, and was wounded, on the other side of those works. The Confederate said, "Our men lay on one side of the breastwork, the enemy on the other; and in many instances men were pulled over. The trenches on the right, in the angle, ran with blood, and had to be cleared of the dead more than once."

Private Norman Johnson, Second Vermont, noted his wounding in a matter-of-fact way in his diary: "Started for another battlefield about nine in the morning. Was hit in the right side and wrist. Got to the hospital about four in the afternoon." In the Third Vermont, Cpl. William Norris was among a group taking punishment from an enemy marksman firing from an aperture along the contested works. Several men were hit before a bullet struck the St. Johnsbury lad in the forehead, killing him instantly. But the flash of the muzzle revealed the Rebel's position, the barrel of his rifle barely poking from between the ends of two logs. Sgt. G. W. Bonner, of St. Johnsbury, directed the fire of eight of his men at the spot, and no more shots came from that source.

Nearby, waiting for a call to go into action that never came, Maj. Lemuel Abbott, 10th Vermont, wrote,

Surely this fierce struggle of armies can't last more than a day more . . . It is wet and depressing for the "Slaughter Pen" will be our portion next without Lee withdraws tonight which God grant he may do if it is His will. The thought that we may have to assault into the jaws of death at the bloody angle in the gray of the morning is appalling . . . The rattle and roar of musketry is dreadful as I write and may continue all night.

Amid all that appalling fury, as it had done for two furious days in the Wilderness and in the Confederate trenches two days previous, the Vermont Brigade hung on. Sgt. Charles Morey: "Fought the enemy for nine long hours, they occupying one side of the parapet and we the other, the most desperate fighting I ever knew of." G. G. Benedict:

> Outside the angle the carnage was less frightful; but in the bushes and along the ground in front of the rebel breastworks, for nearly half a mile, lay hundreds of bodies of men of the Second and Sixth corps, who fell in the assault. The fight at the angle continued with great fury till nearly dark, the rain falling heavily meantime, and the darkness settling early.

Private John Greene, Fourth Vermont, from Williamstown, noted in his diary, "Hard fighting all day . . . Raining day and night. Minnie balls fly some fighting all night." The Vermont Brigade, with troops and ammunition played out, was withdrawn from the salient's west face as darkness came down over the still-raging battle. The fighting would go on until 3 AM, when Lee began to withdraw his exhausted men, having completed new entrenchments across the base of the embattled salient. The Vermonters moved back into the woods, to the right, and at last were permitted to break ranks and rest. It seems likely that they slept, in the rain and mud, almost instantly.

While the fighting at the Bloody Angle raged, off to the east, on the far, or east, face of the Mule Shoe salient, Ambrose Burnside's Ninth Corps had attacked in support of Hancock's assault. Lt. Col. Charles Cummings' 17th Vermont, in Col. Simon Griffin's brigade, was engaged, though Cummings missed the fight. The regimental commander had marched with his men to Spotsylvania, but the head wound sustained in the Wilderness was still troubling, and he was ordered to the hospital by the regimental surgeon.

Cummings was in a field hospital on May 12, when he wrote his wife, Elizabeth, in Brattleboro,

The regiment was ordered forward with the rest of the brigade. Although it rained in torrents, they drove in the enemy's skirmishers and then charged the rifle pits but unsuccessfully. Here the loss was great. I was in the hospital assisting in dressing the wounds of my men as they came in as long as I could stand up, and the sight was fearful. The regiment continued fighting nearly all that day and part of the next, and my report from the Adjutant was that there were less than 130 guns left. Certainly of all that went into the fight that morning of the 6th [the regiment's first day of fighting, in the Wilderness] nearly 3/5ths are killed or wounded! Some of the wounded must have fallen into the enemy's hands when we were forced to retire from the charge on Thursday morning. But the men have sustained the reputation of Vermont. They have not faltered, nor did they lose their colors as others did in the futile charge although they advanced as fast and as far. The mortality among officers is fearful . . .

Later, Cummings wrote a more considered report on his regiment's fighting on May 12. The colonel said that the 17th advanced at 4 AM, with the 31st Maine and Sixth New Hampshire Regiments, and drove a Confederate skirmish line about a mile before coming on the main line of Rebel works. He said the 17th blazed away until 7 AM when, with ammunition gone, it was withdrawn from the front line. At 11 AM, he said, the 17th again moved forward, this time with a Pennsylvania regiment, but was soon driven back to the shelter of "a wooded knoll." The 17th remained there through the day as "the enemy made several attempts to dislodge us, with shell, grape and canister, from a battery distant about four hundred yards from our front." Under cover of darkness, the 17th was able to erect a breastwork of log, rails, and earth, and behind it spent a long and wet night.

Also engaged near the Bloody Angle were Vermont's three sharpshooter companies. Charles Mead wrote,

We charged up to the abatis and lay there. I fired some rounds. We got a heavy fire. I left, almost the last one, and miraculously escaped the bullets and grape. Mattocks was (I fear) mortally wounded. [Pvt. Henry

A Confederate soldier killed at Spotsylvania Court House. HOWARD COFFIN COL-
LECTION

Mattocks, of Tinmouth, died the next day,] Uncle Tom [Pvt. Thomas
Brown, of Ryegate] killed . . . Steady fighting all day. Co. F. looks sadly
small . . . Rainy night.

Company F lost that day three killed and two wounded. Companies E
and H together suffered but one casualty.

The battle for the salient was over. It had been a confused and ter-
rifying slugging match in the mud and rain. The men who were there
knew they had been in a desperate fight, but it was not until the fighting ended and they were able to walk about the battlefield that a full
realization came of what had transpired on that damp and deadly May
day. Wilbur Fisk:

I visited the place the next morning, and though I have seen horrid
scenes since this war commenced, I never saw anything half so bad as
that. Our men lay piled one top of another, nearly all shot through the
head. There were many among them that I knew well, five from my
own company. On the rebel side it was worse than on ours. In some

places the men were piled four or five deep, some of whom were still alive.

Lewis Grant, who had seen many a grim field:

The sight the next day was repulsive and sickening, indeed . . . Many of the dead men were horribly mangled, and the logs, trees and brush exhibited unmistakable signs of a fearful conflict.

The 10th Vermont, and the rest of Ricketts' divison of the Sixth Corps, had been fortunate that day to be held in reserve. The regiment suffered not a single casualty. However, Chaplain Haynes later saw the Bloody Angle, and wrote,

The mutual carnage was frightful. Here it may be said without exaggeration that the dead "lay in heaps" and the soil was "miry with blood." The slain were piled upon each other—packed up so as to form defences for those who prolonged the battle, and the whole field was covered with a mass of quivering flesh.

Pvt. Edwin Hall, also in the 10th, said,

In one spot in their trench, I counted the dead and dying lying 5 deep and on the trunk and in the branches of an oak tree which had been felled before the battle commenced, I counted 27 dead men—shot as they were passing through or over it.

Major Abbott, of the 10th:

The sight of the enemy's dead is something dreadful. There are three dead lines of battle a half mile more or less in length—men killed in every conceivable way. The wounded are fairly bound in by the dead . . . the breastwork is filled with dead and wounded where they fell, several deep nearly to the top in front . . . The dead as a whole as they lie in their works are like an immense wedge with its head toward the works. Think of such a mass of dead! Hundreds and hundreds piled top of each other! At the usual distance in rear of these breastworks—about ninety feet—are two more complete dead lines of battle about one hundred feet apart the dead bodies lying where the men fell in line of battle shot dead in their tracks. The lines are perfectly defined by dead men so close they touch each other. Many of the bodies have turned black, the stench is terrible, and the sight shocking beyond description. I saw several wounded men in the breastworks buried under their dead, just move a hand a little as it stuck up through the interstices above the dead bodies that buried the live ones otherwise completely out of sight . . . Could anything in Hades be any worse?

Private Erie Ditty, Sixth Vermont, wrote,

I went over the works after the battle. It was terrible. In some places the dead lay three deep . . . Gun carriages, horses, and men participating in that 24 hours of leaden rain were literally torn to shreds.

On May 13, writing to his wife in the northern Vermont town of Fletcher for the first time since May 3, Lt. Chester Leach of Company H, Second Vermont, said,

I can say but little what we have done or who is killed or wounded, only that about two-thirds of our Co., Regt. & Brigade are gone. Seven have been killed, & one died from wounds . . . making 8 in all as far as heard from. E. W. Squires is the only one from Fletcher that is killed, but a number are wounded, L. M. Bingham, C. Spaulding, Rob Fulton, Nathan and Wait Scott, slightly wounded. We have but five or six officers left out of over twenty when we left camp. Col. Killed, Lt. Col. Wounded, one Capt. Killed, Capt. Bixby, Co. E. Only one Capt. left with the Regt. We were in a fight nearly all day yesterday, & I don't know what the loss of our Co. was yet, for they were mixed up with other troops, & when we were relieved by other troops, I could get together but six, & now I have but four privates, all told, but they will find their Regt. in time. Fred Marshall was killed yesterday. It is impossible to tell how long the fighting will last, but if we keep at it much longer as we have, there will be nobody left to fight . . .

When the butcher's bill was tallied, it was determined that the Vermont Brigade had sustained 254 more casualties. A total of 42 men had been killed, 186 wounded, with 26 men missing. Historian Benedict calculated the loss of the 17th Regiment to have been lower than Colonel Cummings' battlefield estimate. Nonetheless, it was considerable, being 17 killed, 51 wounded, and 2 missing.

In Vermont, on May 12, rain also fell. William Hoyt wrote, "cloudy . . . and rainy morning. Cool S wind during the forenoon of the day, then to north again at evening." Alney Stone, in the northwestern Vermont town of Westford, wrote: "Went to David Sibley's got 10 bushels of potatoes and six of corn got home at noon plowed in the afternoon." In St. Johnsbury, Henry Herrick was worried about his upcoming vacation, and about events military:

> Have been trying all week to make things come right for Zenas and I to go to Cabot Saturday and stay next week but they do not come fully right yet. The papers tonight announce a severe fight Tuesday near Spotsylvania C. H. in which we are the gainers taking many prisoners. This makes six days continuous and severe fighting. God grant it may not be in vain, there is nothing discouraging about it except the heavy losses.

Back on the battered, blood-soaked earth north of Spotsylvania Court House, Private Fisk concluded his report on the Bloody Angle: "I turned away from that place, glad to escape from such a terrible, sickening sight. I have sometimes hoped, that if I must die while I am a soldier, I should prefer to die on the battle-field, but after looking at such a scene, one cannot help turning away and saying, any death but that."

⌖

The great Mule Shoe salient of the Spotsylvania Court House battlefield is preserved, a quiet place of green fields and pleasant woods. The peacefulness of the place today is in utter contrast to its hours of horror in 1864. Yet the grassy remnants of once deep trenches that wind for miles across the gentle landscape speak of the time of war. Still one may walk the narrow road down which Union soldiers moved on May 10 to launch Emory Upton's brilliant attack. Crossing the fields from the woods to the first line of Confederate trenches, as did the attackers, one may continue through the fields to find the second line of Rebel works, briefly and bravely held by Vermonters. Nearby, the Bloody Angle area remains perhaps the most lovely of all Civil War battlefield places, its soft, muted beauty somehow speaking eloquently to the magnitude of the events, and the depths of suffering, that once occurred there. Move far down the Mule Shoe and one eventually comes to the forbidding, still-deep trenches of General Lee's third line, which the Vermonters and others tried unsuccessfully to assault several days after the Bloody Angle fight.

Chapter Eight

THE WOUNDED

During the night I was taken in an ambulance and carried to the old mining mill. The sun was just rising when I was being laid on the damp ground, without a blanket over or under me. Hundreds of others about me were no better cared for than myself. In the next ambulance that was being laid down was a young soldier. His sighs and groans were dreadful. His thigh was badly shattered, and his hair and face were all covered with dry blood, for he had a bad wound in his head. I did not know him until I heard his voice. I looked at him and exclaimed, "My God, is that you Dan Schofield?" One of our own company boys. I tried to cheer him up by telling him we were all right and would soon be taken to a hospital. "Oh, my leg is nothing," he said, "but my head." The next day, all battle-stained and battle-taken, on a southern field, the patriot died, and his friends know not his resting place.

Thus did one wounded Vermonter, Peter Chase of Weston, describe the death of Daniel Schofield of Hinesburg, a fellow private in Company I, of the Second Vermont Regiment. Both men had been shot on May 5, two of the more than seventeen thousand casualties the Army of the Potomac suffered in the Wilderness. When the great battle ended, the tangled woods and clearings were filled with wounded men, more than one thousand of them Vermonters. The medical staff of the Union army faced an impossible medical challenge.

While Ulysses Grant's Overland Campaign rolled southeast and savage fighting developed around Spotsylvania Court House, another great drama was being played out to the rear. As the fighting of May 5 and 6 ended, the wounded had been taken to hastily organized field hospitals in or near the Wilderness. Private Chase said,

During the forenoon I was taken into the surgeon's tent and lain on the amputating table. I had expected to lose one of my legs. If I had ever been brave or shown any nerve, the sight of the large pile of amputated limbs, which lay outside and in sight, and the thought that I had to give one of my limbs to that ghastly heap, took the courage all out of me and I begged them to spare my leg. "We will not take a hair more than we are obliged to," said the doctor. I took chloroform and they removed the musket ball and some pieces of bone. I was then taken to a large tent where I remained the next day. They were hurrying the wounded back to Fredericksburg. During the afternoon it became known that all of the wounded could not be moved, so those that could stand the journey were moved first. I rode all that night over a very rough road and did not get any sleep or rest. The 8th was Sunday . . . This morning in the ambulance near Piney Creek [Branch] church, we drive out toward Chancellorsville, then toward Fredericksburg.

The private said that on the way,

Several times when the [wagon] train stopped they took men out who had not the strength to endure the dreadful journey. They had answered to the call of death, their torture was at an end. There were hundreds on foot. Many a brave soldier walked the whole distance with an amputated hand or forearm in a sling . . . The suffering which men endured in those two days will never be told . . . The 9th brought us into Fredericksburg about 4 PM. I had seen the city several times, but never did it look so good to me.

Ulysses Grant had planned to move the wounded due north, back across the Rapidan for evacuation to Washington by train. But the threat of raiders along that route caused him to direct the hospital wagons to Fredericksburg, then north to the federal supply bases along the Potomac, where ships would transport them back to the capital.

Virtually all the wounded had a story to tell. A Rebel bullet had torn open the belly of Capt. Edward Carter, and, in agony, he was taken to a field hospital where he came under the care of Surgeon Stevens, of the 77th New York. According to Carter, the doctor, "returned the protruding bowels and sewed the wounds together." Since his wound appeared to be fatal, Carter was told he would not be evacuated to Fredericksburg. But the feisty captain drew a pistol and ordered himself loaded into an ambulance. The rough conveyance jolted through the darkness, only reaching Fredericksburg in the morning. Carter recalled that he was taken from the ambulance and carried into "a negro hut," and laid behind the door. Later, he was "carried to the house occupied by the wounded of the Vermont brigade," where his wounds were dressed. Carter would endure the onset of boils and bedsores, living daily on doses of morphine.

Sergeant Twitchell, of the Fourth Vermont, shot in the head, was carried to a field hospital in the Wilderness. "I was told that when taken back," he said,

> the surgeon insisted that it was only a waste of time to bother with me; but at the earnest solicitations of Ernest Bellamy, a schoolmate of mine, he finally put a bandage around my head . . . The next day about ten AM, I woke up perfectly conscious and found myself lying upon the ground between two bodies from which life had departed . . . Sometime during the day they took off my coat, which was a mass of blood in front, washed it, put it on again, and I was carried into a large tent, where I found Captain Lillie, Amidon, and others of the brigade. My cap was lost and my head swollen so large that I was evidently not a pleasant object to look upon. The pitying looks I was given as I was brought in said plainer than words, "Poor fellow, he can't live."

Twitchell was deemed a hopeless case. "There are no ambulances for dead men," he was told. Yet with a mighty effort, the sergeant roused himself and staggered onto the road, stumbling along until he collapsed at the roadside between two trees.

> My next remembrance is of the morning, when I heard a man say, "I think he belongs to the Vermont Brigade on account of the white cross [Sixth Corp badge] which he has upon his breast. You had better put him into the ambulance." I have since learned that it was a detachment of the 1st Vermont Cavalry which was passing that picked me up . . . My first consciousness after this was of someone putting a new bandage on my head . . . I can recall but little of what passed the next day until I was taken out and carried into a church in Fredericksburg.

The wounded who reached Fredericksburg had endured a torturous trip in springless wagons, jouncing over rutted roads, to arrive in a battle-damaged enemy town. Certainly, a few thousand wounded Yankees was the last thing the four thousand southern residents wanted to see. Bruce Catton wrote a century later:

> It was about one in the morning of May 9 when the head of this great caravan of misery came creaking down into sleeping Fredericksburg, a wrecked, half-lifeless town that lay across the path of war . . . seven thousand wounded men coming in at one in the morning, with no one riding on ahead to announce their coming or to get things ready for them, and not one sullen resident owning the slightest desire to help the Army of the Potomac. Most of them were simply laid on the floor—any floor that was handy. Many buildings were still half-wrecked from Burnside's bombardment of 1862 and contained puddles of stagnant rain water that was coming in through gaping holes in the roof, and men were dumped down in this seepage so that the pools became bloody.

Private Chase said he was

put into a large unfinished brick house in the city. On the morning of the 10th a surgeon with two helpers came into the room to dress the wounds. The worst treatment I received in all my army service was from the brute that called himself an army surgeon. He appeared to be void of all feeling for humanity, and seemed to delight in torturing the wounded men as much as a savage.

But the next day, Dr. William Sawin, of the Second Vermont, came to visit and Chase said, "It was his kind hands that fixed me up, gave me a quieting powder, and spoke cheerful words to me, and I passed through the night very nicely . . . He said to me: 'This is not my place in this room. I am very tired. I have amputated 100 limbs today.'"

Physician Stevens, who had treated the wounded Captain Carter in the field, left one of the best descriptions of the crisis at Fredericksburg:

The process of unloading the wounded at once commenced; all the churches and other public buildings were first seized and filled. Negroes who could be found in town were pressed into the work, yet, with all the help that could be obtained, it was a slow process. All night and all the next day the work went on. The churches were filled first, then warehouses and stores, and then private houses, until the town was literally one immense hospital . . . No sooner were the men removed from the ambulances than surgeons and nurses addressed themselves with all the strength that remained to them to relieve the immediate wants of the sufferers. Never before had such Herculean labors been thrown upon so small a body of men, yet nobly did they accomplish the task. All the buildings in town were full of wounded men, the walks were covered with them, and long trains of ambulances were filling the streets with more. Yet to relieve the wants of all these thousands of suffering men not more than forty surgeons had been sent from the field. It was one grand funeral; men were dropping away on every side. Large numbers of nurses were detailed as burial parties, and these plied the work day after day with hardly time for their needed rest. Surgeons were completely worn out, and many of them had to be sent to Washington, fairly broken down with their labors.

Doctor Stevens included in his account a letter written by another, unnamed surgeon:

All yesterday I worked at the operating table. That was the fourth day I had worked at those terrible operations since the battle commenced . . . Oh! It is awful. It does not seem as though I could take a knife in my hand to-day, yet there are hundreds of cases of amputations waiting for me. Poor fellows come and beg almost on their knees for the first chance to have an arm taken off. It is a scene of horror such as I never saw . . . It is fearful. I see so many grand men dropping one by one. They are my acquaintances and my friends. They look to me for help . . . Mrs. Lewis has just come; what a blessing her presence will be to the colonel [Lt. Col. John Lewis, of the Fifth Vermont], who bears the loss of his arm so bravely. Colonel Barney of the Sixth Vermont died yesterday . . . Major Dudley [Fifth Vermont] lies in the room where I am writing, seriously wounded . . . Hundreds of ambulances are coming into town now, and it is almost midnight. So they come every night.

So help was arriving from Vermont. The wife of Colonel Lewis had arrived from Burlington, and she would nurse her husband back to health. Other Vermonters, on being informed of the desperate situation, that husbands, sons, brothers were suffering in Fredericksburg, headed south. Still others came. On May 12, the day of the Bloody Angle fight at Spotsylvania, in St. Albans, the *Messenger* published the following editorial:

Our readers read with pleasure yesterday the announcement that Governor Smith had gone to Washington to attend to our war wounded. We are glad, and all who have friends who may be among the wounded will be grateful to him that this is so. It is at great personal sacrifice and inconvenience that he has gone. But he will be amply repaid in gratitude of the wounded and of their friends, and in the consciousness of high duty performed . . . He can do a great work there—in seeing that the wounded are well cared for, in getting those who are able into state hospitals, or perhaps their homes . . . in giving the soldiers to feel that they are not forgotten . . .

It seems to have been on May 10, the day of Upton's assault, that Gov. John Gregory Smith, the railroad man, left his hometown of St.

Albans, by train, bound for the war zone. En route, the train may have stopped near Burlington where Dr. Samuel Thayer, Vermont's surgeon general, joined the governor on board. Smith had gone south in response to grim news of heavy casualties at the front. How he learned of the crisis with the wounded is not known for certain, but a good bet is that Adj. Gen. Peter Washburn, in Woodstock, telegraphed him an early alert. Washburn, administering Vermont's war effort from elm-shaded Woodstock, knew more about what was going on in the war zone than anyone in the state. The serious, quiet, workaholic lawyer, who bore something of a resemblance to Abraham Lincoln, was considered by Vermonters to be the finest of all the northern states' adjutant generals. Surely, his early reports on the massive Vermont casualties from the Wilderness would have come from Frank H. Holbrook, who since 1862 had worked in the nation's capital with the title of military commissioner for Vermont at Washington. Also serving Vermont's wounded were two military agents, Robert Corson, in Philadelphia, and Frank Howe, in New York City. Holbrook had been appointed to the job by his father, Frederick Holbrook, who preceded John Smith as governor. The elder Holbrook, during his two terms as

John Gregory Smith, governor of Vermont in 1864, brought Vermont doctors to Fredericksburg to care for the wounded.
HOWARD COFFIN
COLLECTION

Col. Elisha Barney, horribly wounded in the Wilderness, died in a Fredericksburg hospital with his wife at his side. She brought his body to Vermont for burial. VERMONT HISTORICAL SOCIETY

chief executive, had done much for Vermont's wounded, including winning permission for the state to run its own military hospitals. His son now worked energetically in his assignment and he was likely the first Vermont civilian to arrive at Fredericksburg. Indeed, Frank Holbrook likely was responsible for compiling there, on May 11, a list of wounded that was mailed to Washburn's Woodstock office. It was accompanied by a letter from Commissioner Holbrook, which said in part,

> I will send complete reports soon as ever I can do it, but thus far I have been crowded with other matters . . . These are very sad and awful times, but with all more to come. The fighting will not stop and the wounded will necessarily be made of secondary importance.

It seems likely that a summary of the list, at least, was telegraphed to Woodstock. The first page of the document titled "List of Wounded

Collected at Fredericksburg, Va. May 11th 1864," and containing the soldier's name, number of his regiment, company, and nature of wound, read as follows:

Priv. Charles R. Fisk 4 E Rochester, Vt. wound right hip
Sergt. Henry M. Ballard 2 H Georgia wound left thigh
Priv. John McCarry 5 R Underhill side and left arm amputated
Corp. Erastus Worthen 2 B East Rutland right thigh severely
Priv. Ruell R. Wheeler 3 B Brownington both thighs
Alfred Guyett 2 C Burlington left thigh
A Cox 4 G Waterbury right
Reubin Goodwin 3 H Groton left leg
W. R. F. Johnson 2 I Weston right breast
Sergt. H. C. Thomson 3 G Barnet thigh
Geo. Wright 3 G Cabot died May 11
Daniel Skinner 4 H Chelsea left thigh died May 13
Priv. William W. Wheeler 6 A Lincoln left leg to be amputated
Russell Barnes 5 B
Sergt. C. E. Prouty 4 J Townshend
Priv. Chas. Clow 6 K Franklin right thigh
S. G. Conant 2 A Stratton left arm amputated
Corp. Madison Myrick 4 C Ludlow
Priv. Lyman Stoddard 6 G Warren wounded loin
Corp. S. N. Fitch 6 C Windsor left arm amputated 3 fingers left
    Hand
Priv. D. R. Gilchrist 3 H McIntosh Falls leg
James Welch 5 H Brandon left arm and chest
Leverett H. Page 3 C Groton left arm amputated
Merrick G. Page 3 H 4 places died May 13
Sergt. A. W. Ferry 2 F Braintree right leg

The list, in pencil and written in haste, went on for nine pages and contained three hundred names. Obviously, more help was needed. Also traveling to Fredericksburg, perhaps joining Governor Smith when he stopped in Washington, were two Vermont congressmen, Frederick E. Woodbridge, of Vergennes, and Portus Baxter, of the

Canadian border town of Derby. Like the governor, Woodbridge, a longtime mayor of the little city of Vergennes, was a lawyer and railroad executive. Baxter, a sober-faced man of few words, was a friend of Secretary of War Edwin Stanton. He and his wife, Ellen, a native of the east-central Vermont town of Strafford, had already volunteered to help care for the wounded in the Washington hospitals. Baxter would stay longer than any other Vermont public official in Fredericksburg, and on his return to the capital he and his wife would intensify their efforts there on behalf of the casualties.

A man named Thompson traveled to Frederickburg from Vermont, perhaps with Governor Smith. This may well have been John R. Thompson, of St. Johnsbury, who served as a lieutenant in the nine-month 15th Vermont Regiment and had been discharged the previous summer. A letter signed J. R. Thompson appeared in the *St. Johnsbury Caledonian*, giving perhaps the best description that has survived of the governor's mission of mercy. It indicated that the governor had traveled by boat from Washington, down the Potomac River to the army supply base at Belle Plain, where the account apparently begins:

The 14th, Governor Smith, Dr. Thayer of Burlington, F. Holbrook, state agent, and representatives Baxter and Woodbridge, of Vermont arrived, and at last, procuring two ambulances . . . which we loaded with bandages, and such other stores as were most indispensible, we proceeded about ten miles to Fredericksburg. What we had seen at Belle Plain, and on the road, had prepared me to expect much at Fredericksburg, but I was not prepared for the "hell of horror" to which we were introduced here. I could not, if I would, paint you the ghastly picture, nor can your imagination reach the reality. The town, which was a beautiful city, has been mostly burned and stripped by the contending armies, and nearly every building remaining contains, through roof and wall, from one to thirty rents made by shot and shell. Nearly all the large buildings remaining had been converted into so-called hospitals. Here is a large church, there a block of stores, here a warehouse, and there again a large mansion, literally crowded with wounded to the number of 7,000 or 8,000 lying on the hard, dirty floor, and most of them have not even a blanket

over them. Here they had lain for days with scarcely a change in position. Many of them had been wounded eight or nine days, and had lain
on the field and here, with their wounds undressed, and little or no
attention otherwise, since they were first attended to hastily in the field.
As a consequence, many of their wounds were putrid and filled with
worms, and the atmosphere in the rooms was almost intolerable. None
who could get out could endure it more than a few minutes at a time.
This was not confined to one particular room, but it is a type of nearly
all—it seemed as we looked upon them as though we had suddenly left
the bright and beautiful world, where the sun shone, the birds sang, and
men laughed, and been ushered into the grim court of Death, where a
mighty holocaust of blood was being offered, with our friends and brothers for victims. It seemed as though, could the grim tyrant have been
impersonated, and stood with us, he would have been touched with pity
and stayed his hand. But we were reminded that our duty lay not in emotions of pity, but by kind care and prompt treatment in snatching what
we could from his grasp, and at once went to work . . . [Congessman]
Baxter will be specially remembered by the boys in procuring, in spite of
orders and opposition, the immediate transfer of stores . . . The Vermont
surgeons came like angels of mercy, among them Drs. Newell and
Browne of St. Johnsbury, were perfect Godsends. They were given
important charges at once and went to work with a will. A different order
of things could be seen in the hospitals in a short time . . .

Several Vermont doctors hurried to Fredericksburg, where, upon
their arrival, the suffering of the state's wounded had intensified.
Peter Chase wrote,

On the 13th one of our number was taken up stairs in the morning to
have his leg amputated. He was soon brought back without the operation being performed. Tears were in his eyes and he was nearly broken
down with grief so that he could not tell what was the trouble, but we
soon learned that the doctors thought mortification had set in, and it
was useless to do any thing more for him. The poor fellow's greatest
desire was to write a letter home to his wife and children in Massachusetts, but he was destitute of anything to write with. He was soon pro-

Col. John Tyler, Second Vermont, died on his way home to Brattleboro of wounds suffered in the Wilderness. VERMONT HISTORICAL SOCIETY

vided with writing materials, and he sat up and wrote his farewell message to those who were so dear to him.

And Chase wrote,

The 18th the weather was quite warm and the flies became more and more troublesome every day, owing to the odor that arose from the wounds, and one was obliged to exercise great care to keep them off from his wounds . . . About this time Gov. Smith arrived with a force of doctors, from the state, to look after and care for the wounded men. One of these noble men from the town of Brighton was assigned to our room. He was a welcome guest, for he had not been overworked as our army surgeons had been for two weeks, and we now had good care, for our wounds were dressed every day.

Chase added, "Our friend who wrote his farewell letter home to his wife and children was with us as chipper as any of us."

Chase noted that he had been taken to a church, which was serving as a hospital. Though it is nearly impossible today to identify specific buildings in Fredericksburg that housed specific soldiers, it is known that the Baptist Church in downtown Fredericksburg at one time sheltered Sixth Corps soldiers. There the baptismal font was used as a bathing tub, while the pastor's study, in back of the pulpit, became an operating room. A Pennsylvania soldier wrote sometime in May,

> The poor yanks are still dieing. Some of them dies hard and some of them dies easy. One came in and got his wounded head dressed and then he fell asleep and never got awake . . . There is one poor one laying by my side he has been dieing for the last six or eight hours and he is not dead yet nor don't seem to be nearer than he was when he began . . . I am afraid he is not prepared to die. I have heard him sware . . . like a trooper and a chaplain came to him . . . but he cut him off and said he should not bother him . . .

Vermont Surgeon General Thayer:

> Immediately after our arrival we reported to the Medical Director, who gave us permission to go in search of wounded Vermonters. We found them scattered throughout the city, a large proportion of them stretched upon the floors of churches, deserted houses, stores and shops, with nothing underneath them except their tattered and blood-stiffened garments, with amputated stumps, shattered limbs and ugly flesh wounds which had not been dressed for four or five days . . . They did not utter a murmur of complaint—not a murmur escaped their lips—but with patience and heroic endurance bore their sufferings and privations in a manner worthy of the good cause in which they have suffered.

Historian G. G. Benedict wrote years later,

> The thousand Vermonters taken [to Fredericksburg] probably fared better than the majority of this army of unfortunates, owing to the extraordinary efforts put forth by the state authorities for their relief. Governor Smith and Surgeon Thayer went in person to Fredericksburg, and gave able and unwearied effort to the care of the wounded, and the surgical force in charge of them was enlarged by dispatching thither fifteen or twenty of the best physicians and surgeons in Vermont.

Benedict listed the following Vermont doctors who joined Governor Smith in Fredericksburg: G. F. Gale, of Brattleboro; J. M. Knox, of Burlington; C. M. Chandler, of Montpelier; C. G. Adams, of Island Pond; W. M. Huntington, of Rochester; A. C. Welch, of Williston; J. F. Miles, of Hinesburg; D. W. Haselton, of Cavendish; H. Powers, of Morrisville; B. Fairchild, of Milton; S. Newell and H. S. Brown, of St. Johnsbury; and C. S. Cahoon of Lyndonville.

As the Vermont delegation settled in to help the wounded, Dr. Melvin Hyde, assistant surgeon of the Second Vermont, from Isle La Motte, in Lake Champlain, arrived in Fredericksburg with a harrowing tale. Hyde had treated casualties from the Wilderness near Chancellorsville, and after the ambulances had moved most of his patients, the doctor had volunteered to stay with a group of severely wounded men, including thirteen Vermonters. Hyde wrote to his wife, Alice, that Confederate cavalry had suddenly appeared "and took me and my wounded prisoners but they did not disturb my hospital—on the contrary they acted like gentlemen—they surrounded my hospital and the woods about 50 rods off was full of them." Hyde said that after four days as a prisoner, Union ambulances arrived just when "the rebs happened to be out of sight searching for plunder." He added, "We got off all right with our ambulances to Fredericksburg."

Doctor Hyde then wrote,

Gov. Smith, Baxter and Woodbridge (Members Congress) lodged with me in a rebel house in Fredericksburgh. I gave up the sofa which I slept on to Smith and gave my blankets and quilts to Dr. Thayer and the two Members & laid me down on the floor without any. Just like me, wasn't it? They stayed here two days and two nights. Last Monday the 16th they went down to Belle Plains on the Potomac 10 miles from here to take the steamer for Washington. I went down with them with 200 men which I sent to Washington. Baxter is still here, but leaves this morning. They are still fighting desperately about 10 miles from here near Spotsylvania Court House.

A Boston newspaper correspondent who visited Fredericksburg reported that Governor Smith spent his time directing his assistants, laboring with his own hands, hunting up the sick and wounded, giving up his own cot, sleeping on the bare floor or not sleeping at all, cheering the despondent, writing sympathetic letters to fathers and mothers whose sons were in the hospitals, or had given up their lives for their country.

The governor apparently had departed Fredericksburg by May 17, for on that day he telegraphed a letter to the *Free Press* in Burlington that was published the next day, complete with some inflated statistics:

Editors of the Free Press:
I have just returned from Fredericksburg and our wounded, securing all the care possible though suffering badly. The First Brigade entered the field thirty-four hundred and ninety strong, and up to last Saturday lost twenty-seven hundred and ninety. Our men fought with utmost valor and have crowned themselves and the state with glory. I am arranging to get the wounded to Vermont as rapidly as possible. No bodies can be removed from the field at present. Friends desiring to visit the wounded can get passes by applying to Commissioner Holbrook. I send an additional list of wounded and killed.
     J. GREGORY SMITH

Five days later, Surgeon General Thayer had returned to Burlington and told the *Free Press* that the Vermont losses had not been as severe as Smith had been led to believe. Based on what Thayer said, the paper reported,

The sufferings of our wounded at Fredericksburg, from lack of beds, supplies, and medical care, have been dreadful. When Dr. Thayer arrived there, thousands were lying in their bloody garments on the bare floors, and some had not had their wounds dressed for FIVE DAYS. The horrible condition of a wound left undressed for such a time in hot weather, can only be imagined by those who have witnessed such a sight.

Certainly, those words were read by many loved ones of Vermont soldiers with utter horror.

While hospitalized at Fredericksburg, many Vermont wounded wrote home of their situation, and of the circumstances that had brought them there. Capt. Erastus Buck, the popular commander of Company D of the Third Vermont, had been severely wounded in the Wilderness. On May 10, he wrote to his "dear wife and friends" in the northern Vermont town of Coventry:

> I improve a few moments this morning to let you know how I was wounded in two places. Through the left hand and right leg. My wounds are doing well our Brigade is badly cut up nearly half killed or wounded had nine men killed & 23 wounded & 3 missing the rest of the Co. fared about the same. Capt. Bartlett was killed dead J grew was wound. A. Grow was wound through the leg badly. Losson my Co. killed. Campbell the leg badly. Wm. & Geo. Currier not hurt send word to their folks dont worry. About me there is no doubt that I shall get well. We expect we shall be sent to Washington soon, then we shall be sent to Vt., and I shall come home. Lieut Goodall has a wound in the right hand. We have awful fighting the battle commenced Thursday night and still continues we have driven the enemy and think we are all right. But what a slaughter of men . . .

Also on May 10, Sgt. Edward Holton, Sixth Vermont, wrote to his "Dear Katie" in Williston from "Hospital of the 2d Div., 6th Corps, Fredericksburgh, Va.," telling her of the fighting in the Wilderness on May 5:

> Our last charge we gained 40 Rods more than we had had and found a pile of dead Rebs. Just as the last charge was ordered and we had risen up to pour a volley in a percussion bullet struck David in the head, killing him instantly and about 15 minutes after one struck my leg just below the knee and striking the bone. It bounded out leaving me pretty lame and sore yet it is not dangerous and I can get on a trifle on it. As soon as I can get to Washington I shall try and get a leave of absence and come home.

Dr. Melvin Hyde was for a time a Confederate prisoner as he remained with the wounded near the Wilderness battlefield. VERMONT HISTORICAL SOCIETY

Private George Howard, Sixth Vermont, wrote home to Rutland on May 10, obviously glad to be out of the fighting:

> I hasten to inform you of my present comfortable condition. During the battle of the P. M. of May 5th I received a slight but bloody buck shot wound under my right eye which has troubled me but little since the first three days . . . Also when an order came to fall slightly back to relieve us from flank fires, which was partly accomplished and our line nearly steady again when I was struck by a Minnie on the inner side of the left knee causing a sore but not dangerous wound which force me to leave. No bones are broken.

Private Solomon Heaton, Third Vermont from Brighton in northeastern Vermont, shipped to Fredericksburg from the Wilderness, wrote to his mother: "I am in good health at present although I have been wounded in the head be not alarmed for me for I am getting along first rate. I am at work in the Hospital in this City I am in the cook room." Apparently many of the wounded, recovered sufficiently to be of any use, were put to work helping their fellow soldiers.

More wounded rolled into Fredericksburg from Spotsylvania. George Toby, an army teamster, got to Fredericksburg in mid-May, probably transporting wounded from the front. The private from Hinesburg noted in his diary,

> chimbys standes above first met your gaze and as you come into the city you see the church spiris and you see them full of holes that whare made by shell at the Battle of Frediburg as you enter the city you begin to see the wounded the stores are full an the churches a private build-ings and you can not pass a building that is but what is fill with wounded and round the woutskirts you can see where our soldiers are buried from the battle of Freidburg to night makes thirteen days fight—great God when will this end.

On his arrival at Fredericksburg on May 15, Pvt. Darius Priest, Second Vermont, wrote to his wife in Mount Holly: "I am alive but all the boys that you know are either dead or wounded. Some of the wounded are very bad . . . don't fear for I will live a long time yet. Will and Steph are very bad off but they will get well."

Private Norman Johnson, Second Vermont, from Marshfield, was shot in the right side and wrist at the Bloody Angle. He wrote in his diary:

> *May 15: Rained, find myself quite comfortable. There are about sixty in the room where I am. Had coffee and hardtack for breakfast and supper.*
> *May 17: Had another bad night, troubled with bowel complaint. Splendid morning. Went outdoors for first time.*
> *May 18: A large number of wounded came in this evening. Wounds mostly caused by shells.*

The medical crisis persisted. According to surgeon Stevens,

For a time it was almost impossible to obtain sufficient supplies either of food or dressings. Everything that could be spared from the field had been sent, but in the field they were still fighting terrible battles, and there was little to spare. Food was obtained in very limited quantities in town, and men went to the houses of citizens and demanded sheets, which were torn into bandages. But large supplies were sent from Washington by the government in a few days, so that all necessary articles were furnished in abundance, with a profusion of lemons, oranges and canned fruit. The Sanitary Commission was also on hand with large supplies of delicacies, which were joyfully received by the wounded heroes, who not only relished the luxuries, but remembered they were the gifts of friends at home, who had not forgotten the soldiers.

Vermonter Peter Chase noted an improvement in conditions.

The 16th was a day of rejoicing for us all, as the supply train came in, and we received more and better rations. The 17th I received a very delightful treat. I was taken from the floor and put in a rough board bunk, and one of the sanitary commission gave me a white shirt in exchange for mine that I had worn ever since I left camp. I think it was the most lively garment I ever parted with.

By May 17, the father of Capt. Horton Keith, commander of Company K, Sixth Vermont, had reached Fredericksburg, from the family home in Sheldon, to care for his son who had been wounded at the Bloody Angle. That day the captain wrote to his sister,

My wound is in the left shoulder breaking part of bone and is called severe though not any worse and I hope I shall be able to go north soon. Father is out making calls on my wounded and my dear sister if you could see how many more are worse off than I am you would thank heaven that I am as well off as I am . . .

The captain soon went to a Washington hospital, then home to Vermont, where he was discharged from the service.

The attitude of Fredericksburg residents was sometimes a problem. Doctor Stevens:

Many of the people . . . exhibited the most malignant spite against the Yankee wounded, but others, while they claimed no sympathy with our cause showed themselves friends of humanity, and rendered us all the assistance in our power. No men, except Negroes and white men unfit for military duty, were left in town, but the women were bitter rebels. Some of them made fierce opposition to the use of their houses as hospitals, but they were occupied notwithstanding their remonstrances.

Stevens said that at one of the town's finest mansions,

A red-haired woman thrust her head out of the side window, in answer to the ring of the door bell:

"What do you want here?"

"We wish to place some wounded officers in this house."

"You can't bring any officers nor anybody else to this house. I'm all

Wounded Union soldiers in Fredericksburg, after the Wilderness. HOWARD COFFIN COLLECTION

alone. I hope you have more honor than to come and disturb defense-less, unprotected women."

"Have you no husband?"

"Yes, thank God, he's a colonel in the confederate service."

"Well, if your husband was at home, where he ought to be, you would not be a defenseless woman."

Stevens said the woman was forced to admit the wounded men to her home, against her protests at the intrusion of "detestable Yankees."

The New York doctor continued, "Day after day, the gloom of death hung over the town. Hundreds of our brave fellows were dying . . ." Stevens also noted that help was daily arriving. "Physicians and nurses from civil life came to our assistance in large numbers," he said:

Some were earnest men, wholly devoted to the object of relieving the distress which they saw on every side. Others had come for selfish pur-poses. Physicians who had never performed an important surgical oper-ation came armed with amputating cases, and seemed to think that there was but one thing to be done, to operate, as they said. Distressed fathers and brothers wandered about the town, in search of informa-tion regarding some son or friend who had been wounded, or perhaps, as they feared, killed.

Doctor Stevens made special mention of the death of Vermont Major Dudley, who, he said,

After suffering untold agony for many days, finally yielded, and died in the embraces of his youthful wife, who had arrived in Fredericksburg just in time to be present during his last hours. The major had gone into the fight sick with a fever, but his determined bravery forbade him to remain quiet. Receiving a severe wound while thus depressed by dis-ease, he gradually sunk, until his brave spirit took its departure.

The army strove to evacuate the wounded from Fredericksburg to hospitals within the safety of Union territory as fast as possible. The men were to be taken by wagon to the Army of the Potomac's supply base at Aquia Creek on the Potomac River as soon as they were able to travel the twelve miles. There ships transported them to Washington and the many military hospitals in and about the capital city. Sgt. Marshall Twitchell told of his journey from Fredericksburg:

> My place was right over the hind axle, as we were started away from the church door to make room for another wagon, I felt certain I would never be able to stand the jar over the corduroy road to Aquia Creek. Looking out, I saw a Negro woman shyly putting her head out of the cabin window. I motioned to her to come to me and asked if she could give me a bundle of straw to sit on. She said, "No massa, but I can give you my pillow." I took the pillow and gave her what small change I had. It was nearly dark before the train moved out on the road for the Potomac. The only incident which occurred during the night was being halted by guerillas, who quickly detached two fine horses from an ambulance containing General Torbert [Brig. Gen. Alfred Torbert, a cavalryman] and got away with them.

Twitchell said that on the docks at Aquia Creek, he recognized "a son of Governor Holbrook," surely Commissioner Frank Holbrook who made many trips with wounded Vermonters from Fredericksburg to the Potomac. Twitchell said he fell asleep on boarding the boat and slept all the way to Washington. "From the time I was wounded I was in constant fear of losing my mind on account of the wounds being in my head," he said. "I opened my eyes in the hospital, found that I was undressed and in a narrow bed upon which, to my surprise, were white sheets." In his confused state, it was several hours before the sergeant realized where he was.

By May 17, Pvt. Darius Priest had reached Emery Hospital in Washington, and he wrote to his wife,

> I arrived here at three o'clock this morning. I left Allen, Will and Stephen at Fredericksburg. I can't tell when they will get away from thare . . . Fifty of our company have been shot since the fifth of May so there is but ten left in the company now . . . I have shot eight of the devils and killed one with my bayonet. Some of our boys have knocked

out their brains with the butts of their guns. I believe we have lost all human feeling whatever, for to step on a dead man or to kneel in pools of blood and lean over the dead bodyes of our own men a man will get used to it after while . . . I may possibly come to Vermont soon and I may not for six months. I shall not go to the front again at any rate.

Back in Fredericksburg, an unknown Vermonter wrote from a temporary hospital to the *Windsor Journal* on May 25:

I go by this man with an arm off, with but one leg and another shot through the body and knowing that he has but a few hours to live, not one have I heard say I am sorry I have entered the service. One of our company, a boy whose father was opposed to his enlisting, had his right arm amputated at the shoulder, and as I am writing a letter home for him day before yesterday he said, "tell mother if I had heard to father I should have escaped this but as it is I must make the best of it." The wounded are being moved as fast as possible to Washington and vicinity and I think by tomorrow will all be gone from here . . . [Fredericksburg] was a place of considerable trade being situated at the head of navigation on the Rappahannock, there were also several manufacturing establishments of considerable importance but they are all ruins now, and the only business now is with army wagons and ambulances the city in fact is one vast hospital.

Peter Chase, due to the severity of his wounds, was one of the last to be transported. "The 25th all day I laid waiting to be moved," he remembered,

and just at night I was taken out and put into an ambulance and taken across the [Rappahannock] river to Falmouth and placed on a flat car, where I remained until morning. I had been here several times before. Once on a cold night in December 1862 [for the first battle of Fredericksburg], as a wounded soldier, having been wounded on the 13th by a musket ball in the left breast, and a gun shot through the left hand, but I was able to care for myself. Now it took two men to move me . . . On the morning of the 26th the cars were run up to Aquia Creek, during a very hard shower, so we were soaked through, for we had nothing but a woolen blanket to protect us. At the landing we were put on a steamboat and taken up the Potomac river to the city of Alexandria . . . Two men took me out of the steamboat on a stretcher and carried me to the Mansion House hospital, and here I received my first bath and a change of clothes, and was placed on a real bed, with feelings that I was at my journey's end.

"At length," said Dr. Stevens, "by the 26th of May, all the wounded men were sent by transports to Washington, and the hospitals were broken up." The military surgeons who had treated the wounded went south, following the army. Stevens: "Escorted by a squadron of cavalry, crossed the country by way of Bowling Green, and, after a three days' journey, rejoined the army at Hanover."

Private William Johnson of the Second Vermont, shot through the body at Bloody Angle, was sent toward Washington on May 23, according to his diary. He arrived there on May 24 and was placed in the Lincoln Hospital, where he reported himself "well cared for." On May 29, he said that a state agent (probably Commissioner Holbrook) "came to transfer us to Burlington." Johnson said he reached the hospital at Brattleboro on June 4, and then was moved on to the Burlington hospital, reaching there June 6 where he experienced "a very bad night, side and back pained me bad." But two days later he reported having "a comfortable night," and added, "seventy new cases came in last night."

On May 24, Commissioner Holbrook sent to Peter Washburn in Woodstock a list of the Vermont wounded being cared for in Washington-area hospitals. Written in pencil on yellowish tissue paper, the list noted the men's names, ranks, and units, and stated where they were confined. Among the hospitals listed were the Fairfax Seminary and Georgetown Seminary, and the Mount Pleasant, Lincoln, Carver, Campbell, and Armory Square Hospitals. The document, which survives at the Vermont State Archives, is perhaps the most striking surviving testimony to the astonishing price Vermont paid in the opening days of Grant's 1864 campaign. The list totals ninety-three pages and includes more than one-thousand names.

Burials in Fredericksburg on May 12, the day of the Bloody Angle fight. HOWARD COFFIN COLLECTION

Marshall Twitchell, so severely wounded in the head, was at last ready to travel north. He boarded a train at Washington that passed through Philadelphia. He wrote, "After we reached Philadelphia it seemed as though the people could not do enough for us. It was one continual ovation from there to Vermont. Just as I was passing out of Brattleboro I heard a rooster crow." Twitchell finally reached his Townshend home and was greeted by his astonished mother, who believed that her son had died of his wounds.

Not so fortunate was Lt. Col. John Tyler, shot in a leg on May 5. On hearing a report that he was wounded, his uncle, Judge Royall Tyler, had mailed an inquiry to Washington, obviously having access to high places. A telegram came to Brattleboro, from no less a personage than Edwin M. Stanton, secretary of war, stating that the young colonel had indeed been wounded and that "the hospital is to be established at Fredericksburg." There Colonel Tyler was taken, but only briefly, for on May 11 he telegraphed home: "Capt. Wales and myself severely wounded Doing Well, be in Washington Soon Ball in leg."

That message prompted Judge Tyler's departure from Brattleboro. On reaching Washington, the decision was made to start for home with the wounded nephew. They reached New York and sought the assistance of a local physician, Dr. Willard Parker, who promptly performed an operation. Colonel Tyler, however, died on Sunday night, May 22, in the city's Metropolitan Hotel. When news of his death reached Brattleboro, his cousin, Gertrude Tyler Brown, grief-stricken, was moved to write a bit of verse in his honor:

> He fell for his country's good,
> Write neath his glorious name
> And paint in letters of blood
> The scroll of his wondrous fame.

⁂

Fredericksburg today, at least the old part along the Rappahannock River, maintains much of the elegant, shaded beauty of a southern colonial river port. At the edge of the river plain are the famous Sunken Road and Marye's Heights, scenes of furious fighting in 1862 and 1863. But war touched all the old town. Walking about its quiet streets today, near the river, it becomes difficult to imagine how all of those antebellum houses, once battered by battle, were filled with the thousands of wounded who came suddenly in the night into the old town in search of care and shelter. The handsome tall-steepled Baptist Church once held wounded of the Sixth Corps. Many antebellum structures in Fredericksburg today are open to the public, as shops and restaurants. Most of them surely housed the wounded of the Wilderness and Spotsylvania as Grant drove his campaign on toward Richmond.

Chapter Nine

ON THE MARCH

While the Army of the Potomac and the Army of Northern Virginia settled into a stalemate around Spotsylvania Court House, elsewhere men in Union blue were on the move. The biggest force in motion, by far, was the cavalry under the command of Maj. Gen. Philip Sheridan, Grant's handpicked man. As the armies closed in on Spotsylvania, Little Phil, itching for a showdown fight with J. E. B. Stuart, went to General Meade and proposed to take all his divisions off to threaten Richmond. Stuart, he knew, would have to give him battle. Meade was skeptical, and the two fiery men had words. But Ulysses Grant settled the matter by siding with Sheridan, and off he went riding toward the Confederate capital, with twelve thousand mounted soldiers, including Addison Preston's First Vermont Cavalry.

The expedition, known as "Sheridan's Raid," got going early on the morning John Sedgwick was killed, May 9. Sheridan's three divisions at first moved to the east, swinging well away from the infantry. James Wilson's command, including the First Vermont, trotted toward Fredericksburg on a road choked by ambulances. "We marched toward Fredericksburg for several miles," said Horace Ide, "so as to deceive the enemy in regard to our destination, but at the point where the

Telegraph Road crosses Massaponax Run we were joined by the whole command under Sheridan."

The Telegraph Road, an old Virginia thoroughfare, ran due south, into Richmond. Sheridan headed his command down it, looking for a fight. Lt. Walter Greenleaf, from Colchester, said, "The column moved at a walk, with the three divisions on the same road, making a column about 13 miles in length." Merritt's division led the way, Wilson's came next, and then Gregg's. Soon, Rebel cavalry was sniping at the rear of the column. Sheridan moved on. The Rebels tried to slow him, blocking the road, but they were soon brushed aside and the advance continued, slowly and powerfully. After crossing the Ta River at Jerrel's Mill, the column turned into the road leading southwest into Chilesburg. "We camped that night on the north bank of the North Anna," Ide recorded in his diary. So the column had reached the North Anna River, some 25 miles south of Fredericksburg, on the first day's march. The weather was hot and the blazing southern sun took its toll. Several Vermonters were overcome with sunstroke.

Early next morning, Preston's command received a message from Major General Stuart in the form of a cannonball that crashed into its encampment. The colonel hurried his regiment across the river and formed into line of battle to protect the crossing of Gregg's division. But no fighting developed, and soon the long blue column pressed on. Ide noted, "The country we passed through was very pleasant; the trees past leafing out, the orchards in bloom and all looking like a region never before visited by the troops of hostile armies." While the main force marched, George Custer pushed ahead, attacking Robert E. Lee's main supply base at Beaver Dam. There he dealt the Rebel army fighting at Spotsylvania a heavy blow by destroying two weeks of its supplies, and a good deal of railroad track and rolling stock. Also, a brigade under Brig. Gen. Henry Davies galloped down the Telegraph Road and smashed more railroad equipment at Ashland Station. Already, Sheridan was raising a good deal of hell, and Stuart, caught somewhat unawares, was riding hard to intercept him.

The Vermonters bivouacked that night just below the South Anna River, having crossed at Ground Squirrel Bridge. Next morning, May

11, gray-clad cavalrymen galloped into the field where Preston's regiment was preparing for the day's ride, but a few shots turned the outnumbered Confederates away. Sheridan rode steadily south as the morning warmed, covering six more miles along the Mountain Road. Where a dilapidated hostelry known as Yellow Tavern stood by the roadside, James Ewell Brown Stuart waited with some 4,500 dismounted horsemen, badly outnumbered but prepared to receive an attack. Sheridan took his time deploying his divisions, and as he did so a hot skirmish developed.

Horace Ide:

> We moved forward and soon struck the enemy very advantageously [deployed] behind a fence on a knoll while we had no cover and as we came in sight they opened fire and would have driven us back had it not been for Maj. William Wells who rallied the lines and moving to the left a little got us under cover and connected with a Pennsylvania Regt. that had just come up.

Major William Wells, a Waterbury man, had risen from the rank of private to command one of the three battalions in the First Vermont Cavalry. A hero of the battle of Gettysburg, Wells was always cool under fire, and this May morning he quickly steadied the men.

Confederate artillery fire was taking a toll, and finally two Michigan regiments advanced to engage the guns. Somewhere past midafternoon, while that action was in progress, Brigadier General Custer rode up to the Vermont position and, locating one of his favorite cavalry commanders, Colonel Preston, informed him that he was about to make a charge and inquired whether the colonel would care to join. Ever spoiling for action, the Danville man accepted the invitation and aligned his Vermonters for an advance. Custer was a Michigander, and he also ordered horsemen of his own state into action. G. G. Benedict:

> As soon as the Michigan boys moved from the cover of the wood, the enemy opened a brisk fire from his guns. Before the battery could be reached, there were fences to be cleared and a broad ditch to be

George Armstrong Custer, left, with fellow cavalry officer Alfred Pleasonton, at war in Virginia. HOWARD COFFIN COLLECTION

crossed. Surmounting these obstacles, the Vermont and Michigan boys started on at a walk, then increased the pace to a trot, and when within two hundred yards of the battery, charged it with a yell.

The attack captured two cannon, a considerable amount of ammunition, and several prisoners. George Custer wrote in his official report, "The united efforts of the First, Fifth, Sixth, and Seventh Michigan, assisted by Heaton's battery, and the First Vermont, under the gallant Colonel Preston, proved sufficient, after a close contest, to rout the enemy and drive him from his positon." Horace Ide said the Vermonters then dismounted and "followed the enemy for a mile or so." He added to his brief account a telling note, touching on the event that made Yellow Tavern an encounter long remembered in the annals of the Civil War. "Stuart was mortally wounded by a shell and died in Richmond after."

Another member of the Vermont Cavalry, writing to the *Rutland Herald*, gave another version of the attack, not sparing the superlatives:

> Gen. Custar . . . called to Lieut. Col. Preston for the First Vermont—although our regiment is not now in his brigade—and at the head of the First Michigan and First Vermont, followed by a number of other regiments, he led the most daring charge of the war, and with brilliant success, for the result was the capture of three pieces of artillery, two of which could be brought away, one caisson, and a number of prisoners, besides driving the rebels from two strong positions, besides killing their cavalry chieftain Gen. Stuart, and a colonel, who was commanding a brigade . . . Our loss was heavy.

J. E. B. Stuart had been at the front directing the fighting, and as Michigan troops moved back from their attack, Stuart was on his horse behind a low rail fence, sporting his familiar plumed hat and red-lined cape. A Michigan soldier saw him, took careful aim from close range, and shot Stuart in the stomach. The gravely wounded Confederate commander was placed in an ambulance that promptly started for Richmond and expert medical care. Stuart reached the capital city alive, and the best Richmond doctors were summoned. But they all saw that his case was hopeless and, after an agonizing night, he passed away. The loss was a telling blow to the South. When Sheridan heard the news of Stuart's death, he aptly assessed that he had, upon Lee's army, "inflicted a blow from which entire recovery was impossible." Sheridan tested the Rebel battle line through the day, forcing it back in places. Then he simply left the field and, after a brief pause, rolled on, closing on the outer defenses of Richmond. The fight at Yellow Tavern had been a hot one, and the doomed Stuart had given the Yankees a tough match, slowing their march. But on rolled the victorious Sheridan. The Vermonters' cost had been mercifully light, with two men killed and ten wounded.

The ponderous Union column moved in the middle of the night, in the same hard rain that was drenching Hancock's soldiers moving to attack the Mule Shoe salient back at Spotsylvania. The way was now south and east. "Marched till morning," Lt. Eri Woodbury wrote. The Yankees moved along south of the Chickahominy River and penetrated Richmond's outer defenses, close enough to hear the city's bells sound alarm. Sheridan took a long look at attacking the inner defenses, confident that he could bust in and cause a mighty ruckus. But he also knew he could not hold out there for long. Reluctantly, he turned back north, as Rebel opposition intensified, aiming to cross to the north bank of the Chickahominy and put that rising river between himself and Richmond.

"Just as it began to come light," said Vermonter Ide, "we being in line on a hill in a field a Reb battery opened upon us with grape just in front. Action was smart till middle P. M. till we all got across the Chickahominy at 2 PM." Another Vermonter said, "Gen. Custar then started with his brigade and one or two other regiments, dismounted, and after heavy fighting nearly two hours, drove the rebels back out of the way . . . By the middle of the afternoon everything was safely got across." The high Chickahominy, swollen by the prevailing storm, proved a major obstacle, as Rebel cavalry had torched the bridge. Sheridan was forced to fight off Confederate advances while new planks were placed on the still-intact superstructure, and soon the river was behind him. As they rode on, the Vermonters encountered a new Rebel menace. "Torpedoes" buried in the road exploded, killing several horses. The Vermonters then came under fire on the Mechanicsville Pike, and Colonel Preston engineered a flank attack to dislodge an enemy line blocking the way. That night, in camp near Gaines' Mill, some feisty Richmond newsboys came into camp selling papers fresh from the capital. The Vermonters were pleased to learn that the people in Richmond feared a Union drive into their city. One Vermonter wrote that evening, "Gen. Sheridan has won the admiration of his men. When we think we are in a tight place, the boys will be heard to say, 'Well, Gen. Sheridan knows what he is about,' and they say right."

Sheridan's force was now in territory familiar to some of his troopers, in countryside just beyond the outskirts of Richmond, where the bloody fighting of the Seven Days battles had ended George McClellan's

Peninsula Campaign two years earlier. One of the heavy clashes had come at Gaines' Mill. Next morning, Sheridan set a course south and east, bound for the James River. There he planned to obtain supplies from Benjamin Butler's Army of the James, bottled up behind entrenchments on Bermuda Hundred, just across the river. Horace Ide:

> Crossed Bottoms Bridge, passed through White Oak Swamp, and in the afternoon came out on Malvern Hill near the James River. There were some of our gun-boats in sight, and the first thing we knew "swish" came a shell about two feet long right over our heads and buried in the ground displacing a cart-load of dirt. A man was sent to the top of a house to wave a U.S. Flag, which soon caused them to cease the sport.

Malvern Hill, scene of the last battle of the Peninsula Campaign, rose close by the north bank of the James River, below Richmond, where federal gunboats prowled the waters. One of the boats, seeing horse soldiers on the nearby crest, had opened fire.

Sheridan then moved along the James to Haxall's Landing, where his men got a badly needed rest and dined on fresh rations ferried over by General Butler's troops. On May 14, Lieutenant Woodbury reported, "Went to camp upon bank of the River where we drew rations. Report says Rebs are well whipped and scattered in Virginia." May 16, Woodbury:

> *Off before breakfast on "foraging" expedition. Got nothing but oats . . .*
> *May 17: Packed and led into line at 11 a. m. Then were sent back near camp. We are getting nicely rested.*

The night of May 17, Sheridan turned his force, now refreshed and with horses and men well fed, back in the direction of Grant's main army. "Left camp at 8½ . . ." Woodbury wrote. "Marched all night down river. Breakfast & off again by easy march. Camped for night half an hour after crossing Chickahominy." Sheridan crossed that river at Jones Bridge, then camped near Baltimore Cross Roads the night of the 18th. The next day he dispatched part of Gregg's and Wilson's division to Cold Harbor to protect the flank of his marching column. On May 21, Woodbury wrote,

> Hot day. Foraged potatoes and young pigs . . . We leave the districts through which we pass quite destitute of provisions. Men are all absent . . . It seems hard to go in and take it!!! But such is war, & its woes be on the heads of those who brought it on so recklessly.

On May 23, the cavalry was on the move. Woodbury wrote, "Started for White House Landing about 20 miles distant at 3 AM Warm day . . . Into camp at landing at 12 a. m. Bathed in river." The long ride had taken Sheridan's raiders to the banks of the Pamunkey River at White House Landing, where the men enjoyed a swim. The next morning, army transports took them across the Pamunkey, and on they rode, closing on Grant's main force. The expedition was ending. In his memoirs, Ulysses Grant gave it praise:

> Sheridan in this memorable raid passed entirely around Lee's army; encountered his cavalry in four engagements, and defeated them in all; recaptured four hundred Union prisoners and killed and captured many of the enemy; destroyed and used many supplies and munitions of war; destroyed many miles of railroad and telegraph, and freed us from annoyance by the cavalry of the enemy for more than two weeks.

Lieutenant Woodbury seemed to see the raid as a respite. He wrote May 24, "We expect to join Grant's army tomorrow & then our turn comes for fighting again." But the men were tired, after the long miles. Before he went to sleep that night, the lieutenant wrote, "My pants are worn out."

Back around Spotsylvania, the fighting went on uninterrupted, the casualties mounting. Ulysses Grant needed all the men he could get his hands on, so he looked up to Washington where he knew a good many regiments were doing very little, manning forts that protected the city. One of those regiments was the largest that served in the Civil War from Vermont, the 11th Vermont Heavy Artillery.

The brilliant James Ewell Brown Stuart, doomed to fall defending Richmond, at Yellow Tavern. HOWARD COFFIN COLLECTION

In the spring of 1864, back in the northwestern Vermont village of Jericho, there lived a young lady, Miss Wealthy Field, who seems to have been corresponding simultaneously with two soldiers in the Union blue. One, Roswell Hunt, from Burlington, served in the 10th Vermont. The other, Martin C. Clark, from Swanton, served in the big 11th. Private Clark wrote to Miss Field on May 11, "The news is that wee are transferred to the army of the Potomac which of course wee see some hard times for myself I am ready to go . . . The captain said we should have to fight wee have one hundred rounds of cartridges with us."

Private Charles Porter, from the Champlain Valley town of Ferrisburg, wrote,

Spotsylvania convinced Gen. Grant that he must have men to replace those killed, wounded and missing. He telegraphed Washington to send all the infantry that could be raked and scraped together and we had been expecting the call and we were prepared when on May 11th an order was read ordering the men to send all surplus clothing, blankets, etc. to our homes and next morning the regiment was assembled at Fort Slocum . . .

The men of the 11th, who had enlisted as infantrymen only to be made artillerymen, again were foot soldiers. The regiment was led by of one of Vermont's most capable field-grade officers, Col. James Meech Warner. The son of a prominent family living in the Champlain Valley college town of Middlebury, young Warner had graduated from West Point in 1860. With his new commission, Warner was sent west to serve as quartermaster of a frontier outpost, Fort Wise, in Colorado, which was commanded by John Sedgwick, who soon formed a high opinion of the Vermonter. When Sedgwick came east to fight, in 1861, Warner for a time commanded Fort Wise. As the war intensified, the War Department sent Warner home to raise a Vermont regiment. So he assembled and drilled the 11th, taking it down to Washington where his men had served well in the Washington forts. By the time orders came to join the Army of the Potomac, Warner had been put in charge of a full seven miles of the Washington defenses. The regiment would move to the front divided into three battalions of about 500 men each. The First Battalion was led by Lt. Col. Reuben Benton, of Hyde Park, the Second by Maj. George Chamberlin, of St. Johnsbury, and the Third by Maj. Charles Hundson, of Shoreham.

The 11th had seen no combat in nearly two years of military service, though the sound of distant battle sometimes reached its fortified camps. It seems that before his death, John Sedgwick had asked that Warner's regiment be made a part of his Sixth Corps, and he got his wish, though posthumously. When orders reached Warner, at Fort Slocum, he was directed to proceed to the Army of the Potomac via Belle Plain and report to Sedgwick. Historian Benedict wrote,

The order was speedily made known and its full purport was at once understood. All knew that it meant the exchange of a life of comparative ease and safety for hard marching and bloody fighting. It meant weariness, exposure and peril for all, and wounds, imprisonment and death for not a few. It meant, moreover, as they soon learned, that they were to join the "old Vermont brigade," where their conduct would be compared with that of those veteran fighters.

The regiment, 1,550 strong, assembled at 5:30 the morning of May 12 (as Hancock's great assault on the Mule Shoe was rolling forward), in the rain. It marched down through Washington (where spectators mistook the big regiment for a full brigade) to the Potomac docks, and by 10 AM the men were aboard transports. Steaming down the Potomac, past stately Mount Vernon, by 5 PM they had disembarked at Belle Plain, on Potomac Creek, 12 miles from Fredericksburg. That night the men got a rude welcome to life in the field as they slept on wet ground, beneath skimpy shelter tents, as the same storm drenching the Bloody Angle combatants and the cavalrymen down near Richmond gave them a soaking. Charles Porter: "We had our first experience with tents, which were issued to us that night, none of us knew how to pitch a tent and the result was all of us got thoroughly wet." Pvt. George Bridge, of Morristown, said, "We drew rations, getting our first hardtack, sugar, coffee, salt, pepper, salt pork . . ."

The next day, according to Private Porter,

We began our march for Spotsylvania reaching Fredericksburg before sunset and camped on Stafford Heights. Half way between Belle Plain we met 3,000 rebel prisoners who were captured May 12 by Hancock's Corps. They were being taken to northern prisons, escorted by Union cavalry.

Private Bridge:

The mud was fairly deep and sticky, and the sun came out hot and with our heavy loads, we were much distressed. Soon the roadside was strewn with all manner of clothing, everything we thought we could spare, except guns, equipment and rations were dumped. The battle of the Wilderness had just been fought or was being then and we met many of the wounded, those able to walk, doing so. Others in ambulances, one or two from my town, all going to boat landing for Washington.

Private Porter added, "John W. Gardner of my company 'E' said he threw two postage stamps away to lighten his load." Capt. Chester Dodge, from Morristown, said, "Going through Fredericksburg found it full of wounded."

On May 14, Pvt. Seymour Howes, from Northfield, said, "Marched from Fredericksburg . . . 20 miles. Camped in sight of the enemy." Private Porter:

We were guarding a wagon train of supplies to the army on that march, and before we reached our destination we could see the white puffs of smoke and hear the reports of bursting shells which appeared above the tops of the trees. We marched up from our bivouac to join the Vermont brigade, each battalion with colors, the U S flag, the state flag, and the Artillery flag . . . We were greeted by the soldiers who lined the way with "What brigade is that" or "What division is that." On being told it was the Eleventh Vermont they would reply "there have [been] two Eleventh Vermont regiments gone past all ready." The fact being that our regiment with full ranks was larger than many brigades which suffered the useless butchery of the Wilderness and the first two or three days of Spotsylvania. We were placed in line on the left of the brigade, the 2nd brigade, 2nd division of the 6th Corps, which then was the extreme left of the Army of the Potomac . . .

Capt. Charles Buxton, from Rockingham, wrote, "Came up with the 6th Corps at night at Spotsylvania they was shelling the Johneys in front when we got there this is the first we had seen of fighting."

The big new regiment had joined the Old Brigade, its heavy numbers about equaling all the losses suffered by the five original regiments since the Overland Campaign commenced. The old soldiers, as veterans were wont to do, gave the rookies a hard time. Many former artillery units were marching into the Army of the Potomac's lines and were getting the nickname "heavies," being a little stout from life in the forts, and having been the handlers of heavy artillery. What was generally left unsaid was that the old soldiers, in truth, were very glad to see reinforcements of any kind.

Also on the march through that Virginia spring was the Third Vermont Artillery Battery, one of three batteries the state sent to war. The First and Second Batteries had gone off early on, to serve in Mississippi and Louisiana. Recruiting for the Third Battery proved a challenge, as had the raising of men for the last Vermont infantry regiment, the 17th. Again, men who had fought at Gettyburg proved to be reluctant re-enlisters. Finally, it was mustered in January 1864 with 151 men commanded by Capt. Romeo H. Start of St. Albans, a veteran of the Third Vermont Regiment. The battery arrived in Washington on January 18 and, after weeks of drilling and firing, like the 17th Vermont, it was assigned to Ambrose Burnside's Ninth Corps. Then it was attached to that corps' Fourth Division, made up of black troops commanded by Brig. Gen. Edward Ferrero, a former dance instructor at the U.S. Military Academy. Throughout the Overland Campaign, Ferrero's black soldiers, under the command of white officers, were kept out of action, save for a brief skirmish with Rebel cavalry outside Fredericksburg. Their duty was to guard the army's trains.

The Third Vermont Battery crossed the Rapidan the morning of May 6. Sgt. Harlan Closson, from Thetford along Vermont's eastern border, kept a diary that offers a distant view of the main army's operations:

May 6: Marched about three miles beyond the Rapidan which we crossed at Germania Ford. There was heavy firing a short distance beyond. It is said there has been a hard battle and that the loss is great . . .

May 8: Located near Spotsylvania C. H. There has been heavy firing South and East of us. The Vermont Brigade has lost heavily in the fight.

May 9: About two thousand rebel prisoners passed through our camp yesterday . . . I am now sitting in a basement window of the Chancellorsville House. This was Gen. Hooker's headquarters at the time of the Chanc. Battle last May. It is a brick building. The walls were pretty well battered down . . . Several wounded men lie here under the trees who had started for Fredericksburg hospitals but were unable to get through. They have but little care here.

Chancellorsville May 12 . . . We had a wet night and it has rained hard some of the time to day. There has been very hard firing a little southeast of us to day. There has been almost unbroken roar of artillery. I have heard nothing like it before.

The battery remained at Chancellorsville until May 17. Then it marched to Salem Church, near Fredericksburg, before swinging off south and east, remaining well back from Grant's front lines. The Third Battery would not fire a single round during the entire campaign.

And on the move that fateful spring were processions of blue-clad soldiers nearly as sad as the long ambulance trains bearing broken bodies from the battlefields. They moved away from the thunder of the guns, bound far south. Among the Union soldiers headed for Confederate prison camps were two Vermont cavalrymen, Pvt. Charles Chapin, of Williston, and Pvt. George Crosby, of Brattleboro. Both had been captured on May 5, near Craig's Meeting House. Both men kept diaries. First, Chapin's:

May 6, Pleasant and very warm. Marched to Orange Court House . . . laid in the dirt till about midnight. Took the cars for Gordonsville started at day light.

May 7: Arrived at Gordonsville about 8 a. m . . . drew 12 hard tack for six of us got no more till Monday afternoon.

May 8: Started for Lynchburg packed 50 into a car also 2 guards.

May 12: Laid in cars all night, have drawn no rations since Tuesday, feeling very faint. Cars are so full that we suffer some. We have a good feeling crowd and jokes fly freely around.

May 14: Showery, drew 10 loaves bread a bit of bacon and a bucket of soup for 20 men . . . Heard our forces were entrenched at Spotsylvania C. H. also that we were to start for Georgia Monday.

May 16: The days are pretty long shut up in an old brick building 250 men each floor.

May 17: Started at four A.M. rode about 30 miles & then walked about 10.

May 18: Passed through Jamestown at High Point there is a great deal of cotton stored. Passed Glenn Anna Female Seminary at Thomasville. There was a great many young ladies on the piazzas who seemed right glad to see us. Saw Locusts in bloom.

There Chapin's diary ended. Crosby's diary continued:

> *May: 22: Arrived at Macon about daylight. One of the guards fell off the cars and was killed arrived at Andersonville about noon this our destination.*

So the prisoners had reached the dreaded Confederate prison stockade at Andersonville, Georgia. Crosby continued:

> *May 23: . . . this is an awful place [that] beggars description.*
> *May 24: more prisoners came in here to day there must be here now over fifteen thousand men here some have been prisoners more than a year but they hardly look like human beings my prayer is to be delivered from this hell of torment.*

Crosby would survive the hell of Andersonville and return home to Brattleboro. Chapin died at Andersonville in January, and was buried in the prison cemetery, where he rests to this day, one of more than twelve thousand Union soldiers there interred.

As men marched to Yellow Tavern and Haxall's Landing, to Chancellorsville and Todd's Tavern, from Washington to the front lines, and to the horror of a Confederate stockade, back at Spotsylvania Court House the firing, day and night, never ceased, as it began to seem the battle there really might take all summer.

Chapter Ten

TRENCH WARFARE

I am unable to say what was done each day, but I remember that we were under fire most of the time. The fighting at this time was continued every day and we were in a fight every day . . ." So Seth Eastman remembered the combat around Spotsylvania Court House. The soldiers were battered and confused from day after day of relentless warfare. On arrival in the lines at Spotsylvania, Wilbur Fisk described himself as "almost tired to death." Usually an accurate recorder of events, the soldier-correspondent from Tunbridge was befuddled as he attempted to chronicle the early fighting around the courthouse village. In his diary, he said Upton's May 10 assault happened on May 8, and listed May 9 as the day of the Bloody Angle fight, being three days in error. It's no wonder the opening days of Grant's campaign had left soldiers exhausted and dazed. Something like shellshock may have prevailed after the relentless killing and maiming, hard marching, constant exposure, all in the heat of high spring in Virginia. The veteran soldiers had never been in anything like it before.

Pvrivate Tabor Parcher penciled a hurried note to his wife in Waterbury on May 13, while under fire. The letter contained one remarkable sentence.

We are having a hard time and we have been under fire for 8 days and am liable to be as many more before we whip Lee's forces but we are gaining a little the balls are flying over my head as I write but I have been lucky so far.

Writing to his parents the same day, Pvt. Edwin Hall, 10th Vermont, said,

We are expecting to have to make another charge on the breastworks today, but the boys do not crave the job at all. This is the 10th day of the fight and we have been under fire every day. There was a Reb bullet just whizzed past my head. Guess I'll lumber to the rear . . .

And on May 13, Lt. Col. Samuel Pingree, Third Vermont, wrote to his parents:

This is the first time a letter could be sent out of this army for ten days. We have fought the most terrible series of battles ever fought by hostile armies . . . in modern history—Each army must have lost in killed or wounded near 40,000 men . . . if I survive I shall consider myself of singular luck. If not I am sure I shall have died in a cause which commends itself to both judgement and conscience . . .

Major Crandall, in the Sixth, wrote,

Heard of the death of our dear Col. Barney. Among all those who have fallen in this fight no one was better or truer than he. The Earth has lost a faithful servant & a faithful friend. God help his wife.

The day after the Bloody Angle, with Lee withdrawn from the Mule Shoe to a line across its base, the two battered armies eyed each other like two punched-out boxers. Next day, Ulysses Grant moved the Sixth Corps about six miles to the left end of the long Union line. According to the exhausted Private Fisk, the march was a confused affair and the soldiers ended up tramping a good deal farther than the intended distance. "We made a long day's march, though we gained but a few miles, swinging around to our left, and resting on the Ny," he wrote. Chaplain Haynes, in the 10th Vermont, said, "On the fourteenth, we moved with the corps . . . around the second, Fifth, and Ninth Corps, crossing the Fredericksburg pike to the extreme left of the army." Ricketts' Sixth Corps division, including the 10th, engaged in a brief fight at day's end, wading the little Ny River to relieve Emory Upton's brigade, which had been trying to seize a hillock held by the Rebels. "Our men charged through the stream where the water was up to their armpits," said Chaplain Haynes, "swinging their cartridge boxes over their shoulders, they gained the hill with a shout. Then filing back to the right, and drawing back [to] the left, they threw up intrenchments . . ."

The Vermont Brigade was now on the left of the Sixth Corps; indeed, on the left of the whole army, on its flank near the Ny River. The move had taken the Old Brigade from northwest of Spotsylvania Court House to a position a mile and a half east of the village. The Rebel lines were but a short distance off. Sharpshooters were ever at work, and artillery often boomed. Men were in constant danger. Almost every day, some kind of a battle happened. And every day, men died. It was a nerve-racking, exhausting experience. It was, in short, a new kind of warfare that would dominate much of the remainder of the Civil War in the east and become the standard of fighting early in the next century. Trench warfare had been born. Seth Eastman:

At times we were shelled for hours by the Rebels and it seemed to me I never saw such marksmen as these Rebel artillery men were. They could burst a shell at any point they wished to, and did not waste their ammunition, but made every shot count. At the same time, our artillery men were giving them just the same as they were giving us. They would fire until one or the other's guns were disabled, or lost so many men that they could not man the guns. They also had mortars and threw shells about 5 inches in diameter, high in the air, intending to have them fall on us and explode, but we kept out of the way of these by having holes dug in the ground and covered with earth and poles. We could crawl into this ground retreat when such kinds of shells were used. I never knew much damage to be done with this kind of projectile. We also had the same and used it against them. The weather was very hot at this time and we had many thunder showers and rainy nights, all of which we took without any shelter. This we did not care about. It was the hail of musket ball that we were most afraid of, then again we were hard up all the time for food and drink, as it was impossible to get water, as we had to stand in line so much, and the food was all the time of the cheapest and smallest quantity that could be possible used. No teams could come near us for many days at a time, and we were hungry all the time . . . Horses that were disabled were dressed and used for food. There was nothing in the country that could be used for food, as it was all used up by the Rebel army before we got there.

On May 15, reinforcements from Washington joined the Vermont Brigade. "Our arms were strengthened and hearts made glad," Lewis Grant wrote, "by the arrival of the Eleventh Vermont, Colonel Warner, a noble body of men, 1,500 strong. Two companies of conscripts were also added to our number." Seth Eastman described the new men as

all dressed like artillery men with jackets trimmed with red, and a red stripe on the outside of their pant leg. They looked fine, clean, and as if just out of a band box . . . The contrast between them and us was very remarkable. We were dirty, lousy and foot sore, and each of the old regiments numbered not more than 300 men apiece, all tattered and torn by a week solid of battle every day and marching every night, but they were good men and took their places in the front line within an hour after they reached us on the front. They murmured some at the hardtack that was given them for food, and of sleeping on the bare ground, but this was soon forgotten. They acted like trained veterans and did all they ever were called on to do, and began losing men the first day at the front.

Eastman also noted the arrival of two hundred additional troops, Vermont draftees, all assigned to his Sixth Vermont.

They joined us at the same time, and the whole 200 were put with our regiment . . . and it nearly doubled our numbers. They were not such good men on the average as those of the 11th, and they found fault with everything. Some of them would not go into battle, and would sneak to the rear when there was danger.

The 11th had scarcely settled into the trenches when some of its men fell victim to inexperience with front-line soldiering, at a considerable cost. A soldier recalled,

> In the lines at Spotsylvania a man named Patterson [Pvt. John Patterson of Orange] took an unexploded shell [and] was fooling with it by a campfire. Some one told him it will blow your hand off. None of your damned business if it does [he said]. Shell exploded & killed him and another man James Darling [a private, from Westminster] . . . and wounded 5 or 6 others.

Private Charles Porter, in the 11th, said that Patterson actually "dropped a coal of fire" into the shell.

The day the 11th arrived, elsewhere in the Sixth Corps sharpshooter Charles Mead was told that he had lost a friend. He wrote,

> Silas came up and said that Henry [probably Pvt. Henry Mattocks, of Tinmouth] died between four and five o clock on the 13th and was

Lt. Newton Glazier was severely wounded as the 11th Vermont made its first combat assault on Robert E. Lee's tough final line at Spotsylvania. Vermont Historical Society

buried in the dark. He sank away gradually and easily. Another hero has laid his priceless life on our Country's altar. Thy will be done.

That night, Pvt. Alvin Woodward, Third Vermont, wrote a brief letter to his wife in Berkshire that made obvious the strain of the Overland Campaign: "Oh dear how long will this last. We have now been laying still 2 days. Our Regt has been detailed for Pickett . . ." Major Crandall noted that night,

> We had divine service to-day. Alas, for the faces that we used to see in the social gathering. Alas for the voices thus we shall hear no more. I learn that Gov. Smith and other Vermonters are at Fredericksburg with the wounded.

May 16 was a quiet day for the Old Brigade, as Private Fisk said:

> Monday we did but little except clean our guns. This was no small job for they had become awful rusty both outside and in. One could hardly tell what they were made of originally so rusty had they become.

Sgt. Charles Morey, Second Vermont:

> Pleasant and warm. We remained quietly in camp where we started night before last nothing of importance seems to be going on, we have received no mail since we left camp. Wrote a letter to Mother.

That letter, the first of length Morey had written since he left Brandy Station, said in part:

> Through the goodness of Him who over-looks all things and protects us when exposed to extreme dangers I am permitted to write you a few more lines . . . Our division has seen very hard fighting and have met with heavy losses, our losses in this regiment 71 killed, 309 wounded and 30 missing making a total of 400 which is considerable more than half our number when we left camp . . . We are lying quiet yesterday and today on the River Po, the enemy occupying the other side. My

health very good and stand all the hardships very well. I understand there is 40,000 reinforcements on the road to us and when these arrive I am confident we can whip the enemy and drive [him] out of Virginia and if we succeed in doing this the war is virtually ended. My trust is in God and through Him we expect to gain the victory. Pray for us . . .

That day, Samuel Pingree again wrote his parents, updating them on the campaign and mentioning his brother, Stephen Pingree, of the Fourth Vermont:

. . . We are still pressing Gen. Lee from one strong hold to another—are occasionally checked but the general results are every where in our favor and the rebel army are gradually falling back before us.

. . . Our Brigade have been reinforced by the arrival of the 11th Vt. heavy Atillery Reg't. armed as riflemen—they add 1,500 to our strength.

The army have received about 12,000 new troops, from Washington and elsewhere.

We shall fight another great battle in a short time—perhaps tomorrow.

Maj. Gen. John Sedgwick our beloved Corps commander was struck in the face by a rifle ball on the 9th inst. & died in a few hours after.

Maj. Gen. Wright commands the Corps now.

Lieut. Gen. Grant is with this army yet.

Gov. Smith of Vt. is near here with a Corps of 12 Surgeons from Vt. to care for our wounded of that State.

Stephen is now on the skirmish line with his Reg't. & part of the 11th Vt. Reg't.

He relieved me on the same line on his arrival last night. He is well.

On May 17, Edwin Hall, 10th Vermont, wrote to Brookfield, making clear the difficulty front-line soldiers had in understanding overall military strategy:

We are all anxious to see a late paper to find out how the thing is going. We have not seen one since we started except those that came from Vt. last night and there was not much in them. I see the [Vermont] Watch-

Col. James Warner led the 11th Vermont until he was wounded at Spotsylvania. He would return to command the regiment. HOWARD COFFIN COLLECTION

man thought that Lee would not fight much this side of Richmond—but I have a different opinion . . . I must stop and eat some breakfast—can't call it that for all we have got is a few hard tack and a small piece of pork. Wouldn't I like to see Mothers buttery about this time—guess I would. We were in the skirmish line we advanced and one of the Rebs left his knapsack. I found some letters in his portfolio. Will send one home. I got a pipe and an old brass ring. Will send the ring if I can find it—the pipe I use myself.

That night, Ulysses Grant ordered two of his corps, the Second under Hancock and the Sixth under Wright, back to the right, into the vicinity of the abandoned Mule Shoe, to attack a stretch of Rebel works believed weak. The assault was to hit the new line constructed across the base of the salient. The attackers moved in the night to the jump-off point, aiming for a dawn assault. The Vermont Brigade was settling into its new position near the Ny River when orders came. "We had just dressed our line into shape," Private Fisk wrote,

and begun to establish our tents to correspond when the order came to pack up and fall in. It was near night. We marched very rapidly for a few miles in the direction we had come when for some reason or other the column had to halt. Every one of us was sweaty. The air was damp and chilly. The men sat down on their knapsacks or laid down till they got chilly and cold . . . We marched back to where we had come from and charged over the same breastworks once more.

General Getty, still recovering from his Wilderness wound, nevertheless filed a report on the action:

"On the night of the 17th [my] division moved back to the Angle, and having formed in columns of brigades in the following order from front to rear, Wheaton's (first), Edwards' (fourth), Bidwell's (Third), and Grant's (Second), in conjunction with the Second Corps and the remainder of the Sixth, made an attack at daylight on the enemy's position on the right and in front of the Angle."

Due to delays, it was 8 AM before the assault began, and, as Fisk noted, it first rolled over the abandoned lines of the Mule Shoe. The Vermont Brigade, this cool morning, was formed in two lines. The brigade's thin regiments made up the first line, while the 1,500 men of Colonel Warner's 11th Vermont, making their first attack, formed the second. The Second Corps troops came under fire first, hit by massed artillery. "The troops of the 2nd Corps made the first attack, reached the abatis but could get no further and fell back under cover," said Pvt. Henry Houghton. The Vermont Brigade marched through a line of men that had stopped its advance, then the proud Old Brigade came under cannon fire. "The rebels shelled us severely, killing two and wounding ten more," said Fisk. "Scott of Company C [Pvt. Israel Scott, of Newport] was completely torn to pieces by a shell. Ford [Pvt. Hadley Ford, of Brandon] of Company G was killed also." General Getty simply said, "The attack was not successful," as the Union front took heavy casualties and never reached the Confederate earthworks. In the advance, the 11th Vermont suffered its first battle casualty as shrapnel tore away part of a calf of Pvt. Nathaniel Rogers, of Newport. Soon, the regimental commander Colonel Warner was a casualty. Lt. Col. George Chamberlin:

> My noble adjutant, Glazier [Lt. Newton Glazier, of Stratton], who
> stood near me, was hit by a cruel shell, and his left arm torn almost
> completely off. It was a horrible wound. With my own hands I put a
> tourniquet on above it, and detailed a corporal and four men to take
> him off the field. He turned to the colonel [Warner] just as he was leav-
> ing, and said, "Colonel, I hope you will get the victory." In less than half
> an hour the colonel himself, while standing near me with drawn sword,
> and just preparing to advance the battalion over the rifle pit and into
> the open field beyond, was wounded by a sharpshooter, the ball passing
> in behind the ear and coming out in the middle of the back of the neck.
> The vital parts escaped and it proved only a flesh wound.

But the wound was severe, and Warner was soon on his way to a
Washington hospital, then to his Middlebury home for a lengthy recu-
peration. Lt. Col. Reuben Benton, of Hyde Park, commander of the
First Battalion, took command of the 11th. According to Lewis Grant,

> An advance of about half a mile was made under heavy artillery fire. This
> brigade came up on the first line in the advance and halted. No farther
> advance was made and the troops in our front retired. After holding the
> front line for some time, the whole command was ordered to retire.

The effort was given up about 10 AM, according to Wilbur Fisk. The
Old Brigade had taken 37 casualties. The Sixth Corps then marched
back in the direction from whence it had come, back to the left of the
Union line, crossing the Ny River and going into the lines east of
Spotsylvania Court House. During the attack, the 17th Vermont, in
the Ninth Corps, had been briefly engaged but lost no men.

The veterans of the Vermont Brigade took the day's action very
much in stride. Pvt. Carlton Felch, a pioneer assigned to brigade
headquarters, noted in his diary, "Our brigade engaged not hotly . . . at
noon marched back to the front of where we left yesterday. I was
detailed to put up Aunt Lydia's H. Q. tent. Day warm and pleasant

except one or two showers." Felch had made sure that brigade commander Grant would be protected from those showers. Looking back at the battle, Pvt. Elijah Stone, Sixth Vermont, writing to his brother in West Glover, chided the brigade's newest regiment, the 11th: "4 companies came up behind us yesterday," he wrote. "They thought they was a going right into a fight there was the line of battle forward of us and they was behind us . . . They started on a run and hollered and the officers had a hard work to stop them."

The next day, May 19, was relatively quiet for the Vermont Brigade. "In the morning we marched down into the woods and in front of the enemy and built breastworks all day," wrote Capt. Chester Dodge, in the 11th. Pvt. Willard Thayer, in the 10th, told his wife in Warren: "We had the pleasure of having a good knight rest to day we have advanced a mile & have thrown up a good line of Breast Works the talk is that we are not going to have as much chargin but use the Big Guns more . . ." He added,

> you wanted to know if I used profane language I will tell you the truth I don't mean to use much but when I feel a little cras I do some times but I don't use as much as I did at home . . . we have seen some pretty hard times but if I live to get through with it I shant be sorry I came for I never should have been satisfied if I had not come.

Thayer would survive the Overland Campaign, but died of diarrhea in a New York City military hospital in September.

If May 19 was uneventful for the Vermonters, severe fighting erupted in another part of the battlefield. Robert E. Lee, seeing that Ulysses Grant was shifting his forces to the south and east, that afternoon sent Richard Ewell and six thousand troops on a reconnaissance in force. On the Harris Farm near the Fredericksburg Pike, Ewell struck the Yankee lines and, after bitter fighting, was repulsed. At a considerable cost, Lee was now certain that Grant, as he had done in the Wilderness, was moving by the left.

The trench warfare went on. Benedict wrote,

> The opposing picket lines, to the southeast of Spotsylvania Court

House, were pressed closely together, the pickets sheltering themselves behind trees and other cover. The shooting was so close upon any exposure, that the reliefs could only reach their posts during the daylight by crawling out on their hands and knees; and as a rule the line was relieved only at night.

Private Henry Houghton: "In the night if we made a sound or motion it was sure to bring a shot." Private Stone, writing to his brother, described a narrow escape on May 19: "They went [for] me but I had an eye open and saw mister shell a coming and dodged it. We can't see pieces of shell but we can see them sometimes."

At Spotsylvania, it was easy to die. The lines were so close that Yank and Confederate could often see one another. Certainly it was so on picket, where scant yards separated the combatants. The cover of a tree, or a mound of earth, was necessary for survival. In the trenches, nobody was ever entirely safe. A careless movement, the

Lt. Col. Reuben Benton took command of the 11th Vermont when Colonel Warner was wounded. VERMONT HISTORICAL SOCIETY

raising of a head for a quick look to the front, could mean instant death from the rifle of a beady-eyed sharpshooter concealed in a tree even a quarter mile or more away. If a man kept low and out of the sights of some far-off and unseen marksman, there was always the possibility that a chance round of artillery would sail in and strike, or burst, in just the wrong place. The spring heat at times grew to that of midsummer, water was scarce, and food was hardtack with, now and then, a small piece of meat. Trench warfare was tough, dirty, and deadly war. The trenches around Spotsylvania were a place from which the soldiers on both sides would be happy to escape. And by May 20, Ulysses Grant, in spite of his famous pledge to fight it out on those lines all summer, if that was what it took, was ready to move on.

On May 20, Capt. Charles Buxton, in the 11th Vermont, wrote to Rockingham, "Laid in camp all day could see the Rebs from our camp, was not much firing." Dr. Joseph Rutherford wrote to Hannah,

> Lee has entrenched himself at Spotsylvania and Grant is beginning to dig him out, and he will do it . . . This morning I rode around our breast works where the 6th and 9th corps are stationed. I could see the Reb Sharp Shooters in the trees in front of our line and our Sharp Shooters occasionally bring one down faster than he went up. I wanted to pick one off this morning but the Col would not let me. I did want to draw a bead on the skunk I can tell you . . .

That evening Major Crandall, as he was wont to do, wrote of a poignant moment along the lines: "Evening—our bands are playing national & home airs. A rebel band not to be out done just struck up Dixie . . ."

Lieutenant Colonel Cummings, shot in the scalp in the Wilderness, was recovering nicely on May 20, about ready to resume command of his 17th Vermont. He was somewhere well away from the firing line, probably at a field hospital, when he wrote his wife in Brattleboro of the Virginia spring: "Yesterday I saw some Harrison roses. The young peaches are as big as bullets and numberless. Wheat that has not yet been trampled is in blossom."

Capt. Aldace Walker commanded the brave 11th Vermont lads who covered the Vermont Brigade's risky withdrawal from the lines at Spotsylvania. VERMONT HISTORICAL SOCIETY

The next day, May 21, proved to be the last at Spotsylvania Court House. Lt. George Howe, 11th Vermont, from Shoreham in the Champlain Valley, wrote to his fiancée, Lorette Wolcott, that morning:

> There is some difference between fighting a battle & reading about it no one can describe it & I shall not attempt to so far I am unhurt my life was saved by my blankets which were rolled up & over my right shoulder & under my left arm they were struck by a piece of shell which tore three holes in my rubber & eight in my woolen blanket besides one in the blouse it knocked the breath out of me but am well all right again it happened on the 18th of May at Spotsylvania the same shell killed a man & wounded another they belonged to the 2d Vt.

On May 21, Ulysses Grant again had his army on the march, most of it bound initially for a stop along the rail line to Richmond, Guinea Station. The men of the Vermont Brigade were among the last troops to leave the Spotsylvania lines, and getting away was a delicate matter. The wary Confederates, expecting a Union move, were poised to smash forward if they sensed a weakening along the front. Henry Houghton was on picket:

The order was whispered along the line to withdraw half a mile to the rear, to some rifle pits. We could not withdraw without being seen, so at a given signal we started on a dead run, and the bullets were flying thick after us. The enemy chased until we got to the rifle pits then they thought it best to stop, they made several attempts to drive us out but they did not succeed.

Wilbur Fisk described his regiment's withdrawal from the front lines.

We expected the enemy would follow us up and every moment were prepared to hear the picket firing. They commenced to advance about the middle of the afternoon. The picket firing grew nearer and nearer . . . We stood to our arms expecting every moment to receive an attack. By and by their bullets began to whistle over our heads and their guns sounded near by. We anxiously awaited the coming in of our pickets . . . One by one they came until all of our company were in. They were completely out of breath from running and some of them attributed their escape from rebel bullets to their fleetness with which the bullets were no match.

Private Felch, Third Vermont:

Moved to the right or rear built a breast work and then left it and moved to the left were attacked by the rebs making a charge on breast-works but they were repulsed. At ten we marched southeast direction all night a distance of about 8 miles.

The Sixth was the last corps to leave the Spotsylvania lines, and the Vermont Brigade was one of the last units to depart. The delicate job of protecting the brigade's withdrawal was given to the new lads, the 11th Vermont. Lieutenant Colonel Benton, leading the regiment with Colonel Warner out of action, on the evening of May 20 advanced two hundred men under Capt. Aldace Walker, of Middlebury, to reinforce the picket line and defend the Sixth Corps' rear. The line lay low the next day as the army was put in motion. Late that day, the Confederates stormed forward. Benton said,

About an hour before sunset the picket-line was furiously attacked by two full brigades of the enemy. The situation was such that the enemy could approach within a very short distance, under cover of the woods. Notwithstanding this advantage, that part of the line held by Captain Walker sustained three successive charges, repulsing the enemy every time. In one of them the colors of a regiment of the enemy were advanced to and planted on the breast-work.

Benton proudly added, "They were driven back by men who had never seen a line of the enemy before that day."

Capt. Charles Buxton said, "Had a brisk fight about 5½ o'clock the rebs advanced . . . with 3 lines of battle. I think the Johneys got punished very bad. Marched about 9 o'clock P. M. & marched all night."

So in the night the 11th Vermont, the last Vermont unit to leave the battlefield around Spotsylvania Court House, began its march, at the rear of the Army of the Potomac. By the time that army moved from Spotsylvania, it had lost more than thirty-six thousand men in the campaign that had begun the night of May 3 at Brandy Station. Lee's losses, while heavy, were a little more than half of Grant's. But Grant, of course, had far more men to lose. Historian Benedict calculated the campaign's cost to the Vermont Brigade alone, as it left Spotsylvania, as follows:

> The losses of the brigade, in action, in the three weeks since it crossed the Rapidan, were reported by General L. A. Grant on the 23d of May, to be 249 killed, 1,231 wounded, 170 missing, total 1,650, of which 1,634 were from the original regiments. Of the wounded not less than 190 died of their wounds; and to these losses were added about 100 more discharged for disability, and about 300 who had broken down under the fatigues and exposures of the campaign, had been sent to northern hospitals. Less than half the veterans who were in the ranks on the 1st of May, now answered to the roll call, and of the officers but a third remained.

So the loss, counting killed, wounded, missing, and those no longer able to fight, had topped two thousand in the Old Brigade alone.

Adding in the losses in the 10th and 17th Regiments, in the three sharpshooter companies, and among the cavalry, the toll thus far was somewhere around 2,250 for the little state of Vermont. And Grant's Overland Campaign rolled resolutely on.

Chapter Eleven

IN THE LAND OF GOSHEN

In Vermont, as the armies battled around Spotsylvania Court House, lilacs were coming into bloom, beginning to spread their sweet, nostalgic fragrance from dooryard to dooryard. Ducks and geese were back from the troubled south, and also about to come north were the big-city traveling shows. Thus Rutland, Burlington, and Montpelier residents were most excited about scheduled appearances, in the local opera house, of the famous little gentleman Tom Thumb, and his new bride. Brattleboro was bedecked with posters advertising "The Great Show," soon to appear under a large canvas tent on Frost Street. Gymnasts, acrobats, a contortionist, and Whitmore & Thompson's Brass Band would be featured, along with "Broadway minstrels." Things were moving toward a summer level of activity along Lake Champlain, where the ice was gone and steamboats were making regular runs, their proprietors advertising summer excursions with special rates. Summer people would soon be heading toward the state, escaping the warming cities.

Throughout the Green Mountain State, farmers were plowing, and planting corn, potatoes, and early peas, while the first crop of hay was growing nicely. With an eye toward dealing with the first cutting, more and more Vermont families were attending mowing machine demonstrations and purchasing the new contraptions, for most of the young men, who could swing a scythe all day, were off to war. Vermont was a flurry of activity as old men, young boys, and the women did their best to prepare for the always too brief growing season. Along the state's rivers, including the wide Missisquoi and Lamoille in the north, the rushing White and Ottauquechee in midstate, the deep-valleyed Black and West to the south, winding Otter Creek to the west, and on countless splashing, twisting streams, the trout were biting as the waters became less cold. Some brave farm lad might even have already taken a quick plunge in some chill creek at the end of a long day in the fields. Vermonters were enjoying blessed warmth after a long winter, but all the springtime optimism was tempered by the growing concern about events far away. The full import of the Wilderness and Spotsylvania battles was beginning to be realized. More and more families were learning of the death, or wounding, of a son. Others waited and waited for some word on the still-unknown fate of the lad gone off to war whose unit, the papers said, had been "cut up." On May 11, in Woodstock, the local *Standard* ran a list of Vermont wounded that filled half a page, a list likely given to it by neighbor Peter Washburn.

On May 12, the day of the Bloody Angle fight, Henry Herrick stopped briefly at his place of employment and, on receiving his pay, discovered that he had been given a raise. In the Fairbanks shop that morning, all the talk was of military matters. "There came a dispatch to the office," said Herrick, "of the hard-fought battle at Spotsylvania and a great victory and the capture of 40 guns and 10,000 prisoners, and there was a great excitement." Herrick then left the Fairbanks factory to begin his long-awaited vacation. At a St. Johnsbury livery stable he hired a wagon and team of horses and sometime well after dark, driving alone, reached the family home in Cabot, 20 miles distant. Herrick apparently traveled in contentment, relieved that mother Herrick had relented on the subject of Zenas, clearing the way for his friend to soon arrive at the Herrick home. That night, a rainy one in Cabot, Herrick wrote, "Now I am going to have a weeks rest from the confinement of the shop, and with the pleasant sound of running water in my ears, I lay me down to sleep."

That same night, in the nearby town of Peacham, men gathered as usual at the post office in Peacham Corner to wait for the stage and its bag of mail. When the *Boston Journal* was brought in, the best reader among them was chosen to render its contents aloud, cover to cover. The same thing happened nightly in the town's Green Bay district. Papers were expensive, so they were shared. Besides, the nightly event was a social one for the men of the isolated hill town. Thus did many Vermonters in many towns get the latest news, and certainly the focus of attention was on the war.

That May 12 in nearby Ryegate, on the upper Connecticut River, Amos Abbott, a man of few words, noted in his diary: "Commence Planting Potatoes." His next entry would come on May 17: "Finish planting corn." Before turning in the night of May 12, Royal Peake, in Bristol, wrote, "Raining—come off rather pleasant but some cloudy. The Vermont Brigade are said to be badly cut up. R. A. Bird killed. [Capt. Riley A. Bird, of the Sixth Vermont, shot May 5.]" In Peru, near Bromley Mountain in southern Vermont, fourteen-year-old Marshall Hapgood, a farm boy doing a man's work, stated in his diary, "Charley was wounded today, in the head." He was referring to Pvt. Charles Hapgood, Second Vermont, who was hit on both May 5 and May 12. On June 15, Hapgood would write, "Work on road all day go home and while washing me who should stand before me but Charley. Lord my prayers has been answered."

On May 13, in Brattleboro, while the battered armies rested after the Bloody Angle slaughter, the *Vermont Phoenix* reported:

> For a few days past the news has been of the most stirring and impor-
> tant character. The two great armies have been in deadly conflict, and
> thousands of brave men have fallen . . . It appears that our Vermont
> troops have suffered severely. They were in the thickest of the fight,
> and their losses show how hard the fighting was. It is stated that the
> 4th regiment had only 90 men and five officers remaining . . .

The *Phoenix* also ran these brief items:

> PROMOTED—Major John S. Tyler of this village has been promoted
> to Lieut. Colonel of the 2nd regiment. We are sorry to learn he was
> wounded in the recent battles.

KILLED—It is our sad lot to record the death of Captain Dennie W. Farr [of Readsboro] of Co. C. 4th Vermont regiment, and well known to many of this village and neighborhood. He was killed in the great battle of May 5th, by a bullet through the head . . . He has left many friends and a young wife to mourn his death.

The May 13 *Phoenix* also ran the following message:

Executive Mansion, Washington, D.C., May 9, 1864. To the friends of the Union and Liberty: Enough is known of our army operations within the last five days to claim our especial gratitude to God. While what remains undone demands our most sincere prayers to and reliance upon Him, without whom all human effort is vain, I recommend that all patriots at their homes, in their places of public worship, and wherever they may be, unite in thanksgiving and prayer to almighty God.

    Abraham Lincoln

And the *Phoenix* that day stated,

The ladies of this village and vicinity are making preparations to furnish hospital supplies for our sick and wounded soldiers as soon as possible. They wish to forward a box of articles without delay. Lint, old linen, cotton, or any articles fitted for hospital use, may be sent to the Savings Bank for the purpose of being forwarded. Our noble Vermont soldiers have suffered severely in the recent desperate battles, and they must not be allowed to want anything necessary that we can send them.

That May 13, Henry Herrick was up early and spent most of the day working in his mother's flower garden, in the front yard of the family home on Cabot's main street. That evening, after a long snooze in the hammock, Herrick went to the stage stop and waited for the mail's arrival. He wrote,

There is nothing particularly new to-night, only a confirmation, with fuller particulars, of the fight Thursday but bringing the names of killed and wounded of which a heavy account comes in this town, Ed Stone,

Billy Merrill, Geo Wright killed, Scott, two Marshes and some others wounded—well, it is part of the price.

As Herrick passed a quiet evening in Cabot, 70 miles to the north and west, the town of Swanton, on Lake Champlain, was both busy and sad. That evening, Col. Elisha Barney's body came home and was greeted at the railway station by a large number of Swanton folks. "Their arrival was awaited by a large concourse of citizens," said one who was there, "who accompanied them to his father's house, at the hour of twilight, amid the tolling of the bell, the peal of cannon, and the beat of the muffled drum."

That day, at Newport Barracks, North Carolina, where the Ninth Vermont Regiment was stationed, its lieutenant colonel, Valentine Barney, had written to Swanton and his wife, Maria:

Yesterday your letter was received containing the sad intelligence of brother Elisha's death. I had seen in the New York Herald that he was wounded and had been in great anxiety for two days about him but I was not prepared to hear that it was a fatal wound and the news was almost crushing to me, I had not seen him for nearly two years, which makes me feel worse, this is the deepest affliction I have ever experienced . . . I can hardly realize that my DEAR BROTHER is gone, but know of course it must be so . . . the recollections of a thousand things come up as [I] think over my past life and my associations with him. For the past day I have thought over more of my youthful life than for years before, for that time was spent almost entirely with HIM who has given his life for his country . . . A sadness pervades our whole Regiment and almost every one here has lost a brother or a dear friend. Many a prayer has ascended for the fallen as well as for the success of our Army, and we shall continue till rebellion is crushed . . .

On May 13, in Burlington, the *Free Press* ran a list of men who had been drafted into military service in Chittenden, Franklin, Orleans, and Essex Counties. And it contained an account of the death of General Sedgwick. Also in Burlington that day, William Hoyt wrote, "Great news from the Virginia battle fields of the desperate fighting between

Grant & Lee's armies. The tide of success decidedly in our favor now. Planted winter squash, late peas, & early beans today."

On Bible Hill, near St. Johnsbury Center, farmer Lester Styles finished putting in his corn on May 13. Next day he wrote, "Been a warm wet growing week. The trees are getting well covered with leaves the grass never looked any better at this time of the year."

War news dominated the newspapers and on May 14, in Windsor, the *Journal* republished a letter that had appeared in the *New York Times* of May 7. Said to have been written by an aide to General Sedgwick, it read in part: "I am sorry to say the Vermont Brigade is terribly cut up. In the Fourth, Col. Foster is seriously wounded, Adjt. French is wounded, Capts. Farr and Carpenter and Lieuts. Ainsworth and Putnam . . ."

Politics was in the Vermont papers in mid-May as the Republican State Convention, scheduled for Burlington, neared. The *Rutland Herald* editorialized on the subject, opining that it was safe to assume Governor Smith, Lt. Gov. Paul Dillingham of Waterbury, and State Treasurer John Page of Rutland would be nominated by the convention. But it said a far more important question concerned "who shall pilot the Union through the dangerous storms of the coming four years." It went on, "If Mr. Lincoln is the man of the people and the Union, we cannot afford to lose him for the sake of ousting a few postmasters and custom-house officers."

Papers throughout the state were also announcing the holding of conventions in each of Vermont's three congressional districts for the nomination of congressional candidates and the electing of delegates to the Republican National Convention set for Baltimore on June 7.

But not all the news was national in scope: The *Journal* also published the following advice on "How to Choose a Cow":

> There is always some risk in buying a cow, of whose previous character and history we know nothing, for there are no infallible signs of excellence. A rough, scrawny, coarse, ill-shapen cow is often a noble milker . . . a small boned head and light horns are better than large. Long legs make too long a gap between udder and milk pail, and long-legged cows are seldom quiet feeders, but wander about too much.

Horsemen in Windham County took notice of two advertisements in the local *Phoenix*:

ATTENTION ALL WHO LIKE NICE HORSES

The celebrated stock horse Dandy Jack, formerly kept at Shelburne Falls, Mass., by E. W. Wood, will start the coming season commencing May 23d at the stable of the subscriber in Guilford every week except Saturday, on which day he will be at Plumb Hollow in Fairfax. Good pasturing provided for mares coming from a distance. All accidents at risk of the owners.

"Lovers of Fine Stock" were notified that a young stallion named Uncas also would be available for stud services, though Uncas would apparently face a considerably lighter schedule than Dandy Jack. "Will stand for a limited number of mares this season in the Town of Brattleboro," the notice said, "except on Thursdays . . . at the farm of George C. Hall."

The May 14 *Vermont Christian Repository*, published in Montpelier, editorialized on prevalent economic problems, with a bit of religion mixed in:

The signs of this time indicate a pressure with regard to the necessities of life. It may become a question with certain classes, what shall we eat, and wherewithal shall we be clothed? It certainly WILL become a serious question unless this earnest working religion operates with considerable force throughout the country. Our armies are very largely filled with those who were once producers; and in thousands of instances where those have gone who were mechanics or traders, or clerks, THEIR places have been filled by farmers or the sons of farmers. The manufactures of the country are not greatly less to-day than they were four years ago; their CHARACTER is changed, that is all . . . Taking so many men from the farms, and putting them into the armies, must in the end have its effect.

Henry Herrick attended church in Cabot on May 15 and heard the minister "very earnestly implore God's blessing on the soldiers and on those afflicted by the war." Next day, after some garden work, he walked to the center of town, "but it was insufferably dull up there and I could find nobody to be lazy with me. There are so few familiar faces here now and the community seems to be almost entirely changed in the five years I have been gone."

Not all the struggles being waged by Vermonters that troubled spring were on the battlefield or a stony sidehill farm field. Along the Lamoille Valley, teacher Dana, on the eve of another week in the classroom, writing as far away the bullets flew between the deepening trenches at Spotsylvania:

> As the great battle of the war, yes of the age has been fought during the last week, so perhaps I never was called upon to fight a greater battle than last week & I sink from recalling my hard lot; my unpleasant experience in the schoolroom. In the first place I have not been well at all, my bowels have been much out of order my whole system has been out of gear . . . Had occasion to discipline two pupils . . . I wish they might appreciate my kindness and respect my good intentions. God, who protects the right, who are well pleased with those who trust him, who are angry with the wicked every day, be thou my support every hour and every day. Bring me to the dore of work happy, satisfied, cheerful, hopeful . . .

On May 16, the Republican State Convention was held in Burlington, with Vermont railways, largely owned by such Republicans as Governor Smith, offering free trips to attendees. William Hoyt wrote, "Republican State Convention held in town to-day, attended its sittings, not largely attended and its sessions tame and spiritless." The newspapers put the attendance at between six hundred and eight hundred. Next day, the *Free Press* reported that, as expected, Governor Smith, Lieutenant Governor Dillingham, and Treasurer Page had all been nominated. And it stated,

> The main feature of the occasion was the apparently unanimous desire for the nomination of ABRAHAM LINCOLN which found expression in hearty applause whenever his name was mentioned in the conven-

tion; in the resolutions adopted by unanimous vote; and in the election of delegates, unanimously chosen.

All the Vermont delegates bound for Baltimore would, of course, support Lincoln. The convention also passed several resolutions, including a lengthy one that concluded, "We will heartily sustain him and his administration in his efforts to crush the rebellion and the cause of the rebellion, and to restore the nation to union and assured peace."

Though the GOP convention had gone whole hog for Lincoln, within the state there remained a small knot of Lincoln foes. Montpelier's *Argus and Patriot*, a Democratic newspaper, answered news of the Republican gathering with an editorial "The Issue of 1864" that began:

> The fourth, and we trust the last, year of abolition domination has commenced. The three years that are past have been years of carnage, misrule, and mourning. The track of this Administration may be traced to the ever widening stream of blood . . .

On her farm in Stowe, on May 17, Olive Cheney, apparently little concerned with the great issues of the day, wrote to daughter Jane:

> We have had the queerest weather today you ever saw. This morning it was pleasant and very warm, but about the middle of the forenoon it began to rain all of a sudden and poured down GOOD for a few minutes then the sun shone, and finally the clouds and sun have done all sorts of things this forenoon. We have not had a WHOLE PLEASANT DAY this spring, or but a few. Hattie came home from school she cries every night and morning about going to school. Martha McAllaster is her teacher and Hattie thinks she is VERY STRICT, says she don't dare to speak to her . . . The NEW church has been the cause of an AWFUL FUSS among the Universalists, perhaps you have heard about it. There are two parties in the society each determined to keep the other out of the church, and they had a regular battle one night. One or two were injured considerable. They are going to law about it, and they say the church will be closed for a year . . .

On Wednesday, May 18, activity stopped in busy Swanton as funeral exercises were held in the village park for Col. Elisha Barney. The Stars and Stripes shrouded the coffin, and upon it rested the colonel's sword. A huge crowd was present to hear the Rev. D. U. Dayton deliver a eulogy founded on the theme "How are the mighty fallen in the midst of battle." The casket was then borne to the nearby graveyard where, after the singing of "Wrap the Flag Around Me, Boys," it was lowered, as a contemporary account stated, "and dust consigned to dust."

That evening, Henry Herrick went to the Scott home in Cabot to visit Capt. Luther Scott, Fourth Vermont, who had just arrived home to recuperate from a wound suffered May 5. "He has a scalp wound, not apparently serious," Herrick wrote,

> but which may produce inflammation of the brain. He had a ball through his haversack, another through his coat and another through his cap, before he was hit, and thinks sharpshooters were making targets of the officers. He was quite tired and I did not stop long to talk with him.

Perhaps to mother Herrick's consternation, Herrick's friend Zenas arrived at her Cabot home on May 19, bringing tidings that Mrs. Herrick found upsetting. Herrick said,

> Zenas brought the news of another draft soon to come off, and mother is quite in despair about it. The news is not very well authenticated, but is hardly worse than we expected, I suppose. We have decided on going to Montpelier tomorrow and so are going to be early.

In Rutland's town hall on May 18 and 19, a theater troupe performed a stage version of Harriet Beecher Stowe's *Uncle Tom's Cabin*. The *Rutland Herald* found it "deep, thrilling, and solemn."

On May 20, in West Windsor, army veteran Jabez Hammond, certainly glad to be at home and out of his uniform this spring, "finished plowing on the flat & plowed uncle Belas garden." Next day he "Harrowed in forenoon. Planted the watermelons & went to Felchville in afternoon." On a nearby farm on May 20, Miss Julia Blanchard wrote in her diary, "It has been pleasant today. We have cleaned the buttery and cupboard & Mother washed the kitchen floor. About five o'clock Uncle Micah & Aunt Persis and Wain came up here. Made quite a visit . . ." May 21: "It has been pleasant today, but looks a little like rain tonight. I have swept the house most all over and baked a little, besides puttering considerable. Mother has been to Windsor to mill. She bought Aunt Mitty a new dress . . ." Though neither diarist mentioned the other, Jabez and Julia had already fallen in love and would be married within a year.

The morning of May 20, Herrick and Zenas took the family wagon and headed for Vermont's capital city 25 miles distant. The day was clear, but windy, and Herrick said he had a chill by the time they reached the Pavilion Hotel in Montpelier, close to the capitol building, and checked into a room "with a fire in it." Deciding they had time to visit the State House before dinner, the two men found the place locked. However, the Pavilion's proprietor gave them a key and they wandered through the stately domed, columned building by themselves. Herrick wrote,

> Went up stairs and into the galleries of the Senate & House of Representatives, into the Governor's room, also tried to get up in the dome but found the door locked. I had seen it all before, but it was all new to Zenas and I enjoyed it much "for a thing of beauty is a joy forever."

Before leaving they saw the statue of Ethan Allen, on the capitol's portico, arm upraised and demanding the surrender of Fort Ticonderoga, as Herrick noted, "in the name of God and the Continental Congress." On returning to the Pavilion, Herrick said, "There was a soldier from the 4th Regt. at the Hotel wounded in the arm during the late battle, and they were asking him a great many questions concerning it, and those he knew to be wounded."

The next day the two tourists toured Montpelier, then headed for Cabot. Just before departing, Herrick availed himself of the services of the "resident genius" of a local barbershop. He was, said Herrick, "About the blackest and homeliest specimen of 'a man and a brother' I ever saw, but he shaved me very well and brushed and frizzled my hair as well." The trip back to Cabot was uneventful, but cold.

On May 21, Herrick and Zenas were again in the wagon, off to the Moscow section of neighboring Calais, where Herrick had spent his early childhood. Herrick wrote,

> Going down the sand hill, the landmarks grew more and more significant—the little red school-house—the pond and saw mill, but some of the old landmarks are gone—the old red store is gone, and a large house burned down. We drove up past my old home, then down that beautiful winding road to what used to be Grandpa's [house] now owned by strangers, but I almost expected to hear Uncle Harvey's bluff welcome . . . I walked up the sand hill, turning to look at the scenes once so familiar.

That evening, Herrick said he lay on the kitchen lounge with his head in Zenas' lap, and listened to his mother fuss about the possibility of a military draft. "Oh dear," her son wrote, "I wish she could see something more than the dark side of the war . . ."

On May 22, Herrick left Zenas asleep and went to visit the wounded Capt. Luther Scott at his Cabot home, intent on learning details of the death of St. Johnsbury's Captain Carpenter. He discovered that the Scott home had been visited by the death of a soldier son. "He could not tell me much about him [Carpenter]," Herrick said. "Scott had heard of his brother's being killed making six from this town . . . It is very sad and the whole community seems in mourning, and still not without some feeling of rejoicing, I think." That afternoon, after a parting conversation with mother, Herrick and Zenas hitched up the wagon and enjoyed a pleasant journey back to St. Johnsbury. The vacation had ended.

Olive Cheney wrote Jane on May 22,

> The news have not come who were the wounded and killed yet of the last fight only David Marshall son and Houstin killed George Colby wounded. I suppose they are fighting to day. There has a story come William is killed but it has not come in a way we put any dependence on. No one seems to know how the news came. [Her son Pvt. William

Cheney, of the 11th Vermont, would come through the entire war unscathed.] If so he was killed pretty quick after going into action but probably there has a good many out of that Regt been killed some said the report was last night 1000, if so it would be pretty likely some of the Stowe boys were in the number. Your Father was down [in the village] he said there was a good many anxious faces there last night waiting to hear the news . . . it seems they are making a terrible slaughter of our Army but talk as though Grant was advancing toward Richmond. I am afraid we will be overcome and get beat so lose all they have done. Jane we have got to make up our minds to give up our friends that have gone into the Army it will be a miracle almost if their lives are spared, all of the four boys of them. your Father thinks it is asking a little to much of him to furnish so many to the war it wears upon him with his work he looks quite poor to what he did last winter . . . grass looks beautiful fruit trees are blowing full if there does not come a frost and spoil it fruit will be more plenty this fall. Some have planted corn but a good many have not . . .

In his classroom along the Lamoille River, teacher Dana seemed to be getting his pupils under control. May 22:

Praise God from whom all blessings flow . . . The pupils see and with one exception have acknowledged to me personally their wrong . . . We have had a week of warm pleasant weather, almost like summer. Vegetation is getting a fine start. The trees and bushes are as green as in June.

That day, in Burlington, William Hoyt celebrated the birthday of a daughter:

Anna . . . 18 years old to day, and consequently "of age." We have given her a small library of books, a bookcase of pine shelves, and a sewing chair, for presents. She is well and healthy, and as good and pious as a heart could desire.

Far to the south, the armies of Lee and Grant made for the North Anna River. In Montpelier Susan Dewey, wife of Quartermaster

Edward Dewey serving far away with the Eighth Vermont Regiment in Louisiana, wrote to her husband, "Gov. Smith . . . [and Congressman] Woodbridge with nurses have been down to look after the wounded. The governor writes that he shall bring here soon as many of the wounded as are able to be moved." Susan's brother George Dewey was serving in the navy and would one day become a famous admiral of the Spanish-American War, the victor of Manila Bay.

Many Vermont papers reported the progress of construction on the new military hospital at Montpelier for, obviously, the need was about to be great.

The *Brattleboro Phoenix* carried an account of a small consequence of war, surely the result of a union between a soldier and a local young lady:

FOUNDLING—On Tuesday morning . . . about six o'clock, a male child, apparently two or three days old, was found in the shed of G. G. Allen, near the camp ground in this village. It was placed in a basket, properly dressed, and lying on some cotton batting. A new lined hand-kerchief was tied over its head, and some additional clothing placed in the basket. Word was conveyed to the selectmen, who caused the child to be removed and placed under the charge of Mrs. Chaffee on Elliot Street.

In late May, to the Bixby home in Tunbridge, came a letter written at Spotsylvania on May 16 by Lt. Henry Hayward, of the Second Vermont, and addressed to Mrs. Frances Bixby:

Mrs. Bixby

It becomes my painful duty to inform you of the death of your husband Capt. Bixby although I understood the Chaplain of the 2nd Regt. has written to you before this. He was mortally wounded in the 5th of May by a ball in the head. We supposed him killed instantly. I took his watch Diary Pocket book containing $63, several letters and other things all which I gave to Mark Sergent for safe keeping until I could send them to you. Finding him still alive I sent him to the Hospital where he died that night. His trunk is with the train at Fredericksburg which I will send to you the first opportunity if you will write to me where to send it.

It will be some time before we can get it as we are constantly on the move.

Mrs. Bixby I and the Soldiers of this Co. and Regt. mourn the loss of so brave and good officer for he was beloved and respected by every officer and soldier in his command.

As the Army of the Potomac battled its way south, and the Vermont hills became a deeper and deeper green, in Rutland the editor of the *Herald* penned an editorial:

Will anybody read a short paragraph on so common a subject as spring? How can we turn aside from the all engrossing of war and business to contemplate the beauties of nature? We are so absorbed in the stern realities of the hour that we can scarcely spend time, even if we have the inclination, to look upon the smiling landscape, or listen to the song of the robin, the oriole, or the bob-o-link. Never did the grass look greener, the flowers bloom with more charming fragrance, or the thrush whistle more sweetly on the sprig. Vermont, the Switzerland of America, is now in her glory, notwithstanding her sons are pouring out their lifeblood by thousands, she refuses not to appear in her spring attitude.

Let Vermont decorate herself glorious always and forever decorate herself from valley to hill top with the freshest and richest green. Let the people with grateful and chastened emotions enjoy the blessings which the good God has bestowed upon them and fail not to see that he has placed those who have made some honest efforts to keep his commandments in the land of Goshen.

Chapter Twelve

THE NORTH ANNA

The hardest marching of the war" said Charles Porter, in the 11th Vermont, of the move away from Spotsylvania. "The march was what is known as a forced march and we were hurried forward with but stops to cook coffee. We kept going all night of Saturday May 21 being the last troops to leave Spotsylvania & at dark of the 22 we halted—many were completely tired out, threw their blankets on the ground, dropped on them and fell asleep." Capt. Orlo Austin, from Brownington, in the 11th, said, "Many men fell out by the way from fatigue."

Major Crandall of the Sixth Vermont said, "Marched all night constantly halting in the direction of Guinea Station & Bowling Green. Grant is again doubling back Lee in another flank movement. We are getting out of the Wilderness into fair country."

Chaplain Haynes, 10th Vermont:

Crossed a number of small streams which the inhabitants and map makers called rivers. These furnished the waters and syllables for the name of a larger stream below. They were named respectively as follows: Mat, Ta, Po and Ny. Running a short distance to the south, they formed geographically, as well as literally, the Mattapony River. This certainly must have taxed someone's ingenuity for a name.

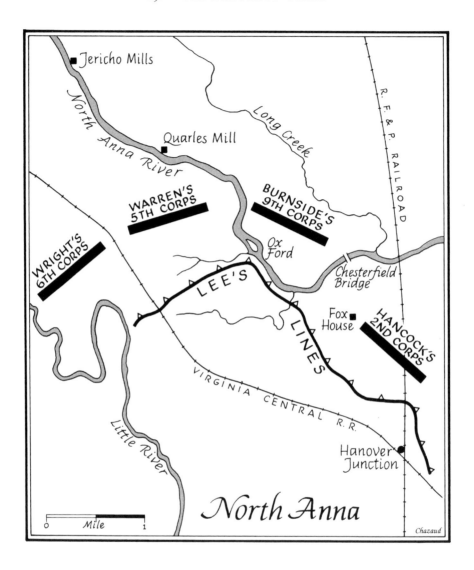

Jericho Mills

North Anna River

Quarles Mill

Long Creek

R. F. & P. RAILROAD

WARREN'S 5TH CORPS

BURNSIDE'S 9TH CORPS

Ox Ford

WRIGHT'S 6TH CORPS

LEE'S

Chesterfield Bridge

LINES

Fox House

HANCOCK'S 2ND CORPS

VIRGINIA CENTRAL R.R.

Little River

Hanover Junction

North Anna

0   Mile   1

Chazaud

The Army of the Potomac was again on the move toward Richmond. But first it swung off east, and for a time as the long columns
tramped past Massaponax Church, Ulysses Grant, George Meade,
and their staffs occupied the yard of the modest brick church, poring
over maps and likely discussing the routes by which the divisions
would march. Photographer Timothy O'Sullivan lugged his big camera
upstairs in the church. Through a window, he took several pictures of
the army brass, sitting on pews taken out into the churchyard for their
comfort.

In departing Spotsylvania, the long columns moved through a mixed landscape of broad fields and dense woods, cut through by sluggish streams. Certainly the appeal of this bland part of Virginia's Tidewater country, not yet severely touched by war, was heightened by its contrast with the shot-torn landscape around Spotsylvania. "This is a beautiful land here," said Major Crandall, ever betraying a poet's soul, with "wide fertile plains extending about as far as the eye can reach."

"From Spotsylvania we marched all night," said Lewis Grant, "and halted a few hours the next day near Guiney's Station . . ." That train stop on the Richmond & Fredericksburg Railroad was already a famous place when the hot and tired Vermonters arrived there the afternoon of May 22. Stonewall Jackson died there the previous spring, on May 10, 1863. Severely wounded at Chancellorsville, he was taken to the railroad stop of Guinea Station and placed in a small house on a plantation there. Under the care of his personal physician and his wife, the general briefly improved. But pneumonia set in and within a week he was dead. Cpl. George Peeler, 11th Vermont, wrote, "Stopped to rest about 10 A. M. on the plantation where Stonewall Jackson died. This is a most splendid country. I am just about played out." Colonel Cummings in the 17th assessed the march, mentioning Guinea Station:

> The country in this region is very fine, but thinly settled and poorly improved . . . The male population are generally absent from their homes, and the females bitter against us, though one gave me a glass of milk the other day, at the house where Stonewall Jackson died.

After the rest stop at Guinea Station, the army's eastward movement ended. The Second and Ninth Corps swung briefly off southeast before turning due south, while the Fifth Corps, and finally the Sixth at the rear of the march, turned due south there. Grant and Lee were again in a race toward Richmond, with Lee having the inside track, most of his troops tramping down the Telegraph Road. His destination was the North Anna River, some 25 miles south, the first sizeable stream that offered a natural defensive position. As in the race from the Wilderness to Spotsylvania, Lee won. Lewis Grant said, "Continued the march to Harris's Store, where we rested for the night."

On May 23, Major Crandall wrote,

Marched from Lebanon Church to North Anna. Hastened the last part of our journey to come to the support of the 5th Corps which was engaged with the enemy. The day was very hot; many of the men fell down exhausted. I wonder if the country knows what she owes to her citizen soldiers.

Sergeant Morey said that his Second Vermont Regiment, along the way, was "Thrown out as guards until the corps had passed along then we went on a mile and drew 5 days rations . . . then we marched on." Lt. Col. Reuben Benton, acting commander of the 11th Vermont, said, "About 4 PM . . . the sound of the engagement at the crossing of the North Anna by the Fifth Corps caused a forced march until 9 o'clock, making forty hours marching out of forty seven." Charles Porter said, "When it became dark with the clouds of dust raised by thousands of tramping feet, we began to feel the effects of thirst, but could get no water for it was too dark to find it . . . Finally at ten or eleven o'clock we reached the North Anna, took a long, deep drink of water and too thoroughly exhausted to get any supper dropped onto our blankets and were asleep . . ." That night, Corporal Peeler said the day's march "came near killing us all," and he added, "It seems as though I should die." Peeler had been part of the skirmish detail left behind at Spotsylvania to screen the departure of the Sixth Corps, and that group had done the hardest marching of all, hurrying to catch up with the Old Brigade and the corps. When it reached the North Anna, Aldace Walker said his detail had marched for 67 of the past 74 hours.

General Lee reached the North Anna the morning of May 22 and surveyed the terrain along the winding, high-banked stream as the bulk of his army came up. It was the next day, toward noon, when the vanguard of the Army of the Potomac approached the river, and long-range firing immediately developed. Warren and his Fifth Corps soon moved upstream, and by late afternoon had crossed the North Anna,

Ulysses Grant, seated in front of the two trees, and his staff outside Massaponax Church en route from Spotsylvania to the North Anna. HOWARD COFFIN COLLECTION

with surprising ease, in the vicinity of Jericho Mills. As Wright's Sixth Corps arrived, it also moved upstream, to support Warren. Meanwhile, Hancock's Second Corps, sent downstream, attacked at Chesterfield Bridge. After only a brief fight the corps routed the South Carolina Rebels on the North Anna's north bank, and the next morning forced its way across the river. So Grant quickly had a sizeable portion of his force below the North Anna, facing both the left and right of Lee's line. Across the river from the Rebel center, Burnside moved his Ninth Corps into position. Late in the afternoon, as Warren edged down the North Anna from the west, he was met by a Confederate force in the riverside woodlands and fields, and a vicious fight occurred. When it was over, fourteen hundred more Union and Confederate soldiers were casualties.

Lee took a long look at the federals and, satisfied that they meant to give him battle and not to now try another flank movement, ordered his army to entrench. It did so in a hurry, throwing up a 5-mile-long line of earthworks in the shape an upside-down letter V. The V's point touched the North Anna at Ox Ford, where the high south bank provided an excellent artillery position. From there, the lines ran off southwest and southeast, about 2½ miles in each direction. One side of the V was nicely anchored on the Little River, the other on a dense swamp. It was a good defensive position. Though Grant had gotten his men across to the right and left of the Confederate center, Lee strongly held Ox Ford, and massed cannon there to support infantry.

Private Hall, Tenth Vermont, in Ricketts' Sixth Corps division:

Our division with the Corps crossed the North [Anna] River at Jericho Mills at 8 AM. The Fifth Corps had fought its way over the night previous. We lay on the bank of the river til 6 PM then we moved toward the South Anna, marching by Grant's headquarters while the Gen. and his staff were having tea.

Chaplain Haynes said,

The newspapers had told us a great deal about the "tooth brush baggage," and the paucity of our commander-in-chief's commissariat. The delusions appeared when we saw the large, airy tents, the splendid outfit of these headquarters, and cast our hungry looks upon the well supplied tables where officers were eating from real crockery plates with genuine knives and forks. This of course was all as it should be, and no man who knew the duties of a soldier could complain of it; but we did not like the newspaper fraud, and did not afterwards commiserate the General of the Army, as we had done before, as he had been represented riding about with the tooth-brush in his vest pocket, living upon hard tack and sleeping at night on the damp ground, with his saddle for a pillow, and with nothing but the deep starry heavens for a shelter . . . We marched through a terrific rain storm to Quarles Mills, where at eight o'clock we run into the enemy's picket lines. After some skirmishing we withdrew, and during the night we took a position and fortified it.

Major Crandall, with the Vermont Brigade, said: "Lay all quiet the troops resting after exhausting toils of yesterday. There has been heavy firing on our right." Crandall had heard Warren's contested advance down the river's south bank.

The Vermont Brigade, with the Sixth Corps, crossed the North Anna the morning of May 24 and moved behind Warren's Fifth Corps to take position near the right end of Grant's long line. There the Old Brigade dug in, within sight of the enemy, and though expecting to be called into action, the men managed to enjoy two days' rest. "Marched across the North Anna River about one mile," said Corporal Peeler, "and stoped and made some coffee and finally pitched our tents . . . we all went down to the river in swimming."

One of the remarkable photographs to emerge from the Civil War shows a dozen naked Union soldiers, waist and chest deep in the North Anna River's cool waters. The Army of the Potomac was made up mostly of farm boys, who knew few greater pleasures than to swim in a cool country brook at the end of a hot and itchy day's work in a hay field. On the North Anna, after nearly three days of relentless hiking down dusty roads through the intense haying-time heat of a Virginia May, they at long last found blessed relief. There they were, cool and happy as in days gone by, boys again amid a man's world of war. They frolicked in the cool waters while above them comrades, ever striving to survive and get back home, dug still more deep trenches. The swimming soldiers took a moment to look at the curious camera, and soon they were back in their blue wool uniforms and were boys no more. For many, this was the last swim they would ever take. Surely, during that blessed break from the business of war, they heard the boom and crack of guns. Newly promoted Cpl. Oscar Waite said, "I had splendid bath in the river; the whole army seemed to be in swimming."

Waite's Tenth Vermont, in Ricketts' division, soon had some work to do. After its morning dip on May 25, according to Chaplain Haynes, the regiment "Marched to Nolan's [Noel's] Station, on the Virginia Central Railroad, which we burned; we also destroyed the track for eight miles beyond." That night, he said, the regiment went on picket below the railroad. "Our post was at a place so wet that those who were allowed the privilege were allowed to pile up fence rails, in order to sleep above water." Haynes said the men were not engaged "except for slight skirmishes." Corporal Waite said, "I was one of the pickets and there was not a sign of a rebel in our front, I managed to put in quite a comfortable night."

Early on May 24, sharpshooter Charles Mead was in breastworks on the north bank of the North Anna, occasionally under fire. Later in the morning he crossed at Chesterfield Bridge, and eventually found himself in some high-ranking company. "We went into the front yard of Dr. Wm. Fox and enjoyed the shade," he wrote. "Got some books. Made hotcakes. The rebs. fell back a little into a better position. They shelled us some P. M. Our men building breastworks, skirmishing all day . . . Gen. Birney, Burnside, Hancock in the yard." That night, Mead said he slept "upstairs in one of the nigger huts."

Major Crandall said May 24: "Still fronting the enemy . . . There has been skirmishing today." So the Vermont Brigade rested and the 10th Vermont held a picket line. The 17th Regiment, with Griffin's brigade of Potter's Ninth Corps division, was sent upstream to support Warren, while the main body of Burnside's force faced the Confederates in the vicinity of Ox Ford. Burnside tested the apex of the Rebel line there, but the attack was easily turned back after a bloody little fight.

As the 17th moved to the North Anna, it was rejoined by its commander, Lieutenant Colonel Cummings, sufficiently recovered from his Wilderness head wound. He wrote to his wife, summarizing his experience along the river:

> Tuesday we drew rations in the morning and in the afternoon crossed the bridge under a moderate discharge of shells. After crossing we lay in line of battle near the stream until 11 o'clock P. M., a drenching rain falling . . . We were put in front and directed to commence intrenching. Just as our breastwork was complete we were ordered to establish a new line further in the front. This we built, with now and then a stray ball whistling by us. The men were now quite tired and were in hopes after breakfast to rest a little; but another line in advance was ordered, so we built, Wednesday morning, our third line. Here we lay on our arms . . . sending out skirmishers and watching the progress of events. Of the skirmishers sent out one was shot through the lungs & will probably not recover; another man was slightly wounded. That day I was Division Field Officer of the Day & had charge of the pickets & skirmishers. We attempted to advance our line of pickets but after an

hour's vigorous firing were compelled to give it up. Before 12 P.M. that night all our troops were withdrawn across the river. At 2 A.M. I went out and withdrew our pickets, so silently that the enemy's pickets did not fire a gun, although in some places they were not ten rods distant. At day light were all across and the bridge was on fire.

While the Vermont units escaped hard fighting along the North Anna, high military drama was being played out. Grant was intent on smashing Lee there, and he prepared to attack the Confederates from both the right and left, along the trenches on both sides of their upside-down V lines south of the river. On May 24 the federals advanced, but quickly came upon powerful entrenchments reminiscent of the Spotsylvania lines.

It soon dawned on the Union high command that the Army of the Potomac was in a mess. Lee had devised a trap, and it seemed ready to be sprung. With Warren's and Wright's corps south of the river to the west, and with Hancock's corps south of the river to the east, Grant's army had very neatly divided itself. Lee, by holding his center at Ox Ford, could attack either wing of the Union army, confident that Grant could move one wing to the support of the other only with many miles, and many hours, of marching. Grant explained it in his memoirs: "To get from one wing [of my army] to the other, the river would have to be crossed twice. Lee could reinforce any part of his line from all points of it in a very short march; or could concentrate the whole of it wherever he might choose to assault. We were, for the time, practically two armies besieging." Despite Grant's glaring vulnerability, Lee never managed to muster a heavy attack on either wing. Lee saw the chance. Indeed, he had created it. But though the Confederate commander fumed at his generals and spoke of going into action, he was incapacitated by illness and never was able to mount an assault. In the end the federals saw their predicament, and after some heavy firing got out of the trap. When it was all over along the North Anna, as Grant moved his forces back north of the river and marched away, Lee may have lost his last great chance to strike his adversary a deathblow.

On May 26, Erie Ditty wrote, "Warm and pleasant in forenoon and until about five P.M. when we had heavy thunder shower. It was found impractical to attack enemy without great disadvantage so recrossed the river and moved to the left." To aid in evacuating the infantry, Grant called on part of Sheridan's cavalry, Wilson's division, including Colonel Preston's First Vermont, which was moved south of the North Anna to relieve the Sixth Corps. Eri Woodbury said that as the regiment approached the river, he saw "a mile or two of 'wounded train' moving from field." Wherever the two great armies came in contact, even if an all-out battle failed to develop, the casualties were always significant.

Behind the cavalry's screen, the Army of the Potomac pulled out of its North Anna lines. Lieutenant Colonel Benton, 11th Vermont:

These Union soldiers enjoyed a swim in the North Anna as the shooting contin-ued not far beyond the high banks. HOWARD COFFIN COLLECTION

Lay quietly until dark. Then marched all night . . . The mud was deep and the night was dark. There had been some rain, and the roads gave the regiment a fair sample of Virginia mud. For several miles of that night's march the mud was literally knee deep.

Lt. Col. Samuel Pingree, in the Third, wrote to "Cousin Augustus" May 26, "We are 27 miles from Richmond, having gained over one half of the distance from the Rapidan by fighting and manoeuvering . . . I hope we may be able to destroy the Rebel Army, before the end of the month, but it is a hard job." Pingree then inquired whether his cousin knew anything of the fate of the Army of the James, under Maj. Gen. Benjamin Butler. He added, "I wish Smith could take command of the active troops there."

Pingree was about to get his wish, in part. While at the North Anna, Ulysses Grant had issued two significant orders that would alter the makeup of the Army of the Potomac. First, Ambrose Burnside's Ninth Corps, including the 17th Vermont, was officially made a part of the Army of the Potomac, and was no longer an independent command. Second, fifteen thousand men in the Army of the James were ordered to move north to join Grant's drive on Richmond. Benjamin Butler's army was hopelessly bottled up south of Richmond, at Bermuda Hundred, so Grant told the hapless general to send him half his force. The 18th Corps would be coming, under the command of a Vermonter, Maj. Gen. William Farrar Smith, of St. Albans. Smith, nicknamed "Baldy," had Grant's confidence, having served him well in the west.

On leaving the North Anna, Ulysses Grant moved, once again, by the left flank. Though the great battle both he and Lee had believed, even hoped, might happen along the quiet river had never really come to pass, more than 2,500 lads northern and southern had become casualties in the woods and fields along the now famous stream.

While the armies began to move away from the river's bloodied banks, back in Vermont, in St. Johnsbury, Henry Herrick had returned to work and was suffering from postvacation blues. The evening of May 23 he took a walk, then came home "feeling quite blue." He explained, "I suppose it is . . . the reaction from my long idleness and something the effect of damp dull weather, but I do feel quite home-sick, blue . . ." Next evening, after work, he read a copy of *Harper's Weekly* and found "a fine picture of Gen. Grant, which presents a fine countenance, in which decision, and determination, are most strongly stamped—the *Weekly* says of it, 'The face of Gen. Grant is of itself a victory, its look of fixed determination is terrible; and his career is the commentary upon it.'" That day, in West Hartford, down in the White River Valley, farmer Orvis Wills wrote in his diary, "A little frost in some places this morn. Frank plowed corn ground today. Mr. Bartell planted corn on narrow flat today." Though Wills carefully made an entry each day, not once did his diary mention war during the entire Overland Campaign. In Vergennes, Mary Tucker wrote, "A lovely day . . . Sue and Bell worked all day in the flower garden. I helped them until noon. Since I have written out a brief review of Longfellow's 'Evangeline.'"

The *Burlington Free Press* reported on the heroic efforts of the Ladies Relief Society of nearby Colchester, since it was formed seven months previous:

> A small initiatory fee was required of every member, and special collec-tors were appointed to solicit money, butter, dried fruits, etc. The con-tributions were liberal, and the meetings well attended. In December, a Concert, under the direction of Col. Munson [Lt. Col. William Mun-son, of Colchester, formerly of the 13th Vermont Regiment], was kindly given for the benefit of the Ladies Society, and $37 was received. This, with other donations, has enabled the Ladies, during the last seven months, to send to the Sanitary Commission four boxes, containing shirts, drawers, socks, quilts, butter, dried fruit and other useful arti-cles, to the value of $152.

Women's groups, organized in towns throughout Vermont, increased their efforts as word of the heavy casualties in Virginia came in.

On May 24, the *Free Press* published a list of wounded in the Sec-ond Vermont alone that took up a column and a half. Each man's name was listed, along with the nature of his wound. Next day, it pub-lished an equally lengthy list of wounded in the Third Vermont. On

May 25, the *Lamoille Newsdealer* in Morrisville printed a list of wounded from the Vermont Brigade that filled a full column. On May 26, the *Free Press* published a message from the office of Secretary of War Edwin Stanton, in Washington, forwarded by Adj. Gen. Peter Washburn, in Woodstock, informing the state that the federal government would, on July 1, conduct another nationwide draft of men. A message from Washburn said the national goal would likely be three hundred thousand, and that Vermont's quota would probably be about seventeen hundred. "It becomes obviously the duty, as well as the interest of every town in the state," Washburn wrote,

> to make immediate and active preparation for the coming draft, by enlisting men and sending them at once into the service, to take the places of the brave men who, by their self devotion upon the field of battle, have so nobly sustained the National Government, and added imperishable honor to the state, making the name of "Vermonter," in the army of the nation, the synonym for unflinching bravery and heroic daring.

The paper contained a great array of advertisements, several aimed at the exploitation of soldiers and their families, including these two:

> HOLLOWAY'S PILLS AND OINTMENT
> All who have Friends and Relatives in the Army or Navy, should take especial care, that they be amply supplied with these pills and ointment . . . They have been proven to be the Soldier's never-failing friend in the hour of need.
>
> FROM THE ARMY HOSPITAL—the bloody battle-field—the mansion of the rich and humble abode of the poor—from the office and the sacred desk—from the mountain top, distant valleys and far-off islands of the ocean—from every nook and corner of the civilized world—is pouring in the evidence of the astonishing effects of DRAKE'S PLANTATION BITTERS . . .

On May 26, Henry Herrick spoke of having read an overly optimistic report in some newspaper:

More news and better from the army to-night. Lee is making for the intrenchments of Richmond and abandoning all his defences between— it seems to show a weakness which would argue well for the final success of our arms, but "the end is not yet," and though we wait with confidence and have strong hope, there is much work yet to be done.

That day, at the military hospital in Brattleboro, Pvt. Augustus Paddock, formerly of the Vermont cavalry, wrote to his brother Ephraim, back home in Craftsbury. Paddock, now assigned to the Veteran Reserve Corps, had worked in the hospital since coming home in late March, recovering from a wound.

A dispatch came to town last night that Lee had crossed the South Anna & was bound for Richmond. If our army can get him pend in and STARVE HIM I think it would be better than to lose so many men driving him out of his strongly fortified places. You say that you are glad I am out of it. The V. R. Corps is being looked over some & I may YET go back . . . I think however that the Surgeon will try to keep me if he can. We are expecting a lot of men in very soon now.

On May 27, the day Grant gave up the confrontation on the North Anna, the *Free Press* noted in its "Vermont Items" that a citizen of Monkton, while visiting Vergennes, "was pelted with rotten eggs for avowing disloyal sentiments." Four convictions on violations of liquor laws were reported in Brandon, including the assessment of a $140 fine against one Widow Burns who, failing to pay, was put in jail.

On May 25, in Westford, farmer Alney Stone had planted corn in the morning. Then he took the wagon to Fairfax and "bought two pigs gave five dollars." That night, across northern Vermont in the village of Island Pond, the local Masonic lodge met and adopted a resolution in honor of Erastus Buck, fellow Mason and resident of nearby Charleston. The popular captain of I Company, Third Vermont Regiment, had died of his Wilderness wounds at the Seminary Hospital near Washington on May 22. The resolution read, in part:

It [becomes] us as worthy brothers and friends to render to his memory

Union soldiers digging in along the north bank of the North Anna at Jericho Mills. HOWARD COFFIN COLLECTION

that tribute of respect and regard so justly due to one who had proven himself worthy, kind and true. He loved the stars and stripes and when his country called, he was one of the first to respond, ever prompt and faithful in the discharge of his duty, brave and resolute in the hour of peril. He has proven his devotion to his country's flag by shedding his heart's blood to uphold it and fell in defending it.

In Brattleboro, Lt. Col. John Tyler had come home, accompanied by his proud and grieving uncle Judge Royall Tyler. The young colonel's body lay in state for a day in the Brattleboro Town Hall, where, according to the local *Phoenix,* "Many of our citizens were permitted to look upon that well-known face." The funeral was held in St.

Michael's Church late the next afternoon. The paper said, "The shadows of the evening hours fell from the darkening sky" as the twenty-one-year-old soldier was accompanied by a military escort to the cemetery and "consigned to the silent dust." As the funeral procession made its way to the grave, more than 500 miles to the south the armies of Grant and Lee were again on the march, again to the south and east, bound for another vast battlefield.

⁂

The state of Virginia makes ever more accessible its Civil War places as the value of heritage tourism increases. Maps are now available that allow one to trace the route of march of Lee's and Grant's armies throughout the Overland Campaign. Grant moved his forces out of Spotsylvania across country to the hamlet of Guinea Station, on the Richmond, Fredericksburg & Potomac Railway, which had become an important Rebel supply depot. Guinea Station is the location of the Jackson Shrine, the small white plantation building in which Stonewall breathed his last in the spring of 1863. A year later, Grant stopped by and spoke words of praise for the Confederate general. At the house, which today still holds the deathbed, a southern lady offered a refreshing drink to a Union soldier from Vermont. From Guinea Station, the route of war wound south through farm country that the Vermonters praised. The sparse look of much of it today makes one wonder whether such praise came mainly as expressions of relief for having escaped the deadly trenches at Spotsylvania.

Drive south on Route 1, the wartime Telegraph Road that runs from Fredericksburg to Richmond, and one eventually reaches the North Anna River. Cross on the aging cement bridge, near the site of the wartime Chesterfield Bridge, and a short way south of the river, on the west side of the road, stands a stately old redbrick plantation house set back from the road. Known today as Ellington, this is the wartime Fox House. It is a private residence and closed to the public, but a good view can be obtained from the roadside. Tradition holds that General Lee received a drink of buttermilk on the front porch from the house's owner. Later several federal generals, including Hancock and Burnside, came under artillery fire in the yard of the house. Also, sharpshooter Charles Mead wrote of spending the night in a slave cabin on the property.

Continue south on Route 1 about a mile and turn right at a historic marker sign, then drive about a mile west to the entrance of the new North Anna Battlefield Park. From the small parking lot, walk on a well-marked trail along some of the best preserved of all Civil War entrenchments. The trail, with interesting interpretive signs along the way, leads about one mile to the apex of Lee's famous inverted V line. At its end, one stands in the deep Virginia woods, looking down at the North Anna River and Ox Ford. Here one sees the point of the ingeniously constructed lines that enabled Lee to divide Grant's army, putting it in danger of being dealt a mortal blow. But Lee, ailing, was never able to bring about the telling attack.

Return to Route 1 and just south of the turn to the North Anna Battlefield, turn left and come almost immediately upon the hamlet of Doswell. Known in wartime as Hanover Junction, here the east–west Virginia Central Railroad, coming in from the Shenandoah Valley, crossed the north–south Richmond, Fredericksburg & Potomac line. The rail junction was throughout most of the war vital to the supplying of the Army of Northern Virginia, as food for men and animals rolled in from the breadbasket of the Confederacy to the west. Hanover Junction today seems the essence of a rural southern village. Some of its old buildings appear to be survivors of the long-ago war. Vines climb the ancient trees, with their low and lazy branches, and obscure old walls and porches, almost as if trying to obscure history. But the past here is vital, and everything seems fixed in some quiet state of preservation. The trains still come and go, up from Richmond, south from Fredericksburg, and in from the beautiful Shenandoah. Throughout the fighting at the North Anna, though Grant made a stab at the place, Lee's army held the railroad junction, though it fell to the federals with the abandonment of the North Anna Line.

Move back north on Route 1 and some three miles north of the

North Anna is the crossroads hamlet of Mount Carmel Church. The brick Baptist edifice for which it is named stands in the southwest corner of the crossroads. Grant set up headquarters in the church during part of the North Anna fighting, and planks set across pews formed worktables. When his armies withdrew from the North Anna, they turned east here, bound for the hell of Cold Harbor.

Chapter Thirteen

TO COLD HARBOR

Nine miles east-northeast of Richmond, at another Virginia place where roads came together in low, sandy country, stood another roadside tavern that had seen better days. Cold Harbor was what the place had long been called, so long that the locals gave little thought to the absurdity of the name. The place was anything but cold, certainly not in the heat of an early Virginia summer, and since it was well out in the fields with no major body of water in sight, nothing that could be called a harbor was within miles. Its name may have been Old English, referring to a low-cost lodging where one might find an unheated room. G. G. Benedict suggested it meant a place of "shelter without fire." The soldiers often misnamed it, some calling it Cool Arbor, or Coal Harbor. Another previously undistinguished point on a Virginia map, this rural location was about to attain worldwide fame because, as May became June in 1864, the varied influences of road networks, stream courses, and military strategy would draw to it, as a vortex, the Armies of the Potomac and Northern Virginia. Getting there from the North Anna proved to be an exhausting, painful toil, with long hot marches, a lot of digging in, and considerable shooting and bloodshed as the armies bumped together on their parallel courses generally south and east. Again, Grant was moving, and Lee was ahead, keeping between his relentless adversary and the Confederate capital.

Wilbur Fisk said he was on the picket line, south of the North Anna and close to enemy pickets on May 26, and shots were occasionally exchanged. He said the pickets were called in about midnight: "The rest of the troops had gone a little while before. We passed back across the North Anna River and turned to the east—another flanking operation. We catched up with the regiment at noon."

Seth Eastman, Sixth Vermont, proud to have just been named a regimental color bearer, described the move to Cold Harbor as "a series of marches and countermarches, intended to deceive the Rebel Commanders as to the real destination of our Army, and many times during the movement, we were put into battle array and entrenched the line as to give battle." He wrote,

> Actually, at the same time, the main part of the Army was in swift motion to gain some advantage of the enemy. But the enemy was very alert and always seemed to know just what we were about to do. We were often so near them that we had conversation with them, they would ask us where we were going next, and would say to us, "You need not be so cunning, we know just what you are up to." We used to talk politics at times . . . They seemed to think the War would be over if George B. McClellan could be president instead of that old barbarian, Abe Lincoln, and so expressed themselves many times in my hearing.

Eastman continued,

> When the army changed its position, it was done with the utmost quietness, so as to get to the place we wanted to occupy before it was known to the enemy. We had to put our canteens inside our knapsacks so they would not rattle. No fire was lighted anywhere, and we would have to be very careful about lighting our pipes for fear of being seen by the sharp-eye outposts of the enemy. And, at this time, only a few men would march away at a time, and the lines would gradually grow thin, while keeping up the show of firing in the direction of the foe . . . Then again, our Cavalry would drag brush along the roads on the other side

of the woods to raise dust to make them think that we were going in an opposite direction from what we were really going.

The route of march for Grant's army was at first on the north side of the North Anna, which, at its confluence with the South Anna, became the Pamunkey River. Grant moved the army downriver in two mighty columns, and on May 27 he had most of two cavalry divisions and Wright's Sixth Corps on the Pamunkey's south side, after crossing on pontoon bridges near Hanovertown and at Nelson's Bridge. "The country along the North Anna," said Chaplain Haynes,

> is barren and destitute of interest, the inhabitants poor and sparse. But as we approached the Pamunkey the soil is rich, well cleared, and culti- vated. The valley is wide and fertile, and wide wheat and corn fields just springing up, gave indication of far more thrift and enterprise than we had seen elsewhere . . . the hungry markets at Richmond needed the utmost kernel they could produce . . . Before the promise of harvest was fairly budded, the heavy tramp of the Union Army came thunder- ing over their fields, and left wide paths, beaten as smooth as a summer threshing floor.

The chaplain of the 10th Vermont had spoken of Richmond and well he might have, for the armies were approaching ever closer to the Confederate capital, now less than 15 miles to the south. While nei- ther Grant nor Lee had yet managed to deliver any kind of fatal blow to his adversary, both commanders knew they were running out of countryside, that something had to give, and soon. Private Fisk said the march to the Pamunkey was "very hot and hard." The Vermont Brigade crossed the river with Neill's division on May 27, three miles upstream of Hanovertown. Sgt. Charles Gould, in the 11th Vermont, informed his parents in Windham, "Crossed the Paminkey River & are now about 15 miles from Richmond. We are on the 'Peninsular' & everything looks promising for the capture of the place." South of the river, the Old Brigade turned west, somewhat in the direction from whence it had come, and tramped several miles to Hanover Court House. Fisk did not like the added marching. "Long after every man had got out of patience," he said, "we stacked our arms and heard the welcome order 'Rest.' After this we had to wait for the beef to be killed and draw our ration of it or else go without. This encroached upon our sleeping hours prodigiously . . ."

Corporal Chandler Watts, 11th Vermont, wrote to his wife, Jane (the daughter of Olive Cheney), from Hanover Court House:

> As it has been a long time since I wrote to you I know that you are worry-ing about me and I have a chance to send I will tell you what sort of time we have had a week ago last Saturday [at Spotsylvania] I went on Picket and most all of the Stowe boys too just at dark the Jonies pitched in to us and we had a smart fight that lasted about an hour George Stevens was killed I saw him soon after he was shot the ball went through his body near his heart he died in an instant all that he said was that he was shot and fell dead . . . in the morning we started on a march Sunday marched all day at night dug rifle pits all night stayed there one day yesterday we came on this ground throwed up rifle pits after a march of 2 days and one night rather tired I tell you . . . I wish that I could see you to night but this is out of the question and perhaps never but I trust that we may see that day sometime the Stowe boys stand the marches first best all but Lamon [Pvt. Lucien Lamson, of Stowe] he is in the rear left sick Geo and Ed & Bill are all well we are having good times as can be expected in the field our army takes a good lot of Stuff as they march along burn a good many houses everything looks like Destruction where we go we are about 15 miles from Richmond the country is handsome if there was no war in the country . . .

The next morning, Private Fisk wrote, "We had to get up this morn-ing at daylight and march on again. Without stopping to get our break-fast or anything of the kind we started off down the river. The roads got clogged up with troops . . ." Charles Mead was on the march with his Second Corps sharpshooter company: "The trains move in the road, and we in the fields," he wrote on May 27. "Halted for the night in a big field, as tired almost as one could be." The next day, he said, "Marching through a country of cornfields. Crossed the Pamunkey on a bridge of six pontoon boats above Newcastle. Passed army headquarters and on about two miles and camped in a cornfield . . . Troops building breastworks. We are now about 14 miles from Richmond."

Chaplain Haynes said the 10th Vermont crossed the Pamunkey at "Widow Nolan's [Nelson's] Bridge" and came to a fine southern plantation. "Our brigade occupied a position south and east of one Dr. Pollard's house," said the reverend,

the works running through an orchard and across a cotton field, where the young plants were about six inches high when we entered it. Pollard's estate was the finest we had seen. He had a splendid plantation, rich in broad agricultural fields, and thrifty orchards; adorned with shade and ornamental trees, and supplied with every domestic convenience. We approached this place through long avenues, shaded by the magnolia and catalpa; and the large egg-shaped flowers of the former, and the clusters of smaller, trumpet-shaped blossoms of the other, variegated with yellow and purple, loaded the air with delicious fragrance, and filled the scene with the most tranquil beauty, strangely contrasting with the smell of powder, the tumult, and the gory exhibition of battle.

Private Oscar Waite said,

We got in a blissful, restful day at the Pollard Place. Much of the time, though, was spent in trying to tame those poor, deluded darkies who were wild as hawks at first. They had been led to believe that the Yankees are all straight from Hades; that we have cloven feet, enormous horns, and a standing contract with Satan to furnish nigger stokers to run his everlasting fires . . . Nearly all the negroes we have seen up to now understand the significance of this war as well as anyone, but we can see by the bulging eyes, the looks and manner of these poor things that they are actually frightened. If it wasn't so pathetic, it would really be amusing."

On May 28, the Old Brigade moved six miles south and dug in on the east bank of Crump's Creek. Lee was waiting, across the Totopotomy, with his army entrenched. The Vermont Brigade guarded the right flank of Grant's army. The next day, a Sunday, the brigade remained in place and Private Fisk said, "Today we have another quiet Sabbath. A few of us got together and had a very interesting prayer meeting. Almost all of our little circle were missing."

As the armies drove south, Charles Cummings, leading the 17th, was becoming more impressed with the scenery. "I saw the scarlet trumpet honey suckle . . . in full bloom," he told his wife:

> I enclose specimens for Lizzie. I also saw the sweet scented honey suckle in bloom, larger holly trees, bigger than our Scotch larch, and a hundred years old, in blossom, much as our hawthorn blossoms. It is a splendid country, peas in pods, beans & melons up & growing finely, corn a foot in height . . . There is no use talking about starving out the rebels.

By the afternoon of May 30, Cummings' regiment, in Burnside's corps, occupied earthworks along the Totopotomy, and he had time to write a long letter to his wife in Brattleboro. "This morning there is skirmishing along the line," he reported. "For the last week we have been on two-thirds rations, and food is at a premium. I saw a soldier pay TWO DOLLARS for six hardtack to one of his comrades who had saved all he could get." But Cummings was living quite well:

> I am now sitting on a rail in the rear of my regt. 3 or 4 rods behind the crest of a hill where the men lay, my back against a tree, a cracker box in my lap . . . I have just eaten breakfast consisting of a nice beaf steak cut an inch & a half thick which I broiled over a twig fire for a time, two hard tack and two cups of tea, all of which I cooked myself. It is the best breakfast I have had for a month. The beef was cut out of a heifer shot by one of my regiment . . . One day my boys foraged for me a chicken, hot hoe-cakes, new butter and milk, but to offset that I have been three days in succession on a diet of six hardtack per day and cold water of a poor quality.

Cummings also discussed the local Virginians:

> The inhabitants are secesh without mitigation in Caroline, Spotsylvania & Hanover Counties—so far as I have learned. There is not to be found a single well man from 16 to 60 at home—all gone to the war.

Their families give them up cheerfully . . . would that the North was as united & committed in this great struggle as the South. They live plain & short of luxuries to carry out their patriotism . . .

While along the Totopotomy, Ulysses Grant probed for a vulnerable point in Lee's well-prepared lines. There was fighting, heavy at times, though the Vermonters generally were spared. There was always danger. Seth Eastman had a close shave: "I was sitting on a seat made of earth," he said,

with my back against the breastwork . . . I had just sat down when I heard a gun go off in front. I sprang up and as I did so, a ball of musket from the enemy entered the middle of the seat where I had been sitting half-a-second before, and it tore a large hole . . . I should have been killed . . . I took out my ramrod and ran it into the hole made by the ball the whole length, and still did not reach the ball, showing that the ball was moving with great velocity.

The Vermont Brigade stayed in its earthworks through the night of May 30 and into the night of May 31. G. G. Benedict wrote,

On the 31st, the skirmish lines were everywhere pressed closely against the enemy and the pickets of Major Chamberlain's battalion of the Eleventh had a lively day of it, though they lost but one man killed, and but three or four wounded.

The sharpshooters were busy, as Charles Mead reported May 30:

Went on picket early in the morning. We have strong breastworks built, found the rebs have ditto and a good position. Dug us a pit with a hoe, under fire, Grover, Kent and I. Sharpshooting on both sides all day, rebel works 600 yards off, battery 900. Some artillery firing . . . After 3 P. M. heard artillery miles away on our left . . . Mortars shelling the rebs in the evening, nice fireworks, but unpleasant for the Johnnies.

While the Rebel and Union infantry growled at each other across the Totopotomy and Crump's Creek, the cavalry of both armies had been in the saddle. Coming down from the North Anna, Eri Woodbury made at least one notation in his diary each day:

May 26: Passed many a new grave—their battles were all o'er, their last sleep is begun, friends may not yet know the sad truths.

May 27: Beautiful day. Went foraging . . . First time I've spoken with a white woman since leaving Vermont.

May 28: Foraging . . . Ninth Corps came past toward the front. [Some of the Vermonters recognized old friends in the 17th Regiment.]

May 30: Marched a short distance then pitched tents upon the banks of the Pamunkey. Abt 12 n . . . crossing on pontoons. About 2 . . . rebs skirmished with us.

As Woodbury noted, Sheridan had his well-rested horsemen moving with the infantry. All went southeast as Grant again moved by the left. On May 28, three miles south of the Pamunkey, the head of Sheridan's advance came up against a line of Rebel horsemen at a country hamlet called Haw's Shop. Both sides dismounted and a battle began that has not been long remembered, despite the fact that it proved to be the second largest cavalry engagement of the war thus far, second only to the massive Brandy Station battle early in the Gettysburg Campaign. Casualties were heavy, and the fight went on for seven hours. Sheridan and his adversaries, Wade Hampton and Fitzhugh Lee, nephew of Robert E. Lee, gave each other all they could handle before the shooting sputtered out. Addison Preston's men brought up Sheridan's rear and were spared the fight. On May 31, Sheridan was in another severe fight, again without the Vermonters. That night, Major Wells wrote home to Waterbury, "It is very hot. The woods are all fire. Dead horses every rod make the air smell any thing like fresh."

Both Grant and Lee were well aware of that strangely named place, off to the east of their lines, where five roads meandered in to meet by an old tavern. Cold Harbor, they knew, had taken on added importance as Grant had relocated his main supply base to White House, on the Pamunkey. The road from White House to the armies led directly through Cold Harbor. On May 31, Grant sent Sheridan to seize Cold Harbor, and when he got there, Little Phil found Rebel infantry had beaten him to it. But he dismounted his troops, who moved forward with their repeating carbines, and he soon seized the crossroads. Sheridan called for reinforcements and was told they were on the way from two directions. From the east, from White House, Vermonter Baldy Smith was on the march with the sixteen thousand soldiers he had shipped up from General Butler's lines below Richmond. From the north and west, out along the Totopotomy, the Sixth Corps was also coming. Men of the Sixth Corps recorded the tramp to Cold Harbor as one of the worst of the war. They had a long way to go, first quietly withdrawing from their position on the far right of the army, then marching along behind the long line, to screen the move. It began well before daylight, in pitch blackness along roads crowded with troops. Then the sun came up and the day became brutally hot. The soil toward Cold Harbor is pale and sandy and with the tramp of thousands of marching feet, a thick cloud of dust rose that nearly choked the men. When the march was over, Carlton Felch, in the Third Vermont, wrote, "Day terrible hot and dusty marching." But up ahead Sheridan kept calling for reinforcements, so the officers were unmerciful. Off to the east, Baldy Smith's reinforcements also were being driven hard, but in the darkness and on confusing rural roads, the column got lost and, for a time, marched in the wrong direction. Sheridan held on against growing numbers of Rebel infantry.

Wilbur Fisk had been out on picket when the move began. "We were relieved at ten o'clock at night," he wrote,

> Taking a very crooked, roundabout way we didn't get back to the brigade till after midnight. Early in the morning again we were ordered to sling knapsacks and trudge. We started to go in the direction of Cold Harbor. So much hard labor, fatigue, loss of sleep and lack of rations had begun to tell on my physical strength and I found it impossible to keep up with the regiment.

Charles Porter, in the 11th:

Vermonter Baldy Smith led the 18th Corps to Cold Harbor. HOWARD COFFIN COLLECTION

At night of May 31 we started on another forced march. The rebs were at Cold Harbor, an important position as several roads radiated from that point. We reached there at 3 o'clock p m and were put in a wheat field to cook coffee. Cold Harbor was . . . an old hotel with a pump house across the road.

Chester Leach, Fourth Vermont, called the tramp to Cold Harbor "the worst march we have had this year for heat & dust, for it was awfully dusty and hot." Major Crandall: "We marched today to Cool Harbor. It has been a hot and dusty journey. Found the enemy in force . . ."

Chaplain Haynes put the distance to Cold Harbor at 15 miles. He said that when the 10th Vermont came on the battlefield, the cavalrymen

received us with wild demonstrations of joy; they had been hard pushed, fighting dismounted all the morning . . . General Custer had his brigade band out on the skirmish line playing "Hail Columbia." As we approached I thought these gay troopers were celebrating a victory, but on the contrary they had been roughly handled, and did not mean to let the enemy know it, even if they themselves were aware of it.

Captain Lemuel Abbott said,

He [Custer] had a goodly number killed and wounded who lay on the field uncared for because all his men were absolutely required for fighting in order to hold the place. Soon the dry grass and underbrush took fire and the helpless wounded were roasted to death, their charred remains being found afterwards.

While Sheridan fought Confederate cavalry and infantry on June 1 in the heat and dust of Cold Harbor, and infantry reinforcements struggled his way, the Vermont cavalry was in a fight miles to the north and west. Early that morning, Brig. Gen. James Wilson had taken James Chapman's brigade back in the direction from whence the army had come, to destroy bridges on the Richmond & Fredericksburg Railroad. Some bridges had already been torched, near Ashland, when the head of the column was attacked by Confederate cavalry under old foe Tom Rosser. Maj. William Wells and his battalion of Vermonters galloped to the rescue and soon came on the First Connecticut Regiment, in fast retreat. Wells at once attacked their pursuers and, temporarily, halted the Rebels. But soon the Confederates came on in a well-organized assault and Wells was forced to give ground. Then along came Addison Preston, with the rest of the Vermont regiment, and he quickly launched an attack on a Confederate flank. The sudden move knocked the Rebels back for a short time, enabling the Vermonters to retire under fire. Chapman's entire brigade was soon in retreat.

Eri Woodbury said, "Fell in with a strong force of enemy near Ashland Station. I went on skirmish line. We were finally flanked completely & had to retreat in haste. Lost largely in prisoners I expect." Among those lost, temporarily, was Preston. The fearless colonel, in making his flank attack, had bulled ahead of his troops and become separated. It was not until the next morning, after a long and dark ride through the Virginia countryside, that Preston and a small group of fellow officers returned to their regiment. The loss for the Vermonters that day was put at seven wounded and twenty-four missing. The next day, the First Vermont Cavalry rested near Hanover Court House until just after dark when orders came from Sheridan. Preston's men, too, would move toward Cold Harbor, where a mighty battle had begun.

While the blue and gray hosts gathered for the last great confrontation of the Overland Campaign, in Vermont on May 27, after a day of rain, Henry Herrick went for an evening walk and found the streets filled with people also enjoying the night air. He and a friend named Ed took seats on the porch of Burns's Store. "Zenas came along," Herrick wrote, "and after stopping awhile asked me to go and walk, which I was very glad to do. Don't know but Ed thought I took rather quick leave of him, but I can't help it, for though I like Ed, Z is my associate." Next morning, Herrick was wakened at 4 AM by "a splendid matinee musicale from the bird chorus." Later, he went to church and heard a Mr. Eastman, from Danville, preach. "I thought him very tedious," said Herrick, "one of the old school in theology, and of the blue-light kind." That evening, after a long walk with Zenas, Herrick

Addison Preston, commander of the Vermont cavalry.
Francis Guber Collection, Vermont Historical Society

came home and mended a shirt, calling the task "a serious job, and making me wonder if I don't need a wife."

In Manchester, in southwestern Vermont, the local paper reported on an incident at "the Seminary" involving a student who came to the dining hall wearing a pin that indicated his sympathies were with the southern cause. The paper said:

> The other students chose to regard it as an insult. After dinner was over, one of them, whose name is Evans, informed the "gentleman from Bradford" that he had worn that pin about long enough. The latter immediately drew a knife from his coat-pocket . . . and made a plunge at Evans. Other students interfered, and after a short but sharp struggle, succeeded in getting possession of the knife as well as the obnoxious badge. Evans' coat and shirt sleeves were cut through, and his arm was slightly scratched. Another student had his wrist slightly cut. No other damage done. The copperhead will probably be dismissed.

In Rutland, excitement was reaching a fever pitch as the visit by Tom Thumb and his new bride neared. The *Herald* said the little entertainers would arrive in a tiny coach drawn by miniature horses for afternoon and evening performances in the town hall.

In Bennington, the *Banner* announced a happy ending to the story of a Vermonter shot in the Wilderness:

> Gen. P. Harwood, who left this place some two weeks since, to look for his son Martin, who was wounded in the leg in the late battles at the Wilderness, has arrived home, accompanied by his son, who, we are happy to learn, is doing as well as can be expected—although his wound is still very troublesome. The Judge gives a painful account of the sufferings experienced by the wounded a few days after the battles, for the want of proper surgical treatment and good nursing . . . But the wounded he says are now all removed from the scenes of the battles, and are well cared for in the Washington and Philadelphia hospitals.

Private Harwood, Second Vermont, was wounded on May 5. Finally, some of the men shot in the Wilderness and Spotsylvania were coming home. But surely not all, as the *Rutland Herald* made clear in its report on a funeral in Bridport, up along Lake Champlain. The paper said that services would be held the following Sunday for Lt. Albert Crane, also shot on May 5 in the Wilderness. The paper said, "We learn that Lieut. Crane . . . was not killed instantly, as first reported, but died in an ambulance while being moved to hospital, about an hour after receiving his death wound. His body has not been recovered."

❋

Following the route of Grant's army from the North Anna, one notices that as the miles are traveled, the fields become larger and more lush. Past Mangohick Church, where Grant set up headquarters for a time, and which survives, one turns south and soon comes to a bridge across the sluggish Pamunkey River, which flows through a lush river valley. The bridge stands at the site of Nelson's Bridge, where many of the Vermonters crossed the river on pontoons. On a bluff to the north stands the imposing "Wyoming" plantation house, home of the Nelson family for which the bridge is named. The Nelsons lost a son not long after the Union army passed by in fighting near Richmond. He was a cavalryman in a Virginia regiment. Look on the high ground south of the river for entrenchments, on private property. Moving on, one soon comes to Salem Church, which survived the war, standing at a wartime place known as Haw's Shop. A short distance away is another wartime house of worship, Enon Church. Somewhere between the two churches, Colonel Preston of the Vermont cavalry fell. Moving south, the sluggish Chickahominy is soon crossed, and more trenches can be seen on the high ground south of the river. Cold Harbor is nearby.

Chapter Fourteen

A MARK THAT WILL SHOW
FOR AGES TO COME

The enemy had a strong position in our front, and from appearances we were going to try to hit that position," Wilbur Fisk said concerning the late afternoon of June 1. "Our regiment was formed into the front line, skirmishers were ahead firing continuously. Our batteries got into position and soon we had a furious fight with artillery. By and by the order came to advance."

Sheridan's cavalry had held Cold Harbor until relieved by Horatio Wright's Sixth Corps. From the east came Baldy Smith's 18th Corps, at long last tramping in from White House, after a confused trek that brought them to the field hours late. Grant was impatient, and though planning a heavy attack next morning, he ordered the Sixth and 18th Corps forward. The aim was to push up close to the Confederates, seizing an advantageous position for launching a big morning assault. The battle of Cold Harbor, already a tough fight, was about to become brutal.

Lewis Grant said of the June 1 action, "The attack was made by the Sixth and Eighteenth Corps, the Sixth on the left and the Eighteenth on the right; this [Neill's] division and brigade having the extreme left. The plan of attack was in four lines, and this brigade was placed on two lines in front, with two brigades in its rear." To protect his exposed south flank, Grant positioned the Third Vermont to the left, in the direction of the Chickahominy. "While the preparations for the attack were being made the enemy opened a heavy artillery fire in our front," said Grant, "and at the same time attempted a diversion of the left by attacking our skirmish line and opening artillery from that direction." To meet the new threat, Grant also ordered the Sixth Vermont to the left, to help the Third Regiment; a bit later he sent the Fourth Vermont over to further strengthen the flank. The brigade commander also dispatched the Fifth Vermont to the support of a battery firing to protect that endangered end of the line. Those troops guarding the flank, though under fire, were thus kept out of the attack, certainly sparing them many casualties. The Vermont Brigade's advance fell on the Second Vermont and the big 11th Regiment. To the front was a low hill, then a stretch of uneven ground, on the far side of which were the Rebel works. Benedict wrote, "It was no holiday work. The enemy was well posted, his lines covered and concealed by woods, while the attacking troops moved over open ground . . . Both the artillery and musketry fire in front was terrific."

Wilbur Fisk:

> We moved slowly to the crest of the hill, then double quick. Our regiment went altogether too fast. The ground was rough and we became more broken than we needed to. The rebs poured a terrible fire into us of grape and canister besides a line of rifle pits filled with infantry that rained their bullets among us in a perfect shower.

Lieutenant Colonel Benton, leading the 11th, said his men advanced to within about 100 yards of the enemy under heavy fire, both from Rebel infantry and Union artillery. Charles Porter:

> We were ordered forward, through a patch of pine woods, the trees scattered, and after a couple of hundred yards came into open ground and 500 or 600 yards away down a slope and across a flat on which corn three or four inches was growing, and at the edge of heavy timber was the rebel breastworks, and as soon as we emerged from the pines, the

enemy opened a fire of musketry and canister. I had a man hit, Joseph Bean [of Hinesburg], a Canadian French man hit in the leg. Directly in front of E Company was a house and garden. Capt. Sears [Richard Sears of Wilmington] gave the order, "By the right flank file left," and while going in four ranks another got hit and at the foot of the slope was the head of what is known in the west as a slough, and here we found the first brigade of our division hugging the ground. Our battery . . . was dropping shells among us, some would explode behind us and the pieces would hit the men. The lieutenant colonel . . . then ordered a charge on the breastworks in front, and directly in front of us, close enough to reach with our hands, was a New Jersey brigade, and when ordered to charge their officers told them to stay where they were . . . Musketry came fast and furious, cutting men down rapidly. When about half way to the reb breastwork we found that those on our right were not advancing but had halted and lain down. We were therefore ordered to halt and lie down and presently the order was given to return . . .

Corporal George Peeler, in the 11th, wrote, "Went into the fight and fought . . . until after dark our Co. awfully cut up. Dug entrenchments all night." Fisk added, "Our flank gave way and we had to retreat over the crest of the hill to a place near where we had started from, when we rallied and advanced once more."

Again, the Vermonters' mettle under fire was proven, for though driven back by heavy fire, they rallied and resumed the attack. But not for long. Fisk said his regiment was under "severe fire" for 300 yards both in advancing and retreating. "Had the movement been started with proper care," he said, "it seemed to me it might have been a success." To the right, or north, along the federal line of battle, another division of the Sixth Corps was having considerably more success. James Ricketts' regiments, including the 10th Vermont, battled into the Rebel works and came back with 600 prisoners. Chaplain Haynes: "The advance was made through [a] belt of pine woods . . . over a ploughed field, where the rebel skirmishers had erected temporary breastworks of fence rails, through a shallow ravine and swamp, and into a thick woods where the rebel intrenchments were forced and carried." The 10th rushed across the open ground, under fire, and leaped into the Confederate earthworks. Haynes said that a sergeant from St. Albans, Silas Lewis, "Sprang over the works capturing single-handed a major, a lieutenant and several men." Another St. Albans man, Pvt. Edward Skeels, according to historian Benedict,

> was among the first to mount the works, saw a Confederate major and two lieutenants leaving an underground shelter, almost at his feet, as he sprang inside the breastworks, and ordered them to surrender. They gave him their arms, and were sent to the rear, while he remained and emptied the major's revolvers at the retreating enemy.

In the midst of it all, the commander of a North Carolina unit, apparently the 54th Regiment, surrendered his sword to St. Johnsbury's Capt. Edwin Frost, serving that day as regimental major. Haynes said, "When this regiment surrendered, Colonel [William] Henry jumped upon a log and called for three cheers, which were given with a will."

Hundreds of Rebel prisoners were passed through Ricketts' division to the rear, and the 10th Vermont felt it should have been given credit for capturing a large share of them. But since those Confederates ended up in the hands of other units, the 10th received little official due. The cost to the regiment was high. In the midst of the close-in fighting along the Rebel works, Lt. Ezra Stetson, of Montpelier, commanding B Company, was killed by a bullet to the face, and minutes later Lt. Charles Newton, of Company G and Williamstown, was struck in the throat, falling dead. Also, Colonel Henry, soon after leading the cheers, had a finger shot away. Lt. Col. Charles Chandler, of St. Albans, quickly took command. Lt. William White, from Sheldon, said the attack was "through a sheet of fire." He later wrote from a hospital bed,

> When we got within yards of the rebel rifle pits . . . a ball struck my saber, then glanced cutting a hole in the outside of my pants, bruised the main artery in my left groin enough to break the skin & make it very sore, but the ball did not go in, so you see I have great cause to thank & bless the Lord.

Chaplain Haynes:

The captured works were strengthened, and others thrown up. This business was not attended to a moment too soon, for an hour afterwards the rebels made a desperate attempt to regain their works and capture ours. In this attempt they were fearfully repulsed; repeating it several times during the night, they met with the same ill success.

When at last the fight died, men all along the Union line dug in as best they could. In their advanced position, G. G. Benedict wrote that along the 11th's front,

> Throwing themselves flat, the men secured partial shelter from the bullets which whistled over and around them by digging shallow trenches with their bayonets, tin plates and cups, and held their ground till nightfall. The sun sank red in the west, on a field veiled by clouds of smoke and dust, and the stretcher-bearers were busy along a front of over two miles.

Private Ellery Webster, from Irasburg, was in the fight with the 11th. "Image how it looks on smooth water when it rains," he said, "and you have something of an idea how the ground looked around us, when the bullets struck. It is a great wonder to me how so many got off without being killed or wounded." The day had been hard fought and deadly, but the Union army, Grant believed, had positioned itself well for the morning. Charles Morey, Second Vermont, wrote that night, "Fortified our position within good rifle range."

Private Fisk concluded his report on the day,

> That night we built breastworks out in the field pretty close to the enemy. The whole army appeared to be doing the same. The field was covered with haversacks and knapsacks that the men had thrown away. I picked up a half tent and all the hard tack I wanted.

The loss to the two attacking corps that first afternoon of June 1864 had been about 2,200 men. The 11th Vermont was hard hit, with 119 men shot. Of them, 32 died, or soon would, of their wounds. The artillerymen from the Washington forts had taken their first severe casualties as infantrymen. The 10th Vermont's losses were nearly as heavy. In the Second Vermont, nine men were wounded.

The next morning, the brigade lay low behind what protection its men had managed to scrape up. "We stayed in our works," Private Fisk wrote,

> [until] ten o'clock when we were relieved by some of the Second Corps. This was a rather ticklish place for a timid person to be in. Bullets were flying continually. A man must keep his head down or he would be sure to get hit. Only that bank of dirt was between us and death. Our rifles made the rebels' predicament but little better. When the Second Corps came to relieve they came along with their heads up as if nothing was the matter. But when the bullets began to "Zip" "Zip" amongst them pretty lively they curled down and got up to the works in their respective places as quickly as possible. Several were hit as they were relieving us. We filed carefully out so that a building would cover us and none of our men were hit. Royal Sanborn [a private from Tunbridge] got it nearer right when he said we were to be taken from one nasty hole to be put into another nastier one. We were shoved around on the right expecting to go to the front, but another regiment took the front lines and we built breastworks further to the rear.

Brigade Commander Grant:

> The division moved to the rear, then marched to the right of the Sixth Corps and relieved a division of the Eighteenth Corps. This position was a very unpleasant one. A part of the enemy's works had been carried at this point and was now held by us under a very destructive front and flank fire.

Obviously, the daybreak mass attack planned by Grant had not materialized. Hancock's Second Corps was slow getting into position. Meanwhile, Baldy Smith was complaining because many of his men still had not reached the field after their difficult march of the previous day. Finally, an exasperated and testy federal high command postponed the whole thing until the following morning. All the while, the

Confederates were busy deepening their trenches, cutting lines of fire to cover all fields of fire, and carefully positioning artillery—in short, creating about the best defensive line the Civil War produced. And it was all sited along a low line of hills, mostly with open country or thin woods to the front. Lee waited, even hoped, for another federal advance. All day long the Union soldiers stayed low, ever under fire in their advanced positions, waiting for orders to again rise up and move forward. But morning became afternoon, then evening. The firing never stopped, but the lines remained in place. The night of June 2–3, the rains came, a sullen storm that some soldiers said had sleet mixed in, at least serving to dampen the parched earth and give temporary relief from the heat. Richard Crandall noted, "The foe is throwing shot and shell among us with some rapidity. An order to charge the enemy's works has been countermanded, it has been delayed until daylight." Along the Union lines it was noticed that some veteran soldiers wrote their names and homeplaces on slips of paper. These were pinned to the backs of their uniforms, to be used in identifying their bodies the next day. The old soldiers had taken a daylong look at the strengthening Rebel positions and knew the dawn would bring deadly work.

The force that had come up from Ben Butler's Army of the James included two generals who had once led the First Vermont Brigade, and one former commander of the Second Vermont Brigade. The 18th Corps was led by Baldy Smith, who three years previous had won permission from another Army of the Potomac commander, George McClellan, to go against army policy and form a brigade composed entirely of regiments from a single state. Thus Vermont's Old Brigade had been born. The brigade's second commander had been William Brooks, a tough Ohio native, now leading Smith's First Division. And commanding the First Brigade of the 18th Corps' Second Division was George Stannard, recovered from a serious wound received while his men assaulted the right flank of Pickett's Charge at Gettysburg. Indeed, word that Stannard was again fit for duty was big news in Vermont. When the commander of the Ninth Vermont, Edward Ripley, heard of it in North Carolina, he wrote Stannard, "I have heard with a great deal of pleasure of the recent girding on of your armor once

more, knowing so well with what intense satisfaction you must have
obeyed the summons." When word reached Vermont that the 18th
Corps had joined Grant's forces, several newspapers carried chatty
items about the Old Brigade being reunited with its former commanders, and with the great Vermont hero of Gettysburg. Smith's corps
was about to go into battle beside the Sixth Corps, including the Vermont Brigade.

For the morning attack, Burnside's Ninth Corps held the army's
right flank, to the north up near the Totopotomy. Burnside's left flank
connected with Warren's Fifth Corps, and Warren's left, in turn,
linked up with Smith's 18th Corps, in the center of the Union line.
South of Warren was Wright's Sixth Corps, and below it, stretching
down toward the Chickahominy, was Hancock's Second Corps. Hancock, Smith, and Wright would make the initial assault. In preparation, Neill's Second Division, with the Vermont Brigade, was shifted

*Brig. Gen. George
Jerrison Stannard, said
to be the first
Vermonter to enlist
when the war began,
led the Second Vermont
Brigade to glory at
Gettysburg. He fought
at Cold Harbor, leading
an 18th Corps Divi-
sion.* HOWARD COFFIN
COLLECTION

to the right of the Sixth Corps. Beside them were the new men in town—Baldy Smith's 18th Corps. Neill's division was formed in three lines, with the Vermont Brigade making up the second. In the front line was Wheaton's brigade. Action began as Union artillery opened on the Confederate lines in a heavy 10-minute bombardment. The big attack at Cold Harbor came just before dawn. Pvt. Oscar Waite, 10th Vermont, described its commencement:

> At half past three this morning the orderly sergeants quietly told the men to fall in for roll call; the names were called and the answers given in tones not louder than ordinary conversation, and the men dismissed for breakfast of pork, hardtack and coffee, made over tiny fires in some sheltered ravine. Then the companies were formed into regiments; from these came brigades; and from the brigades, divisions . . . Some of the men were just leaning on their guns; others quietly pinned tags to their coats, with the names and addresses of friends at home: but at the same time, all were watching a gray streak of light creeping along the horizon, and were listening for that bugle call which, whatever its military significance, means to us boys, "More childless parents; more weeping maidens; widows and orphans, widows and orphans." At 4:30 they heard it; the brazen-toned order to Charge! Far flashed the red artillery, and the line moved on.

The day's first light was gathering in the east, to silhouette the men in the long blue lines, as Grant's divisions moved across the damp earth, through the pines and trampled fields, on a six-mile front. Ahead, in the gloom, was the long, low rise that held the Rebel earthworks, a thin scar of fresh-turned earth all that betrayed the presence of an army. Beyond it, not a half day's walk distant, was Richmond. As Grant's men advanced, many of them were guided by an old dirt road that ran less than 10 miles into the Confederate capital.

The advance was ill planned and irregular, far from a solid line of battle, and the Confederate riflemen and cannoneers, encountering it, came alive piecemeal. But soon the Rebel trenches were lit with thousands of muzzle flashes sounding forth a rolling crash, while the roar of artillery added its thunder. The heavy blue lines were ripped, not

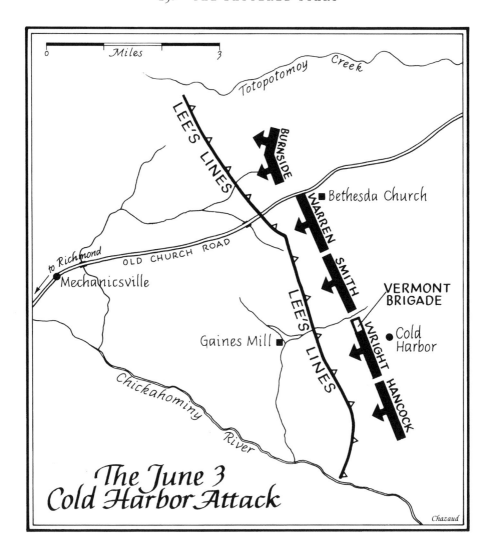

The June 3
Cold Harbor Attack

Chazaud

unlike the Vermont Brigade had been so suddenly and horribly shattered in the Wilderness. Ulysses Grant, two decades later in the waning days of his life, would write, "I have always regretted that the last assault at Cold Harbor was ever made . . . At Cold Harbor no advantage whatever was gained to compensate for the heavy loss we sustained." Brig. Gen. Evander Law, in the Confederate works on that June 3, also recalled it 20 years later:

Our troops were under arms and waiting, when with the light of early morning the scattering fires of our pickets . . . announced the beginning of the attack . . . I had seen the dreadful carnage in front of Marye's Hill at Fredericksburg, and on the old railroad-cut which Jackson held at the Second Manassas, but I had seen nothing to exceed this. It was not war, it was murder.

Captain James Franklin, Fourth Alabama:

We stood there three and four deep in the works, which we had strained every nerve and muscle during the night to complete, the men in the rear handing up loaded guns and taking empty ones from their comrades in front. We had never had nor desired a better chance to protect ourselves and damage an enemy. Line after line came out of the opposite woods, only to melt away under our continuous fire . . .

As Neill's division advanced, Wheaton's men to the front overran a Rebel picket line. But facing the fusillade pouring forth from the main Confederate line, they quickly came to a halt and lay low. "The first line was wasted away before they got out of the woods and the others halted," said Major Crandall. The Vermont Brigade was close behind, and when Wheaton asked Lewis Grant for help, saying he could not hold his position, Grant moved his men up in close support. Then he sent the Third and Fifth Vermont Regiments to replace Wheaton's front line. Grant said, "No farther advance was made." Wilbur Fisk, in the Second Vermont, perhaps mistakenly, said the Sixth Vermont was to his regiment's front. "Shot and shell and bullets were flying," he said:

The Sixth Regiment was just ahead of us. As fast as they advanced, we were to follow. They were in the works just ahead of us. Pretty soon we saw them leap over their breastwork and advance to the next one. We advanced and took the one they left. Their Lieut. Bailey [Hiram Bailey, of Brandon] was killed. A piece of shell hit him in the forehead. He lived to nearly night when he was buried. The Sixth Regiment advanced to another line and we followed them as before.

The Vermonters, in their brief attack, had carried some Rebel rifle pits. But they got nowhere near Lee's main line.

Remarkably, Fisk seemed to feel that no major engagement had yet taken place. Apparently the brevity of the attack had deceived him. "Everything indicated that a regular engagement was going to take place," he wrote:

> Colonel Pingree came around and told the company commanders to instruct the men to keep closed up and maintain as straight a line as possible in going through the woods. We were going to make another charge as soon as the 18 Corps advanced our right. Well we could make another charge and do it bravely but after so much hard fighting we did not feel that enthusiasm that we did at first. At least it was so with me. I dreaded the contest. If there had been an honorable way for me to get out of it I should have done so. But duty said go forward and trust in God and so I determined to do. But the order to advance was not given. They discovered the enemy had too strong a position for us to carry. So we remained there all day.

The popular and eloquent Maj. Richard Crandall died from a sharpshooter's bullet in the trenches at Cold Harbor. VERMONT HISTORICAL SOCIETY

Charles Porter, in the 11th Vermont, wrote, "The order to assault was countermanded and a sickening list of killed was avoided." Nonetheless, musketry and artillery fire poured in toward the Vermonters. Porter kept low, but not low enough. "I was lying on my right hip and elbow," he said,

> keeping my head low, I was struck on the shoulder blade quite hard. My first thought was that some Johnny had up and either kicked, or struck me with the but of his gun. I involuntarily exclaimed Oh! As it hurt very much, as the force of the blow was sufficient to roll me down the embankment. I heard some of the boys say, "Porter is hit," and two or three crawled to where I lay and offered me help to the rear, but I said "If the bullets gone in where it hit, there is no use moving me," but on looking there was no hole in the knapsack and the bullet was found on the ground.

Porter was taken to a field hospital, and survived.

Though the Vermont Brigade had not experienced the worst of Cold Harbor on June 3, still the day was for them a bloody one. Pvt. Alvin Woodward, Third Vermont, chronicled the loss of his tent mate, Pvt. Horatio Hogaboom, also of Berkshire, that day. "After we had been on the line about two hours," he wrote to his wife,

> Horatio was killed shot through the head by a sharpshooter the ball went in just below the left eye and passed out at the back side of the head. He died instantly, and without any pain. He did not even groan & there was not even a contraction of the muscles. He stood a little to the right and about 10 feet to the rear of me and I did not know that he was hit until the Capt told a man to take his things and give them to Woodward . . .

Lewis Grant: "The Third and Fifth Regiments were much more exposed than the rest of the brigade. They had no protection except the trees at the edge of the woods." Grant then risked disobeying orders to protect his endangered front line:

> I asked for authority to withdraw these regiments, leaving only a skir-

mish line to hold the edge of the woods. This authority was refused. Being, however, satisfied that men were needlessly exposed, and that a skirmish line would hold the position as well as a line of battle and with less loss of life, and having obtained the direction of the assistant adjutant-general of the division in the matter, I withdrew those regiments, leaving a skirmish line for each, which held the position the remainder of the day.

In the center of the Sixth Corps' advance that morning was Ricketts' division, with the 10th Vermont, under Lt. Col. Charles Chandler, replacing the wounded regimental commander Colonel Henry. The division moved under heavy fire to a point within 40 yards of the Rebel line before being repelled. Pvt. Oscar Waite wrote:

We did not go far, only for six rods . . . soon, in spite of a hot fire from the front, by the lively use of bayonets, frying-pans, tin plates, and cups, we had a temporary protection, and the satisfaction of holding practically all the ground we had been over. Soon, we had our turn; while one half of the company was digging, the other half was trying to shave the top of the rebel breastworks just under every hat that showed itself. The range was short—like shooting across a broad highway—and our loop holes were small. Next we turned our attention to the sharpshooters and, not liking such short range, they finally backed off; not so far, though as to prevent our hearing from them occasionally. Every puff of our smoke draws perhaps a dozen bullets, which, in one case at least, brought a fellow sprawling from a pine tree top.

Among the scores of 10th Vermonters who fell on June 3 was the popular Capt. Edwin Frost, a Thetford resident who had attended nearby Dartmouth College. He died that night from two horrible wounds, saying as he slipped away that he was "happy to die for my country and my God."

On the far right of the army, the 17th Vermont, in Burnside's corps, was spared the morning attack. However, the regiment was moved forward into a field in the afternoon, and came under fire. Regimental commander Cummings, like Lewis Grant, apparently bucked orders to spare his men. "In the midst of a galling front and infilading fire," he wrote,

> word came that we were to charge and take a battery that had been silenced by our sharpshooters but could not be withdrawn. Being the senior officer of the three regiments on the ground I declined to order the charge so we remained and poured in as smart and well directed fire as we could. It was evident that the enemy had a very strong line in an extended rifle pit in our front and sharp-shooters on our right.

Cummings said that he soon brought his men back to a more sheltered position, along a road somewhat to the rear. But in retreating, he said, "A fire opened from the whole length of the enemy's rifle pit, which had been supposed to be nearly or quite empty, and a masked battery threw grape & canister, the whole movement was an error."

Cummings put his loss at 1 killed and 15 wounded, 5 of whom later died. Among them was a Corporal Scott [probably Oscar Scott, from Townshend], who was hit by a shell that severed his foot at the ankle. The former Middlebury College student told his company commander, Lyman Knapp, also of Townshend, "Captain, you don't know how that hurt."

The Vermont Brigade lay low through the morning, doing its best to dig in, as any movement drew fire. In the early afternoon came orders for a second attack. But after a long and anxious wait, the Union high command thought the better of it. So the long day passed at Cold Harbor, as the cruel sun rose high and blazed hot. The Union attack had been a miserable failure, conducted at a frightful cost, destroyed within minutes. In places, some Union units briefly, miraculously, gained the Confederate lines. Some troops in the 18th Corps, led by a Vermont combat veteran, nearly got a foothold. Brig. Gen. George Stannard's brigade, advancing to the right of the Sixth Corps, struck a shallow ravine leading toward the Rebel works. Benedict said,

> Stannard made three gallant and desperate charges. Twice he nearly reached the breastworks in front; but the raking fire from both flanks was too deadly to be endured, and he relinquished the attempt; but not

till after every regimental commander but one, sixty per cent, of his line officers and fifty per cent of the men of his brigade had fallen. Stannard was himself wounded in the thigh, but kept his saddle, and he lost every member of his personal staff, killed or wounded.

Baldy Smith said, "Stannard's Brigade [was] repulsed in three gallant assaults."

In a way, the Vermont Brigade got off easy that bloody morning. Still, 104 casualties were suffered, mostly in the Third and Fifth Regiments. The Sixth Corps had lost more than eight hundred men, and nowhere had it reached the main Rebel line. In the entire army, nearly eight thousand men had been killed, wounded, or captured. More than half had fallen in the first few furious minutes of the assault. Firing went on through the long, slow day, the heat increasing as the sun moved across the pale sky. The Union men tried to hold the ground they had gained, scooping out shallow earthworks, ever under fire. To the front, out in the open between the lines, lay wounded and dying men, their comrades helpless to aid them.

Just as darkness mercifully began to envelop the battlefield, a hot fight developed to the left of the Sixth Corps. The Vermonters were not engaged. During the night, Lewis Grant was ordered to send half his brigade, the Third and Fifth Regiments, and two battalions of the 11th to the left, where they were placed in the front line with Russell's Sixth Corps division. The Second, Third, and Fourth Regiments, and the remainder of the 11th Regiment, stayed on the front of Neill's division.

In the slaughter of the early morning of June 3, Vermont lost some of its finest, including a young man heading a regiment from another state. Franklin Aretas Haskell had become one of the best-known soldiers in the Army of the Potomac since Gettysburg, where the young officer had dashed about under fire bringing troops into line on Cemetery Ridge to confront Pickett's Charge. After the battle, he had written a lengthy letter about it that remains probably the best eyewitness account of the battle by a participant. Haskell was born on a farm high in the hills of Tunbridge, just over the ridge from where Wilbur Fisk grew up. He graduated from Dartmouth, then went west to Wisconsin to read law. When the war began, he enlisted in a Wisconsin regiment that became part of the famed Iron Brigade. As the big June 3 attack rolled forward at Cold Harbor, Haskell, now a colonel, was leading his 36th Wisconsin Regiment. His men had just started forward when they came under heavy fire. Their colonel was standing amid the leaden storm, shouting to his men to lie down, when a bullet struck him in the temple. He was dead in three hours. When he heard the news, former Iron Brigade commander Brig. Gen. John Gibbon said, "This sad event cast a gloom over us all."

So bloody June 3 ended at Cold Harbor with Richmond still a vain hope, off behind those trenches now known to be impenetrable. The Confederate victory had been the most one-sided of the war. Though the Union high command was slow to realize the magnitude of the disaster, and talked of renewing the attack, all those broken blue-clad bodies between the lines grimly, pathetically displayed the Union failure. As was certainly becoming clear to the men in the trenches, Grant's costly spring offensive would not end in the fall of the Confederate capital. Captain Abbott, 10th Vermont, summed up the day: "We never even reached the enemy's works . . . We advanced under a murderous fire in our front from the enemy's artillery, sharpshooters, and when in range of its main line of battle were simply slaughtered."

As the two great armies faced each other in the darkness, out on the right of the Union line, near Haw's Shop where the big cavalry fight had raged seven days earlier, the First Vermont Cavalry Regiment was in mourning. The Vermonters had been in action that day, in support of the infantry attack at Cold Harbor, and the cost had been high. Col. Addison Preston, the handsome daredevil commander so popular with his men, had as usual been at the front and had taken a bullet near the heart that proved fatal. Indeed, as George Benedict noted, the loss was felt throughout the entire Union cavalry corps. Preston's regiment had been engaged June 3 because James Wilson's division of Sheridan's cavalry had gotten orders the previous day telling them to attack the extreme left of the Confederate line at Cold Harbor as the grand assault went forward. Thus, the division had taken a lengthy ride out to Hanover Court House and, crossing the Pamunkey, closed on Haw's Shop, where it waited through the remainder of the stormy night. As Wilson advanced in the morning, he came on a part of Fitzhugh Lee's cavalry dug in and waiting. Wilson formed for an attack, placing the Vermont regiment on his division's left. About 10 AM, after some skirmishing, the Vermonters were moved forward, dismounted, to the edge of a wood. Preston was at the front, and looking ahead into a field, he saw a line of men midway toward the main Rebel line. Apparently thinking them Union soldiers, the colonel started across the open ground. Alas, they were Confederates. Maj. William Wells, who would take command of the Vermont regiment, wrote home to Waterbury,

> He had just ordered me where to put my Battalion in line on our left. he says Maj don't allow your men to fire, for our men (from other Regt) are in your front. I saw nothing more of him until I was informed that he was wounded in front of my line. several times I attempted to advance my line to get his body but was driven back, but the third time I got his body off. he was alive, not conscious, died about 15 minutes after we got possession of him. He was shot in the left side near the heart. We also had a Captain killed Oliver F. Cushman Co. E. he was instantly killed, one of the best officers in the Regt. beside one of the finest men, was very badly wounded in the face just 11 months before at Gettysburg.

Private Wayland Bishop wrote to his mother in Ludlow, "Col. Preston and Capt. Cushman were killed, two of the bravest officers in the regiment. They were shot almost the same instant . . ." Another casualty of the fatal moment was Pvt. Hiram Danforth, shot as he carried Preston's body in, doomed to die two months later of his wound.

The fight went on, and Wilson's cavalry recovered and drove the Rebels from their lines. The Confederates fell back in the direction of Enon Church, but as Wilson failed to connect with Burnside's infantry, as hoped, the advance was suspended. The Vermont regiment had lost three killed and five wounded in the fight at Haw's Shop. Horace Ide recalled years later, "I stood beside the wagon the 4th of June, 1864, when General Custer viewed the remains of the gallant Preston, and heard him say, 'There lies the body of the best colonel in the cavalry corps.'"

At Cold Harbor, there would be no more big attacks. But day by day the killing went on, night by night the works were dug deeper and became more complex. In places, the Union positions were seven lines of entrenchments deep, and more. Artillery was brought up in support, and frequently opened fire. In daylight, the shooting never stopped, and any man raising his head on either side was inviting a bullet. The sharpshooters did especially devilish work. All the while, between the lines lay the dead and wounded, the corpses rotting, the agony of the shot men increasing as the long hours of suffering became days. There was no relief, not even water for the parched throats of the shattered men. The weather was hot, the stench almost unbearable, buzzards circled relentlessly, often landing. Rescue efforts were usually suicidal, even those tried in the night. The plight of the wounded was reported to Lee and Grant, and the two commanders began an exchange of messages, aimed at arranging a truce. The negotiations dragged cruelly on. Major Crandall wrote on June 4, "Lay in the works all day that we built last night under the fire & firing upon the enemy. The range was short and we kept their heads well down, but day by day our gallant boys are growing less and less."

Lieutenant Charles Gould, in the 11th, wrote home of the rescue of a wounded man. "The boys in the 3d Vermont," he said,

> got one inside the works in the following manner. They tooke several tent ropes, tied them together, tied a canteen of water to the end, and threw it over the works to him. After drinking he revived so that he tied the rope around his body & was hauled to the works, when one of the boys jumped over the work & handed him over the top, a perilous undertaking to perform within 150 yards of the enemies sharpshooters and in plain sight.

The Union soldiers took turns occupying the front ranks. Units would be moved to the front in the night, where they lay low through the day. Hopefully, they would be relieved the next night, moved back to the third, fourth, or fifth line, or to a camp well back from the lines. "The command was constantly under fire," Chaplain Haynes wrote. "No man could show his head above the breastworks, or go twenty yards from them to the rear, without exposing himself to the same fate." Pvt. Londus Haskell, in the 11th Vermont, told his mother in Woodbury,

> Our lines are prety near to theirs some places they are not even twenty rods apart the brestworks whare the skourmishers are that is not over thirty rods apart & behind them three lins battle we are in the second we have got good brestworks and batteries every whare they can put them in to do good business and every good tree thar is a sharp shuters station . . .

In the 10th Vermont, Captain Abbott said,

> As I sat on the ground this morning with my back against a sapling in the woods, a sharpshooter planked a bullet about an inch from the calf of my right leg which covered me with flying dirt. He could see my blue pants through the green foliage.

Writing to the *Green Mountain Freeman*, Wilbur Fisk described trench warfare at Cold Harbor:

> The breastwork against which I am leaning is not more than 200 yards from the enemy's lines, and in front of us are skirmishers and sharp-shooters still nearer. Our line is just outside the edge of a woods, and theirs partly in an open field, and partly covered by timber in our immediate front. The field is open between us, but it is a strip of land across which no man dare to pass. An attacking party from either side would be mown down like grass. We have abatis in front of our works, and so have they . . . I believe if the enemy should attack us we could kill every man of them before any could get into our works . . . Our skirmishers and the rebels keep up a continual firing. Bullets are whistling over our heads all the time. A man's head isn't safe a moment above the protection of the breastwork. Our work here is built zigzag

like a common rail fence, which gives us a chance to protect ourselves from a cross fire. We can only get from place to place, or from one part of our works to another, by walking in trenches that we have dug for that purpose. There is a breastwork in our rear and a winding sap connects them so that we can pass from one to the other in safety . . . This is what I call a charming place to sit and write letters . . . since I commenced this one, a bullet has struck the breastwork behind me, spattering the dirt all over my sheet, and another pierced Col. Pingree's tent just in front of where I am sitting . . . A sharpshooter has gone out to discover the offender and take care of him. The bullets have a peculiar sound. Some of them come with a sharp "clit," like striking a cabbage leaf with a whip lash, others come with a sort of screech, very much as you would get treading on a cat's tail. Then there are others, the sharpshooters bullets we suppose, that whistle on a much higher key, and snap against a tree with as much force as if the tree had been struck by a sledge hammer. Some strike in the dirt with a peculiar "thud," others fly high in the air and make a noise similar to a huge bumble bee. They do not tarry long by the way. What they do is done quickly, and woe to the man that stands in their way. To add to the beauties of our situation here we are in an ash heap, as it were. The earth is like a pile of dust, and it dances before every breeze like Vermont snow in midwinter. A man may spread down his rubber blanket for a seat, and one puff of wind will cover it so completely with dust that it will be difficult to distinguish it from the ground around it. Our clothes are filled with dust, and our coffee and everything else we cook is sure to get a clever sprinkling of this fine sand. This dirt goes everywhere. It gets into our haversacks and knapsacks, it fills our hair and mingles with the sweat on our faces. It is universal, and there is no getting rid of it.

Orvin Leach remembered:

Now and then a bullet would come down the line among us. I lay flat on my face. Sergeant George Fitch [from Windsor] was sitting, leaning against a tree, about a foot and a half from me, when a bullet just skipped over me and struck him in the leg, shattering the bone all to pieces.

Tabor Parcher, on June 6:

We are behind our brest works whare thare is not much danger but the balls come whipping into our works every minute but we are getting use to them . . . thare are at least 50 guns going off every minute & every little while a shell goes boom down the line . . . It would make you laugh to see the cooks come with the coffee for us they come all curled down & they dodge & fly around scart half to death . . . This is a very unhealthy place here whare we now are we are on one side of a swamp that leads to the Chickahominy & than thare are a good many dead buried near hear & they begin to smell bad & we will all be sick if we lay here a week.

Private Carlton Felch, Third Vermont, made the following interesting entry in his diary: "I was detailed to . . . help build shade over Gen. L. A. Grant's H. Q. Then to help bury some dead when I was wounded with a sharpshooters ball through the leg just above the knee." Felch survived and was back in the ranks before the war ended.

So long as the daylight revealed targets, the sharpshooters were at their deadly work. Charles Mead wrote,

Col. Somebody ordered us to drive away rebel S. S. Passed a line of heavy art. Pickets. Drove the rebs away some . . . shot over eighty or ninety rounds, flanking shots on the right and left—close calls. Bickford wounded in the shoulder slightly. [Pvt. Joseph Bickford, of Windsor, would die of the wound 10 days later.] At night went back to the regt. Tremendous picket firing, and a few volleys with shelling of our lines, shells coming unpleasantly near.

Seth Eastman recalled that a Rebel marksman was zinging in very troublesome shots from a tree to the front, and a group of sharpshooters was summoned. He said they arrived "splendidly armed with the telescopic ranges on their long-range rifles." Said Eastman,

We pointed out to them . . . the location of the Rebel marksman in a tree, with a very large top, not very high, and in open ground. Our marksmen observed this tree very closely. At last they located him and began firing into the tree-top where they thought he was. In a few minutes, he was hit and he fell head over heels out of the tree-top to the ground. He lay there all day, as no-one on either side dared to go out to him. At night, one of our men went out to him and they said he was dead when he fell, as he had never moved. They brought back his gun or rifle. It was an old-fashioned affair, but good and heavy. It had over 20 notches cut in the stock.

One night, at Cold Harbor, George Chamberlin wrote to his wife in St. Johnsbury,

My thoughts are with you almost every moment. I dream almost every night of seeing those beaming eyes, and oft in the midst of those happy dreams I am awakened by the rattling of a thousand muskets, or the roar of the murderous cannon. What an awful leap, from sweet thoughts of home, and of her who is home's chief ornament and attraction, to the murder of the battle-field.

On June 7, a long-distance shot claimed one of the Vermont Brigade's finest, Maj. Richard Crandall, who often noted the softer side of war, such as the playing of a Union band and the answering back of a Rebel band: "A rebel sharpshooter picked off one of our bravest and best men today," wrote Erie Ditty. "He was Major R. B. Crandall who went out as First Adjutant of the Regiment. He will be sadly missed by the regiment." Crandall's body was soon on its way home to Vermont, to rest in the upland cemetery at Berlin. The major's diary was sent home to his father, who added the following notation, written in a shaky hand, for the June 7 entry: "This morning my dear dear Son was mortally wounded by a rebel sharp shooter, and died in the evening. His remains were embalmed and sent home by the kindness of Quarter Master Clarke."

All the while, in the burning heat, the casualties lay to the front. Pvt. Oscar Waite said, "The dead . . . in many places still lie between the lines, and the stench is getting to be terrible." Finally,

Lee and Grant agreed to a cease-fire, too late for most. Chaplain Haynes:

On the seventh, there was a flag of truce . . . and many officers of these contending armies sprang over the high intrenchments to witness the bloody work they had done. Enemies met as friends. There was no boasting, no bandying of words—the event was too solemn for jokes between those who had fought with such stern bravery for so long. No one can adequately describe the scene presented here. Hundreds of dead men, and many wounded and helpless, before beyond the reach of friends by night or day, lay stretched along between the lines, that were, in some places, not more than one hundred and twenty yards apart, reaching from Totopotomy Creek to the Chickahominy River. Some had lain here dead since they fell, six days before, but now swollen and torn by the leaden and iron tempest, that had swept over and beaten around them, thicker than the flakes of a blinding snow storm, so as to be scarcely recognizable by friends who eagerly sought them. There were some wounded, who yet survived all the shocks that meted death to so many others, sheltered in some sunken part of the ground, to be brought off now and saved. The dead were hastily buried or taken away; then this sublime hour—holy for its brief lease of life, an hour of peace, when the earth was calm, and the air so still that the gods of war slept—was at an end, friends were enemies again, and they hurried back to renew the carnage.

Lieutenant Charles Gould, 11th Vermont:

One of the rebs said to our boys on exchanging papers "well we are friends now, but in half an hour we will shoot at one another." Two or three of the rebs took the liberty to walk into our lines and give themselves up . . . Our boys got in one of the wounded men while I was with them that had been shot through both legs & the shoulder. One of his legs was broken and he was wasted away almost to a skeleton. He felt chipper as could be & talked & laughed with the boys. He had an eye as bright as any one, & on hearing it mentioned remarked that it would brighten any ones eye to get among friends again after giving up in

Diarist Erie Ditty, Sixth Vermont. COLLECTION OF MARK JENKINSON

despair all hopes of anything but a miserable death of hunger, thirst, and wounds, in the burning sun.

Orvin Leach:

The pickets took advantage of it and had a meeting between the lines, spending the time swapping coffee, tobacco, etc. Soon our men came running back, saying the Rebs had given them five minutes to get into their holes. As soon as the five minutes were up they fired a shell which just went over us. They fired five or six times, but did no damage. Then we began to fire bullets at them and made it so hot for them that they had to stop.

Captain Orlo Austin, 11th Vermont, wrote,

Crowded into a narrow ditch—great heat & dirt & discomfort. Widened the pit—could not raise our heads above the works. After dark burial of the dead under flag of truce. Clouds, thunder, and lightning.

Sharpshooter Mead wrote June 8, "No firing on our front. The boys talk with the rebs, and exchange coffee for tobacco, eat dinner together etc. In front of Barlow's Div. the pickets are firing all the time." So the truce, along portions of the long lines, led to other, local and informal cease-fires. On June 11, Mead noted,

> Johnnies and we ratify the treaty—no firing. Trading stationery for plug tobacco. Talking with them. Their officers stopped the trading much till near night when they skulked more, and I had a good chat with one of Co. E, 22 N. C. . . . About a dozen of the 22d deserted, and more would if they dared.

Tabor Parcher wrote a letter to his parents the night of June 7:

> The trees are all full of ball holes & the tree tops are cut off by shell & sollid shot but the old ones are not so numerous as the new ones I tell you whare the armeys go now they make a mark that will show for ages to come.

Parcher went on to express, at some length, his faith in Generals Grant and Meade, and the Army of the Potomac. Then he wrote,

> Wall the cannonading has comenced & the shells are flying so I will have to put up this for a while for they may be making a charge & I want to be prepared for them wall the shelling has petty much stoped but the minneys fly some but I doant care for them half so much as I do for the great shells & then have them burst & fly all around & over you & if a peace hits you you are pretty sure gon up . . .

Lieutenant Colonel Samuel Pingree wrote of the routine in the trenches:

> Each Reg't. holds the front line 24 hours & the line next the front . . . also 24 hours—then is relieved for 48 hours and goes about a half mile to the rear to straighten up, wash up, sleep up & clean up arms . . . Our sharpshooter trenches are in our front & within 100 rods of those of the

enemy—These holes are dug at night—men put in them who remain next night and are relieved by other Sharpshooters—If one of them gets wounded we dig a sap to him & bring him in—this don't pay unless he is wounded in fore noon for it takes half a day to dig to them generally & if afternoon we let him lay till dark then get him in.

Wilbur Fisk:

Saturday night we went to the front line to relieve the Sixth. We went carefully to the front just after dark and the Sixth went as carefully back. We were in good musket range of the enemy and our safety as we went from one work to another depended on the enemy's not knowing where we were. As soon as we got into our places a detail was made to work on another breastwork in front of that. The field was open to the enemy's works not a hundred yards distant. We worked very quietly and occasionally a bullet would come whistling over fired by some suspicious picket, but they were chance shots and did us no harm. As soon as daylight revealed to them what we had done they gave vent to their temper and attacked away at us for a considerable length but finding it poor business they finally "dried up."

The long hours in the trenches afforded many Vermont soldiers their first opportunity to get caught up on letter writing. Pvt. Bradford Sparrow, Fourth Vermont, wrote home to Elmore,

I don't wish to discourage you but you may as well know the truth, News Paper reports are very flattering but they are false. If Richmond is taken in another month Grant will do a great thing & if he does it in 2 months he will do WELL. Infantry can do no harder fighting than we have done.

Private Jonathan Blaisdell wrote his first letter to Cambridge since the 11th left Washington, and reported on soldiers from his town.

Edwin Gallup has lost his right leg it was taken off below his knee. John Safford is well that Co. has suffered as bad as any they have lost

about 30 & 3 killed here has been 10 wounded in our Co. James Knee-
land is wounded Gideon Wood I suppose is dead . . . I should be glad
when we get out of this place . . .

The 10th Vermont's Pvt. Henry Burnham wrote sister Emma, in
Williamstown:

I will try and tell you how the Williamstown boys are wounded as near
as I know [Pvt. Almon] Boutwell was wounded in the shoulder, pretty
bad. [Pvt. Ira] Badger in the face slightly (so that he is with us no
more). Decamp [Pvt. Leander, who would die June 14] in both hands
(lost five fingers and in the shoulder). [Pvt. David] Jillson in the back
(or seat) pretty bad. John Poor the ball went into his left shoulder and
passed down through his left lung and the ball stayed in him. Joseph
[Pvt. Joseph Williams] the ball went into his right leg and lodged near
the groin. The surgeon said it was mortal . . .

On June 6, Martin Clark, 11th Vermont, wrote Miss Wealthy
Field,

The Rebel Sharpshooters are a firing at us but they cannot hit because
we are in our entrenchments and they can't hit us wee have been in
some hard fighting since we left the fort wee have lost six in our company killed in all 25 killed missing and wounded that is not much to
what some have lost wee are in sight of the Battle Field where the ded
ly now it looks hard to think of how many are in sorrow for their lost
friends who will never come home again.

On June 6, Maj. Charles Chandler wrote a report to Adjutant General Washburn, in Woodstock, from the headquarters of the 10th Vermont, well behind the front lines, which summarized the state of his
battered regiment and spoke to the tenuous state of life at Cold Harbor. "I have the honor to report," he began,

the effective force of the regiment present with it is twelve officers and
352 enlisted men. I forward herewith a statement of casualties on &

since June 1st which shows several vacancies caused by the loss of commissioned officers killed in action. The regiment now is so much reduced in officers that its efficiency is severely impaired. I add with pain that Captain Samuel Darrah lately commanding Co. D has just been killed in front of Regimental Head Quarters by a sharp shooter.

Captain Aldace Walker, 11th Vermont, wrote of the arrival of an artillery battery at the front:

A company of regular engineers threw up in the midst of our brigade a little earthwork for the use of a section of artillery which was placed in position just at daybreak. The enthusiastic artillerists had great expectations in regard to the damage about to be inflicted upon the enemy by their two little field pieces, and at "sun up," as our colored brothers say, they opened vigorously. It was intended for a surprise . . . It could not have been more than ten minutes, before, to their consternation and our amusement, the whole concern, earthworks, guns, gun-carriages, platforms and artillery had disappeared in a cloud of dust and smoke, literally knocked to pieces by the concentrated fire of half a dozen hidden rebel batteries. At night the poor artillerists gathered up the fragments of their field pieces, and quietly retired, sadder but wiser men.

The Overland Campaign was taking a heavy toll on everyone, including twenty-year-old Seth Eastman, who recalled years later:

Some days . . . I fired as many as 200 times in a single day. I was tired, hungry, dirty and lousy with no change of clothing, and no chance to wash what I had on. I had not half enough to eat, and the procuring of water was very difficult and had to be done mostly at night . . . I never expected to see Vermont again . . . I could not see that a fellow could live much longer amid such strife and carnage as I was in most every day. The comrades were falling one-by-one, and more than half of them were either killed or wounded since the Campaign began. I could not see when it was to end, so I gave up all hope of ever seeing home and friends again.

In the ranks of the Fourth Vermont was a young private, William Stevens, from East Montpelier, who had paid an especially dear price to enlist. Stevens' family was Quaker, very much opposed to war, and closely related to the prominent abolitionist Robinsons of Ferrisburg, who harbored fugitive slaves in their home, called Rokeby. Young Stevens had enlisted against the wishes of his family and, because he had donned a uniform, had been voted out of his Society of Friends. Captured in the fall of 1863, he survived imprisonment in Richmond, though he left there an ill man. But after hospitalization at Brattleboro, he rejoined his regiment in the trenches on June 8, and that night he composed a letter to his mother, Rachel Stevens, telling her he was back at the front. "There has been little firing," he wrote,

> except from Sharp Shooters, tho at about nine their shells came over to encounter our works—only one did any damage to us. This struck a tall

A Vermonter killed at Cold Harbor on June 1, Lt. Ezra Stetson of Montpelier and the 10th Regiment. HOWARD COFFIN COLLECTION

Pine about twenty feet from where I was and am sitting. Tho it was four-teen inches through it was cut completely off . . . The minnies are now coming over, semi-occasionally and striking the bushes around us.

The next day, Stevens wrote from a hospital behind the lines, telling his family he had been wounded:

I am once more in my old position, & have leisure. I will improve it. I came here about two hours since; am feeling first rate mentally, but have some, I hope, slight body aches, do not be alarmed in the least about me; it is not dangerous, only serious and painful. My 3d day's duty favored me with a Minnie ball thro the fleshy part of the thigh, in front, and just below the groin, & one inch outside the main artery of the leg. I was able to walk off the field, hope soon to be able to return there.

On June 9, Charles Cummings of the 17th Vermont told his wife:

Remained in position all day without moving. Went to the 18th Corps and called on Gen. Stannard. He inquired kindly after you . . . The 17th got quite a compliment the other day which came to my ears last night. Gen. [Robert] Potter cmdg the division said in the hearing of the Medical Director that he thought highly of the 17th Vermont . . . it's a G-d d-n good fighting regiment. Leaving out the profanity, I am satis-fied. Rumors are rife that we are to abandon our present position . . . Enclosed I send what I call a High Japonica. Its petals are white, thick, and of wax like finish. Of course this specimen gives no adequate idea of such flowers for petals like these cannot be pressed. In their natural state they are pure white. The swamps are full of them and their fra-grance is delicate, sweet & delicious. Lizzie may like it as coming from the Chickahominy swamp.

The stalemate along the Cold Harbor trenches dragged on. Chap-lain Haynes reported that Ricketts' division was moved on June 11

to the left, into some works vacated by the Second Corps, which were very high, and so close up to the enemy's line that "Yank" and "Johnny" could easily converse with each other,— so near indeed

"That the fixed sentinels almost receive

The secret whispers of each other's watch."

Behind these works were vast excavations, covered with logs, in which officers burrowed; they served the double purpose of shelter from the shells of the rebel mortar batteries, and protection from the burning heat of the sun.

Major William Reynolds, of the 17th, wrote to Adjutant General Washburn on June 10 stating that, despite receiving fifty four reinforcements, his regiment numbered just 178 men. "I really wish the Regt. could be filled up and given to the 'Old Brigade,'" he said. "I can not speak very well of what our prospects are, having been these 'forty days' in the Wilderness and seen little outside my own sphere. However, I do anticipate this is our decisive field."

The First Vermont Cavalry Regiment had a new commander, William Wells, who described his selection in a letter to his father:

At a meeting of the officers of the Regt to consult upon what should be done for a Col for the Regt a committee was appointed to ascertain the feelings of the officers. A paper was submitted to them by the committee asking for the Govt to commission your humble Servt as Col stating the reasons . . . It was a very strong paper.

Lieutenant George Howe, 11th Vermont, wrote to Lorette Wolcott in Shoreham, on June 12, "It is just one month today since we took the field and the old Soldiers Say they never had a harder time, when we first joined the Brigade a great many of the old Soldiers thought we could not Stand fire and they laughed at Heavy Artillery but they have said nothing about our standing fire since the 18th of May."

Many soldiers seemed to be getting used to the dreadful routine of Cold Harbor. Lt. Artemas Wheeler, in the 10th, wrote to his wife in Weathersfield,

The balls of the Sharp Shooters continue flying over our heads with occasionally a solid shot or shell that we are become so accustomed to we mind no more than you would to have a stone thrown over your head.

As the deadly standoff dragged on at Cold Harbor, Pvt. Peter Abbott, Third Vermont, wrote to his family in West Barnet up in northeastern Vermont.

There was a man shot out of the 11th Vermont he was going out to the fire to lite his pipe . . . The sharp shooters are picking off men every day . . . Well since the 3d day of June thare has not been any advance on either side to mark a charge here, would be nothing but a useless loss of lives. I don't [know] what is going to be dun here any more than you do thare at home. The road to Richmond is a hard road to travel . . .

⁕

Some of the best preserved of all Civil War entrenchments still scar the Cold Harbor battlefield. Unfortunately, most lie on private property and cannot be visited. Efforts continue to make them, one day, part of the battlefield park. Those entrenchments mingle with fortifications thrown up during the 1862 battle of Gaines' Mill, and thus the ground around Cold Harbor is some of the most bloodied in all of America. The battlefield park at Cold Harbor, though small, is still one of the great Civil War places. Its entrenchments are in the vicinity of where the Vermont Brigade, the 10th Vermont, and George Stannard's 18th Corps brigade all fought. Cold Harbor Battlefield is a quiet, lovely place. Line on line of Rebel trenches face a level field of fire, all shaded by tall pines. In touring the park, one soon comes to the Union lines, dug out by prone men after the ill-fated June 3 attack. One can still see the remnants of the rifle pits where men lay day after day, keeping low to avoid sharpshooter bullets. Behind them are line on line of trenches, daily improved by Union soldiers as the standoff at Cold Harbor continued. Walk the dry, sandy soil between the lines and know you walk where wounded Union boys once lay, many of them for days in the awful heat, all waiting for the truce, and help, that for many came too late. Cold Harbor is a good place to spend some quiet time, amid the haunted stillness, hearing the whisper of breezes through the pines in a place once filled with utter violence and long agony. In the nearby walled and shaded Cold Harbor National Cemetery lie thirty-five Vermont soldiers.

Chapter Fifteen

ALL MY HOPES IN LIFE
ARE O'ER

Long after the Civil War, America would lose much of its dignity. The quiet forbearance with which trials and sufferings
of the mighty rebellion were endured would become a thing
of the past, as the nation made the revealing of what once was private, and personal, almost a national pastime. But in 1864, the individual dignity of Americans, though severely tested by blood and
grief, fire and anger, very much endured. People suffered and
mourned in the quiet of their homes, with the support of relatives
and neighbors, save for the brief external event of the funeral or
memorial service.

Today, when from the mists of seven score years there emerges an
expression of deep and private grief, it touches us deeply, not only
because it reminds us that those long-ago people felt pain fully as
deeply as do human beings today, but because its rarity speaks so
profoundly to their dignity and forbearance. On the night of June 2,
1864, Mrs. Margaret Scott wrote a brief letter to her sister, Harriet.
Margaret had just learned that her husband, Erastus Scott, a Cabot
lad serving in the Third Vermont, had been killed on May 12 in the
vicious fighting at Spotsylvania's Bloody Angle. Erastus had written
to his parents just before the Old Brigade marched into the Wilder-

ness, expressing the concern that should he die, they would have to help his wife for she had no money, or "not the first thing to show," as he put it.

Then came the message that this farm lad, so obviously deeply cherished by his young and loving wife, was no more. She wrote:

Sister Harriett

He is dead I never shall see him again Oh I cannot have it so all my hopes in life are oer There is nothing but disappointment and trials in this Wourld He was shot in the head and died instantly oh how like a knell it rings in my ears I lay in a fainting condition most all night and am so weak in body and mind have pity on me to think he lays on the Battle field far away without one moments warning and could not send no message to the wife he loved so well My poor mother is almost beside her self they all loved him so well

I cant write any more

Margaret

write your father

All that ever came home of Pvt. William Stevens, to his family's Quaker home in East Montpelier, was his diary. Stevens died of his Cold Harbor wound in an Alexandria, Virginia, hospital, and his body was buried nearby. The family learned of his death on receipt of his last letter, written from a hospital tent behind the lines at Cold Harbor: "I was able to walk off the field, hope soon to be able to return there. Sister Mary, Please read this & use thy own good judgement re-garding mother—in haste truly. W. B. Stevens." To the letter was added this notation:

P. S. It is my painful duty to inform you that the wound of your son became gangrenous a few hours ago in consequence of which he died . . . He was cheerful until within an hour before he died—enclosed please find list of his effects.

The letter was signed by surgeon Henry Janes, of Waterbury. Dr. Janes, who had overseen the care of all the wounded at Gettysburg, would soon be on his way home to take charge of the new military hospital at Montpelier.

At the home of Hiram Jones, in the Mad River Valley town of Waitsfield, a letter arrived during the Cold Harbor fighting written from "Camp in the Field, May the 20, 1864," concerning his son, George Jones, a private in Company H, Second U.S. Sharpshooters. The letter was written by Pvt. Leonard Berry, of Waitsfield:

Mr. Jones Dear Sir,

I now sit down to pen you a few lines. I not being acquainted with you personally but your son I got well acquainted with having tented with him 4 months and now to my sorrow as well as yours, he has been cut down in battle. He was a good soldier. He was killed instantly while helping a wounded soldier from the field. He was hit in the head. He was faithful to his country and very faithful to his God . . . He was much respected in his company and now we mourn his absence . . . he fell into the hands of the enemy and it was impossible to get to him . . . May the blessings of God rest with you both now and forever . . .

This from

L. C. Berry

By late May, the full extent of the losses, at least in the Wilderness and at Spotsylvania, were becoming obvious to all Vermonters. On May 27, the *Vermont Standard* in Woodstock filled page one with a list of Vermont casualties and an account of the 17th Vermont's fighting in the Wilderness. On page two, an editorial tried to shed as kind a light as possible on the grim news:

The front page of our paper is wholly devoted to the casualties in the Vermont regiments during the late engagements in Virginia . . . It is a sad tale, which will cause thousands of loving hearts to bleed, and yet it has a cheering as well as sorrowful aspect. Of the nearly fourteen hundred casualties we have published, two hundred and nineteen are classed as slight . . . There were comparatively few killed or taken prisoner, and very few were missing.

Augustus Paddock and friend Molly Scott, in a scratched old photo taken just before the war began. He ended his wartime service working in the military hospital at Brattleboro.
VERMONT HISTORICAL SOCIETY

In Brattleboro, at the state military hospital, faithful aide Augustus Paddock received a letter in early June from a friend named Molly, back home in Craftsbury, that certainly took his mind off his duties for a time. It read in part:

So you are 24 are you? What an old batch you are. Is your hair gray? Or do you dye it? I am anxious to know for I suppose I shall have to dye it for you when—

I am very youthful you know just "sweet sixteen." I think you would be surprised if you should see me. I am getting to be famed for my BEAUTY . . . Mr. Augustus won't you send me that note L wrote you? NOW DO. I want to see it. Besides it is not proper for you to be carrying around notes from other ladies. No I shall not consent to your answering Jane's letter OF COURSE. It is VERY DANGEROUS to have any thing to do with one's last love . . . Evening—how warm it is: I wish I could be rafted into the Arctic sea where the gentle wintry breezes would sensibly cool my fevered brow . . .

In St. Johnsbury, as trench warfare raged at Cold Harbor, Henry Herrick continued to pour out his soul, and record the everyday events of his life and his community, in the privacy of his rented room, to the silent listener that was his journal. In early June, he was much concerned about his special friend Zenas. On June 3, Herrick had walked about town looking in vain for him. The next day, he wrote, "While I was in the barber's I saw Zenas . . . with a fellow I didn't know who, who I have seen him much with lately, and my infernal jealous temper came up a little after I got home." The next day, Herrick confronted his friend at work and got the response, "Can't I speak with anybody else? If I can't I want to know it."

On June 5, Herrick attended church and said, "The singing went very well." But he noted that the minister "choked, coughed, and I thought he would break down, but he finally got over it and preached very well." That evening, Herrick was back in church and heard former governor Erastus Fairbanks read "a very interesting extract from a letter in the *Congregationalist,* by an agent of the Sanitary Commission with the Army of the Cumberland." After church,

> Zenas came down to the St. Johnsbury House and we went to walk. He appeared quite cool and disturbed and I asked him if he wished it to be all over between us, which appeared to startle him somewhat and he disclaimed any such wish.

In reading passages like this in the Herrick diaries, one comes to the inescapable conclusion that Herrick and Zenas were gay.

On June 6, Herrick wrote,

> To-day the hottest day of the season I think, but has grown cool since sunset and the wind is howling and blowing equal to December . . . the shutters are slamming, the wind howls and the house rocks like a December storm . . . Oh dear the wind makes me lonesome and homesick. I wish it would stop. The news came by telegraph to-day that Col. Preston of the First Vt. Cavalry is killed, it is a great loss for he was a fine fellow and a brave officer, his reputation was an honor to the state and himself.

In Rutland, on June 3, the day of the suicidal assault at Cold Harbor, Tom Thumb and his bride, "accompanied by Commodore Nutt and Miss Minnie Warren," arrived in town. The local *Herald* had helped to build excitement, and had testified to its Republicanism by getting in a shot at Abe Lincoln's Democratic rival for president, with such notices as:

TOM THUMB AND TROUPE—This troupe of little folks is expected here to-day. They have been drawing immense crowds at Montpelier and Burlington. The Montpelier Freeman says that General Tom Thumb is a smaller general even than General McClellan.

Look out for the "magnificent miniature $2,000 coach with the four smallest ponies in the world" which is to appear in the streets.

Mr. And Mrs. Tom Thumb, Commodore Nutt and Miss Minnie Warren hold levees in the Town Hall at from 3 to 4½ o'clock this afternoon, and from 8 to 9½ this evening.

The next day, the *Herald* reported,

The advent of the little folks created a tremendous excitement in town yesterday, which the severe rain storm of the afternoon could dampen but not extinguish. It broke out afresh, as the storm ceased toward evening's "reception." Everybody with his wife and baby, from Rutland and adjoining towns, was present, crowding the Town Hall and blocking up the street in front of it, afternoon and evening, and all were delighted with the show, of course . . .

That night, the diminutive star paid a surprise visit to the Rutland Masonic Hall to commune with fellow Masons. There, he introduced himself as Charles F. Stratton, his true name.

In Westford, on Sunday, June 5, Alney Stone scribbled, "Marcia Billie & I went to meeting. Dr. Foster preached forenoon, in afternoon preached funeral sermon for Lieutenant John G. Macomber." Lieutenant Macomber, of the Sixth Vermont, had been mortally wounded in the Wilderness on May 5.

On June 7, in St. Johnsbury, Herrick wrote,

The news came to-day that Capt. Frost [Edwin Frost, Fourth Vermont, of St. Johnsbury] is killed and the news seems to have made a profound sensation for he was well known and much liked here. What a fearful price we are paying for the maintenance of the government, our best and our bravest offer up their lives as willing sacrifice, may we be worthy of it all.

That night Herrick watched the town firemen drill, and

> saw Col. Foster [George Foster] of the 4th Vermont . . . he was wounded at the battle of the Wilderness and just got able to come home . . . The National Convention meets at Baltimore to-day . . . there is no doubt who will be nominated and the people (most of them) say "amen."

The Republican National Convention, billing itself the "National Union Convention," met at Baltimore on June 7 and, as expected, nominated Abraham Lincoln. On the eve of the gathering, the Vermont delegation met at Barnum's Hotel, in the room of U.S. Sen. Solomon Foot, of Rutland, and took a vote on its preference for vice president. The vote was unanimous in favor of favorite son Senator Foot, but the senator quickly set the thing to rest, saying that a vote for him would be wasted. The Vermonters again took a poll, and the vote this time was unanimous for incumbent Vice Pres. Hannibal Hamlin, of Maine. The next day, amid the hurly-burly of politics, that vote would change.

As the convention opened, considerable attention focused on Senator Foot, being touted by some for election as chair of the convention. But what effort there was on Foot's behalf fizzled, and Gov. William Dennison of Ohio was selected. In the matter of the vice presidency, Hamlin's hopes for nomination quickly faded, and his demise was reflected in the Vermont delegation. On the first ballot, the Vermonters cast one vote for Daniel S. Dickinson, two for Maj. Gen. Benjamin Butler, two for Hamlin, and five for Andrew Johnson, of Tennessee. As Johnson's strength increased, the Vermonters threw all their votes to Johnson, as he became the nominee. The Vermont delegation voted unanimously for Abraham Lincoln. G. G. Benedict was there and reported on the moment of the president's nomination for the *Free Press*:

It was on the motion of the chairman of the Missouri delegation that the nomination was made unanimous. The enthusiasm now broke over all bounds. The members sprang to their feet with swinging hats, and handkerchiefs waving from the galleries, and cheering long and loud enough to lift the roof. Hail Columbia, by the Band, almost unheard at first, broke in on the tumult, and the mighty volume rose and swelled and fell till music and shouting died away.

Vermont papers were also carrying a list of the 10 delegates, and an equal number of substitute delegates, chosen to attend the Democratic National Convention, set for Chicago on July 4. The Democratic *Argus Patriot* in Montpelier editorialized:

There is every indication that this convention will be the largest, most enthusiastic, and patriotic political gathering that ever assembled on this continent. The Fourth of July, 1776, was not a more important day for mankind than the day of this Convention. God speed the right!

On June 2, the paper ended an editorial it titled "The Virginia Campaign":

We confidently look, in due time, for the fall of the Confederate capital, and the dispersion of Lee's great army. More blood will yet be shed, we doubt not. Fiercer yet will be the conflict. The rebels will fight for their capital—for their own firesides—if for anything. We do not look for the end just yet; a still more sanguinary battle must yet be fought. We deprecate the loss of so many brave men, but the radicalism that rules the day compels the sacrifice.

On June 7, the *Rutland Herald* said Commissioner Holbrook had reported that 225 Vermonters in Washington, D.C., area hospitals, another 84 in Baltimore hospitals, and an undisclosed number in Philadelphia hospitals were ready for transfer to Vermont. The hospitals at Brattleboro and Burlington, and the Montpelier facility just nearing completion, were making ready.

June 8, Henry Herrick:

Capt. Charles Morey, Second Vermont, diarist and letter writer, survived the Overland Campaign. He was killed a week before Lee's surrender at Appomattox Court House, as the Vermont Brigade led the assault that broke the Confederate lines at Petersburg. VERMONT HISTORICAL SOCIETY

Went over to the street this evening and pretty soon Zenas came down, we walked about there awhile and then came up to my rooms, I gave him the scarf which he appeared much pleased with, but demurred at taking it as a present. We sung some, till it was too dark to see, and talked for some time . . . There is news of heavy skirmishing at Coal Harbor with a loss of about 7500 men.

On June 9, he wrote:

Col. Preston's body came up in the train to-night and Zenas and I came out of the shop at 5 and went over to the Depot for it was intended to pay some respect to his memory. The train had come in and a procession was forming to escort the body as we got down there, it was headed by a drum and fife, and a flag draped with crape . . .

Herrick said that the "prominent men" of the town, including former governor Fairbanks, were present. "These headed the procession," he wrote,

> and the coffin, covered with the flag, and followed by a long line of wagons from Danville, followed—the flag was hung at half mast on the flagstaff at the Depot, and the bells were tolled as the procession moved slowly up the hill—at the head of Western Av. the St. Johnsbury delegation opened and stood with uncovered heads while the other passed through them . . .

Another St. Johnsbury resident, Sue Warner Gould (sister of Charles Gould in the 11th Vermont), wrote to a friend,

> The body of Col. Preston of the Vt. Cavalry arrived here to night. His remains was carried to Danville his native place followed by a large number of his townspeople and many from this place. (The bells tolled and they had muffled drums and a fife.) Aron [her husband] and I went down to the depot. A new flag was wound about the coffin—or box, it was a sad sight and I wanted to get home again.

The body was escorted up the long hills to Danville, where Preston's widow and infant daughter waited.

On the night of June 10, Herrick noted,

> After tea I opened the Journal and looking down a long list of killed and wounded almost the first name that arrested my attention was that of C. H. Perry [Pvt. Charles Perry, of Cabot, Fourth Vermont]—died of wounds received June 3d. I sat for a moment utterly stupefied and incapable of taking in the truth of which the types declared—unable to realize that among that "noble army of martyrs" was the friend that I had known and loved so well; then as the bitter truth came plain, I

cried out in bitterness of spirit . . . I know not how he died, but of this
I am sure—it was doing his duty manfully, and faithfully . . .

On June 9 the *Rutland Herald* reported the arrival, at the Brattleboro military hospital, of 216 wounded soldiers, "mostly from Vermont, New Hampshire and Michigan." It stated that another 50 were
expected within days.

The June 6 *Free Press* contained a letter signed with the initials
M. C. A., making certain that the folks back home knew of the labors
of Congressman Baxter in caring for the Vermont wounded at Fredericksburg:

> Among the noble men who . . . have been doing all in their power to
> mitigate this awful sum of human suffering is Portus Baxter, your repre-
> sentative in Congress. He has come back the shadow of himself, so
> worn is he in body and soul, with the sight of wounds which he could
> not heal—of agony, which he could not eliminate . . .

Several papers carried the text of a telegram sent from Washington, by
Baxter's wife, to her friends at Derby Line, on the Canadian border:
"Go to your house and take every article in the shape of linen, cotton,
etc., etc., and all preserves and jellies and forward them at once to the
front for the use of the soldiers."

The papers continued their usual reports on everyday life
throughout the state. The June 3 *Rutland Herald* said, "Two gentlemen went trouting yesterday not far from here. One of them caught
eighty trout, and the other caught one. Good for the one." The *Herald* also noted, "E. F. Cook drove a lady to one of the trout streams.
She very properly resented such conduct by beating him." And, the
Herald said, "Clothes line thieves are at work in Shoreham. S. L.
and E. L. Bissell, on Monday night, lost about $50 worth of cloth-
ing by the depredations of the villains." The *Burlington Weekly Sentinel* said that an outbreak of diphtheria had occurred in the
northern Vermont town of Walden. The paper said, "Cyrus and
Martha Smith have within twelve days buried three children with
this terrible disease."

The *Rutland Herald* ran the following items in early June:

SAD AND FATAL ACCIDENT—We are informed that a young son of Mr. Geo Eayres of Pittsford, accidentally shot his little sister, aged about six years, day before yesterday. It appears that the boy took a gun which was standing near where he, his father, and sister were at the time, asked his father if the gun was loaded, and on receiving a negative reply, snapped it at his sister. The gun, which was loaded, was discharged and the bullet pierced the little girl's head, killing her. It seems that a man in the employ of Mr. Eayres had loaded the gun without Mr. Eayres' knowledge.

VERMONT OFFICERS—We learn that Capt. M. T. Samson, Co. I, 5th Vermont regiment, was instantly killed being shot through his head on Friday last near Cold Harbor. He was at the time on the skirmish line, keeping the enemy in check, while our forces were making an important movement . . . Several officers of the regiment aided in recovering his body, which was buried in a place well marked so there is a strong hope of obtaining it. He was from Weybridge, 23 years of age, a man of good character and a gallant officer. He leaves a young wife.

While the firing went on at Cold Harbor, the mother of Sgt. Charles Ross, 11th Vermont, wrote him from the family home in Lower Waterford, on the upper Connecticut River, giving assurance that the home folks were doing their part.

You are pretty near Richmond now & pretty near the swamps I should judge by the maps . . . We are at work doing all we can for the wounded soldiers. Have sent two barrels of hospital articles & shall continue to work as long as we are furnished with means to work with, which I hope will be as long as there are sick & wounded soldiers to need the things we make . . .

In Vergennes on June 3, Mary Tucker wrote,

Our friend Mrs. Ellen Campbell was married last evening to a Mr. Butler of Colton, N. Y., and left today for her home . . . Our cow has a fine large white calf today, we can soon make our butter. Charles McAllister was killed in a recent battle in Virginia [a private from Vergennes in the 6th Vermont killed May 6] . . . Anna and William Bradley attended the exhibition of the dramatic club this evening, it is for the benefit of the Soldiers Aid Society.

The Tuckers had been busy with a family project, moving the family dead to the new Vergennes cemetery. "Friday 10 June," she wrote,

> a clear but very cool day for the season, so that we have sat by fires. Mother and I rode to the cemetery this morning to see the vault and the foundation of the monument soon to be erected for our Father. Soon after our return his remains were disinterred from the old cemetery where they had rested for thirty-eight months, and were deposited in the new vault.

A few days later:

> Been to the old cemetery and saw uncle Joseph disinterred after he has been buried 23 years, his coffin was well preserved, but only his skeleton remained, oh what a comment on human strength and permanence.

Vermont newspapers daily carried lengthening lists of Vermont casualties, with shorter accounts of individual tragedies. The *Free Press* of June 10 stated, "The remains of Maj. Crandall of the Sixth Vermont have been sent home for interment, and will probably reach Montpelier on Saturday." The *Rutland Herald* carried the following remarkable account:

> Henry Amblo, Co. G., 2d Vt., reported missing in the official list of losses of the Vermont Brigade, was found lying helpless for eight days in the Wilderness, during which time he had nothing to eat but the food in his haversack. His ankle had been shattered by a Minnie ball, and when found his wounds had been so long neglected that mortification had set

in, so that the amputation of his foot became necessary. At last accounts he was doing well. [Pvt. Globe Amblo, of Burlington, died June 6.]

In Montpelier, the *Journal* said,

Corp. Geo. Lawrence, Berlin, died in the hospital at Fredericksburg May 20th, of a wound received in the first day's fight of the Wilderness. "He was as good a soldier as there is in the army," writes a comrade, and how truthfully. With true devotion to his country and a sacrificing spirit, he left home and friends as its defender, and laid down his life without a struggle . . .

The *Rutland Herald*:

Lewis Young of Company F, Fifth, Vt., whose name appears among the wounded, called at our office yesterday. He has been in all the battles of the Potomac Army, except the first Bull Run, and was wounded in the left hand in the Wilderness. He says that all previous battles, not excepting Savage Station and Gettysburg, were mere skirmishes compared with the battle of the Wilderness . . .

The *Herald* published a letter written June 5 in the Cold Harbor trenches by a local soldier serving in the 11th Vermont:

It is almost impossible for our side to charge against such strong breastworks and carry them, and it is always terribly destructive of life, especially so, if repulsed. Some regiments go in with 1600 or 1700, and come out in about ten minutes with less than half their number, such is the result of charging against strong works. About four weeks of active campaigning has led me to believe that the peaceable citizens of Vermont know but little of the horrors of warfare, although they read the papers . . .

On June 10, as Grant's army began to stir at Cold Harbor, Henry Herrick was still struggling to come to terms with the death of his friend, Charlie. He wrote,

Has been cold all day and a bleak uncomfortable wind blowing, luckily it is cloudy and windy to-night or we should get a sharp frost . . . I looked over my letters and picked out all I have received from Charlie since I came back from the army . . . I cannot get reconciled to his death as if he were my one brother . . .

Also on June 10, the *Windsor Journal* ran an editorial on "The Military Situation":

There is a doubtful and half despondent spirit abroad, in regard to the military situation of affairs between ours and the rebel armies in Virginia, which we are sorry to see. There is no just occasion for it, and it should be dismissed from the minds of all. We expected too much, and that too soon, from General Grant's army movements, and now we oscillate to the other extreme . . . Let us think hopefully and act hopefully, therefore, in regard to the prosecution of the war under his leadership. Let us be patient if it takes a comparatively long time yet, and the cruel loss of many more of our brave soldiers. It is the future of war, and cannot be shunned.

Chapter Sixteen

TO CROSS THE RIVER JAMES

O n June 10, in the Cold Harbor trenches, Lt. Col. Samuel Pingree wrote,

> The moment a head is shown above the parapet a sharp shooter's ball is directed to it—In this way we loose two or three careless men in each regiment every day, and the enemy do the like. It is estimated that each army loose 1500 per day this way . . .

In those trenches, Pvt. Alvin Woodward indicated that he'd had about enough of Ulysses Grant's Overland Campaign. The veteran of nearly two years of service in the Vermont Brigade wrote,

> I don't wish to have it understood that we think this regt has been used any worse than any other in the Brigade or that we have lost any more men according to the number when we started. But I do think our Brigade has been in more engagements than any other in the whole army since this campaign commenced. But I understand that Gen. Grant has issued an order there is to be no more Chargeing on the enemies Breast works and I hope so—I am willing to work night and day to siege them out or I am willing to fight Beehind Breast works or if nec-

essary I can go on a charge where there is a clear field. But I am not willing to go against their Breast works, one more charge would utterly annihilate what there is left of our Old Brigade . . .

Wilbur Fisk wrote of the monotony of trench warfare, and its effect on Yankees and Confederates:

A few minutes ago there was a lull in the firing, and the boys hallooed, "Wake up there, Johnnies! It is getting dull here." A half dozen shots was the only reply. The other night after it was safely dark, the rebels were as "bold as sheep." They jumped upon their breastworks, and invited the "Yankee sons of b_____" to come on. They said it would take a long time for us to dig into Richmond. Our boys replied that we should dig them into hell and walk into Richmond.

Historian G. G. Benedict well summed up the Vermont Brigade's situation as the standoff at Cold Harbor dragged on:

The health of the men, especially of those in the front lines, began to suffer from overwork, constant watching and exposure to the scalding sun while lying in the trenches, as well as from the scantiness of the supply of water, want of vegetable rations, insufficient cooking of their food—for the cooking was necessarily of the rudest—and from the contamination of the air by the numbers of unburied bodies of dead men and animals between and behind the lines. Under these circumstances, for ten days, the Vermont brigade held the front trenches at two important points, the regiments relieving each other, but the brigade as a whole having no relief. During all this time hostilities were in progress except for an hour or two on the 7th, when a flag of truce brought a brief respite. During this period the brigade lost 48 men killed and wounded by the enemy's pickets and sharpshooters, each regiment having its share of the loss.

Private Erie Ditty, 11th Vermont, summed it up well: "We were under fire for 13 days and nights while at Cold Harbor. Awake and asleep you were liable to get hit by a stray bullet."

Ulysses Grant had seen the futility of trying to break through Lee's Cold Harbor lines, and consequently gave up any hope of the capture of Richmond being the result of his Overland Campaign. So he began to move his forces away from the killing ground, and the first units to depart were two of Phil Sheridan's three cavalry divisions. Grant had received encouraging news from the Shenandoah Valley, where a Union force under David Hunter had won a victory at Piedmont and was now moving up the valley, already at Staunton. Sheridan was sent west, hopefully to link up with Hunter and destroy railroad track and a canal leading in from the valley, keys to the supply of Richmond and Lee's army. Sheridan was under way early on June 7, with two divisions, riding back in the direction from which the Army of the Potomac had battled its way to Cold Harbor. The route was to the north and west, to swing around Lee's army. When Lee found out that Sheridan was on the move, he dispatched his own cavalry, under Wade Hampton and nephew Fitzhugh Lee, off due west to put a stop to the whole thing. The collision came at Trevilian Station, and Sheridan would soon be riding back toward Grant. Back at Cold Harbor, James Wilson's cavalry division, including the Vermont regiment, was left to mind the flanks of Grant's lines.

Grant had also determined to put his battered infantry on the march, once again by the south and east, bound for the James River and a swift crossing that would bring it in on the key railroad center of Petersburg, 20 miles south of Richmond. To make certain that Petersburg was seized, Grant ordered Baldy Smith and his 18th Corps to march back to the landing at White House, on the Pamunkey. There, they would board steamships for a ride back south, to make a quick strike at the undermanned Petersburg lines. The rest of the army would march cross-country to the James, where army engineers would construct a pontoon bridge across the wide river.

On June 12, Capt. Charles Buxton, 11th Vermont, made the following entry in his diary:

> Ora Howe [a private from Jamaica] was shot—was buried. Lt.
> Macomber [Lt. John Macomber of Fair Haven] officiated at the burial.
> Lt. Bemis [Lt. Warren Bemis of Vernon] got his discharge. Wish it was

mine. Marched from the rifle pits the rebs throwed some shells after us as we left. marched all night made coffee at 4 PM.

As Buxton noted, it was the night of June 12 that Grant's infantry left Cold Harbor. The Fifth, Ninth, and 18th Corps were first to go, with the Sixth and Fifth Corps holding the lines to mask the departure from the Army of Northern Virginia's watchful eyes. The Vermont Brigade was concentrated behind the lines, expecting to move with the rest of the army. But according to Wilbur Fisk, the brigade got a surprise.

> Instead of marching off to the left, we started out "right in front" and marched back on to the right flank. It soon became evident that we were sent there only as a rear guard, and after remaining behind good breastworks till midnight, we changed our course toward the Chickahominy.

For a few uneasy hours, Grant's brigade had the same dangerous duty that Aldace Walker's picket detail had endured at Spotsylvania, holding a thinly manned line and hoping the Confederates wouldn't notice its vulnerability. But the Vermonters got away with it, and some of them had to make a very hasty exit. "For the first five miles," said Orvin Leach in the Second Vermont, "we went on the double quick, through woods and over fences, and it was dark and cloudy. We marched all night and all the next day. Everybody who could not keep up was left behind. Maxham was one of these." (Pvt. Isaiah Maxham, of Bridgewater, died at Andersonville in September.)

The 17th Vermont also departed the lines that night and moved with Burnside's corps in the dark. Before leaving, the corps had spent four days back from the forward trenches, in reserve behind the Union center, and had gotten a break from the action. Also on the move was the 10th Vermont, and as it prepared to march, Chaplain Haynes said,

> The Tenth now began to appear like a veteran regiment. Scores of the men who had fought through the battles of the Wilderness and Spotsyl-

vania unhurt, had fallen at these fatal crossroads, and as the command filed silently out of their works on the night of the twelfth, their thinned ranks plainly told the sad brave story of their last twelve days' work.

G. G. Benedict said the armies faced "a march of 55 miles across the Peninsula and the crossing of a large River." Wilbur Fisk:

We left Cold Harbor the night of the 12th. It was a bright moonlight night, just right for marching, except that the air everywhere was filled with choking dust, which the dampness of the evening could not belay. At daylight we halted an hour for breakfast, then pushed on through the dust and heat till night. We crossed the Chickahominy at Jones' bridge just before sundown, but continued our march a number of miles further before we came to a halt. I don't know exactly how far we marched, it is variously estimated at from twenty to twenty-five miles, but the choking dust and heat and the many crooked turns we made, made the march doubly difficult. We were completely exhausted before we bivouacked for the night. The last miles were doled out in suffering by inches.

Fisk was tired and irritable, and that night he questioned the whole thing. "One blunder of General Grant's may make final victory forever impossible and all our lost toils go for nothing. I tell you some of the hard marches put our patriotism to the test . . ." That night Cpl. George Peeler, 11th Vermont, wrote, "2 miles from the Chickahominy. awful tired."

The first stretch of marching had taken the Sixth Corps, the first night, to Despatch Station, where it halted for a rest in the morning. Then the corps moved down along the Chickahominy until sunset, when it turned south and crossed the river at Jones Bridge. The men slept the night of June 13 on the river's south bank. Though the army was exhausted, its spirits were beginning to rise, with the Cold Harbor trenches far behind and the countryside becoming more pleasant. "The men are nearly all jaded out," Pvt. Artemas Wheeler wrote to Weathersfield that night. "The only thing that keeps them in good spirits is their near approach to Richmond." The next morning, the Vermont Brigade closed on the James River. "Here fields of tasseled corn and grain already yellow," Benedict wrote, "varied the green of the meadows; and old mansions, surrounded by noble groves, showed how much ease and wealth had provided before the war." Maj. Lemuel Abbott, 10th Vermont, spoke of "a fine country and community with fine old plantations and houses surrounded with lovely flowers and beautifully embowered." That night, the Old Brigade reached the village of Charles City Court House, which it found nearly deserted.

Tabor Parcher wrote his wife on June 14, from "near Charles City C. H.," saying,

> Wall old gall once more I have got out of reach of Rebel Balls and shell. Grant has commenced another flank movement on Old Lee his men will swear worse than ever . . . As long as we lay near the James River we can be protected by the gun boats. I can hear the steamers a whistling from our base at Harrison's Landing.

On June 14, the 10th Vermont, after an exhausting march, reached Wilcox Landing, where Major Abbott wrote,

> Very cool and comfortable for this season; marched about six miles this morning and went into camp . . . We are only a short distance from the James river; can hear the steamboats whistle plainly. It does seem SO good not to hear musketry and picket firing, but from force of habit I hear both in my sleep nights. It took one hundred pontoons to construct the bridge which is held in place by large vessels at anchor above and below the bridge, especially during the ebb and flow of the tide which is about four feet.

George Chamberlin: "Encamped on a wide plain on the left bank of the James River. It is a half mile wide here, and filled with boats of all descriptions, and it was very cheering to come in sight of a scene so lively and home-like."

On June 16, the 10th was loaded onto boats. Major Abbott said that the regiment was favored by going on the dispatch boat; had plenty of room and a fine time. The quiet moonlight night and cool river breeze were delightfully enchanting after such war experiences as we had passed through. It seemed heavenly! I withdrew to a lonely corner by myself and gave myself up to reflection and feelings of thankfulness; has been hot all day. It has been reported that General W. F. Smith has taken the outer works of Petersburg, Va., captured sixteen pieces of artillery and twenty-five hundred prisoners. I hardly believe it. I know what such fighting means too well. Such victories don't grow on bushes to be plucked by everyone passing.

Private Henry Burnham said the 10th got on steamers

at Wilcox Wharf on the James River. There we took the steam boat and went up the river about 15 or 20 miles. We landed at Bermuda Hundred and we started from there about two in the morning to this place some six or eight miles. I don't know where this place is. I guess it is no place in particular, but it is not far from several places near here.

The regiment had landed on Bermuda Hundred, then moved toward Petersburg, coming in behind Baldy Smith's lines.

On the 15th, the Old Brigade was moved to Wilcox Landing, where it dug in facing to the west. The Sixth Corps had the job of guarding the James River bridgehead while the rest of the army crossed, either on Ulysses Grant's 2,100-foot pontoon bridge, or by boat. Whether the men in the ranks knew it is unclear, but off to the west, facing the Sixth Corps' defenses, was the corps of A. P. Hill, making certain that Grant made no last-minute lunge toward Richmond along the north bank of the James. It was perhaps fitting that as the Overland Campaign came to an end, the Vermonters faced the same Rebel corps they had battled in the Wilderness on the campaign's first day of fighting, May 5.

The night of June 15, Oscar Waite wrote, "There is a mile-wide river separating us from the main army, but it doesn't matter, as we can hold anything that is likely to tackle us here; if not, we will call in a few gunboats, the same as McClellan did." The same night, Lt. Chester Leach, Second Vermont, wrote his wife, "Our Corps is all that marched on the road we took, but I suppose the Army is still somewhere around here, but farther up the river. I have heard very distant cannonading today, & I should judge it was on the south side of the river."

The evening of June 16, while much of the Sixth Corps was ferried across the river on transports, the Vermont Brigade crossed on the famous pontoon bridge at Windmill Point. Virtually every soldier who kept a diary or wrote a letter took note of the remarkable construction. G. G. Benedict said the bridge "Swayed and tossed with the river's tide, but held fast till it had borne across the larger part of the army and its train of wagons and artillery ambulances, which poured over in a continuous stream fifty miles long." Henry Houghton: "We crossed the pontoon bridge which I thought was the longest pontoon bridge ever laid. It swayed so that several men pitched overboard but they only lost their guns and got thoroughly wet themselves." That night, Pvt. Charles Wells stated, "Crossed the river on Pontoon Bridge at sundown. Marched till 12 fell out and slept till morning . . . moved on near Petersburg."

The First Vermont Cavalry, William Wells commanding, walked its horses across the famous pontoon bridge on June 17, after a circuitous ride from Cold Harbor often interrupted by skirmishing. Wilson's cavalry division and Warren's Fifth Corps had been given the task of screening the army's move to the James, making sure that Lee didn't launch a sudden attack on the long blue columns. The Vermonters' horsemen left Cold Harbor the evening of June 12 and moved south to White Oak Swamp, where early the morning of June 13 they ran into Rebels at White Oak Bridge. Eri Woodbury said,

> Firing opened about 6 AM 1st Vermont ordered out on skirmish line at 9. Drove Rebs a mile then built Breast work of rails to hold him. But they outnumbered and flanked us and we fell back. Infantry relieved us. Fight continued all day. Very hot. Moved again at evening.

The Vermonters rode in the night down to the James, to Harrison's Landing. Soon after arriving, Wells' regiment was sent on a reconnaissance to Malvern Hill where, on June 14, Woodbury said it took up position "inside the fortifications built by McClellan two years ago." The next morning, the Vermonters were along Turkey Island Creek, south of the hill, where they again came on Rebels. The regiment suffered several casualties in a lengthy firefight, doing the job, according to Woodbury, of "keeping their attention while our forces cross the James . . ." On June 16, the Vermonters rode down to Wilcox Landing, and after a day of patrolling, Woodbury wrote, "Crossed on pontoons at early hour and encamped on bank of James. Beautiful spot. Few moments had elapsed ere the water was alive with bathers. How soft and luxurious felt the clear waters to our dusty and sweaty limbs!" The next day, the Third Vermont Battery became the last Vermont unit to cross the river. So by the end of June 17, all the Vermont units serving in the Army of the Potomac were on the south side of the James.

Sharpshooter Charles Mead, with Birney's Second Corps division, had made his usual diary entry each day on the march down from Cold Harbor. On June 13, he wrote, "At 2 p. m. made a frantic but vain attempt to find water . . . Birney now 'struck his gate' and for over two hours we marched without a halt as fast as we could march." June 14: "Drew fresh beef and washed . . . About 10 AM packed up and marched about a mile to the James River. It looked GOOD to us." The next entry in Mead's little diary was written in another man's hand, that of his brother, Pvt. Eugene Mead:

> *June 17 Charles was shot at about 7 A. M. and died at 8:30 A. M. he did not speak a word after he was hit the ball struck him over the right ear and came out the back side of his head taking a right oblique cource it passed through a yellow pine log six inches in diameter before it hit Charley. I write this not knowing whether I can ever be permitted to write a mor particular account hoping it may reach home.*
>
> *Eugene*

That "more particular" account arrived at the Mead family's Rutland home several days later: "We were aroused," the brother wrote, before light, and marched in front of our position to silence the sharp-shooters. We made rifle-pits, and as soon as it was light began to shoot them. It was about 7 A.M. as we were all watching, that Charlie was hit. I was in the same pit, also, David Loran, the Indian. We had a pole on sticks to shoot under, and just room enough to stick our guns through. The ball went through the rail. The Indian said, "A good shot." Charlie did not say anything about it. I looked around at him, he was lying on his knapsack on his side as though asleep. I spoke to him, but he did not answer. I went to him and the blood was trickling down from his head. He was shot in the top of his head, about an inch above and behind the ear. I took him back a little, and into a small hut and staid with him. He never spoke after he was hit, but moaned, and was not sensible that anything was going on around him. He died at half past eight . . . With the aid of three others, detailed to assist him, a place is selected, a strong box made, and when the darkness will allow, the body is brought away, and at the hour of ten is deposited in its lonely grave. Thus suddenly and thus sadly, in its freshness and in its strength, his noble life is laid as a sacrifice upon his country's altar.

Charles Mead was shot soon after arriving along the lengthening battle lines outside Petersburg, the victim of another sharpshooter's bullet. In his history of Company F, First U.S. Sharpshooters, the company's first commander, William Y. W. Ripley, a fellow Rutlander, wrote of Mead, "He was a young man of rare promise, and his early death brought sadness, not only to his comrades in the field, but to a large circle of friends at home." The year before the Civil War began, Mead, ever the writer, had scribed a composition he called "Life," which concluded:

Life has been compared to a ship, a book, the drumming of a partridge, the seasons, a journey, and to many other things, but all are inadequate to express in its full sense the true meaning of the term life; nor is mortal capable of showing all its reality by the use of feeble words. When we can look back through the "dim vista of the years" passed, may there be few things to regret. And when we have passed innumerable and now incomprehensible years in the next-world, we shall look back to this life as but a drop in the ocean of time, then we shall just begin to know something of the reality and meaning of the term of life.

Charles Mead's death by the bullet of another sharpshooter was one the young man would well have understood. When the missile that bore his death ripped across the new no-man's land between the deepening trenches at Petersburg, Ulysses Grant's campaign, from the Rapidan River to Petersburg, had ended. The young Vermonter was one of the more than eighty thousand casualties, North and South, suffered during its forty days.

Private Alvin Woodward wrote to his parents in Berkshire soon after reaching the Petersburg lines.

> The cloud that has hung over our beloved Country is beginning to rise around the horizon and ere another year rolls around I Believe we Shal have peace on the basis of Universal freedom without regard to color. Negro Slavery the only cause of this war and the Greatest Blot that ever was or ever will be in our National History will be done away with forever. Then let the Negro take the place that belongs to him & if God made them to be the equal of the White man, they will be in spite of all the White Men do & if he did not then they won't. But I believe that a Negro in Heaven will have a seat as high as the White man.

⁂

The route of the armies from Cold Harbor to the James at first leads through a broken, woodsy, and often wet land. Crossing the Chickahominy, one sees the historic river as a swampy, murky stream. On approaching the James River, the landscape becomes one of wide fertile fields and grand plantation houses. Certainly, any farm boy would have been impressed by the beauty and vitality of the land. On arrival at Wilcox Landing, the wide James stretches impressively away to a far-off bank. Part of Grant's army boarded steamers there to be ferried to the south bank, not far from Petersburg. It is not surprising that Union soldiers' letters often speak of the beauty of the place, the wide river and the clear air in stark contrast to the filthy, deadly battlefields through which they had passed. A small park is located today at Wilcox Landing, and a fishing pier extends well out into the river. For those who wish, a drive upstream along the James' north bank soon brings one to a bridge that crosses the river to Petersburg. There, at the national battlefield park, one can walk along miles on miles of trenches of the new battleground the men who survived the Overland Campaign had to face.

Chapter Seventeen

AS THE SUN GOES DOWN
AT EVENING

On Friday, June 17, Sgt. Charles Morey wrote,

> Clear and hot. We halted for breakfast at 5 o'clock within hearing of the boat whistles. Then marched on and arrived in sight of the city of Petersburg, which is held by the enemy. We go on picket near the right flank, heavy firing on our left after dark but the enemy were repulsed and we held our position through the night.

Wilbur Fisk said,

> We had positive assurance that Petersburg was taken, and of course felt highly elated at the cheering news, but we found when we got here that the news was not quite so good as reported, although we captured their outer line of fortifications and were almost within musket range of the city.

While the battered Army of the Potomac marched down to and crossed the James River, Baldy Smith had brought his 18th Corps in on Petersburg, just as Ulysses Grant had planned. But Smith failed to overwhelm the badly outnumbered Confederate defenders and capture the vital railroad city. Smith found himself facing trenches that reminded him too much of the last great battlefield, and while he could see few Confederates manning them, the specter of the June 3 attack and all its helpless casualties lying between the lines caused a fatal hesitation. Later the Vermonter said, remembering Cold Harbor, "I lost too many good men ever to forget the battle." And he said, "Very little infantry could be seen, but that was not positive proof that it was not there, and it was not probable that the number of guns at work against us would be without strong support." Smith scouted the Rebel defenses, launched a less-than-full-scale attack, then waited for reinforcements. By the time a heavy assault rolled forward, Lee had rushed in enough veteran troops to make Petersburg secure. Baldy Smith was soon removed from command of the 18th Corps by his old comrade in arms, Ulysses Grant.

The Overland Campaign, the great 116,000-man, forty-day effort that the North hoped would end in the capture of Richmond, or in the defeat of Lee's Army of Northern Virginia, was history. To those ends, it had failed, at a terrible cost. It had, of course, brought about the siege that would eventually realize both objectives, 10 months later, at Appomattox Court House. What had been the cost? Grant's Army of the Potomac had suffered more than 57,000 casualties, while inflicting some 27,000 on Lee's divisions. The cost to Vermont is impossible to determine exactly, but it had been heavy. Including the astonishing 1,234 killed, wounded, or missing in the Wilderness within the Vermont Brigade alone. Lewis Grant, on May 23, after Spotsylvania, put the Old Brigade's loss to that time (counting the losses of the newly arrived 11th Vermont) at 1,650. Historian G. G. Benedict also states that, by that time, another 400 Vermonters had left the ranks, either discharged for disability or "broken down under the fatigues and exposures of campaigning, and had been sent to Washington hospitals." Of course, bloody Cold Harbor was ahead. In his two-volume history *Vermont in the Civil War,* Benedict usually mentions casualty totals at the end of battles and skirmishes, but not always. Among the five original regiments of the Old Brigade, plus the 11th Vermont, the 10th Vermont, the 17th Vermont, the First Vermont Cavalry, and the three companies of Vermont sharpshooters, he makes mention of 2,471 men killed, wounded, or missing during the forty days. Add to that the four hundred worn-out men who, he says, were "broken down," the total of loss of the state's regiments in the campaign reaches 2,771. But Benedict makes no mention, after the early fighting, of more men having been sent north due to disability and breakdowns. Surely, there must have been more. And at times he seems to neglect mentioning casualties in smaller actions. With that in mind, the total casualties would surely approach 3,000 Vermonters. The state of Vermont records the names of each of its 34,238 men who served, and a brief summary of his record, in the voluminous *Roster of Vermonters Who Served in the Civil War*, compiled under the direction of Adj. Gen. Theodore S. Peck, and published in 1892. A careful search through its nearly 900 pages, checking the Vermont regiments involved in the Overland Campaign, turned up 2,576 men identified as having been killed, wounded, or taken prisoner during the 40 days. Some 50 men are listed as missing, bringing the total to more than 2,600. Again, the 400 total mentioned by Benedict as having been forced out of the campaign, after the Wilderness and the early fighting at Spotsylvania, tempts one to add that number. Benedict mentions a total of 668 men having been killed in action, or dying of wounds soon thereafter. Peck's *Roster* seems to list 614 men having been killed in action, or having died of wounds and disease, during the 40 days. The discrepancy in the number killed may be due to Benedict's possible counting of some who suffered wounds during the campaign, but died after the 40 days. At any rate, it appears that the total loss of the state of Vermont in the Overland Campaign approaches 3,000 men. Thus, the little state of Vermont, with a wartime population of about 315,000, saw nearly 1 in every 100 of its people become casualties of Ulysses Grant's drive from the Rapidan to Petersburg.

The story of Vermont in the Overland Campaign seems to be a story without an end because the war would drag on. Indeed, some of the famous battles in which Green Mountain State units took part were yet to be fought. The first heavy casualties, after the 40 days, would come on June 23 at the Weldon Railroad, near Petersburg, where 401 Vermonters were taken prisoner, many to perish in Confederate prisons. At the Battle of the Crater, in late July, the 17th Vermont was cut up in the bungled attack launched under the leadership of the incompetent Ambrose Burnside. On western Maryland's Monocacy River, on July 9,

Maj. Charles Buxton, who fought bravely from the Wilderness to Petersburg, died on September 19, 1864, at the third battle of Winchester. VERMONT HISTORICAL SOCIETY

the 10th Vermont, shipped up from Washington with Ricketts' division, suffered heavily in the hard fight that delayed Jubal Early's advance on Washington for a crucial day. The entire Vermont Brigade, the 10th Vermont, the First Vermont Cavalry, and the Eighth Vermont Regiment, up from Louisiana, fought in Phil Sheridan's Shenandoah Valley Campaign in the late summer and fall of 1864. Vermonters played key roles at the third battle of Winchester, and at Cedar Creek. The wounding and dying went on.

In the trenches at Petersburg, the siege dragged on through the winter, with the firing seldom stopping. Finally, on April 2, 1865, the Vermont Brigade led a Sixth Corps assault that ended the siege by breaking, after 10 months, Lee's Petersburg lines. The surrender at Appomattox came one week later.

Many Vermonters who survived the Overland Campaign fell in subsequent battles. A few among the many were Lieutenant Colonels Charles Cummings and George Chamberlin. Chamberlin died of wounds received in late August at a heavy skirmish near Charles Town, in the Shenandoah Valley. Cummings fell at Petersburg in September. Charles Buxton was killed on September 19 at the third battle of Winchester, where George Peeler was mortally wounded. Henry Burnham died a month later at Cedar Creek.

But back to mid-June, 1864. On June 19, William Wells, the new commander of the Vermont cavalry, wrote his parents: "The Grand Army of the Potomac is South of the James and I hope it may never be obliged to do any more fighting North of that river again . . ."

At first, news of the advance to Petersburg was greeted in Vermont with hope. In St. Albans, Judge James Davis wrote in his diary on June 18,

> The telegraph reports that the whole of the army of the Potomac is on the south side of Richmond and that Petersburgh is in possession of the Union troops. Gen. William F. Smith, one of our St. Albans boys, at the head of one of the army corps, is in possession. It is said that Richmond will soon be surrounded and all communication with the sources of supply cut off.

Yet 10 days later, the judge wrote, "The news from the south does not seem to indicate that the war is near to its termination. The rebels claim as many victories as the federal troops do. Indeed, they do not admit any reverses."

To the veterans of the Army of the Potomac now facing Petersburg, it must all have seemed too reminiscent of Cold Harbor, or Spotsylvania. The night of the first Sunday after crossing the James, Charles Gould wrote to Windham,

> The moon shines so bright and am writing by its light and can see quite plainly . . . As it is the first day for two weeks that we have rested in and I had got very dirty on the march, I washed myself, put on a clean shirt & washed my dirty one. Then we had a meeting which I attended and which was very interesting. They sung "America" at the close and I never heard anything half so grand and solemn as that piece of music, sung by hundreds of men who felt every word and line. The Chaplain had just pronounced the Benediction when the Rebs opened on our advanced line with grape & which our batteries had to silence for a short time the Canonading was terrific . . . There is pretty heavy musketry & I can see

Charles Gould, who on April 2, 1865, would be bayoneted in the face as he became the first Union soldier to enter the Confederate works as the Union army finally broke the rebel defenses of Petersburg. VERMONT HISTORICAL SOCIETY

the flashes of the guns very plainly as it is on our left but a short distance. Our men work with their guns by them & so are ready for anything that comes along . . . Our band is just playing "The Star Spangled Banner" to the rebels. Perhaps they dont like the sentiment of the piece but they cant help liking the style of playing as it is a very fine band.

While the trench warfare developed, the grim reality of the Overland Campaign's cost came home daily to Vermont. In Brattleboro, on a Sunday evening, Pvt. Augustus Paddock wrote home from the military hospital,

The surgeon is having beds enough put up to accommodate 1200 men. There are but four hundred here now, but more expected every day . . . It is very hot here today but when I think of the poor boys in Va. I do not feel like complaining much . . . I do not go away from the hospital at all, but just stay & do all I can to make the wounded men compatible.

On June 16, the *Burlington Free Press* stated, "One hundred fifty wounded soldiers arrived at hospital here yesterday over the Central Vermont R. R. More are expected. There are now about 1000 at Brattleboro." On June 18, the new Sloan Hospital at Montpelier officially opened. It immediately began to fill with wounded soldiers. On June 22, Commissioner Holbrook wrote to Adjutant General Washburn:

> I learned when there (New York) Monday last at the office of the Medical Director of Transportation, that the following Detachments had been forwarded, viz:
> June 4th 212 to Brattleboro
> 6th 75
> 13th 157 Burlington
> 17th 150 Brattleboro
> 18th 300 Montpelier
> 18th 44 Brattleboro
> 19th 20
> 958 in all. A detachment of 110 or more of our men to be transferred Monday (20th) to Brattleboro. My humble opinion on the subject is, as ever, that the best thing that can be done for our soldiers in particular is their transfer to Vt. hospitals, practically it amounts to more than anything else that is done for them.

Private Paddock wrote from Brattleboro on August 11, "This hospital is full and more too, over 1200 here now." By late summer, some two thousand wounded soldiers filled all three Vermont military hospitals to capacity. On August 16, the surgeon in charge of the Brattleboro hospital wrote to Commissioner Holbrook, "In reply to yours of the 12 & 13 inst. would say that we now have 129 vacant beds . . . our whole number of beds now is actually 1150 but we manage to accommodate 1200 when hard pressed."

Wounded Vermonters still in hospitals far from home, and their families, flooded Holbrook with requests. William Felch wrote the commissioner from the village of Felchville, in southeastern Vermont:

> I write you to learn the fate of my grandson, Wm. E. Amsden of Co.

C 6th Vt Vols, who was wounded May 5 in the Wilderness battle . . . His chaplain Rev. A. Webster reported to me that he learned indirectly that he died in the 2nd Corps hospital in the Wilderness . . . We have had a report from P. T. Washburn, our state adjt gen, saying that in his last monthly return, which was for May, Wm E. Amsden was in the Fairfax Seminary Hospital on the 11th of May . . . If you can have the facts about him and write without delay, you will receive my thanks, and relieve a long and anxious suspense of his friends.

A note was written on the bottom of the letter, probably in a clerk's hand, "He died May 5 of wounds received the same day."

Lewis Reya, a private in the Fifth Vermont, from Sheldon, wounded in the Wilderness, wrote Holbrook:

I take the opportunity to inform you I am able to be transported to Vermont State at any time now. I believe you was over to the hospital week or two ago you said whenever I was able to let you know so I do so. I like to be transferred to Burlington.

Reya got his wish, and a discharge.

In Vermont on June 17, Vergennes' Mary Tucker noted in her diary:

Mr. Hobbs has brought us a quarter of veal, and six pounds of butter. Thank God for food we eat in these perilous times of civil war . . . I feel his precious promise mine. "I will never leave thee or forsake thee" "Leave thy fatherless children to me."

In Rutland, the *Herald* reported:

Wilson, the great "Cagliostro" is drawing larger and larger audiences each successive evening. The lucky ones in drawing prizes last evening were Jane Cain, who received a set of bedroom furniture, and John Buckbee, who drew a barrel of flour and a pig. The "Magician" and company hold forth at the same place tonight.

In Brattleboro, the *Phoenix* said,

> Everybody and his wife has heard of and perhaps heard that comical William B. Brown, the irrepressible, side-splitting son of the nurses, who goes about making people happy, drawing crowded houses, and putting much filthy lucre in the trouserloon pockets. We are happy to announce that Mr. Brown will give one of his brownest concerts at the Town Hall, Saturday evening next—he will be assisted by Miss E. A. Marsh, the pretty contralto.

The newspapers reported that in Ripton, high on the west side of the Green Mountains, Mr. E. S. Kirby shot and killed a brown eagle that measured seven feet from wingtip to wingtip. The June 17 *Vermont Phoenix* said, "A party lately angling on Whitingham Pond for pickerel, caught a pike which weighed 150 pounds. This is considered the largest catch ever made in Vermont waters."

In West Windsor, Miss Julia Blanchard's mind was much on her impending marriage to neighboring farmer Jabez Hammond. She wrote,

> It has been a nice day, just cool enough to wash. We got through washing before noon. Aunt Cynthia has been here. She said that Sam Lamson asked her if it was true that Jabe Hammond was going to be married and take his wife home. I shall have to tell him of that. What pains other folks take to find out other folks business.

Up along the Lamoille River, teacher Dana was well pleased on June 19:

> The wheels of time continue to roll. Life and a comfortable degree of health are yet vouched safe to me . . . In school and out of school all has gone quite well the past week . . . Grant has made another flank movement. He is now across the James River south of Richmond. I fear to hear the next intelligence, but I have much confidence in our leader. He knows what is best. May victory attend him. This is and shall be my prayer.

In St. Albans, it was announced that "a war meeting" would be held at the town hall. Many Vermont communities were holding such events encouraging young men to enlist for the coming military levy imposed on the state by the federal government. The *Rutland Herald* said, on June 15,

> We understand a petition is being circulated for calling a Town Meeting in this town, to take into consideration what should be done towards filling our quota under the expected new call. This movement is commenced none too soon, and in fact is considerably behind similar movements in other towns of the state.

While Vermonters were rallying to another call for men for Mr. Lincoln's armies, in Montpelier, the Democratic *Argus Patriot* took the newly renominated president, and his running mate Andrew Johnson, to task in a June 16 editorial:

> The age of statesmen is gone, the age of rail-splitters and tailors, of buffoons, boors, and fanatics has succeeded. God forbid that we should reproach Mr. Lincoln, or Mr. Johnson, with the narrowness of their early circumstances, which precludes opportunities for culture. But when men are proposed for the highest and most responsible offices in the Republic, there necessarily arises the question of fitness . . .

But in Brattleboro, the *Vermont Phoenix* opined, "The nomination of Abraham Lincoln for President, and Andrew Johnson for Vice President, seems to give universal satisfaction to everyone but 'secesh' and 'copperheads.'" Most Vermont papers praised the president's nomination.

In Cavendish, the family of Pvt. John French, a cavalryman killed in the running fight from Craig's Meeting House on May 5, received in the mail an affidavit signed by Pvt. John Buckley, of Chester. The document concerned French's death and said, in part:

> I was very near him when he was shot from his horse . . . I immediately went to him and found he was dead and . . . assisted in making a coffin

and in burying him with two others of our company. They were buried three or four miles south of Chancellorsville and near a shop called Todds or Dodds Shop. Said road leads from Chancellorsville to North Anna and the place of their burial, perhaps a mile south of Todd's Tavern, near a large walnut tree, and near a spring . . . On [his] headboard, I think his age was marked 19 . . . He was buried in his ordinary dress, or uniform. No portion, not even his boots, were taken off, and as we had conversed with an embalmer previous to his burial, in view, if practicable, of having his body disinterred, embalmed, and sent to his friends . . . I have passed by and seen said graves within the last six or eight weeks and they remain as we left them . . .

On learning of French's death, Murray Closson, a family friend, sent the family a poem he had written in the young soldier's honor:

Above the loud din of the red battle field
Where thousands lay dead with their high mission sealed,
A whispering voice came down from the skies,
To bid our young hero's freed spirit arise.
His lead shattered body moved not to the word,
But presently something bright, winged as a bird,
Arose from the clasp of its cumbersome clay,
And soared where the angel now beckoned away.
And then in my mind, I went back to the place
Where a fond father's hand and a mother's embrace,
Would never again in the transports of joy
Welcome their beloved and returned soldier boy.
In spite of the strength that I thought I possessed,
The tears filled my eyes and my heart felt oppressed;
And I cried from the depths of an agonized soul,
How long, Oh My Lord, shall this war carnage roll?

In Rutland, Charles Mead's funeral was held in a packed church. The Rev. Henry Grout delivered the eulogy, and declared that Mead's name "has been added to the list of the fallen: patriotic martyrs, who counted their country's weal dearer than life itself . . ." Pastor Grout then read excerpts from letters written home by Mead, including one sent from somewhere south of Spotsylvania:

> I am still alive, and well. I can hardly realize that I have passed untouched through the bloody battles of the past few days. God's mercy alone has given a safe direction to the streams of lead and iron that I have passed through.

And another:

> I am sad, I am sick, at the slaughter in our company and army. I have seen enough to sicken any one to the very soul. We are winning victories, but at a fearful cost. I feel the danger at every skirmish I go in . . . Never fear for me, but pray for the country.

The reverend continued,

> Life is short or long as it affects the great interests of the world. His life, therefore, as linked with the great struggle of our country for existence; in comparison with that of those who abide needlessly at home, was NOT short, but long. So it will seem in the memories of others. It will be associated with the defense of principles of undying value, with events that must unfold with a still widening influence, not upon a nation only, but upon the world. And measured thus his life was long.

Soldier funerals, or memorial services when no body was present, were being held in virtually every village and hamlet in Vermont. At Londonderry, on May 29, the Baptist Church was filled for a service for George Lyon, of nearby Winhall, killed May 5 as the Vermont Brigade advanced in the Wilderness. Back at Brandy Station, with less than three days to live, the eighteen-year-old private had written home to tell a friend of a night on picket, in the rain. "It was dark as a pocket and rained quite hard. Made me think of home a little but I commenced to whittle and sing . . ." The Rev. J. S. Goodall preached on the subject, chosen from the Book of Matthew, "To what purpose is this waste?" Pastor Goodall went on at great length, thundering forth from the pulpit of the little church mighty words dealing with great issues. It all would likely have embarrassed young Lyon a bit, but surely he would also have found, in the words, true honor. The reverend posed the question, had the life of this one young soldier from Vermont been wasted? His answer was, of course, "No," for Lyon had died for a noble and historic cause, which Goodall went on to describe:

> American citizen, stand fast therefore in this liberty wherewith you have been made free. Millions who have been in bondage have been proclaimed free as a military necessity. Over a million are now within our lines; one hundred and thirty thousand are employed in the military service of our country; eighty thousand freedmen are fighting valiantly for our institutions, and for the liberation of our brethren. We have prayed to God to remove the accursed system from our land. The bondmen are fixing their lips to shout the song of liberty. Shall we disappoint them? The echo of our prayers, their cruel sufferings, the God of heaven, all say, in language unmistakable, "No." Shall we disappoint the hundreds of thousands in the old world, who are looking to this land as the asylum for the oppressed, a home for the free? Weekly five thousand crowd our shores. Let them come, and let them find a patriotic, a free, a Christian people . . . We will embalm his memory in our minds as a noble, patriotic youth, who gave his life to defend his country—to preserve the privileges we this day are permitted to enjoy; and we pray they will be kept unsullied, and handed down to the last generation for them to enjoy.

On June 13 in St. Johnsbury, as the Army of the Potomac moved south from Cold Harbor, Henry Herrick wrote:

> Col. Preston's funeral yesterday is said to have been very imposing, though it was NOT a military funeral as his wife did not desire it. Capt. Fisher was the marshall and Mr. Cummings made the address, not a sermon—a horse wearing his horse equipage—his sabre, boots and equipments was led behind the hearse . . .

Herrick wrote on June 15,

Got a letter from mother giving the particulars of Charlie's death. I can best write them by quoting from Dr. Goodwin's letter. "Dear Sir. It has become my duty to announce to you the unhappy news of the death of Charles Perry. He was wounded by a shell while faithfully doing his duty in the engagement at Cool Harbor yesterday afternoon and died at half-past 12 last night. He felt it hard to leave this world so soon but said, 'Tell my folks I died doing my duty.' I was with him when he died. His loss is severely felt by all his associates . . ."

Throughout Vermont, such letters were arriving at hundreds of homes. The anguish, suffering, and hardship they produced, for the most part, remain locked in the past, veiled by the mists of time and shielded by the quiet dignity of a people long known for their few words, and fortitude.

News of the death of an Overland Campaign casualty was not always greeted with quiet resignation. In September 1864, Joseph Brainerd of St. Albans was informed that his son, Cpl. Joseph Partridge Brainerd, of the First Vermont Cavalry, had died at Andersonville after being captured on May 5 near Craig's Meeting House. Young Brainerd's father was a founder of the Republican Party and had been a delegate to the Republican National Convention in Chicago that nominated Abraham Lincoln for president in 1860. Joseph Brainerd had staunchly supported the Illinois man's candidacy. But when it came time, four grim years later, to erect a memorial stone in the St. Albans cemetery for a boy buried in the Georgia soil just outside the Andersonville stockade, the father vented deep feelings in the inscription he chose:

Joseph Partridge Brainerd, son of Joseph A. and his wife Susan Partridge, a conscientious, faithful, brave Union soldier, was born on the 27th day of June, 1840; graduated from the University of Vermont in August, 1862; enlisted in Co. L of the Vermont cavalry, was wounded and taken prisoner by the Rebels in the Wilderness May 5, 1864; was sent to Andersonville Prison Pen where he died on 11th day of September, 1864, entirely and cruelly neglected by President Lincoln, and murdered with impunity by the Rebels with thousands of our loyal soldiers by starvation, privation, and exposure and abuse.

Abraham Lincoln, a target of that inscribed sentiment, who perhaps bore the greatest weight the war imposed on any single human being throughout the North, spoke of the suffering of his people in a speech delivered, as the Overland Campaign ended, where the American nation had been born. Addressing a fair held in Philadelphia on June 16 to raise funds to help the Sanitary Commission in its care for soldiers, and with the fighting having resumed at Petersburg, the president said:

> War, at the best, is terrible, and this war of ours, in its magnitude and in its duration, is one of the most terrible. It has deranged business, totally in many localities, and partially in all localities. It has destroyed property, and ruined homes; it has produced a national debt and taxation unprecedented at least in this country.

Then the Emancipator, tall and tired, brought forth some of his mighty words in describing the agony of his people. The war, he said, "Has carried mourning to almost every home, until it can almost be said that the 'heavens are hung in black.' Yet it continues . . ."

Certainly Miss Mary Lance, of Cabot knew the mourning of which Abraham Lincoln spoke. In the winter of 1864 she had been engaged to marry Abel Morrill, a local lad who enlisted in the Third Vermont. Lieutenant Morrill was killed May 6, leading his men into the green horror of the Wilderness. Apparently, for all intents and purposes, Mary Lance's life ended that day as well. "She lived the life of a recluse," it was recalled many years later by a Cabot resident. "She rarely, and I think I am correct in saying, never was seen in public afterward. She lived and died in the large white house back of the grist mill dam . . ."

The mourning was most evident in a letter published in the *Caledonian Record* on June 17. The paper explained that it had come from surgeon C. P. Frost, and been sent to him by a chaplain in the 11th Vermont, giving details of the death of the surgeon's brother, Capt. Edwin Frost, of St. Johnsbury and the 10th Vermont Regiment:

> He died at half past one, on the afternoon of the 3d of June, from wounds received two hours before. The regiment were lying down

behind their works while Edwin, who was a little in the rear, got up and walked forward a little to see if all was right. At this moment a bullet from a sharpshooter hit him in the bowels on the right side pretty low down, and instantly another ball struck him a little further up under the ribs and passed straight through him . . . He was brought about a mile to the rear, to the house of one Kelly. The loss of blood was very great, and yet he was perfectly conscious. His suffering was agonizing, intense. We gave him large doses of morphine. He knew me perfectly, and arranged more or less of his business affairs. He spoke freely about dying and expressed his desire for a speedy relief from suffering, and spoke of being in heaven with Jesus, and said he was willing to die for his country. He felt that he was reconciled to God. He spoke of being through with fighting and going to his rest. He has an excellent record during this campaign, according to Col. Henry. He fought with the greatest bravery, and has earned a good name as a soldier. His regiment captured 300 rebels on the evening of June 1st, and one rebel captain surrendered his sword to Edwin. This he desired to send to you; I shall try and get it to you if possible. We buried him very decently under a large tree, by the side of Lt. Newton of the same regiment, and marked well the spot. I buried him in his clothes, with two blankets about him and an old coat of his under his head and an overcoat over him besides. He rests in a good spot, if he must be away from home. We buried him while the cannon were roaring about him his requiem. His life went out as the sun goes down at evening.

In St. Johnsbury, on June 17, with more and more blue- and-gray-clad soldiers filing into the Petersburg lines, the *Caledonian Record* ran an advertisement for artist F. B. Gage:

LOST IN BATTLE

Large beautiful portraits of those

LOST IN BATTLE

Can be made at the St. Johnsbury Po Gallery, from

Old Daguerreotypes, ambrotypes, cards,

Pictures, or card negatives.

The paper also announced the death, from "canker rash" (scarlet fever), of four children in Wheelock.

Years after the Civil War, the 10th Vermont's Chaplain Edwin Haynes said of the Overland Campaign, and of his (and Captain Frost's) regiment,

> In the steady advance from the Rapidan to Petersburg, there had been scarcely a day that some one did not fall from our ranks, and oftentimes scores yielded themselves willingly to the country's needs. Among the fallen were some of the bravest and best.

The mourning always touched Henry Herrick, in the rented upstairs room where, nightly, he made his very personal journal entries, through the remainder of the Civil War and for several years afterward. On June 11, the last day of fighting at Cold Harbor, he wrote, "Got a letter from the Claremont Co. in answer to mine, written so long ago about binding my 'Journal.'" Fortunately, Herrick did have his journal bound, and it exists today at the Fairbanks Museum in St. Johnsbury, by far the finest of all home front accounts yet discovered from the Civil War period in Vermont. Former private Herrick knew war, having seen the carnage on the peninsula. He had not witnessed firsthand the surpassing horrors of the Wilderness, Spotsylvania, and Cold Harbor, but he surely had seen something of pain-filled deaths such as that suffered by fellow St. Johnsbury resident Captain Frost and so many other sons of Vermont. Herrick wrote the night of June 19 of Ulysses Grant's Overland Campaign,

> In the last sad weeks the reaper whose name is Death has gathered a terrible harvest, we look wearily down the long lists of that noble army of martyrs who have given their lives to the country and sometimes a familiar name, perhaps of a dear friend, sends a ping like a sword-thrust to our hearts and benumbed, stupefied for the moment, we are unable to realize the crushing weight of sorrow which the words bring to us.

The night of June 24, Herrick wrote his reaction to a notice in the local paper announcing that some local patriots were preparing for the usual Fourth of July festivities, these to be the four-score-and-eighth since the Republic's founding. That news did not sit well with the former soldier, now grieving for the loss of a soldier friend, and as always closely following the course of the great war that had turned, in the past month and a half, so terribly bloody. No, it had all been too much, with tens of thousands of broken American bodies the price, and countless American homes and families deep in mourning. Herrick turned to his journal, and concluded his response to this call for celebration at the end of the Overland Campaign with a metaphor based on his beloved music, a line from Shakespeare's *Macbeth,* a work from which Abraham Lincoln was fond of quoting. Herrick wrote,

> There is a call for a meeting of citizens at the Town Hall to-morrow evening to consult in the matter of celebrating the coming 4th, but I don't see how they can feel like it—for my part anything of the kind seems to jar on my feelings, while it is such a time of intense anxiety, and the fate of the nation seems trembling in the balance, and while there is such wide-spread sorrow in the land, mourning for loved ones who are not. A time of rejoicing and merrymaking seems like "sweet bells jangled out of tune and harsh."

Conclusion

OUR THINNED RANKS

The evening of Wednesday, November 15, 1876, the 13th annual gathering of the Reunion Society of Vermont, an organization of Civil War veterans, was held at the State House in Montpelier. After the business meeting Redfield Proctor, former commander of the 15th Vermont Regiment, delivered the keynote speech. He concluded:

> The war is over, but let not its lessons soon be forgotten. We preserve in these corridors the battle-torn flags that tell their silent story. I would that by enduring monuments in the daily haunts of men the memory of the fallen might be perpetuated, and the lessons of their lives and glorious sacrifice be kept ever before the people. The war is over, and let us trust its marks and scars may soon be healed; but never at the cost of any of the dearly bought principles for which you fought. The duties of peace are crowding upon us, in which it is often more difficult to guide our steps aright, than in the rougher paths of war.

The applause was "hearty," the "Battle Hymn of the Republic" was sung by the St. Albans Glee Club, then the society adjourned to the dining room of the nearby Pavilion Hotel for a banquet. Late in the evening, the speaking resumed and Brig. Gen. Lewis A. Grant was introduced, having traveled, it was noted, 1,000 miles from his post-war home in Des Moines, Iowa. After long applause, Grant began his brief remarks by saying that he loved the First Vermont Brigade and its officers and men, and took pride in its fame. He expressed hope that a history would soon be written, for lacking one, he felt the Old Brigade stood at a disadvantage as compared with many other combat units. Grant noted that the nine-month Second Vermont Brigade had been accorded far more recognition for its part in the battle of Gettysburg than his command had ever received, "though it remained in the field, fighting on and doing its duty." Grant then deemed it perhaps not strange under the circumstances, yet hardly fair, that while the Vermont General Assembly had passed a resolution thanking Stannard and his men, a like resolution for the First Brigade lay without action on the legislative table.

The general said he believed two achievements of his command were worthy of fuller recognition than it had received. One was its leading of the April 2, 1865, attack of the Sixth Corps that broke the Rebel lines at Petersburg. The other, he said, was "the engagement on the Plank Road, in the Battle of the Wilderness." Grant concluded his remarks:

> While I live, let me live in the regard of my comrades, and in the enjoy-ment of the civil liberties secured by our arms; and when I die, it will be enough, if they wrap me in the old flag, and write on my grave stone: He once commanded the First Vermont Brigade.

So far as is known, the Old Brigade never received such a tribute from the legislature was accorded the Second Vermont Brigade. The State House's official Civil War memorial, the grand Julian Scott painting, portrays the Vermont Brigade advancing in the final attack at Cedar Creek. Monuments to Vermont deeds stand on many battle-fields, at Antietam, the Monocacy, Cedar Creek, Winchester, and at Gettysburg, where no less than nine stone tributes honor Green Mountain State units that fought there. At the Wilderness, Spotsylva-nia Court House, and Cold Harbor, only one monument makes any mention of Vermont, and that is at Spotsylvania, where a small marker stands where Emory Upton launched his May 10 assault. The participating Vermont units are listed, as are those of other states.

Perhaps, because of the horror of it all, in the postwar years Vermonters simply chose to forget the Overland Campaign and its terrible cost. After the war, year after year, Vermonters boarded excursion trains for Gettysburg, to attend reunions and show friends and families where they had fought. On one occasion, veterans of Stannard's brigade even visited their campsites in Northern Virginia, but no written record seems to exist of any group of Vermont veterans having paid postwar visits to the battlefields of the Overland Campaign. However, in 1911, nearly a half century after its bitter conflicts, two Waitsfield brothers, Charles Jones and Matt Jones, headed south to Fredericksburg, Virginia, intent on seeing the Wilderness Battlefield and locating the spot where Pvt. George Jones, their uncle, had been killed. Jones, a member of Company H, Second Regiment of U.S. Sharpshooters, died the morning of May 6, near the Orange Plank Road, shot in the head while helping a wounded comrade. The Joneses had in their possession a map marking the spot where their uncle had fallen, drawn by a comrade who served with him, former private Eugene Joslyn.

On reaching Fredericksburg, the Vermonters hired a horse and wagon and the services of their owner, a black man well acquainted with the nearby battlefields. Matt Jones wrote a lengthy letter about their explorations to his father, Hiram, the brother of George Jones, and in it he said of their reaching the Wilderness:

Uncle Georges regiment lay along this Brock road probably not more than a quarter of a mile from the Orange Plank and in the morning they charged diagonally across the corner between the roads. Just as they got to the Orange Plank road they met the rebels in the woods . . . We could identify the place where they struck the Orange Plank for there it runs through a little cut & there are banks up on both sides & there is no other such place on the road within a long distance. Just at this point also the road which is quite level goes up a little hill and Eugene Joslyn wrote us that he was next to Uncle George & they were just south of Orange Plank road & at the top of a little hill.

The Joneses were driven to the intersection of the Brock and Plank Roads, and

At the crossing we turned & drove slowly west along the Orange Plank facing the same way our troops faced. We soon saw (⅜ mile perhaps) the cut in the road which members of the company said was where they came out of the woods onto the road. We also saw the little hill but to be sure of our ground we drove on for some distance but found no other cut & no other hill. We passed the breastworks thrown up by the Vt. Brigade the day before . . . a little beyond the rebel breastworks occupied by Hills men. Then we turned back to the brow of the little hill, left our carriage & walked out into the woods and along the crest on the south side of the Orange Plank. There is nothing here to show a battle ever took place but the topography corresponds exactly with what the men had told us. We both believe that we were standing within 10 or 15 rods of where Uncle George fell and beyond doubt the spot was within the very limited circle of our vision as we stood among the thickly growing scrub oaks. There was a single laurel bush growing here and I broke off a branch to sent to you. For ourselves we cut sticks for canes. Our errand was done . . .

The Joneses spent the night in the hotel at Spotsylvania Court House. The next day Matt wrote,

This morning after an early breakfast we turned east and drove 12 miles back to Fredericksburg. There we went over the field of that battle of Dec. 1862 when Burnside made his colossal mistake [the first battle of Fredericksburg]. Of course we covered only a bit of the 5 or 6 miles of lines but we climbed Marys [Marye's] Heights where the fiercest fighting was and went into the National Cemetery where over 15000 union soldiers are buried. Over 12000 are unknown and we feel that the probabilities are that Uncle Georges body lies here. You see the killed at the Wilderness and Spotsylvania were buried where they fell but in 1866 the govt opened this cemetery and every grave upon these battle fields that could be found was opened & the remains carried to F[redericksburg]. As we were leaving the cemetery it began to rain . . .

A total of sixty-six Vermonters rest in marked graves in the Fredericksburg National Military Cemetery. Certainly many more lie there in anonymous burial plots. It is a beautiful hilltop place with tall trees and lush grass, though its quiet, in recent years, has been increasingly disturbed by the growth of Fredericksburg and the building and widening of ever busier roads that run near the base of the hill. In the much smaller walled cemetery at Cold Harbor, thirty-five Vermonters lie in marked graves, and probably many more in unmarked plots. It is believed that soldier bodies are yet to be found in the Wilderness, and at Cold Harbor.

Twenty years after the Wilderness Campaign, Maj. Gen. Andrew Humphreys, who served as General Meade's chief of staff, wrote a book on the Virginia campaigns of 1864 and 1865. Humphreys summed up the Overland Campaign thus:

It was one battle day and night and day and night. No cessation! No cessation! Often we wished for the darkness to close around us that we might have rest. But, alas! With the darkness came not the rest so ardently desired, but work, fight, and march. The flash of the rifles and muskets, as well as of the cannon, together with the fiery parabolas of the fuses and bursting missiles of the mortars, would illuminate the heavens all around the battle-field. Thus the night struggles were frequent and arduous, and at times again we often wished for the return of the morning, but its return still brought no change from our toils of marching and working and fighting. Our thinned ranks told us the sad story of the deadly conflicts through which we were passing. The long lines of graves told the stranger the direction of our marches and the dispositions of our battles. At each morning roll-call fewer and fewer numbers responded to well-known names. Where are they? The reply came from the newly-made graves!

Not only on the battlefields of Virginia did the new-made graves tell the story of the Overland Campaign, but nearly 140 years later, in Vermont, the gravestones and memorial stones of 1864 still speak to its cost and fury. Monuments to the men who fought with Vermont units from the Wilderness to Petersburg stand throughout Vermont, in hill-

WAR DEPARTMENT,

ADJUTANT GENERAL'S OFFICE,

Washington, *June 30th*, 1864.

SIR:

Final statements in the cases of deceased soldiers are required to be sent to the Adjutant General's Office in duplicate, with one copy of the Inventory of Effects. The Descriptive List should also be sent in cases where the soldier was absent from his Company at the time of his death. Where there were no effects, it should be so stated on a blank for Inventory.

Certificates of Disability should be sent in duplicate. Special care should be taken that the date of discharge and signature of the discharging officer should be affixed.

No copies ~~Inventory~~, of the Final Statement, has been received in the case of *Pt. Oliver Davis*, of Co. *"F,"* *3d* Regiment of *Vt. Inf.* Volunteers, whose papers were forwarded to this office. You will please forward the missing papers without delay.

I have the honor to be, sir,

Very respectfully,

Your obedient servant,

Saml. Breck

Assistant Adjutant General.
(110)

COMMANDING OFFICER

Co. F 3d Vt. Inf. Vols.

This print document, issued by the War Department on June 30, 1864, concerned the effects of Pvt. Oliver Davis, of Wilmington. Davis, in the Third Vermont, was wounded June 3 and died June 26 at the Judiciary Square Hospital in Washington. He was buried in Arlington, Virginia. HOWARD COFFIN COLLECTION

side, mountainside, and lakeside burial grounds, in cemeteries in towns and cities, by rivers and streams, in pastures and deep in woodlands. Maj. Richard Crandall lies in the cemetery just south of Berlin Corners beside a handsome old white church. His impressive stone faces the Northfield Mountains, along whose crest more than 50,000 sunsets have counted the years since his burial. Where two old roads meet in the shadow of Blueberry Ledges, near Bridgewater Corners, in the Topliff Cemetery, lies Pvt. J. Henry Eaton, Fifth Vermont. His stone, in which a hand bearing a flag is carved, tells that he was just nineteen when mortally wounded in the Wilderness on May 6.

The lovely Dewey Wright Cemetery overlooking the Dog River, a few miles south of Montpelier, contains several Civil War soldier gravestones. There stands a granite stone for Pvt. George Wright, who was thirty-one when he died in Fredericksburg of a wound suffered May 5 in the Wilderness. Nearby is Pvt. Edwin Dewey, who perished on August 7, 1864, after being shot in the June 1 attack at Cold Harbor. In the Davenport Cemetery, on the road from Wolcott to Craftsbury in Vermont's Northeast Kingdom, Oramel Tillotson's granite stone says, "Co. C 3d Vt. Vols. Missing at the Battle of the Wilderness."

In Williamstown's lovely maple-shaded and stone-walled East Hill Cemetery, words on the Hopkins family monument honor a soldier son. Denison Hopkins, 10th Vermont, was less than three weeks from his twentieth birthday when, the stone says, he "died June 19, 1864, of wounds received in the battle of Cold Harbor." Close by lies David Jillson, who was wounded three times in the Civil War, once in the trenches at Spotsylvania. Twice he recovered to fight on until the great breakthrough at Petersburg on April 2, 1865, where he was hit again. He came home to Vermont terribly wounded and died five days after Christmas. (Private Jillson was the author's great-great-uncle.) In the Roxbury Village Cemetery, just north of the village, is the gravestone of Byron A. Cheldor, Company C, 17th Vermont. The inscription says that he died at age 22 in Washington's Armory Square Hospital on May 30, 1864, of wounds received in the Wilderness. To those sad facts are added the words, "We have not buried thee in a strangers land."

In a Bristol cemetery, along the Green Mountains' western flank, lies

Capt. Riley Bird, Sixth Vermont. His handsome stone, with carved crossed swords, states that he was killed in the Wilderness on May 5, at age 28. Below are the words:

Lee's Mills, Williamsburg, Seven Days Before Richmond, South Mountain, Antietam, Fredericksburg 2nd, Gettysburg, Rappahannock Station, Battle of the Wilderness. These are his Epitaph.

Not until Memorial Day 1914 did Waterbury dedicate a monument to its Civil War soldiers, a solid granite stone, with brass plaques, on which are inscribed the names of all the Waterbury men who served. Thus the wish of Reverend Parker, expressed in 1861, that a memorial honor the town's soldiers was fulfilled. No mention of Parker was made in the lengthy dedicatory speech delivered on May 30 by U.S. Sen. William P. Dillingham of Waterbury. The senator quoted the Gettysburg Address and declared the Civil War "the greatest war of the Nineteenth Century" which "demonstrated to the world the ability of a free people to maintain free institutions upon a scale so gigantic as to challenge the wonder and admiration of all nations." On the monument, Reverend Parker likely would have recognized the thirteen names of men killed during the Overland Campaign, perhaps recalled them from his memorable days at Brandy Station.

When the Waterbury stone was dedicated, Cabot's Civil War monument was nearly four decades old. To mark the centennial of the American nation, on July 4, 1876, at 2 PM, a large crowd gathered on the village green to dedicate a granite obelisk in memory of the Cabot boys who died in the Civil War. The Montpelier band played, the Rev. B. S. Adams prayed, and members of Montpelier's Brooks Post of the Grand Army of the Republic conducted services. J. P. Lamson, Esq., then spoke. "We meet to-day around this monument of the fallen heroes of Cabot to join in the ceremonies of its dedication," he said.

By the people of Cabot this structure has been reared in commemoration of those noble men, who, when rebellious hands were raised against their country's life, bade a last farewell to kindred and home, and went forth to die in its defense. Their sacred names are enshrined in our memories, and engraved on the tablets of our hearts; as long as life shall last, we, of this generation, shall cherish the recollection of their heroic deeds and noble martyrdom with a devotion which no monument can kindle, and no inscription can keep alive. But time will pass, and memories and traditions shall fail, and the tablet of flesh must moulder into dust. It is fit, therefore, that we should carve on the everlasting granite the names of that noble band, that our children and our children's children may learn by whose blood our country was bap-

Henry Herrick in later years. The identity of the young man is unknown.

tized into new life, and the bonds of its union were cemented for all coming time. Let this monument stand, then, a proud memorial of the dead, and may time touch it with a gentle hand as it bears to succeeding generations its just and deserving record.

He continued,

At this time I am oppressed with a sense of the impropriety of uttering words on this occasion. If silence is ever golden, it must be here beside this monument, which bears the names of 36 men whose lives were more significant than speech, and whose death was a poem, the music of which can never be sung. For love of country they accepted death. That act resolved all doubts, and made immortal their patriotism and their virtue.

What lies beyond death is not known. But it seems safe to speculate that had the Cabot boys who were honored that day been listening, they would have been touched by the words. But it is also possible to imagine them standing in the ranks, nudging each other and chuckling at the reference to golden silence, which, of course, triggered more rhetoric. "Nobly did they fall, and in a righteous cause," Lamson went on:

Their country called, and in the great cause of humanity they died. And though their bones lie bleaching on a Southern soil, far away from friends and home, yet ever fresh will be their memories in the hearts of the living and the loved. And their records will remain from everlasting to everlasting, after this monument dedicated to them shall have crumbled to dust.

With the 150th anniversary of the Civil War becoming visible on the horizon of the 21st century, the Cabot monument still stands erect and barely crumbled at all, with its sad, proud listing of the 36 local men who died to free their fellow men and suppress the great rebellion. Among them are an even dozen who perished in the Overland Campaign: Lt. Abel Morrill, Cpl. George Wright, and Privates

Nathaniel Bailey and Parker Swasey, all killed in the Wilderness; Privates Henry Marsh and George Stone, mortally wounded in Upton's attack at Spotsylvania; Privates Anson Writer and Wallace Page, killed in the deadly June 3 assault at Cold Harbor; Pvt. John Rudd, dead on June 7 of wounds received in either the Wilderness or Spotsylvania; and Henry Herrick's friend Pvt. Charles Perry, killed by a sharpshooter on June 5 in the trenches at Cold Harbor. And there are Privates Samuel Thompson and Erastus Scott, shot dead amid the fury of the Bloody Angle. Scott is the same young man whose death brought such heartfelt grief to his young widow, Margaret. All the names constitute a heavy toll for so short a time in so small a town.

Not inscribed on the Cabot monument, of course, is the name of native son Henry Herrick. He enlisted in St. Johnsbury, served a year hitch, survived, and came home to keep a journal. Herrick died on December 12, 1894, in Boston, at age fifty-six, apparently while on a trip there to hear music. He was fond of attending Boston opera performances. The *Caledonian Record* published an obituary on December 20 that stated:

> His early life was spent in Cabot and he came to St. Johnsbury 38 years ago. He lived here ever since then with the exception of 18 months service in the war. In the war he was a musician in the band of the Third Vermont regiment. He was foreman of the sealing of weights at the scale works and performed his duties there with rare skill and faithfulness. This was a very responsible position, requiring patience, accuracy and a thorough knowledge of all the complications that might arise.
>
> Mr. Herrick was best known to our townspeople as a musician and he was a thorough lover of good music and in a quiet and unassuming way did much in all these years to keep up a high musical standard in the entire community. For over a dozen years he was leader of the North Church choir and during the time he was leader, singing tenor in the quartette. During most of his residence here he was leader of our band and to this organization he gave many faithful works in spite of many discouragements. Though of a quiet and retiring nature he had a great many warm friends who deeply mourn his loss.
>
> The funeral was held at the residence of Abijah Smith on Friday

afternoon and was attended by many of his old associates at the scale works, Chamberlin Post [G.A.R.], and the St. Johnsbury Band. The funeral was conducted by Rev. Dr. A. H. Heath . . . Music was furnished by the Mahogany Quartette. His two nearest relatives were present, a brother, L. Herrick of Cabot, and a cousin, H. H. Scribner, of Montpelier. The body was escorted to the depot by a delegation from Chamberlin Post, and the band, and the body taken to Cabot for interment.

Henry Herrick was buried in the Cabot Village Cemetery, a lovely and hilly burial ground just southwest of the village. He lies in the family plot, beside his mother and father, and a sister who died in 1855 at age twenty-six. His name appears on the family monument. A small stone inscribed "Henry" marks his grave. He rests in the shade of a huge maple, perhaps as old as the Civil War, whose leaves, in autumn, turn fire red and yellow. The stone faces west, toward a tree-covered Vermont hillside. Some 30 yards away, along the ridge and in sight, is the grave of friend Charlie, whose stone notes that he was killed at Cold Harbor. Whatever became of Zenas, or Zenas' full name, remains a mystery. His was a common name at the time, and several Zenases were employed at the Fairbanks enterprises during the Civil War.

Henry Herrick lived to see a time when Vermonters set about honoring their Civil War soldiers in earnest. The erecting of monuments became something of a common occurrence in the 1880s, with the shock of the great war having subsided. In the summer of 1884, to mark the 20th anniversary of Chelsea's Highland Cemetery, Civil War veterans and their sons and wives planted maples along its drive. "Consecrated in 1864" are the words on the arch spanning the entry to the handsome hillside burial ground, with its postcard view of Chelsea Village and the valley of the White River's First Branch. Not far inside the gateway stands the gravestone of Capt. Orville Bixby, killed in the Wilderness on May 6, 1864. The stone lists all the battles in which Bixby fought, a litany of the Vermont Brigade's history up to and including its worst and, perhaps, most glorious conflict. It reads: Bull Run, Lee's Mills, Williamsburg, Golding's Farm, White Oak

Swamp, South Mountain, Antietam, Fredericksburg, Marye's Heights, Banks Ford, Franklin's Crossing, Funkstown, Rappahannock Station, Mine Run, Wilderness.

But for the determined efforts of Orville Bixby's widow, Frances Bixby, the captain's body would lie in a faraway grave, probably in the Fredericksburg National Cemetery, or perhaps lost and lonely in the Wilderness. The latter possibility recalls the words of Herman Melville, who visited the battlefields not long after the fighting and wrote a brief poem "An Uninscribed Monument on One of the Battle-fields of the Wilderness." It concludes:

Take in the import of the quiet here
The after-quiet—the calm full fraught;
Thou too will silent stand—
Silent as I and lonesome as the land.

But Frances Bixby was a determined woman, and in 1864 she set about having her husband's burial site, near a Union field hospital near the Brock and Plank Road intersection, discovered, and his body sent home. She contacted his fellow soldiers and their families in her endeavor, and had her hopes falsely raised for a time when, in August 1864, a letter arrived in Chelsea from the wife of another Second Vermont soldier. "Capt. Bixby may be in rebel hands," she wrote, though the letter contained the caution, "I do not want to give you too much hope for fear that it may be dashed to the ground yet if it only could be true." Of course, it wasn't true, and the determined widow kept about her search. Mrs. Bixby finally located a soldier taken to the same field hospital as the captain, who drew her a map of the burial site. In December 1864, she received information from an undertaking firm about "air tight caskets" and the shipment of remains. It appears to have been in the spring of 1865 that Orville Bixby's body was raised from the Virginia earth and shipped north. The modest, handsome stone, into which is carved a waving flag, was waiting when the captain's remains came home.

A half century later, on May 30, 1915, Frances Bixby died and was buried beside her husband. She never remarried, through 51 years of widowhood. Just down the hill from the Bixby graves, in Highland Cemetery, stands another stone, erected by another widow of a Vermont soldier who fought in Grant's Overland Campaign. Pvt. Francis Skinner, Fourth Vermont, also a Chelsea man, survived the Wilderness, Spotsylvania, and Cold Harbor only to be captured on June 23 at the Weldon Railroad. Taken to Andersonville, he died seven weeks later and his body was buried in the prison cemetery, where it remains. His widow had a memorial stone placed in the family plot at Chelsea, a place she no doubt visited countless times during her 40 years of widowhood, which ended with her death in 1904. Certainly Frances Bixby, and other First Branch Valley people who lost loved ones in the Civil War, saw and well understood her chosen epitaph for her beloved husband. Private Skinner's stone reads:

God has marked every sorrowing day
And numbered every secret tear

APPENDIX:

THE BATTERED STARS

Surgeon Henry Janes kept records on the progress of soldiers he treated at his Sloan Hospital in Montpelier, photographing many. Janes glued the photos next to the men's case histories in a large record book that is preserved at the University of Vermont's Special Collections. Ten of them are reproduced on the following pages.

Pvt. George Abbott, of Londonderry and the Fourth Vermont, suffered the amputation of an arm afer his wounding on May 5. UNIVERSITY OF VERMONT

Pvt. Lyman Hulett, of Shaftsbury and the Second Vermont, was 25 when he was shot in the arm on May 5. UNIVERSITY OF VERMONT

Pvt. John Aldrich, 45, of Granville and the Fourth Vermont, had an arm shot away on May 5. UNIVERSITY OF VERMONT

Azariah Grant, a private in the Second Vermont from Shaftsbury, was crippled for life at age 27 on May 5. UNIVERSITY OF VERMONT

Pvt. John McGowan, 25, was shot on May 5. The Woodstock man, who served in the Sixth Vermont, is shown with his artificial limb. UNIVERSITY OF VERMONT

Pvt. Willard Lilley, of East Calais, lost his lower left arm on June 4 at Cold Harbor. The 11th Vermont soldier was probably the victim of a sharpshooter. UNIVERSITY OF VERMONT

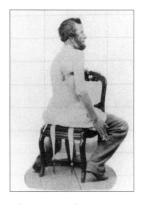

Corp. Herman Knowlton, 22, of the 11th Vermont, shot during the June 1 attack on Cold Harbor. He went home to Rochester without a left foot. UNIVERSITY OF VERMONT

Constantin Chadwick, a private in the 11th Vermont from Bethel, was 40 when he lost an arm in the fighting of June 1. UNIVERSITY OF VERMONT

Alonzo Amsden, of Westmore and the 10th Vermont, displays the bullet wound that ended his military service on June 1 at Cold Harbor. UNIVERSITY OF VERMONT

Corp. Charles Woodruff, 19, needed a walking stick after taking a bullet in the lower right leg. The 10th Vermont soldier went home to Burke, in northeastern Vermont. UNIVERSITY OF VERMONT

SOURCES AND REFERENCES

Abbott, Maj. Lemuel. *Personal Recollections and Civil War Diary 1864*. Burlington, Vt.: Free Press Printing Co., 1908.

Argus & Patriot. Editions of 1864. Vermont State Library, Montpelier, Vt.

Austin, Pvt. Orlo H. Civil War letters. Vermont Historical Society, Montpelier, Vt.

Barney, Colonel Elisha. Account of his funeral from *Vermont Historical Magazine*. Courtesy of Eunice Gates.

Bassett, T. D. Seymour. *The Growing Edge: Vermont Villages 1840–1880*. Montpelier, Vt.: Vermont Historical Society, 1992.

Benedict, G. G. *Vermont in the Civil War*, vol. I. Burlington, Vt.: Free Press Association, 1886.

———. *Vermont in the Civil War*, vol. II. Burlington, Vt.: Free Press Association, 1888.

———. Civil War papers. University of Vermont Special Collections, Bailey/Howe Library, Burlington, Vt.

Bennington Banner. Editions of 1864. Vermont State Library, Montpelier, Vt.

Bishop, Pvt. Wayland. Civil War letters. Courtesy of Ken Bishop, Springfield, Vt., and Linda Welch, Dartmouth College, Hanover, N.H.

Bixby, Capt. Orville. Civil War letters. University of Vermont Special Collections, Bailey/Howe Library, Burlington, Vt.

Blaisdell, Pvt. Jonathan. Civil War letters. University of Vermont Special Collections, Bailey/Howe Library, Burlington, Vt.

Blanchard, Julia. 1864 diary. Hammond family papers. Vermont Historical Society, Montpelier, Vt.

Bogart, Ernest L. *Peacham: The Story of a Vermont Hill Town*. Montpelier, Vt.: Vermont Historical Society, 1948.

Brattleboro Phoenix. Editions of 1864. Brooks Memorial Library, Brattleboro, Vt.

Bridge, George A. Civil War memoir. Vermont Historical Society, Montpelier, Vt.

Brown, Thomas H. Civil War letters. Vermont Historical Society, Montpelier, Vt.

Burlington Free Press. Editions of 1864. Vermont State Library, Montpelier, Vt.

Burnham, Pvt. Henry. Civil War letters. Vermont Historical Society, Montpelier, Vt.

Buxton, Capt. Charles. Civil War diary. Vermont Historical Society, Montpelier, Vt.

Byrne, Frank L., and Andrew T. Weaver, editors. *Haskell of Gettysburg: His Life and Civil War Papers*. Madison, Wis.: State Historical Society of Wisconsin, 1970.

Cabot, Mary R. *Annals of Brattleboro 1691–1895*. Brattleboro, Vt.: Press of E. L. Hildreth & Company, 1922.

Caledonian Record. Editions of 1864. Vermont State Library, Montpelier, Vt.

Carter, Capt. E. W. *A Remarkable Man: His History*. Privately printed 1886. Vermont Historical Society, Montpelier, Vt.

Chadwick, Albert G., editor. *Soldiers Record of the Town of St. Johnsbury, Vermont: The War of the Rebellion*. St. Johnsbury Athenaeum, St. Johnsbury, Vt.: C. M. Stone & Company, 1883.

Catton, Bruce. *A Stillness at Appomattox*. Garden City, N.Y.: Doubleday & Co., 1952.

———. *Grant Takes Command*. Boston: Little, Brown & Co., 1968.

Chamberlin, George. *Letters of George Chamberlin*. Springfield, Ill.: H. W. Rooker's Publishing House, 1883. St. Johnsbury Athenaeum, St. Johnsbury, Vt.

Chandler, Maj. Charles. June 6 report to Peter Washburn. Vermont Military Archives, Middlesex, Vt.

Chapin, Pvt. Charles. Civil War diary. U.S. Army Military History Institute, Carlisle Barracks, Pa.

———. Civil War papers. Vermont Historical Society, Montpelier, Vt.

Chase, Peter. "In the Wilderness." *Vermont Phoenix* May 4, 1888. Brattleboro Historical Society, Brattleboro, Vt.

————. *Reunion Greeting Together with Historical Sketch and a Complete Descriptive List of the Members of Co. I, 2nd Regt., Vt. Vols.* Brattleboro, Vt.: *Brattleboro Phoenix* Job Printing Office, 1891. Brattleboro Historical Society, Brattleboro, Vt.

Cheney Family, of Stowe, Vermont. Family Letters. Cheney/Watts collection. Vermont Historical Society, Montpelier, Vt.

Closson, H. P. Civil War Diary. Dartmouth College Special Collections, Hanover, N.H.

Cobb, Pvt. Curtis C. Civil War letter. Vermont Historical Society, Montpelier, Vt.

Coffin, Charles Carleton. *Redeeming the Republic: The Third Period of the War of the Rebellion in the Year 1864* (including accounts of Confederate resistance to the Union attack at Cold Harbor on June 3 by General Law and Captain Franklin): New York: Harper & Brothers, 1889.

Crandall, Richard B. Civil War diary. Vermont Historical Society, Montpelier, Vt.

Crosby, Pvt. George. Civil War diary. Vermont Historical Society, Montpelier, Vt.

Cummings, Charles. Civil War letters. Charles Cummings papers. Vermont Historical Society, Montpelier, Vt.

Cutler, Jerome. Civil War letters. U.S. Military History Institute, Carlisle Barracks, Pa.

Dana. Teacher's diary. Vermont Historical Society, Montpelier, Vt.

Davis, Judge James. 1864 diary. St. Albans Historical Society, St. Albans, Vt.

Dewey, Susan. Letters to her husband in the Eighth Vermont. Vermont Historical Society, Montpelier, Vt.

Destler, C. M., editor. "A Vermonter in Andersonville: Diary of Charles Ross." *Vermont History* XXI (July 1957): 229–245.

Ditty, Erie. Civil War diary. Special Collections, University Libraries, Virginia Tech., Blacksburg, Va.

————. Civil War memoir. Courtesy of Mark Jenkins, Wilbraham, Ma., and Alan Will, San Diego, Ca.

Dodge, Chester W. Civil War diary. Private collection.

Dowden, Albert R. "John Gregory Smith." *Vermont History* XXXII (April 1964): 79–96.

Eastman, Seth. *The Civil War (As Recollected by an Ordinary Soldier)*. Groton Historical Society, Groton, Vt.

————. Civil War papers. Vermont Historical Society, Montpelier, Vt.

Eddy, Mercy. Diary. Vermont Historical Society, Montpelier, Vt.

Eisenschiml, Otto, editor. *Vermont General: The Unusual War Experiences of Edward Hastings Ripley, 1862–1865*. The Devin-Adair Company, 1960.

Faust, Patricia L., editor. *Historical Times Illustrated History of the Civil War*. New York: Harper & Row, Inc., 1986.

Felch, Carlton. Civil War diary. Fairbanks Museum, St. Johnsbury, Vt.

Felch, William. Letter to Commissioner Holbrook. Vermont Military Archives, Middlesex, Vt.

Ferguson, Ernest B. *Not War But Murder: Cold Harbor 1864*. New York: Alfred A. Knopf, 2000.

Field, Miss Wealthy. 1864 letters. Vermont Historical Society, Montpelier, Vt.

Fisk, Wilbur. Civil War diary. Library of Congress, Washington, D.C.

Foote, Shelby. *Red River to Appomattox*. New York: Random House, 1974.

French Family letters. Courtesy of Linda Welch, Dartmouth College, Hanover, N.H., and the Calvin French family, Cavendish, Vt.

Frost, Robert. "A Prayer in Spring." New York: Henry Holt and Company, 1939.

Gallagher, Gary, editor. *The Wilderness Campaign*. Chapel Hill, N.C.: University of North Carolina Press, 1997.

Getty, Brig. Gen. George. Note of May 5 and Report on Wilderness Fighting. *War of the Rebellion Official Records*, Series L, Vol. XXXVI, Part I, Government Printing Office, Washington, D.C., 1891.

Gilbert, Cordelia L. 1864 letters from Woodstock, Vt. Gilbert Papers, Woodstock Historical Society, Woodstock, Vt.

Gilman, Pvt. Samuel. Civil War diary. Courtesy of Will Gilman of Chelsea, Vt.

Godfrey, Pvt. George. "Reminiscence of the Wilderness." *National Tribune*, Jan. 22, 1884. Fredericksburg and Spotsylvania National Military Park archive.

Goodall, Reverend. Eulogy at Private Lyon funeral. Vermont Historical Society, Montpelier, Vt.

Gould, Lt. Charles, and Sue Warner Gould. Letters. University of Vermont Special Collections, Bailey/Howe Library, Burlington, Vt.

Grant, Lewis A. "In the Wilderness." *The National Tribune*, January 28, 1897.

———. *War of the Rebellion Official Records*, Series L, Vol. XXXV, Part I, Government Printing Office, Washington, D.C., 1891.

Grant, Lt. Gen. Ulysses. Letter to General Meade on eve of Overland Campaign and letter written at Spotsylvania. *War of the Rebellion Official Records*, Series L, Vol. XXXVI, Part I, Government Printing Office, Washington, D.C., 1891.

———. *Personal Memoirs of U.S.*, chapter 55 (Grant's comments on the June 3 assault at Cold Harbor). Cleveland: World Publishing Co., 1952.

Greene, Cpl. George. Civil War diary. Vermont Historical Society, Montpelier, Vt.

Greenleaf, Lt. Walter. Talk on Sheridan's Raid Given at the Bardwell Hotel in Rutland in 1883. Benedict Papers, University of Vermont Special Collections, Bailey/Howe Library, Burlington, Vt.

Grout, Reverend Henry. Eulogy at Charles Mead funeral. Rutland Historical Society, Rutland, Vt.

Hall, Pvt. Edwin C. Civil War letters. Vermont Historical Society, Montpelier, Vt.

Hammond Family, of West Windsor, Vt. 1864 diary. Vermont Historical Society, Montpelier, Vt.

Harris, Pvt. Luther. *A Prison Story*. Unpublished manuscript, University of Vermont Special Collections, Bailey/Howe Library, Burlington, Vt.

———. *The Wilderness*. Unpublished manuscript. Fredericksburg and Spotsylvania National Military Park archive, Fredericksburg, Va.

Harrison, Noel G. *Fredericksburg Civil War Sites*. Lynchburg, Va.: H. E. Howard, Inc., 1996.

Haskell, Pvt. Londus. Civil War letters. U.S. Army Military History Institute, Carlisle Barracks, Pa.

Haynes, Rev. Edwin D. *A History of the Tenth Regiment Vermont Volunteers*. Montpelier, Vt.: Tenth Vermont Regimental Association, 1870.

Hemenway, Abby Maria. *History of Vermont*. Information on Civil War casualties taken from her town histories of Brandon, Charleston, Chelsea, Greensboro, Guilford, Middletown Springs, Pawlet, Stowe, Tunbridge, Roxbury, and Waitsfield. Vermont Historical Society.

Herrick, Henry. Diary. Fairbanks Museum, St. Johnsbury, Vt.

Hinchey, Angela, editor. "Charles B. Mead: A Young Man of Rare Promise." *Rutland Historical Society Quarterly* 37, no. 1 (1997): 3–22.

Holbrook, Frank. List of wounded sent to Adjutant Gen. Washburn with letter. Vermont Military Archives, Middlesex, Vt.

Holton, Pvt. Edward. Civil War letters. Fredericksburg and Spotsylvania National Military Park archive, Fredericksburg, Va., and University of Vermont Special Collections, Bailey/Howe Library, Burlington, Vt.

Hopkins, John H. III. *The Early History of the Diocese of Vermont*. An address at the 150th anniversary of the Diocese of Vermont. Diocese of Vermont archive, Burlington, Vt.

Horton, Edwin. Civil War letters. Vermont Historical Society, Montpelier, Vt.

Houghton, Henry. *Recollections of the War*. Unpublished manuscript. Woodstock Historical Society, Woodstock, Vt.

———. "The Ordeal of the Civil War: A Recollection." *Vermont History,* Winter 1973: 31–49.

Howe, Lt. George. Civil War letters. Howe/Wolcott correspondence. Sheldon Museum, Middlebury, Vt.

Hoyt, William Henry. Diary. University of Vermont Special Collections, Bailey/Howe Library, Burlington, Vt.

Humphreys, Maj. Gen. Andrew A. *The Virginia Campaign of '64 & '65*. New York: Charles Scribner's Sons, 1883.

Hyde, Dr. Melvin J. *In the Field*. Geraldine Francis Chittick, editor. Newport, Vt.: Vermont Civil War Enterprises, 2000.

Ide, Lt. Horace K. Manuscript History of the First Vermont Cavalry. University of Vermont Special Collections, Bailey/Howe Library, Burlington, Vt.

———. Account of George Custer viewing Addison Preston's body. G. G. Benedict Papers, University of Vermont Special Collections, Bailey/ Howe Library, Burlington, Vt.

Johnson, Pvt. Norman W. Civil War diary. Brooks Memorial Library, Brattleboro, Vt.

Johnson, Pvt. Norman William. Civil War diary, courtesy of Harold Hayward, Marshfield, Vt.

Jones, Matt. Letter on exploring Wilderness and Fredericksburg battlefields. Civil War letters and family papers. Courtesy of David E. Jamieson, Calais, Vt.

Joslyn, Eugene. Civil War letters and family papers. Courtesy of David E. Jamieson, Calais, Vt.

Kelly, John T. "The 1864 Diary of Private John T. Kelly, Second Vermont Regiment." Don Wickman, editor. *Rutland Historical Society Quarterly* 24, no. 6: 18–22.

Kuntz, Norbert A. "A Brookfield Soldier's Report: The Civil War Recollections of Edwin C. Hall." *Vermont History.* Fall, 1989.

Law, Maj Gen. Evander. G. G. Benedict. *Vermont in the Civil War*, vol. II.

Lamson, Rev. J. P. Speech at Cabot Civil War monument dedication, *Caledonian Record*, St. Johnsbury, Vt., July 8, 1876.

Leach, Pvt. Chester. Civil War letters. Transcribed by Edward Feidner. University of Vermont Special Collections, Bailey/Howe Library, Burlington, Vt.

Leach, Pvt. Orvin. *Personal Reminiscenses of the Civil War*. Unpublished manuscript. Woodstock Historical Society, Woodstock, Vt.

Lee, Robert E. Report of the action of May 5. *War of the Rebellion Official Records,* Series L., Vol. XXXVI, Part I, Government Printing Office, Washington, D.C., 1891.

Lewis, Lt. Col. John. Speech of 8 January 1880. In *Proceedings of the Reunion Society of Vermont Officers, 1864–1884.* Burlington, Vt.: Free Press Association, 1885.

Lewis, Theodore Graham. *History of Waterbury Vermont 1763–1915.* Waterbury, Vt.: The Record Print, 1918.

Lincoln, Abraham. *The Collected Works of Abraham Lincoln,* vol. 8. Roy P. Basler, editor. New Brunswick, N.J.: Rutgers University Press, 1953.

Lyman, Ellen. Diary kept in Burlington, 1864. University of Vermont Special Collections, Bailey/Howe Library, Burlington, Vt.

Lyon, George S. Civil War letters. Vermont Historical Society, Montpelier, Vt.

Manchester Journal. Editions of 1864. Vermont State Library, Montpelier, Vt.

Marcot, Roy M. *Civil War Chief of Sharpshooters Hiram Berdan.* Irvine, Cal.: Northwood University Press, 1989.

Marshall, Jeffrey D., editor. *A War of the People: Vermont Civil War Letters.* Hanover, N.H.: University Press of New England, 1999.

Matter, William D. *If It Takes All Summer: The Battle of Spotsylvania.* Chapel Hill, N.C.: University of North Carolina Press, 1988.

McFeely, William S. *Grant: A Biography.* New York: W. W. Norton, 1981.

McMahon, Martin. Speech including remarks on Vermont Brigade's "Town Meeting" at Spotsylvania. *The Society of the Army of the Potomac, Report of the Eleventh Annual Reunion at Burlington, Vt. June 16, 1880.* New York: McGowan and Slipper Printers, 1880.

Mead, Charles B. Civil War diary, 1864. Courtesy of State Sen. Hull Maynard and Taffy Maynard, Shrewsbury, Vt.

Melville, Dorothy Sutherland. *The Tyler-Browns of Brattleboro.* (Includes the letters of Lt. Col. John Tyler and family.) New York: Exposition Press, 1964.

Melville, Herman. "An Inscribed Monument on One of the Battle-fields of the Wilderness. Battle-Pieces and Aspects of the War." Sidney Kaplan, editor. Amherst, Mass.: University of Massachusetts Press, 1972.

McMahon, Martin T. *Gen. John Sedgwick, An Address, Montpelier Nov. 11, 1880.* Rutland, Vt.: Charles Tuttle & Co., 1880.

Middlebury Register. Editions of 1864. Sheldon Museum, Middlebury, Vt.

Miles, Pvt. Lorenzo. Civil War diary. Vermont Historical Society, Montpelier, Vt.

Morey, Pvt. Charles C. Civil War diary and letters. U.S. Army Military History Institute, Carlisle Barracks, Pa.

Morrisville Newsdealer. Editions of 1864. Morristown Centennial Library, Morrisville, Vt.

Noyes, Sgt. William. Medal of Honor citation. Vermont State Military Archive, Middlesex, Vt.

Paddock, Pvt. Augustus. Civil War letters. University of Vermont Special Collections, Bailey/Howe Library, Burlington, Vt.

Parcher, Tabor. Civil War letters. University of Vermont Special Collections, Bailey/Howe Library, Burlington, Vt.

Parker, Rev. Charles Carrol. Letters from the winter encampment. Parker Family papers. Vermont Historical Society, Montpelier, Vt.

———. *Early History of Waterbury: A Discourse*. Waterbury, Vt.: Waterbury Job Printing Establishment, 1867.

Parker, Pvt. Samuel. Civil War letters. National Archives, Washington, D.C., and courtesy of Will Gilman, Chelsea, Vt.

Parker, Pvt. William. Civil War letters. National Archives, Washington, D.C., and courtesy of Will Gilman, Chelsea, Vt.

Peake, Royal W. 1864 Diary kept in Bristol, Vt. University of Vermont Special Collections, Bailey/Howe Library, Burlington, Vt.

Peck, General T. S. *Revised Roster of Vermont Volunteers*. Montpelier, Vt., Press of the Watchman Publishing Co.

———. Letter recommending Pvt. William Noyes for a Medal of Honor. Vermont State Military Archives, Middlesex, Vt.

Peeler, Cpl. Charles. Civil War diary. U.S. Army Military History Institute, Carlisle Barracks, Pa.

Pingree, Lt. Col. Samuel. Civil War letters. University of Vermont Special Collections, Bailey/Howe Library, Burlington, Vt.

Pingree, Lt. Col. Stephen. Civil War letters. University of Vermont Special Collections, Bailey/Howe Library, Burlington, Vt.

Pitkin, Caleb, editor. *Cabot Vermont, a Collection of Memories from the Centuries Past*. Barre, Vt.: Brown & Sons Printing, 1999.

Poirier, Robert. *The Blood of our Alumni; Norwich University Citizen Soldiers in the Army of the Potomac*. Mason City, Iowa: Savas Publishing Co., 1999.

Porter, Charles. *Memoirs of the Civil War*. Unpublished. Written at Grinnell, Iowa, 1908. Vermont Historical Society, Montpelier, Vt.

Priest, D. D. Civil War letters. Courtesy of Dennis Devereaux, Belmont, Vt.

Proceedings of the Reunion Society of Vermont Officers, 1864–1884 With

Addresses Delivered at Its Meetings. Burlington, Vt.: Free Press Association, 1884.

Reya, Pvt. Lewis. Letter to Commissioner Holbrook. Vermont Military Archive, Middlesex, Vermont.

Reynolds, Maj. William. Report on the Wilderness action. *War of the Rebellion Official Records*, Series L, Vol. XXXVI, Part I, Government Printing Office, Washington, D.C., 1891.

Rhea, Gordon. *The Battle of the Wilderness, May 5–6, 1864*. Bloomington, Ind.: Indiana University Press, 1985.

Ripley, William Y. W. *Vermont Riflemen in the War for the Union, 1861–1865, A History of Company F*. Rutland, Vt.: Tuttle & Co. Publishers, 1883.

Rosenblatt, Emil, and Ruth Rosenblatt, editors. *Hard Marching Every Day: The Civil War Letters of Private Wilbur Fisk*. Lawrence, Ks.: University of Kansas Press, 1992.

Rumrill, Haskell B. Civil War letters. U.S. Army Military History Institute, Carlisle Barracks, Pa.

Rutland Courier. Editions of 1864. Rutland Historical Society, Rutland, Vt.

Rutland Daily Herald and *Rutland Weekly Herald*. Editions of 1864. Vermont State Library, Montpelier, Vt.

Rutherford, Dr. Joseph. Civil War letters. University of Vermont Special Collections, Bailey/Howe Library, Burlington, Vt.

Saint Albans Messenger. Editons of 1864. Vermont State Library, Montpelier, Vt.

Scott, Erastus. Civil War letters. University of Vermont Special Collections, Bailey/Howe Library, Burlington, Vt.

Scott, Robert Garth. *Into the Wilderness with the Army of the Potomac*. Bloomington and Indianapolis: University of Indiana Press, 1992.

Seaver, Col. Thomas. Report on operations of the Third Vermont from May 4 to June 12, 1864. *The War of the Rebellion Official Records*, Series L, Volume XXXVI, Part I, Government Printing Office, Washington D.C., 1891.

Smith, Sgt. John A. Civil War letter and verse. Collection of Msgr. John McSweeney, Burlington, Vt.

Smith, Gov. John Gregory. *Message of the Governor to the General Assembly of Vermont. October Session, 1864*. Montpelier, Vt.: Walton's Steam Press, 1864.

Smith, Maj. Gen. William F. *Autobiography of Major General William F. Smith 1861–1864*, edited by Herbert M. Schiller. Dayton, Ohio: Morningside Press, 1990.

Sparrow, Pvt. Bradford. Civil War letters. University of Vermont Special Collections, Bailey/Howe Library, Burlington, Vt.

Starr, Stephen Z. *The Union Cavalry in the Civil War,* volume II. Baton Rouge: Louisiana State University Press, 1981.

Stevens, Pvt. William. Civil War letters. Sheldon Museum, Middlebury, Vt., and Rokeby Museum, Ferrisburg, Vt.

Stevens, Dr. George T. *Three Years in the Sixth Corps.* Albany, N.Y.: S. R. Gray, 1866.

Stiles, Lester D. Diary kept in St. Johnsbury Center. Courtesy of Graham S. Newell, St. Johnsbury, Vt.

Stowe, Elijah. Civil War diary and letters. Private collection.

Thayer, Esther M., and Willard Thayer. Civil War letters. University of Vermont Special Collections, Bailey/Howe Library, Burlington, Vt.

Tinkham, Edson. Diary. University of Vermont Special Collections, Bailey/ Howe Library, Burlington, Vt.

Tillison, Pvt. Charles. Civil War letters. University of Vermont Special Collections, Bailey/Howe Library, Burlington, Vt.

Toby, George. Civil War diary. Transcribed by Donald Phanz. Fredericksburg and Spotsylvania National Military Park archive, Fredericksburg, Va. Gift of Allen Kittredge, North Reading, Mass.

Towle, Pvt. Ransom W. Civil War diary. Vermont Historical Society, Montpelier, Vt.

Vermont Journal, Windsor, Vt. March through July, 1864. Windsor Library, Windsor, Vt.

Trudeau, Noah Andre. *Bloody Roads South.* Baton Rouge: Louisiana State University Press, 2000.

Tucker, Mary. Diary 1864. Vermont Historical Society, Montpelier, Vt.

Tunnell, Ted, editor. *Carpetbagger from Vermont: The Autobiography of Marshall Harvey Twitchell.* Baton Rouge: Louisiana State University Press, 1989.

Twitchell, Sgt. Marshall. Civil War letters. Vermont Historical Society, Montpelier, Vt.

Tyler Family letters, including those of Judge Royall Tyler and Col. John Tyler. See Dorothy Sutherland Melville book listed here.

Vermont Christian Repository. Editions of May and June, 1864. Vermont State Library, Montpelier, Vt.

Vermont Phoenix. Editions of 1864. Brooks Memorial Library, Brattleboro, Vt.

Vermont Standard. Editions of 1864. Woodstock Historical Society, Woodstock, Vt.

Vermont Watchman. Editions of 1864. Vermont State Library, Montpelier, Vt.

Waite, Pvt. Oscar E. *Three Years with the Tenth Vermont*. Unpublished manuscript. University of Vermont Special Collections, Bailey/Howe Library, Burlington, Vt.

Watts, Pvt. Lorenzo. Civil War diary. Vermont Historical Society, Montpelier, Vt.

Webster, Pvt. Ellery. June 7 letter from Cold Harbor. *Morrisville Newsdealer* of May 22. Morrisville Public Library, Morrisville, Vt.

Wells, Pvt. Charles. Civil War diary. Fairbanks Museum, St. Johnsbury, Vt.

Wells, Maj. William. Civil War letters. University of Vermont Special Collections, Bailey/Howe Library, Burlington, Vt.

Wheaton, Brig. Gen. Frank. Comments on assuming command of Getty's Division in the Wilderness. *War of the Rebellion Official Records*, Series L, Vol. XXXVI, Part I, Government Printing Office, Washington, D.C., 1891.

Wheeler, Pvt. Artemas H. Civil War diary and letters. Constitution House, Windsor, Vt.

White, Capt. David. Civil War letters. University of Vermont Special Collections, Bailey/Howe Library, Burlington, Vt.

Williams, Lt. Lyman S. Civil War letters. University of Vermont Special Collections, Bailey/Howe Library, Burlington, Vt.

Wills, Orvis. 1864 diary. Vermont Historical Society, Montpelier, Vt.

Windsor Journal. Editions of 1864. Windsor Library, Windsor, Vt.

Woodbury, Eri. Civil War diary and letters. Dartmouth College Special Collections, Hanover, N.H.

Woodward, Pvt. Alvin. Civil War letters. University of Vermont Special Collections, Bailey/Howe Library, Burlington, Vt.

Worthen, Pvt. Erastus. Civil War letters. University of Vermont Special Collections, Bailey/Howe Library, Burlington, Vt.

INDEX

Note: Page numbers in italics indicate photographs.

Bridport, Vermont, 288

Briggs, James, 69

Brighton, Vermont, 195, 200

Bristol, Vermont, 61, 69, 144, 244, 374–75

Brock–Plank Road Battle, map of, 94

Brookfield, Vermont, 27, 77, 231

Brooks, William, 295

Brown, Gertrude Tyler, 209

Brown, Thomas, 35, 179

Brown, William B., 358

Browne, H. S., 194

Brownington, Vermont, 91, 192, 257

Buck, Erastus, *143*, 199, 270–71

Buckbee, John, 357

Buckley, John, 359–60

Burke, Vermont, 385

Burlington, Vermont, 15, 53, 54, 56, 60, 61, 62, 64–65, 66, 71, 74–75, 87, 89, 126, 140, 147, 189, 192, 193, 197, 198, 218, 242, 246, 254, 330, 336

Burlington Free Press, 15–16, 55, 56, 59–60, 64, 65, 66, 67, 71, 74–75, 91, 126, 147, 198, 249–50, 268, 269, 270, 329–30, 333, 335, 355–56

Burlington Weekly Sentinel, 333

Burnham, Henry, 316, 344, 354

Burnside, Ambrose, 47, 49, 65, 90, 99, 141, 171, 177, 261, 264, 267, 296, 306, 341, 352

Burt, Aruniah, 116

Butler, Benjamin, 48, 168, 216, 267, 295, 329

Buxton, Albert, 89, 146

Buxton, Charles, 221, 237, 240, 340, 353, 353–54

C

Cabot, Vermont, 62, 91, 182, 192, 243, 245, 248, 251, 253, 323, 333, 364, 375, 379

Cady, Capt., 43

Cady, Deliza, 52

Cagliostro, 357

Cahoon, C. S., 197

Cain, Jane, 357

Calais, Vermont, 253

Caledonian Record, 193, 364–65, 378–79

Cambridge, Vermont, 42, 69, 315

Campbell, Ellen, 334–35

Campbell Hospital, 56

Carpenter, Joseph, 171, 247, 253

Carter, Edward W., 36–37, 114–15, 186

Castleton, Vermont, 119

Cathedral of the Immaculate Conception, 61

Catton, Bruce, 84, 105, 117, 120, 187

Cavendish, Vermont, 197, 359

Chadwick, Constantin, 385

Chamberlin, George, 219, 234, 281, 311, 343, 353

Chancellorsville, Virginia, 155

Chandler, Charles, 292, 302, 316–17

Chandler, C. M., 197

Chapin, Charles, 98, 223, 224

Chapin, D., 70

Chapman, George, 83, 95

Chapman, James, 285

Charleston, Vermont, 270

Chase, Peter, 111, 118, 119–20, 124, 184, 185, 187–88, 194–95, 202, 206

Cheldor, Byron A., 374